FIFTH EDITION

Counseling American Minorities

Donald R. Atkinson
University of California—Santa Barbara

George Morten, PhD
California State University—Northridge

Derald W. Sue, PhD
*California School of Professional Psychology, Alameda
and California State University—Hayward*

Boston, Massachusetts   Burr Ridge, Illinois
Dubuque, Iowa   Madison, Wisconsin   New York, New York
San Francisco, California   St. Louis, Missouri

P9-DBY-788

McGraw-Hill

A Division of The McGraw-Hill Companies

COUNSELING AMERICAN MINORITIES: A CROSS-CULTURAL PERSPECTIVE

 This book is printed on recycled, acid-free paper containing 10% postconsumer waste.

2 3 4 5 6 7 8 9 0 DOC/DOC 9 0 9

ISBN 0-697-20171-6

Publisher: *Jane Vaicunas*
Editor: *Sharon Geary*
Project manager: *Ann Morgan*
Production supervisor: *Sandy Ludovissy*
Designer: *Lu Ann Schrandt*
Cover designer: *Lu Ann Schrandt*
Cover photo: Photogear: *Fancy Fabrics*
Compositor: *ElectraGraphics, Inc.*
Typeface: *10/12 Times Roman*
Printer: *R. R. Donnelley—Crawfordsville*

Library of Congress Cataloging-in-Publication Data

Counseling American minorities : a cross-cultural perspective /
   [edited by] Donald R. Atkinson, George Morten, Derald Wing Sue. —
   5th ed.
     p.   cm.
   Includes index.
   ISBN 0-697-20171-6
   1. Minorities—Mental health services—United States.
2. Minorities—Counseling of—United States. 3. Cross-cultural
counseling—United States. I. Atkinson, Donald R. II. Morten,
George. III. Sue, Derald Wing.
RC451.5.A2C68   1997
362.2′04256′089—dc21   97-12937
                                      CIP

http://www.mhcollege.com

PART 4

The Asian American Client   199

10 The Interplay of Sociocultural Factors on the Psychological Development of Asians in America—*D. Sue*   205

11 Facilitating Psychotherapy with Asian American Clients— *M. P. P. Root*   214

12 Psychotherapy with Southeast Asian American Clients— *K. Nishio & M. Bilmes*   235

PART 5

The Hispanic American Client   249

13 Providing Services to Hispanic/Latino Populations: Profiles in Diversity—*G. M. Castex*   255

14 What Do Culturally Sensitive Mental Health Services Mean? The Case of Hispanics—*L. H. Rogler, G. C. Malgady, & R. Blumenthal*   268

15 Counseling Cuban Americans—*J. Altarriba & L. M. Bauer*   280

PART 6

Implications for Minority Group/Cross-Cultural Counseling   301

16 Current Issues and Future Directions in Minority Group/Cross-Cultural Counseling   303

Appendix   Multicultural Counseling Competencies   361
Author Index   377
Subject Index   389

CONTENTS

Preface   *v*

PART 1
Racial/Ethnic Minorities and Cross-Cultural Counseling   1

1 Defining Populations and Terms   3

2 Within-Group Differences Among Racial/Ethnic Minorities   21

3 Addressing the Mental Health Needs of Racial/Ethnic Minorities   51

PART 2
The African American Client   81

4 African-American Women and the Male-Female Relationship Dilemma: A Counseling Perspective—*P. D. Bethea*   87

5 Psychosocial Development and Black Male Masculinity: Implications for Counseling Economically Disadvantaged African American Male Adolescents—*S. M. Harris*   95

6 Culturally Sensitive Therapy with Black Clients— *L. L. Wilson & S. M. Stith*   116

PART 3
The American Indian Client   131

7 American Indian Mental Health Policy—*T. D. LaFromboise*   137

8 Counseling Intervention and American Indian Tradition: An Integrative Approach—*T. D. LaFromboise, J. E. Trimble, & G. V. Mohatt*   159

9 The Path of Good Medicine: Understanding and Counseling Native American Indians—*J. T. Garrett & M. Walkingstick Garrett*   183

PREFACE

This fifth edition of *Counseling American Minorities: A Cross-Cultural Perspective,* like the four editions that preceded it, is designed to help counselors and mental health practitioners and researchers to maximize their effectiveness when working with ethnic minority clients and research participants. A major thesis of this book is that culturally sensitive counselors can establish the necessary and sufficient conditions of a helping relationship with many clients who come from cultural backgrounds different from their own. While similarity of race/ethnicity and culture between the counselor and client may be highly correlated with counseling success, we believe that other attributes (e.g., shared attitudes and values; awareness of one's values, attitudes, and biases; knowledge of the client's culture; use of appropriate counselor roles) also contribute to a productive counseling relationship and may help overcome barriers that can result from ethnic and/or cultural differences.

The purposes of this edition remain the same as those of the earlier editions. First, the book is intended to sensitize counselors to the life experiences and within-group differences of four racial/ethnic minority groups. It is also our hope and expectation that increased sensitivity to these four populations will generalize to other racial/ethnic minority groups. A second major purpose is to examine how counseling has failed in the past and, despite increased attention to multicultural concerns, continues to short change the mental health needs of racial/ethnic minority groups. A third purpose is to suggest new directions for counseling and mental health professionals when serving ethnic minority clients.

This fifth edition represents an extensive revision of the fourth edition. Although the format remains the same as earlier versions, most of the chapters are new or have been extensively revised. The first three chapters and the last chapter of the book were written by the editors, as in past editions. For this edition, we updated chapter 1, added significantly to chapter 2, and completely revised chapters 3 and 16. Parts 2 through 5 include readings that address the specific counseling needs of African Americans, American Indians, Asian Americans, and Hispanic Americans. In part 2, both chapters 4 and 5 are reprints of journal articles that are new to this edition. In part 3, chapter 7 is a reprinted article that has been updated by the author for the current edition and chapter 9 is a reprinted article that is new to this edition. In part 4, both chapters 10 and 11 are original chapters that have been updated for the current edition.

In part 5, chapter 13 is a reprinted article that is new to this edition, while chapter 15 is an original chapter.

When we started working on the first edition of *Counseling American Minorities: A Cross-Cultural Perspective* in the mid-1970s, we naively thought that the momentum of the 1960s and 1970s would produce a society largely free of racism, sexism, and other forms of group discrimination by the new millennium. Unfortunately, this has not been the case. Although some gains have been made within the mental health professions (as documented in chapters 3 and 16), society at large appears to be slipping back into the conditions that existed before the civil rights movement of the 1960s. Violent crimes against racial/ethnic minority people are on the increase according to a report by the Southern Poverty Law Center, which tracks crimes of hate. Although some gains have been made, racial/ethnic minorities continue to experience discrimination in employment, housing, and education. The income gap between the wealthy (largely European Americans) and the poor (disproportionately composed of racial/ethnic minorities) has grown considerably since our first edition. Publication of the *Bell Curve* in 1994 gave White supremacists' views support from within the academic/scientific community. Legislative and judicial achievements with respect to nondiscrimination and affirmative action of the 1960s and 1970s came under attack in the 1980s and early 1990s. Attacks on affirmative action programs have undermined efforts over a thirty-year period to level the playing field and bring racial/ethnic minorities into the educational and employment mainstream. In the mid-1990s in California, the University of California Board of Regents did away with affirmative action efforts in admissions, hiring, and contracting, and voters passed one initiative (Proposition 187) to deny services, including education for children, to undocumented people, and another (Proposition 209) that does away with any type of affirmative action in the state. Elsewhere across the country similar attacks on affirmative action are taking place in board rooms, in legislative halls, and in court chambers. In a 1996 decision by the United States Court of Appeals for the Fifth Circuit that is likely to affect affirmative action around the country, the University of Texas Law School was restricted from using race or ethnicity in admissions decisions. This decision, in effect, represented a frontal assault on the 1978 Supreme Court decision in Bakke v. The Regents of the University of California that disallowed the use of quotas but allowed race/ethnicity to be considered in making admissions decisions. At the national level, political candidates for presidential and congressional offices used affirmative action and legal and illegal immigration as "hot button" issues to bolster their campaigns. As we went to press, a bill was moving through Congress that would deny all public services (including education and medical care) to undocumented immigrants.

These events suggest to us that the need for counselors to be knowledgeable about, and sensitive to, the experiences of ethnic minorities is as great as it ever has been. We hope this text contributes to the knowledge and sensitivity that counselors and other mental health workers will need when working with racial/ethnic minority clients.

D. R. A.
G. M.
D. W. S.

PART 1

Racial/Ethnic Minorities and Cross-Cultural Counseling

1
Defining Populations and Terms

The Diversification of the United States

Earlier writers have referred to the "greening" (Reich, 1970) and the "graying" (Sheppard, 1977) of America in reference to the changing demographics in the United States. The current population trend might be referred to as the "diversification" of the United States. This trend started in the late 1960s and is a function of two major forces: (a) current immigration patterns and (b) differential birth rates among racial/ethnic groups.

The current immigration wave, which consists of documented immigrants, undocumented immigrants, and refugees, is the largest in U.S. history. Unlike earlier migrations that originated primarily in Europe and whose members were readily assimilated into the mainstream U.S. culture, the current wave consists primarily of Asian (34 percent), Latin American (34 percent), and other visible racial/ethnic groups who historically have not been so readily assimilated. When combined with the higher birth rates among these and other ethnic groups already in residence (e.g., European American = 1.7, African American = 2.4, Mexican American = 2.9, Vietnamese = 3.4, Laotians = 4.6, Cambodians = 7.4, and Hmong = 11.9 births per mother), the current immigration wave is resulting in dramatic increases in the non-White populations. During the 1980s the Asian American population increased by 79.5 percent (some sources, Ong & Hee, 1993 and U.S. Bureau of the Census, 1991, say this increase was as high as 108 percent), the Hispanic American population by 38.7 percent, the American Indian population by 21.6 percent, and the African American population by 14.4 percent (U.S. Bureau of the Census, 1992b). With European Americans increasing by only 7.0 percent during this time, the complexion of the U.S. populace began to change rapidly.

The diversification of the U.S. is expected to continue well into the twenty-first century. According to Census Bureau population estimates (Bennett, 1995; Byerly & Deardorff, 1995), non-Hispanic Whites made up 74 percent of the U.S. population in 1994, followed by Blacks at 12.5 percent, Hispanics at 10.0 percent, Asian and Pacific Islanders at 3.5 percent, and American Indians at 0.8 percent. An earlier Census Bureau report (U.S. Bureau of the Census, 1992b) projected that by the year 2000, non-Hispanic Whites will decrease to 71.6 percent of the population, while Blacks will increase to 12.3 percent (a figure already exceeded according to the 1994 figures), followed by Hispanics with 11.1 percent, Asian Americans with 4.2 percent, and American Indians with 0.8 percent. By the year 2050, the Census Bureau projects that non-Hispanic Whites will barely constitute a majority of the population at 52.7 percent, while Hispanics will become the largest ethnic group at 21.1 percent, followed by Blacks (15 percent), Asian and Pacific Islanders (10.1 percent), and American Indians (1.1 percent). While official projections provided by the U.S. Bureau of the Census suggest that racial/ethnic minorities will constitute a numerical majority some time after the year 2050, the Census Bureau is notorious for undercounting and underprojecting persons of color.

In some states, the diversification will occur even more rapidly. In California, for example, African Americans, Asian Americans, and Hispanic Americans made up 40 percent of the population by 1990 and are expected to comprise over 50 percent of the citizenry by the year 2000 (C. Jones & Clifford, 1990). California attracted 35 percent of the international migrants in the 1980s, and is projected to attract 39 percent of the immigrants between 1990 and 2020. In addition, Texas, New York, and Florida are expected to experience large net gains in culturally diverse groups through 2020. However, ethnic minorities are expected to comprise a substantially larger share of the total population in all regions of the United States by 2020 (Campbell, 1994).

The diversification trend will have a significant impact on a number of U.S. institutions. For example, the number of African Americans in the labor force is expected to increase over 29 percent between 1986 and 2000 (Kutscher, 1987). Similar figures for Hispanic Americans and Asian Americans are 75+ percent and 70+ percent, respectively. Education will be significantly impacted by the changing demographics. In California the number of European American students dropped below 50 percent of the public school enrollment for the first time in 1988. By 1990, one in every four students in California lived in a home in which English was not spoken and one in every six was foreign born.

The diversification of the U.S. population also has important implications for counselors, psychologists, and other mental health service providers. These professionals need to increase their cultural sensitivity, knowledge of cultures, and culturally-relevant counseling skills to meet the needs of a culturally diverse client population. Mental health services need to be structured to optimize utilization by and effectiveness for racial/ethnic populations. Professional organizations need to press for policy and legislation at the local, state, and national level that will address discrimination against culturally diverse groups. This book is intended to facilitate the development of counselors and mental health service providers who can meet these needs.

To discuss the experiences and counseling-related needs of the racial/ethnic populations that make up a growing proportion of the U.S. population, it is necessary to begin with a common terminology.

Defining Terms

It is important for counselors to become familiar with terminology relevant to cross-cultural counseling because the misuse of some terms may be interpreted by some clients as cultural insensitivity. It is also important for counselors to recognize that not all terms are universally accepted across or within racial/ethnic populations.

Culture, Race, and Ethnicity

There is much confusion in the general public and the counseling profession about the meaning of the terms culture, race, and ethnicity. Moore's (1974) attempt to resolve the confusion is often cited in any discussion of these three terms:

> Sometimes we tend to confuse race and ethnic groups with culture. Great races do have different cultures. Ethnic groups within races differ in cultural content. But, people of the same racial origin and of the same ethnic groups differ in their cultural matrices. All browns, or blacks, or whites, or yellows, or reds are not alike in the cultures in which they live and have their being. The understanding of the culture of another, or of groups other than our own, demands a knowledge of varied elements within a culture or the variety of culture components within a larger cultural matrix. (p. 41)

We have some difficulty with this discussion of culture, race, and ethnicity. First, we are not sure what is meant by "great races." Are some races "greater" than others? Also, we are not convinced that ethnicity is a classification schema that should be subsumed under race, as seems to be implied in Moore's (1974) statement. We have some difficulty with the concept of race itself (as will become evident). In our own attempt to shed some light on these issues we offer the following discussion.

Numerous definitions of *culture* have been developed by anthropologists over the years, including Kroeber and Kluckhohn's (1952) attempt to synthesize many of them:

> Culture consists of patterns, explicit and implicit, of and for behavior acquired and transmitted by symbols, constituting the distinctive achievement of human groups, including their embodiments in artifacts; the essential core of culture consists of traditional (i.e., historically derived and selected) ideas and especially their attached values; culture systems may, on the one hand, be considered as products of action, on the other as conditioning elements of further action. (p. 181)

The myriad of confusing definitions that Kroeber and Kluckhohn set out to eliminate was only augmented by their earnest efforts. The most succinct and useful definition, for our purposes, is that offered by Linton (1968), who defined culture as, ". . . the configuration of learned behavior and results of behavior whose components and elements are shared and transmitted by the members of a particular society" (p. 32). Thus, culture is not, as an Andy Capp cartoon suggests, something that "my crowd has and yours doesn't have." Every society that shares and transmits behaviors to its members has a culture.

According to the *Oxford Dictionary of Words*, the term *race* first appeared in the English language about three hundred years ago. In that brief time race has come to be one of the most misused and misunderstood terms in the American vernacular (Rose, 1964). Race has been defined in two ways. The first definition is based solely on physical or biological characteristics. "To the biologist, a race, or subspecies, is an inbreeding, geographically isolated population that differs in distinguishable physical traits from other members of the species" (Zuckerman, 1990, p. 1297). Some social scientists also have adopted a biological definition. For example, Rushton (1995) defines race as ". . . a geographic variety or subdivision of a species characterized by a more or less distinct combination of traits (morphological, behavioral, physiological) that are heritable" (p. 40). Basic to a biological definition of race is the view that humans can be divided into a set number of genetic groups on the basis of physical characteristics. Physical differences *(phenotypes)* involving skin pigmentation; facial features; and the color, distribution, and texture of body hair are among the most commonly applied criteria assumed to distinguish races of people.

As Anderson (1971) points out, however, this system is far from ideal, in that not all racial group members fit these criteria precisely. While three basic racial types—Caucasoid, Mongoloid, and Negroid—are commonly accepted, a great deal of overlapping occurs among these groups. When we look beneath the superficial characteristics used to categorize racial types, we find there are more similarities between groups than differences (owing to the fact that all humans originate from a single genus species, *Homo sapiens*), and more differences within racial groups than between them (Littlefield, Lieberman, & Reynolds, 1982).

Race as a biological concept can be questioned on other grounds as well. For example, the idea that races result from common gene pools can be questioned. As Schaefer (1988) points out, "given frequent migration, exploration, and invasions, pure gene frequencies have not existed for some time, if they ever did" (p. 12). In the United States, the number of biracial babies is increasing faster than monoracial babies and this disparity will rapidly increase even if interracial marriage rates remain constant (Alonzo & Waters, 1993). The reality is that most African Americans have White blood in them (going back to the days when White slavemasters raped Black female slaves with impunity). Furthermore, the Bureau of the Census classification of "Hispanic" is really multiracial. The vast majority of Latinos in the United States are indigenous (Indian), mestizo (Indian and Spanish), or mulatto (African and Spanish). Those of Mexican origin in the United States are indigenous or mestizo and many have African blood stemming from the colonial period. When we add Puerto Ricans, Cubans, Dominicans, and others from the Caribbean, the mixture of African, Spanish, and Indian ancestry is evident (Root, 1992; 1996). The paradoxical nature of racial categorization is evident with respect to African Americans; an individual is commonly identified as Black if he/she has any African American blood. Similarly, an individual is judged to be an American Indian if he/she has at least one grandparent who is American Indian. So much for isolated gene pools.

Also, there is no biological explanation for why some physical features (e.g., skin color) have been selected to determine race while others (e.g., eye color) have not. As Zuckerman (1990) suggests, "many of the features are not correlated and none by themselves could furnish an indisputable guide to the anthropologists' definitions of racial groups" (p. 1298). Furthermore, the fact that scientists cannot agree how many races there are, with estimates ranging from three to 200 (Schaefer, 1988), suggests that there is little agreement about the criteria defining race. As a result of these and other concerns, a number of social scientists have urged their colleagues to either redefine race or refrain from using the term in their research and writing (Allen & Adams, 1992; Dole, 1995; Yee, Fairchild, Weizmann, & Wyatt, 1993).

A second definition of race includes a biological and a social component. Cox (1948) was among the first to provide a social perspective by defining race as "any people who are distinguished or consider themselves distinguished, in social relations with other peoples, by their physical characteristics" (p. 402). The social component is dependent on group identity, either evolving within the group or assigned by those outside the group. However, the term race has been applied to cultural groups whose members share little or no unique physical characteristics. As Thompson and Hughes (1958), points out:

> . . . (Jews) . . . are not a biological race because the people known as Jews are not enough like each other and are too much like other people to be distinguished from them. But as people act with reference to Jews and to some extent connect the attitudes they have about them with real and imagined biological characteristics, they become a socially supposed race. (p. 67)

Regardless of its biological validity, the concept of race has taken on important social meaning in terms of how outsiders view members of a "racial" group and how individuals within the "racial" group view themselves, members of their group, and members of other "racial" groups. In other words, the concept of race has taken on important dimensions in terms of how individuals identify who they are. The concept of racial self-identification is one that we will have more to say about in chapter 2.

A review of the literature on *ethnicity* reveals that this term also has two different interpretations, one broad and one narrow (Feagin, 1989). In the broad sense, ethnicity is determined by physical and/or cultural characteristics. Thus, Bernal (1990) defines an ethnic group as "a group of individuals who interact, maintain themselves, have some social structure and system of governing norms and values, are biological and cultural descendants of a cultural group, and identify as members of the group" (p. 261). Similarly, according to Nagel (1995) "ethnicity refers to differences of language, religion, color, ancestry, and/or culture to which social meanings are attributed and around which identity and group formation occurs" (p. 443). This broad definition includes physical characteristics, therefore ethnicity is often used interchangeably with race.

The more narrow definition of ethnicity is taken from the Greek root word *ethnos,* originally meaning "nation" (Feagin, 1989). Thus, Schaefer (1988) identified ethnic groups as "groups set apart from others because of their national origin or distinctive cultural patterns" (p. 9). Similarly, Barresi (1990) defined ethnicity as referring to "a large group whose members internalize and share a heritage of, and a commitment to, unique social characteristics, cultural symbols, and behavior patterns that are not fully understood by outsiders" (p. 249). According to this narrow definition of ethnicity, ethnic differences involve differences in nationality, customs, language, religion, and other cultural factors; physical characteristics are not used to identify ethnic differences. If one accepts the view that ethnicity is the result of shared social and cultural heritage, then Jews, for example, are an ethnic group but not a racial group.

Despite the limitations inherent in the concept of race, federal agencies continue to collect data on racial and ethnic groups. The rationale for doing so appears legitimate enough, to monitor the socioeconomic progress and well-being of racial groups (U.S. Bureau of the Census, 1992a), given our earlier observation that racial designation has social consequences. However, by employing racial categories to collect these data, the federal government (as well as various other entities, including well-intentioned multicultural researchers) perpetuates a questionable construct. Several authors have suggested that using race as an experimental variable is an example of the "new racism" (see the section on racism), which takes the category of race for granted (Henwood, 1994, Reicher, 1986).

The Census Bureau and other federal agencies follow the guidelines put forth by the Office of Management and Budget (OMB) regarding the collection of race and ethnic group information.

> OMB requires the collection of information on race (i.e., "American Indian or Alaskan Native," "Asian or Pacific Islander," "Black" and "White") and ethnicity (i.e., "Hispanic origin" and "not of Hispanic origin"). OMB requires that Federal statistics distinguish between Whites and Blacks who are not of Hispanic origin. . . . Federal agencies are allowed to use one or more questions to collect race-ethnic information as long as it is possible to derive the required groups outlined above. (U.S. Bureau of the Census, 1992a, p. 1)

Thus, according to the OMB, there are four categories of race and only two categories of ethnicity. It will become evident in our discussion of terms associated with specific culturally diverse groups, that the OMB policy is inconsistent with emerging practice in the professional psychology literature.

What can be concluded from this examination of the various definitions of culture, race, and ethnicity? For one thing, the validity of the concept of race is called into question. We are not convinced that race is a valid term, although it may be useful, as Johnson (1990) has suggested, to document the effects of racism and the progress in eradicating it. As Zuckerman (1990) points out, "geographical isolation may have been a significant factor producing inbreeding in the distant evolutionary past, but now the barriers that separate populations are political, cultural, and religious rather than geographic" (p. 1297). Ethnicity, in the narrow sense, seems to be a more useful term because it is descriptive (with regard to nationality and/or culture) but without the problems associated with defining race. The difficulty is that the concept of race is so pervasive in the United States that it contributes significantly to how most (if not all) of us identify ourselves. In other words, some of us choose to identify ourselves racially and counselors must recognize the important role that race plays in self-identification.

We prefer the term ethnicity to race when referring to groups of people who are distinguished by their ancestry and/or culture. Race assumes a unique, isolated gene pool that clearly does not apply to many people who identify as African American, American Indian, Asian American, or Hispanic American. The broader definition of ethnicity discussed earlier includes people who share common ancestors and those who share a common culture. For example, we believe it is more accurate to refer to a woman's ethnicity as African American when she has three White grandparents and one Black grandparent but is raised by her Black grandparent and identifies as African American, than to say she is racially Black or African American. However, in recognition of the role that race plays as a social construct, and given that racial self-identification is important to some ethnic minority people, we have elected to use the term race/ethnicity to signify groups of people who share a common ancestry and/or cultural heritage.

It is also important to recognize, that due to the process of acculturation, individuals of the same ancestry may or may not share the same cultural values and behaviors. As Sue and Zane (1987) pointed out, it is important for counselors to "avoid confounding the cultural values of the client's ethnic group with those of the client" (p. 41). Similarly, Phinney (1996) noted that although psychologists have treated ethnicity as a categorical variable, ethnicity may or may not identify one's culture, identity, and minority status. She points out that "ethnic cultures, rather than unified structures to which one belongs, can be thought of as clusters of dimensions along which individuals or samples vary" (p. 922). We will return to the topic of variability within ethnic groups in chapter 2.

Before leaving this discussion of culture, it is important to dismiss two terms, *culturally deprived* and *culturally disadvantaged,* that have been widely used in conjunction with racial/ethnic groups. The term culturally deprived implies the absence of culture, a (perhaps hypothetical) situation that has no relationship to the groups addressed in this book. Despite the effects of the larger society's culture on racial/ethnic groups through the mass media, the groups discussed in this book clearly possess and transmit their own distinct cultures.

The term culturally disadvantaged suggests the person to whom it is applied is at a disadvantage because he/she lacks the cultural background formed by the controlling social structure. The use of "disadvantaged" rather than "deprived" is intended to recognize that the individual possesses a cultural heritage, but also suggests it is not the *right* culture. While slightly less noxious than culturally deprived, culturally disadvantaged still implies a cultural deficiency, whereas the real issue is one of ethnocentrism, with the values of the majority culture viewed as more important than those of ethnic cultures. A person may be economically disadvantaged because he/she has less money than the average person or educationally disadvantaged due to inferior formal education. We seriously object, however, to any inference that racial/ethnic groups have less culture.

Even the more accepted terms *culturally different* and *culturally distinct* can carry negative connotations when they are used to imply that a person's culture is at variance (out-of-step) with the dominant (accepted) culture. The inappropriate application of these two terms occurs in counseling when their use is restricted to ethnically diverse clients. Taken literally, it is grammatically and conceptually correct to refer to a majority client as culturally different or culturally distinct from the counselor if the counselor is a minority individual.

Melting Pot, Acculturation, Assimilation, and Cultural Pluralism

Throughout the early stages of its development, the United States projected an image of the cultural *melting pot,* a nation in which all nationalities, ethnicities, and races melted into one culture. Many Americans took pride in the melting pot image and a play by British playwright Israel Zangwill, entitled *The Melting Pot,* enjoyed widespread popularity in this country when it was first performed in 1908. According to the melting pot theory, a new and unique culture continually evolves as each new immigrant group impacts upon the existing culture (Krug, 1976).

Not everyone in the United States, however, subscribed to the melting pot theory and philosophy. The Chinese Exclusion Act passed by Congress in 1882 was the first of a number of federal and state laws established to ensure that certain immigrant groups would have minimal impact on the emerging American culture. In 1926 Henry Pratt Fairchild, a noted American sociologist of the time, wrote that the melting pot philosophy and unrestricted immigration were "slowly, insidiously, irresistibly eating away the very heart of the United States" (Fairchild, 1926, p. 261). According to Fairchild and others, the "heart of the United States" was an (equivocally defined) American culture based primarily on the values and mores of early immigrants, principally English, Irish, German, and Scandinavian groups. Instead of melting all cultures into one, opponents of the melting pot philosophy argued that an effort should be made to acculturate ("Americanize") all immigrant groups. To reduce the effects of the melting pot phenomenon and increase the probability of acculturation, immigration quotas were developed for those countries whose culture diverged most from the American culture. Public education, with its universal use of the English language, was viewed as the primary institution for perpetuating the existing American culture (Epps, 1974).

Before moving on to a discussion of cultural pluralism, an alternative to the melting pot and assimilation philosophies, it is helpful to distinguish between *assimilation* and *acculturation.* Gordon (1964) has identified acculturation as one of seven different types of assimilation. Acculturation refers to cultural assimilation or the acquisition of the cultural patterns (e.g., values, norms, language, behavior) of the core or dominant society. We will discuss the theoretical underpinnings of acculturation in greater detail in chapter 2. However, assimilation implies more than the adoption of the dominant culture. In addition it requires that structural assimilation be achieved, or, as suggested by McLemore (1983), that "members of the two groups interact with one another as friends and equals and that they select marriage partners without regard to ethnic or racial identities" (p. 35). Even though some immigrants (and their descendants) may desire to become acculturated and may make every effort to adopt the culture of the dominant society, total assimilation may be beyond their grasp since it requires acceptance by members of that society. Thus, for some racial/ethnic persons, assimilation may be a desired but unachievable goal.

For others, assimilation may not be a desired goal. Many members of racial/ethnic groups find the cultural assimilation philosophy objectionable because it calls for relinquishing their traditional racial/ethnic values and norms in favor of those of the dominant culture. With the civil rights movement of the 1960s and 1970s came a growing interest in *cultural pluralism.* According to the theory of cultural pluralism, individual racial/ethnic groups maintain their cultural uniqueness while sharing common elements of American culture (Kallen, 1956). Cultural pluralism is often likened to a cultural stew; the various ingredients are mixed together, but rather than melting into a single mass, the components remain intact and distinguishable while contributing to a whole that is richer than the parts. Cultural pluralism enjoyed some popularity and acceptance during the 1970s as evidenced by the passage of the Ethnic Heritage Studies Bill by Congress in 1973 and the implementation of bilingual, bicultural education in many metropolitan school districts. Some of the gains in bilingual, bicultural education made in the 1970s were lost in the 1980s and early 1990s; by pure force of numbers, however, the current immigration trend presents a strong argument in favor of continuing or reinstituting such programs in the future.

Ethnocentrism, Racism, Prejudice, Stereotypes, and Oppression

Individuals who advocate the acculturation of racial/ethnic groups into American culture can be said to share a characteristic with individuals who seek to exclude these groups from American society; both are ethnocentric. Sumner (1960) defined *ethnocentrism* as the "view of things in which one's own group is the center of everything, and all others are scaled and rated with reference to it" (p. 27–28). Individuals who expect racial/ethnic groups to acculturate are in essence saying that the existing U.S. culture is superior to any culture or mix of cultures that could result from the melting pot or cultural pluralism philosophies.

Believing racial/ethnic groups other than your own are intellectually, psychologically, or physically inferior is a characteristic of *racism*. In a strictly literal sense, racism applies only to racial differences; in common use, however, racism has been applied to cultural differences as well. Belief in racial inferiority also provides a rationale for oppressing racial groups. Identifying racism as a disease, Skillings and Dobbins (1991) proposed that "racism is characterized by (a) the belief that one's own cultural or racial heritage is innately superior to those of others and (b) the use of power, either overt or covert, either intentionally or unintentionally, to enforce prejudices and preferences" (pp. 206–7). J. M. Jones (1972) identified three types of racism: individual, institutional, and cultural. *Individual racism* involves the personal attitudes, beliefs, and behaviors designed to convince oneself of the superiority of one's race/ethnicity over other races/ethnicities. *Institutional racism* involves the social policies, laws, and regulations whose purpose it is to maintain the economic and social advantage of the racial/ethnic group in power. *Cultural racism* involves society beliefs and customs that promote the assumption that the products of the dominant culture (e.g., language, traditions, appearance) are superior to other cultures.

When we think about racism, we think about acts of violence or blatant acts of discrimination by clearly racist individuals or White supremacist groups. However,

> racism also involves the everyday, mundane, negative opinions, attitudes, and ideologies and the seemingly subtle acts and conditions of discrimination against minorities, namely, those social cognitions and social acts, processes, structures, or institutions that directly or indirectly contribute to the dominance of the white group and the subordinate position of minorities. (Van Dijk, 1993, p. 5)

Furthermore, when we think about the consequences of racism, we usually think about acts of physical violence. However, one of the more insidious outcomes of racism is the subtle effect on the thinking of individuals against whom the racism is directed. Through indirect but effective socializing influences, group members are taught and come to accept as "social fact" a myriad of myths and stereotypes regarding skin color, facial features, and other physical characteristics. As we will see in chapter 2, this can have a profound effect on the individual's racial/ethnic identification. Also often overlooked is the effect of racism on the privileged group. As Tatum (1992) has pointed out, racism contributes to a climate in which European Americans feel discomfort or fear in racially mixed settings. Thus, racism restricts the options and experiences of the privileged group and the oppressed group.

Several authors have raised concerns about the *new racism,* a subtle form of racism that facilitates discrimination in liberal, democratic societies.

> Unlike old style racism, which tends to posit crude notions of 'racial' and cultural inferiority, the new racism asserts that differences between groups are simply natural, intractable and non-negotiable, and that for this reason groups are best kept apart. It is proving itself to be a potent means by which dominant groups can discriminate, and yet apparently save face by denying racism. (Henwood, 1994, p. 44)

As we suggested in the earlier discussion of race, researchers may be unwittingly contributing to the new racism by using race as an accepted means of categorizing people.

Ethnocentrism and racism inevitably result in *prejudice,* which refers to negative attitudes, thoughts, and beliefs toward an entire category of people (Schaefer, 1988). Allport (1958) defined prejudice as "an antipathy based upon a faulty and inflexible generalization. . . . It may be directed toward a group as a whole, or toward an individual because he [or she] is a member of that group" (p. 10).

Prejudice is an attitude or belief, therefore it is not always evident in a person's behavior. Prejudice may manifest itself in subtle, covert ways. Counselors who unconsciously treat clients differently based on their racial/ethnic background may be doing so as the result of their unrecognized prejudices.

A *stereotype* is an overgeneralization about a group of people. Some authors define stereotypes as a function of prejudice (Schaefer, 1988) while others conclude that it is an inevitable and necessary coping mechanism for avoiding cognitive overload (Brown, 1965). Stereotypes in general have been criticized for being incorrect generalizations, generalizations of unspecified validity, products of faulty thought processes, characterized by rigidity, and conditioned beliefs based on limited experience (Brigham, 1971). Stereotypes can be negative or positive but, as McCauley, Stitt, and Segal (1980) point out, all stereotypes can have negative repercussions if they are used to make predictions without gaining more information about a person. For example, a positive stereotype of Asian Americans is that they are high achievers who experience few emotional/social problems. However, a school counselor who assumes on the basis of race/ethnicity that a Chinese American student needs no personal (only academic and career) counseling without knowing the student's socioeconomic background, peer relationships, past performance record, and so forth would be, in effect, discriminating against the student on the basis of a racial/ethnic stereotype.

Oppression is a state of being in which the oppressed person is deprived of some human right or dignity and is (or feels) powerless to do anything about it (Goldenberg, 1978). Oppression can manifest itself in many ways. European Jews during World War II and African Americans and American Indians throughout much of U.S. history are examples of groups that have experienced oppression in its most extreme form, genocide. Insidious forms of oppression that continue to plague groups of Americans in the 1990s include political, economic, and social oppression. Examples of oppression currently experienced by racial/ethnic groups include underrepresentation in the 1990 census, subminimum wages paid to undocumented workers, the racial/ethnic slurs that permeate written and oral communication, and physical attacks upon individuals by racist perpetrators.

Minority, Ethnic Minority, VREG, and Third World

As Cook and Helms (1988) suggest, social scientists continue to look for a word or words with which to collectively refer to oppressed and/or ethnic groups in the U.S. population. Several terms have been used by authors in the counseling literature; each has one or more drawbacks.

Some authors have used the term *minority* to refer to physically or behaviorally identifiable groups that make up less than 50 percent of the U.S. population. Included in this definition are racial/ethnic minorities, the aged, and disabled persons. In common use, however, numerical size alone does not determine minority status. Over 80 percent of the population of South Africa is non-White, yet this group is frequently referred to as a minority by individuals within and outside South Africa (Rose, 1964). Wirth (1945) has offered a definition of minority based on the concept of oppression that is preferred by the present authors and is employed in this book. According to Wirth, a minority is ". . . a group of people who, because of physical or cultural characteristics, are singled out from the others in society in which they live for differential and unequal treatment, and who therefore regard themselves as objects of collective discrimination" (p. 347).

We have already established that culture is characterized by shared and transmitted behavior, therefore this definition allows us to accept all those groups included in the racial/ethnic and numerical definitions, plus other groups that are oppressed by society *primarily because of their group membership* as minorities. Most importantly, this definition allows us to include women as minorities, a group of oppressed individuals who constitute a numerical majority in the United States.

According to Bernal (1990), an *ethnic minority group* is a minority group with the added criterion of genetic and/or cultural group membership. Thus, an ethnic minority is an ethnic group singled out for differential and unequal treatment and who regard themselves as objects of collective discrimination. In the United States, this definition is applicable to the four racial/ethnic groups that are the focus of this book.

Some authors prefer the phrase *"visible racial, ethnic group" (VREG)* over the term racial/ethnic minority when referring to persons of color or linguistic diversity (Cook & Helms, 1988). However, this designation emphasizes the use of visible physical characteristics as acceptable criteria for determining a racial/ethnic group, a concept that we questioned earlier in the discussion of race. Also, some individuals may self-identify as a member of a racial/ethnic minority group based on ancestry even though they are not visibly members of the group.

Another term that sometimes is used interchangeably with the word racial/ethnic minority is *Third World.* The term Third World enjoyed international acceptance as a means of describing the nonindustrialized nations of the world that were neither Western nor Communist (Miller, 1967); now it is used in reference to nonindustrialized nations. Many of these countries are located in Africa, South America, and Asia, primarily non-White portions of the world. It has also been used as a symbol of unity among oppressed people. In the United States, therefore, people of color are sometimes referred to as Third World persons. The term is used less frequently than it was in the 1960s and 1970s to identify U.S. minorities, perhaps because this U.S. interpretation is at odds with international use.

Wirth's (1945) definition notwithstanding, many people object to the term minority because it implies "less than." We are sensitive to this issue but have elected to continue using the term at this point because: (1) minority continues to be widely used to describe groups subjected to oppression; (2) no other more appropriate and equally descriptive term has emerged; and (3) we are reluctant to change the title of our book until a more positive term has gained acceptance.

Terms Associated with Specific Racial/Ethnic Groups

Just as there is disagreement about the terms to refer collectively to non-Whites, there is a lack of unanimity about the best terms to use when referring to specific racial/ethnic groups. Some terms may be accepted in some regions of the United States or by some generations within a racial/ethnic minority group but not by others. Furthermore, terms associated with specific racial/ethnic groups are problematic because they fail to recognize ethnic and cultural differences within the group.

African American, American Indian, Asian American, and Hispanic American have emerged as the standard, although by no means universally accepted, references for the four major racial/ethnic minorities in the United States. As suggested, however, some individuals object to these terms because they are too broad and fail to recognize important ethnic differences that exist within the groups. For example, the term Asian American technically includes all Americans who can trace their ancestry to the continent of Asia (including such disparate cultural groups as Iranians, Asian Indians, Koreans, etc.), although common use is restricted to descendants of Eastern Asia. To recognize these distinctions, many researchers and writers refer to the specific country of origin, particularly when discussing Asian American and Hispanic American populations (e.g., Japanese American, Vietnamese American, Mexican American, Cuban American). Similarly, American Indians point to the fact that, depending on how one categorizes tribal affiliations, there are as many as 500 tribes in the United States as evidence that any single term glosses over the cultural variation within their population.

Other objections have been raised to these general terms. Some individuals who can trace their ancestry to Africa prefer the term Black to African American, although Ghee (1990) points out that "The term African American is currently being used interchangeably with the term Black and is increasingly being advanced as a self-referent for Americans of African descent" (p. 75). Controversy also exists over the terms Latino and Hispanic as they apply to people from Central and South America (Hayes-Bautista & Chapa, 1987; Trevino, 1987). Some individuals object to the use of Hispanic for the same reason that they find Latino offensive; both terms refer to countries that conquered and oppressed the indigenous people of Central and South America. We used the term Latino in earlier editions of this book because it emerged from within the population to which it was applied (as opposed to Hispanic, a label created by the U.S. Bureau of the Census). However, a recent PsychLit search revealed that Hispanic is used four times more frequently than Latino in professional psychology articles, so we have elected to follow this convention.

An increasing number of people have mixed ancestry and many of them prefer not to be identified with one specific racial/ethnic group. Many of these individuals self-identify as biracial, biethnic, bicultural, multiracial, multiethnic, or multicultural. Increasingly, the U.S. Office of Management and Budget, the overseer of Census Bureau categories, is coming under attack for the five-race framework used for classifying people. Persons of mixed race are increasingly demanding that they be allowed to choose or integrate their identity as evidenced by the fact that many will check more than one box of a racial designator or write in a multiracial descriptor. Perhaps the biggest challenge to our simplistic system of racial classification comes from multiracial people.

In view of this lack of unanimity regarding racial/ethnic group terminology, it is important that the counselor is sensitive to the client's preferred term for self-identification. If the issue of race/ethnicity emerges in counseling, the counselor may want to ask the client how he/she self-identifies. In other situations, the terms African American, American Indian, Asian American, and Hispanic American are generally acceptable, although every effort should be made to acknowledge specific ethnic groups and to recognize individual preferences. We use these four terms for the purpose of organizing our discussion of cross-cultural counseling in this book, but we readily acknowledge that such groupings are an oversimplification, and we apologize to readers who find any of them offensive.

We also prefer the term European American to the terms White, Caucasian American, and Anglo. Although they are widely used and at times we find it necessary to fall back on them when referencing earlier writing incorporating these terms, we find White and Caucasian American objectionable because they assume racial differences that, as we suggested earlier, we feel are questionable. We feel Anglo is the least appropriate term to use because technically it refers to people of English descent (or more distantly, of Germanic descent). People who trace their ancestry to Italy, France, and the Iberian peninsula, for example, often object to being called Anglo American. White is probably least objectionable of the three terms but it is not particularly descriptive. We have elected to use the term European American because it is the most congruent with the emerging trend of identifying the region (or more specifically, country) of ancestry (e.g., African American, Asian American, Chinese American). The reader should be aware, however, that many (particularly elderly) individuals of European descent will object to European being inserted before American when they are asked to identify their ethnicity.

Cross-Cultural Psychology, Cross-Cultural Counseling, Multicultural Counseling, and Minority-Group Counseling

Cross-cultural psychology is sometimes confused with cross-cultural counseling. Cross-cultural psychology refers to "the systematic study of behavior and experience as it occurs in different cultures, is influenced by culture, or results in changes in existing cultures" (Triandis, 1980, p. 1). A major purpose of cross-cultural psychology is to determine which psychological laws have universal application and which are culture specific. The terms *etic* and *emic* have been used to describe phenomenon that have, respectively, universal application or culture-specific application.

By common practice, *cross-cultural counseling* refers to any counseling relationship in which two or more of the participants are *racially/ethnically* different. If the term were applied in a literal sense, it would refer to those counseling relationships in which two or more of the participants are *culturally* different. In this more literal sense, cross-cultural counseling could be applied, for example, to a counseling dyad consisting of a low-acculturated Mexican American client and a high-acculturated Mexican American counselor. We will use cross-cultural counseling in the broader, more conventional sense, but try to clarify when race/ethnicity and culture do not go hand-in-hand. Cross-cultural counseling includes situations in which both the counselor and client(s) are ethnic minorities but represent different racial/ethnic groups (African American counselor—Hispanic American client; Asian American counselor—American Indian client, and so forth). It also includes the situation in which the counselor is a racial/ethnic minority person and the client is European American

(African American counselor—European American client, Hispanic American counselor—European American client, and so on). Although some authors make a distinction between cross-cultural counseling and *multicultural counseling*, we will follow the more conventional practice of using these two terms interchangeably.

Minority-group counseling, by way of contrast, can be defined as any counseling relationship in which the client is a member of a minority group, regardless of the status of the counselor. The term "minority" can be and is applied to any group that is singled out for differential and inferior treatment, therefore minority-group counseling could be applied to situations where the client is a woman, a gay man or lesbian woman, a person with a disability, and so on. However, by convention, minority-group counseling is often used when the client is a member of an ethnic minority group, regardless of the counselor's ethnicity.

References

Allen, B. P., & Adams, J. Q. (1992). The concept "race": Let's go back to the beginning. *Journal of Social Behavior and Personality, 7,* 163–168.

Allport, G. (1958). *The nature of prejudice* (Abridged ed.). New York: Doubleday, Anchor Books.

Alonzo, W., & Waters, M. (1993). *The future composition of the American population: An illustrative simulation.* Paper presented at the winter meeting of the American Statistical Association, Fort Lauderdale, FL.

Anderson, C. H. (1971). *Toward a new sociology: A critical view.* Homewood, IL: The Dorsey Press.

Barresi, C. M. (1990). Ethnogerontology: Social aging in national, racial, and cultural groups. In K. F. Ferraro (Ed.), *Gerontology: Perspectives and issues* (pp. 247–265). New York: Springer Publishing Co.

Bennett, C. E. (1995). *The Black population in the United States: March 1994 and 1993,* U.S. Bureau of the Census, Current Population Reports, P20–480. Washington, DC: U.S. Government Printing Office.

Bernal, M. E. (1990). Ethnic minority mental health training: Trends and issues. In F. C. Serafica, A. I. Schwebel, R. K. Russell, P. D. Isaac, & L. B. Myers (Eds.), *Mental health of ethnic minorities* (pp. 249–274). New York: Praeger Publishers.

Brigham, J. C. (1971). Ethnic stereotypes. *Psychological Bulletin, 76,* 15–38.

Brown, R. (1965). *Social psychology.* New York: Free Press.

Byerly, E. R., & Deardorff, K. (1995). *National and state population estimates: 1990 to 1994.* U.S. Bureau of the Census, Current Population Reports, P25–1127. Washington, DC: U.S. Government Printing Office.

Campbell, P. R. (1994). *Population projections for states, by age, race, and sex: 1993 to 2020.* U.S. Bureau of the Census, Current Population Reports, P25–1111. Washington, DC: U.S. Government Printing Office.

Cook, D. A., & Helms, J. E. (1988). Visible racial/ethnic group supervisees' satisfaction with cross-cultural supervision as predicted by relationship characteristics. *Journal of Counseling Psychology, 35,* 268–274.

Cox, O. C. (1948). *Caste, class, and race.* Garden City, NY: Doubleday.

Dole, A. A. (1995). Why not drop race as a term? *American Psychologist, 50,* 40.

Epps, E.G. (1974). *Cultural pluralism.* Berkeley, CA: McCutchan Publishing Co.

Fairchild, H. P. (1926). *The melting pot mistake.* Boston: Little, Brown, & Co.

Feagin, J. R. (1989). *Racial & ethnic relations.* Englewood Cliffs, NJ: Prentice Hall.

Ghee, K. L. (1990). The psychological importance of self-definition and labeling: Black versus African American. *Journal of Black Psychology, 17,* 75–93.

Goldenberg, I. I. (1978). *Oppression and social intervention.* Chicago: Nelson-Hall.

Gordon, M. M. (1964). *Assimilation in American life.* New York: Oxford University Press.

Hayes-Bautista, D. E., & Chapa, J. (1987). Latino terminology: Conceptual bases for standardized terminology. *American Journal of Public Health, 77*(1), 61–68.

Henwood, K. L. (1994). Resisting racism and sexism in academic psychology: A personal/political view. *Feminism & Psychology, 4,* 41–62.

Johnson, S. D. Jr. (1990). Toward clarifying culture, race, and ethnicity in the context of multicultural counseling. *Journal of Multicultural Counseling and Development, 18,* 41–50.

Jones, C., & Clifford, F. (1990, August 28). Census puts state near 30 million. *Los Angeles Times,* pp. A1, A18.

Jones, J. M. (1972). *Prejudice and racism.* Reading, MA: Addison-Wesley.

Kallen, H. M. (1956). *Cultural pluralism and the American idea.* Philadelphia: University of Philadelphia Press.

Kroeber, A. L., & Kluckhohn, C. (1952). *Culture: A critical review of concepts and definitions.* New York: Vintage Books.

Krug, M. (1976). *The melting of the ethnics.* Bloomington, IN: Phi Delta Kappa Education Foundation.

Kutscher, R. (1987, September). Projections 2000: Overview and implications of the projections to 2000. *Monthly Labor Review.* Washington, DC: U.S. Department of Labor.

Linton, R. W. (1968). *The cultural background of personality.* New York: Appleton-Century Co.

Littlefield, A., Lieberman, L., & Reynolds, L. T. (1982). Redefining race: The potential demise of a concept in anthropology. *Current Anthropology, 23,* 641–647.

McCauley, C., Stitt, C. L., & Segal, M. (1980). Stereotyping: From prejudice to prediction. *Psychological Bulletin, 87,* 195–208.

McLemore, S. D. (1983). *Racial and ethnic relations in America* (2nd ed.). Boston: Allyn and Bacon.

Miller, J. D. B. (1967). *The politics of the third world.* London: Oxford University Press.

Moore, B. M. (1974). Cultural differences and counseling perspectives. *Texas Personnel and Guidance Association Journal, 3,* 39–44.

Nagel, J. (1995). Resource competition theories. *American Behavioral Scientist, 38,* 442–458.

Ong, P., & Hee, S. (1993). The growth of Asian Pacific American population: Twenty million in 2020. In LEAP Asian Pacific American Public Policy Institute and UCLA Asian American Studies Center (Ed.), *The state of Asian Pacific America* (pp. 11–24). Los Angeles: LEAP.

Phinney, J. S. (1996). When we talk about American ethnic groups, what do we mean? *American Psychologist, 51,* 918–927.

Reich, C. A. (1970). *The greening of America: How the youth is trying to make America livable.* New York: Random House.

Reicher, S. (1986). Contact, action and racialization: Some British evidence. In M. Hewston and R. Brown (Eds.), *Contact and conflict in intergroup encounters* (pp. 152–168). Oxford, England: Basil Blackwell.

Root, M. P. P. (1992). *Racial mixed people in America.* Thousand Oaks, CA: Sage.

Root, M. P. P. (1996). *The multiracial experience.* Thousand Oaks, CA: Sage.

Rose, P. I. (1964). *They and we: Racial and ethnic relations in the United States.* New York: Random House.

Rushton, J. P. (1995). Construct validity, censorship, and the genetics of race. *American Psychologist, 50,* 40-41.

Schaefer, R. T. (1988). *Racial and ethnic groups* (3rd ed.). Glenview, IL: Scott, Foresman and Company.

Sheppard, H. L. (1977). *The graying of working America: The coming crisis in retirement-age policy.* New York: Free Press.

Skillings, J. H., & Dobbins, J. E. (1991). Racism as a disease: Etiology and treatment implications. *Journal of Counseling and Development, 70,* 206–212.

Sue, S., & Zane, N. (1987). The role of culture and cultural techniques in psychotherapy: A critique and reformulation. *American Psychologist, 42,* 37–45.

Sumner, W. G. (1960). *Folkways.* New York: Mentor Books.

Tatum, B. D. (1992). Talking about race, learning about racism: The application of racial identity development theory in the classroom. *Harvard Educational Review, 62,* 1–24.

Thompson, E. T., & Hughes, E. C. (1958). *Race: Individual and collective behavior.* Glencoe, IL: Free Press.

Trevino, F. M. (1987). Standardized terminology for Hispanics. *American Journal of Public Health, 77*(1), 69–72.

Triandis, H. C. (1980). Introduction to handbook of cross-cultural psychology. In H. C. Triandis & W. W. Lambert (Eds.), *Handbook of Cross-Cultural Psychology: Perspectives, Vol. 1* (pp. 1–14). Boston: Allyn & Bacon, Inc.

U.S. Bureau of the Census (1991). *United States Department of Commerce News.* Washington, DC: U.S. Government Printing Office.

U.S. Bureau of the Census (1992a). *Exploring alternative race-ethnic comparison groups in current populations surveys* (Current Population Reports, P23–182). Washington, DC: U.S. Government Printing Office.

U.S. Bureau of the Census. (1992b). *Population projections of the United States, by age, sex, race, and Hispanic origin: 1992 to 2050* (Current Population Reports, P25–1092), Washington, DC: U.S. Government Printing Office.

Van Dijk, T. A. (1993). *Elite discourse and racism.* Newbury Park, CA: Sage.

Wirth, L. (1945). The problem of minority groups. In R. Linton (Ed.), *The science of man in the world crisis.* (pp. 347–372). New York: Columbia University Press.

Yee, A. H., Fairchild, H. H., Weizmann, F., & Wyatt, G. E. (1993). Addressing psychology's problems with race. *American Psychologist, 38,* 1132–1140.

Zuckerman, M. (1990). Some dubious premises in research and theory on racial differences. *American Psychologist, 45,* 1297–1303.

2
Within-Group Differences Among Racial/Ethnic Minorities

In chapter 1 we discussed how the United States is being diversified due to the high immigration and birth rates of ethnic minority groups. This process of diversification, while accelerated at the current time, is not new to the United States. Earlier waves of immigrants from Europe created a tapestry of ethnic and cultural diversity. However, for most families that can trace their ancestors to Europe, these cultural and ethnic differences faded within two or three generations as they assimilated into the dominant culture through acculturation and interethnic marriages. Immigrants of color, however, have always found it difficult to assimilate into the dominant culture and, conversely, many individuals and families of African, Asian, Latin American, and Native American background have chosen to maintain their distinct cultural identification, at least in part. By the third decade of the twentieth century, social scientists began to recognize that the assimilation process was not always a smooth, predictable one, even for those who chose to adopt the dominant culture. It also became evident that not all ethnic groups were equally successful in attaining educational and economic goals.

To explain the differential success rates of the various racial/ethnic groups, researchers began to examine intergroup differences. Research prior to 1970 compared scores of racial/ethnic minority subjects to those of European American subjects on a variety of psychological and behavioral measures. Whether intended, implicit in this practice was the assumption that European American performance on these measures represented the norm or desired performance because they were most successful in achieving "the American dream." Deviations from the norm could be used to explain why some racial/ethnic minority groups were not "succeeding" in the United States. Several hypotheses were offered to explain this phenomenon, including the hypothesis that some racial/ethnic groups were genetically inferior (racism) to others and the hypothesis that some cultures were inferior (ethnocentricism or cultural racism) to others.

By the 1970s, however, critics of this research methodology and the genetic and cultural deficit theories were arguing that comparative data have limited usefulness, could be misleading, and, in some cases (e.g., use of standardized

IQ tests to measure intelligence), were divisive and destructive. Rather than comparing the scores of racial/ethnic minorities on behavioral and psychological measures to those of European Americans, these critics argued, social scientists should examine ethnic minority performance within the context of their own culture. For example, tests should be normed for each racial/ethnic group and individual performance should be contrasted with ethnic group norms, rather than to European American norms. In the counseling and mental health literature, this resulted in a shift from studies that compared subjects' responsiveness to counseling across racial/ethnic groups to studies that described responsiveness to counseling within a specific racial/ethnic group.

Studies that described responsiveness to counseling by a single racial/ethnic minority population were useful because they pointed out the need for ethnically similar counselors, culturally sensitive counselors, and culturally compatible counseling strategies. However, they too were misleading because normative responses of the participants often were generalized to an entire racial/ethnic minority group. Reviewers of this cross-cultural counseling research began pointing out by the late 1970s the need to include within-group differences as variables of interest in future research with racial/ethnic minorities.

An underlying thesis in these reviews was that counselors needed to recognize diversity within racial/ethnic groups and diversity between racial/ethnic groups when working with an racial/ethnic minority client; in particular, the counselor needed to understand both the client's cultural heritage and the degree to which the client identified with his/her cultural heritage. While it is undeniable that each minority group has a unique cultural heritage that makes it distinct from other groups, this has erroneously been interpreted as evidence of cultural conformity—a monolithic approach that views all African Americans, American Indians, Asian Americans, and Hispanic Americans as possessing the same group attitudes and behaviors. Clearly, uniformity of attitudes and behaviors is no more true for minority individuals than it is for members of the dominant culture. About the issue of cultural distinction, racial/ethnic minority attitudes may vary from desire for total assimilation into the dominant culture to total rejection of the dominant culture and immersion in the minority culture (Parham & Helms, 1981). Each of the major racial/ethnic populations in the United States manifests great diversity, including but not limited to diversity of attitudes, values, behavior, education, income, acculturation, and racial/ethnic identity. By ignoring within-group diversity, researchers promote the view that the group is homogeneous and that modal data from a single sample can be generalized to an entire racial/ethnic group.

It is important that counselors and other mental health workers recognize that ethnicity, culture, and minority group status all contribute to ethnic minority experiences (S. Sue, Chun, & Gee, 1995). Ho (1995) argues that to really understand an ethnic minority client, the counselor must gain insight into the client's internalized culture, which he describes as the individual's unique internalization of cultural characteristics. Ho is concerned that by stressing cultural differences between ethnic groups, some authors have contributed to overgeneralization and stereotypes about minorities. We share his concern and feel that an understanding of an ethnic minority client's internalized culture can be facilitated by understanding some of the variables that contribute to within-group differences among minority group members.

In this chapter we examine several variables that account for differences within ethnic groups. In particular, we focus attention on two within-group variables, acculturation and racial identity development, that the cross-cultural counseling experts surveyed by Heath, Neimeyer, and Pedersen (1988) predicted would play an increasingly important role in theory and research publications during the last decade of the twentieth century. We start by briefly drawing attention to cultural differences that exist within the four ethnic minority groups covered in this book and then move on to acculturation, a within-group variable that exists even within families.

Cultural Differences within Major Ethnic Groups

As suggested in chapter 1, the major ethnic categories of African American, American Indian, Asian American, and Hispanic American include many culturally diverse groups. Although these four major ethnic populations have cultural features that distinguish them from each other and from the dominant European American culture, they are each umbrella categories that include many diverse ethnic/cultural groups. It is important to recognize these cultural differences within the major ethnic categories because failure to do so may project the image of a "psuedosensitive" counselor, someone who is knowledgeable about cultural similarities generalizable across the client's umbrella ethnic group, but ignorant of the client's specific ethnic group and culture. This may have the same effect on the client as ignoring culture altogether, because it communicates a lack of understanding of the client and the client's culture.

Unfortunately, cross-cultural researchers have contributed to the profession's failure to recognize specific ethnic and cultural differences within a larger umbrella ethnic group. When researchers are unable to find a representative sample of a specific ethnic population they often lump representatives of diverse groups together to obtain adequate sample sizes for statistical purposes (Sue et al., 1995). Another problem occurs when they attempt to interpret their findings, and generalizations are made about the umbrella ethnic group that may only be applicable to one or two specific ethnic/cultural groups (those most readily available to the researcher).

Although a thorough discussion of cultural differences between specific ethnic groups within the general ethnic categories would take up many volumes, we will cite a few examples to make our point. Consider the diverse ethnic groups and cultures within the umbrella category of Asian Americans. According to Yoshioka, Tashima, Chew, and Maruse (1981), there are at least twenty-nine distinct Asian American subgroups that differ from each other in language, religion, and values. Within the general category of Asian Americans are ethnic groups whose ancestors for generations were enemies due to ethnic/cultural differences. Even among the more specific ethnic group identified as Chinese Americans there are major cultural differences between those who have immigrated from Hong Kong, Taiwan, and mainland China. Similar observations can be made about African Americans, American Indians, and Hispanic Americans. For African Americans, within-group ethnic/cultural differences are most evident among those who are recent immigrants from Africa, the Caribbean, and other parts of the world. However, regional differences also exist within the African American population that, in effect, constitute cultural differences.

Even within specific ethnic groups, cultural differences can exist between recent immigrants and those whose ancestors immigrated many generations ago that are not due to acculturation. Cultures in the home country change over time and the cultural values handed down through four or five generations in this country may be quite different than the cultural values currently practiced in the home country. For example, the cultural values of Japanese Americans whose ancestors immigrated in 1910 may be more similar in some ways to those practiced in Japan in 1910 than to those currently practiced in Japan. Thus, cultural values within an ethnic group may vary due to time of immigration as much as to length of time since immigration, a variable that correlates highly with acculturation.

Phinney (1996) has also cautioned against drawing conclusions about culture based solely on ethnicity, citing "the tremendous heterogeneity among members of American ethnic groups" (p. 921):

> Ethnic cultures differ in terms of particular country of origin within a broad cultural group (e.g., Asian Americans of Japanese vs. Korean ancestry), generation of immigration, region of settlement in the United States, socioeconomic status, and community structure. . . . Furthermore, because of their dispersion and mixing with both mainstream American culture and with other ethnic groups in the United States, ethnic cultures are not discrete entities but rather part of a diverse cultural mix. . . . Finally, even if particular subcultures can be described with some accuracy, cultures are not static, but continually evolving and changing. (p. 921)

Acculturation scales provide one measure of cultural differences within ethnic groups. Acculturation is such an important source of cultural differences within ethnic groups that we devote a major portion of this chapter to discussing it and its impact on ethnic minorities.

Acculturation As a Within-Group Variable

According to Olmedo (1979), acculturation is "one of the more elusive, albeit ubiquitous, constructs in the behavioral sciences" (p. 1061). Keefe (1980) suggests that "acculturation is one of those terms all social scientists use although few can agree upon its meaning" (p. 85). However, there is general agreement that acculturation is a process of change that occurs when two or more cultures come in contact with each other (Redfield, Linton, & Herskovits, 1936).

Anthropologists became interested in acculturation as early as the 1880s (Berry, 1990); however, it was not until the 1920s that anthropologists began studying acculturation at the population level in earnest. Early anthropological models of acculturation focused on changes in social structure, economic base, and political organization when two cultures came in contact. The assimilation model developed by Park and Burgess (1921), among the first to describe the process of acculturation, was widely accepted by social scientists in the past. This model implied that the United States was a melting pot in which immigrant groups contributed elements of their own culture to an evolving U.S. culture. According to the model, complete assimilation usually occurred within three generations after immigration (Neidert & Farley, 1985).

As suggested in chapter 1, the concept of melting pot acculturation has been criticized for several reasons. First, critics point out that total assimilation has been limited in the past to European immigrants and that people of color are expected to acculturate, but never allowed to completely assimilate (Novak, 1972). Also, most contemporary social scientists describe acculturation in the United States as a unilateral or unidirectional process in which immigrant groups are expected to adopt the dominant culture but contribute little or nothing of their indigenous culture (Keefe, 1980). Conceptually, acculturation speaks to an unequal status relationship between the majority and minority cultures. As such, many persons of color believe that the melting pot concept may actually be describing a form of cultural oppression in that racial/ethnic minorities are forced to comply rather than given the choice in adopting the ways of the larger society. The melting pot model of acculturation can only become a reality if there is an equal power relationship between the two groups.

Another criticism of the early assimilation model has to do with the assumption that all immigrants experience the negative effects of being "caught between two cultures." Park (1928) coined the term "marginal man" (or more accurately, marginal person) to describe this condition. According to Park (1950), the marginal person lives in a permanent state of crisis due to an internalized cultural conflict; he suggested that some of the psychological manifestations are "intensified self-consciousness, restlessness, and malaise" (p. 356). Stonequist (1961) expanded upon this, suggesting that "the marginal situation produces excessive self-consciousness and race-consciousness" and "'inferiority complexes' are a common affliction" (p. 148). Contemporary acculturation theorists agree that some immigrants may experience marginalization, but most reject the idea that all immigrants experience the marginal person syndrome. Also, most contemporary theorists point out that many immigrants and their descendants achieve a positive, bicultural resolution to acculturation (Valentine, 1971).

A related issue has to do with the conceptualization of acculturation as a unilinear or monocultural concept. Early models of acculturation conceptualized acculturation as a process occurring along a single continuum, with the indigenous culture on one end and dominant U.S. culture on the other. According to this model, cultural traits (e.g., attitudes, values, behavior) of the indigenous culture were gradually lost while cultural traits of the dominant society were gradually adopted over time.

Although anthropologists and sociologists have studied acculturation for many decades, few psychologists have engaged in a sustained program of psychological research related to acculturation. An exception to this rule is John Berry (Ward & Kennedy, 1994). Berry (1990) makes a distinction between acculturation at the population level (ecological, cultural, social, and institutional changes) and at the individual level (changes in the behavior and traits of individuals, also known as *psychological acculturation*). Research on psychological acculturation, initiated in the 1960s, has focused on the process by which individuals change their behavior, identity, values, and attitudes as a result of coming in contact with another culture, and as a result of "being participants in the general acculturative changes under way in their own culture" (Berry, 1990, 235).

Berry, Trimble, and Olmeda (1986) diagrammed how the process of acculturation operates at both the population and individual levels, and their diagram is presented in figure 2.1. The diagram demonstrates the process and effect of acculturation at a given time. As seen in figure 2.1, Culture A is the dominant culture and exerts a stronger impact on Culture B and Individual B (from Culture B) then they, in turn, exert on Culture A. Culture B and Individual B also exert an impact on each other; the influence of Culture B on Individual B is referred to as *enculturation,* a process of socializing the individual to their indigenous culture that is typically the responsibility of the individual's family. The result of the acculturation (and enculturation) process that takes place between Culture A, Culture B, and Individual B is a transformation of Culture B into Culture B¹ and Individual B into Individual B¹. If Culture A, Culture B¹, and Individual B¹ remain in contact, additional changes are likely to occur (Berry, 1990).

While some people may disagree, Berry and Kim (1988) suggest that individuals have some choice about how they will respond to this acculturation process. Berry and Kim have identified four models of acculturation based on attitudes (labeled *"acculturation attitudes"* by Berry, Kim, Power, Young, and Bajaki, 1989) members of acculturating groups have about accepting the identity, attitudes, and behaviors of the cultures involved. Some individuals may choose to give up their identity and the cultural attitudes and behaviors associated with Culture B and embrace those associated with Culture A (Assimilation option). Others may choose to maintain their identity and the cultural attitudes and behaviors associated with Culture B while rejecting those of Culture A (Separation option). Still others may give up their identity and

Figure 2.1 Framework for Identifying Variables and Relationships in Acculturation Research

Psychology of Acculturation

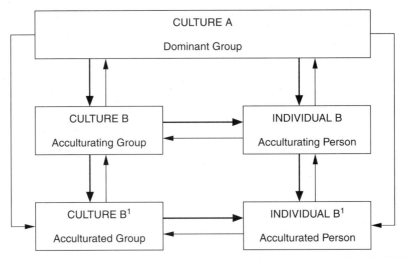

W. J. Lonner and J. W. Berry. *Field Methods in Cross-Cultural Research.* London: Sage © 1986 by Sage Publishers.

cultural practices from Culture B while at the same time rejecting those of Culture A (Marginalization option). Some individuals will choose to maintain their identity and many of the cultural practices of Culture B at the same time that they identify with and adopt the attitudes and behaviors associated with Culture A (Integration or Bicultural option).

Berry (1994) has pointed out that with psychological acculturation, there are two basic phenomenon that impact the individual. One is that *behavior shifts* occur, that is, individuals often change their values, attitudes, and behavior. Generally, although not universally, the behavior shift is away from patterns of behavior learned in the indigenous culture and toward those more frequently found in the host culture. The other phenomenon that occurs is *acculturative stress,* what some authors refer to as culture shock (Oberg, 1954; Winkelman, 1994).

> There is often a particular set of stress behaviors that occur during acculturation, such as lowered mental health status (especially confusion, anxiety, depression), feelings of marginality and alienation, heightened psychosomatic symptom level, and identity confusion. Acculturative stress is thus a phenomenon that may underlie a reduction in the health status of individuals (including physical, psychological, and social aspects). (Berry, 1990, 246–247)

Berry (1990) has identified a number of factors that may influence the degree of acculturative stress experienced by the individual. For example, mode of acculturation experienced by the individual may be one factor related to degree of acculturative stress. Berry and Kim (1988) report that people who feel marginalized or separated experience the most stress, while those who seek assimilation experience intermediate levels of stress and those who seek to integrate the two cultures feel the least stress. Another factor is the general tolerance for ethnic diversity in the dominant culture; in general, pluralistic societies have less acculturative stress associated with them than monistic societies. Societies that exclude acculturating groups from full participation may generate more acculturative stress, at least among those who aspire to acculturate. As Berry (1994) points out, conditions that affect adaptation to acculturation are often under the control of policy makers and health professionals; therefore, the probability of successful adaptations can be enhanced by making appropriate policy decisions and by implementing appropriate programs for immigrants. Berry (1994) suggests that psychologists can play a role in promoting successful adaptation by addressing these issues through research and by lobbying legislatures regarding social programs that produce successful adaptations.

Other psychologists have made important contributions to our understanding of psychological acculturation. For example, Padilla (1980b) was among the first psychologists to develop a model of acculturation and then subject it to empirical verification. He conceptualized a multidimensional model of acculturation for Mexican Americans that consisted of two underlying "elements" and five "dimensions."

> Our model of acculturation involves two essential elements—cultural awareness and ethnic loyalty. Cultural awareness refers to an individual's knowledge of specific cultural material (e.g., language, values, history-art, foods, etc.) of the cultural group of origin and/or the host culture. By loyalty we mean the individual's preference of one cultural orientation over the other. (p. 48)

By identifying acculturation as a multidimensional process, Padilla (1980b) drew attention to the fact that the generation since immigration, often used as a unitary measure of acculturation, was not the only dimension that should be taken into account in assessing level of acculturation. Padilla hypothesized that there were at least five dimensions of acculturation: (a) language familiarity and usage; (b) cultural heritage (knowledge of culture); (c) ethnic pride and identity pride; (d) interethnic interaction; and (e) interethnic distance and perceived discrimination. To test this model of acculturation, Padilla developed a questionnaire that "tapped awareness and loyalty information on the five dimensions of the model" (p. 53) and administered it to Mexican Americans representing a variety of generation levels. After factor and cluster analyzing the data from this study, Padilla concluded that:

> Cultural awareness is composed of: respondent's cultural heritage as well as the cultural heritage of the respondent's spouse and parents, language preference and use, cultural identification and preference, and social behavior orientation. Ethnic loyalty consists of: cultural pride and affiliation, perceived discrimination, and social behavior orientation. (p. 81)

Padilla (1980a) suggests that while the acculturation process may be unique to every immigrant group, "many of the psychological processes underlying acculturation are probably similar" (p. 3). Although the acculturation and biculturalism concepts can be applied to all racial/ethnic minorities, acculturation as a process of adopting the dominant culture seems most applicable to American Indians, Asian Americans, and Hispanic Americans. Recently, however, the concept of acculturation has been applied to African Americans, even though most African Americans are many generations removed from immigration and despite their long-standing history of impacting the U.S. culture.

The concept of biculturalism is particularly important to current theories of acculturation. Bicultural socialization can be conceptualized as two continua, one representing involvement (low to high) with the indigenous culture and one representing involvement (low to high) with the dominant culture. According to the bicultural process model of acculturation, the marginal person and the bicultural person respond differently to their socialization in two cultures. The marginal person feels caught between the conflicting values of two cultures and consequently feels little commitment to either. In contrast, the bicultural individual feels committed to both cultures and selectively embraces the positive aspects of each culture.

De Anda (1984) suggests that six factors contribute to the development of a bicultural rather than a marginal perspective: (a) degree of cultural overlap between the two cultures; (b) the availability of cultural translators, mediators, and models; (c) the amount and type of corrective feedback regarding attempts to produce normative behaviors; (d) the compatibility of the minority individual's conceptual style with the analytical cognitive style valued by the dominant culture; (e) the individual's degree of bilingualism; and (f) the degree of dissimilarity in physical appearance between the individual and those representative of the dominant culture.

In the United States, numerous scales have been developed to measure acculturation among Hispanic Americans and, to a lesser extent, among other racial/ethnic groups. Typically, acculturation measures include items measuring language usage and preference, ethnic identification, knowledge of culture, and so forth. Some of the more widely used measures of Hispanic American acculturation include the Acculturation Rating Scale for Mexican Americans (ARSMA) (Cuellar, Harris, & Jasso, 1980), the Short Acculturation Scale for Hispanics (SASH) (Marin, Sabogal, Marin, Otero-Sabogal, & Perez-Stable, 1987), Short Acculturation Scale for Hispanic Youth (SASH-Y) (Barona & Miller, 1994), and the Padilla Acculturation Scale (Padilla, 1980b). The most widely used scale for measuring acculturation among Asian Americans is probably the Suinn-Lew Asian Self-Identity Acculturation Scale (SL-ASIA) (Suinn, Rickard-Figueroa, Lew, & Vigil, 1987), an instrument modeled after the ARSMA.

Marin (1992) has criticized instruments measuring Hispanic acculturation for

(a) lacking sound psychometric qualities; (b) relying heavily on language use, dominance, or preference as a valid measure of acculturation; (c) operationalizing the measurement of acculturation on a single scale with a different culture on each end (Marin refers to this as unidimensional measurement; to avoid confounding this issue with the unidimensional concerns raised by Padilla, 1980b, we refer to it as unilinear measurement); and (d) failing to include such variables as cognitive style, personality, attitudes, and levels of stress as measures of acculturation. He also criticized researchers for making changes to the wording of items or dropping items on acculturation instruments based on personal preferences and then assuming that the psychometric properties of the original instrument still hold.

Of the concerns raised by Marin (1992), the problem with operationalizing acculturation as a unilinear measurement represents perhaps the greatest problem for contemporary theorists and researchers. Several instruments have been developed to measure Hispanic acculturation that provide for bilinear, orthogonal measures of acculturation. The Bicultural Involvement Questionnaire developed by Szapocznik, Kurtines, and Fernandez (1980) measures the degree to which a person is involved in Hispanic and European American cultures independently of each other. The two separate scores can be used independent of each other to represent acculturation to each of the two cultures, or, the European American score can be subtracted from the Hispanic score to create a conventional, unilinear score for acculturation. More recently, Cuellar, Arnold, and Maldonado (1995) revised the ARSMA to address concerns with the unilinear approach of the original instrument. The instrument, identified as ARSMA-II, consists of two scales. Scale 1 is composed of an Anglo Orientation Subscale (AOS) and a Mexican Orientation Subscale (MOS); scores on the AOS and MOS can be used independently as orthogonal measures of acculturation. However, by subtracting the MOS mean rating from the AOS mean rating, administrators of the instrument can also obtain a linear acculturation score. Scale 2 is identified by the authors as an optional, experimental scale that consists of three subscales: ANGMAR (Anglo Marginality); MEXMAR (Mexican Marginality); and MAMARG (Mexican American Marginality). Cuellar et al. (1995) offer a rather complicated but promising procedure for categorizing respondents into five major types and eleven subtypes. After administering the ARSMA-II to a sample of university students representing five generation levels of Mexicans, Mexican Americans, and White non-Hispanics, Cuellar et al. concluded that the instrument is a "reliable, [and valid] measure applicable with a culturally diverse population of individuals of Mexican origin or descent" (p. 294). Interestingly, they also concluded that their study "indicates the power of linear acculturative measures derived from orthogonal identification theory and suggests that researchers should not be too hasty in abandoning linearly derived indices" (p. 294).

Four reviews of the research have reported a growing number of studies that have found a relationship between Hispanic acculturation and measures of mental health status, depression, anorexia, generational conflict, stress, social support, social deviancy, juvenile delinquency, alcoholism, drug use, political and social attitudes, consumption of cigarettes, and the practice of preventive cancer screening (Casas & Casas, 1994; Marin, 1992; Moyerman & Forman, 1992; Rogler, Cortes, & Malgady, 1991). However, some of the studies reported a positive relationship between acculturation and adjustment, some a negative relationship, and still others found no evidence of a relationship.

A second line of research has examined the relationship between acculturation and counseling process and outcome variables for these racial/ethnic groups. Acculturation among Hispanic Americans has been found to be related to preference for an ethnically similar counselor (Sanchez & Atkinson, 1983), perceptions of counselor trustworthiness (Pomales & Williams, 1989), expectations for counseling (Kunkel, 1990), and willingness to self-disclose in counseling (Sanchez & Atkinson). Similarly, acculturation among Asian Americans is related to attitudes toward seeking professional psychological help (Atkinson & Gim, 1989; Gim, Atkinson, & Whiteley, 1990) and perceptions of counselor credibility (Gim, Atkinson, & Kim, 1991), although not always in the direct relationship hypothesized (Gim et al., 1990).

Although few in number, these studies provide consistent documentation that acculturation is related to how racial/ethnic minority clients perceive and respond to counseling services. In general, they suggest that less acculturated racial/ethnic minorities are more likely to trust and express a preference for and a willingness to see an ethnically similar counselor than are their more acculturated counterparts. For Asian Americans the findings suggest a direct relationship between acculturation and willingness to see a counselor for concerns perceived as "nonpsychological" (e.g., academic or career problems, financial problems, relationship problems). Less acculturated Asian Americans may also prefer a racially/ethnically similar counselor who is culturally sensitive over other types of counselors.

In summary, acculturation is a measure of within-group diversity that is related to a number of counseling process variables. Counselors working with an ethnic minority client should be aware not only of the client's ethnic background but the extent to which the client identifies with and practices the culture of his/her ancestors.

Racial/Ethnic Identity Development As a Within-Group Variable

One of the most promising contributions to the field of multicultural counseling is theory and research on racial/ethnic/cultural identity development. When we first published our Minority Identity Development Model in the original (1979) edition of this book, we were aware of only three earlier models of identity development, all three addressing Black identity development (Cross, 1971; Jackson, 1975; Vontress, 1971). Since our original edition, however, we have become aware of numerous other models for Black (Gay, 1984), Latino (Ruiz, 1990), White (Helms, 1985, 1990; Ponterotto, 1988), female (Downing & Roush, 1985), homosexual (Cass, 1979; Troiden, 1989), biracial (Poston, 1990), ethnic (Ford, 1987; Smith, 1991), racial/cultural (D. W. Sue & D. Sue, 1990), and general minority identity development (Highlen et al., 1988; Myers et al., 1991). In her book on Black and White racial identity, Helms (1990) listed eleven identity development models for African Americans alone!

Helms (1990) cites the Cross (1970, 1971, 1978, 1991, 1995) model of Black racial identity development as "the primary means of investigating racial identity in the counseling and psychotherapy process" (p. 19). Cross originally described his model as a "Negro-to-Black Conversion Experience" (1971) and later as a process of psychological nigrescence (1978). The original Cross (1971) model consisted of five stages: preencounter, encounter, immersion, internalization, and internalization-commitment. Helms (1990) cites problems with differentiating internalization-commitment from other stages on instruments measuring racial identity development as a reason why the fifth stage was dropped in subsequent refinement of the model. According to the original model, Blacks at the preencounter stage are "programmed to view and think of the world as being nonblack, anti-black, or the opposite of Black" (Hall, Cross, & Freedle, 1972, p. 159). At the next stage, the encounter stage, the Black individual becomes aware of what being Black means and begins to validate himself/herself as a Black person. During the immersion stage, the Black person rejects all non-black values and totally immerses himself/herself in Black culture. Finally, in the internalization stage, the Black person gains a sense of inner security and begins to focus on ". . . things other than himself and his own ethnic or racial group" (Hall et al., p. 160).

More recently, Cross (1995) described revisions to his original model that are based on research findings. Most notably, he argued that Black self-hatred is not a defining characteristic of the preencounter stage. Although some Blacks at the preencounter stage may reject their Black identity, Cross suggests that self-hatred previously associated with individuals at this stage of identity development have been exaggerated and that "persons in the Pre-Encounter stage hold attitudes toward race that range from low salience or race neutrality, to anti-Black" (p. 98). Cross also modified earlier suppositions that ideological unity is a defining characteristic of the internalization stage and suggests that "people in the advanced stages are quite divergent in their ideological perspectives" (p. 97). He also retracted earlier differences in value structures (individualism v. communalism) between preencounter Black and Blacks in more advanced stages of development. "I now believe that although they hold radically different value orientations, Pre-Encounter persons do not necessar[ily] differ in their value structures from persons in advanced stages of Black identity development" (p. 103).

Helms (1995) has also updated her earlier thoughts regarding racial identity development (Helms, 1984, 1990); her updated model applies to both Whites and people of color. The process by which Whites develop their racial identity will be discussed briefly in chapter 16 when we examine models for training counselors. For people of color (individuals who can trace some of their ancestry to Africa, Asia, or pre-Columbus America), the other group discussed in Helms (1995), the central racial identity developmental theme is "to recognize and overcome the psychological manifestations of internalized racism" (p. 189). Helms derived her People of Color Racial Identity (PCRI) model from Cross's (1971) original psychological nigrescence model and our own minority identity development model (to be discussed later in this chapter).

The PCRI model consists of five statuses; the term status has replaced the term stage used in earlier writings in an attempt to represent mutually interactive and dynamic processes rather than mutually exclusive categories. In the *conformity (preencounter)* status, individuals tend to devalue their own ethnic group and look up to White standards of merit. Individuals in the *dissonance (encounter)* status are ambivalent and confused about their commitment to their own socioracial group. Idealization of their socioracial group and denigration of White standards is associated with the *immersion/ emersion* status. In the internalization status, individuals have a positive commitment to their own socioracial group and respond objectively to White people. Individuals in the *integrative awareness* status value their own collective identity but also "empathize and collaborate with members of other oppressed groups" (Helms, 1995, p. 186). Helms (1995) suggests that most people do not express their racial identity in pure forms but more typically have one status that is stronger than others.

Research on the application of racial/ethnic minority identity development to counseling process and outcome has largely involved the original Cross model and most of it has been conducted by Janet Helms and Thomas Parham. They developed the Black Racial Identity Attitude Scale (RIAS-B) to measure the first four stages of Cross' (1971) model (Parham & Helms, 1981). They and other researchers have used the RIAS-B to examine the relationship between Black identity development and (a) psychological adjustment and (b) counseling process and outcome. Parham and Helms found that preencounter attitudes were associated with a preference for White counselors while encounter and internalization attitudes were associated with a preference for Black counselors and a rejection of White counselors. In a subsequent study, Parham and Helms (1985a, 1985b) found that pro-White/anti-Black (preencounter) attitudes and pro-Black/anti-White (immersion) attitudes were inversely associated with mentally healthy self-actualizing tendencies. Encounter attitudes, on the other hand, were directly related to self-actualization tendencies and inversely related to feelings of inferiority and anxiety. Ponterotto, Alexander, and Hinkston (1988) found that the relationship between racial identity development categories and preferences for counselor characteristics were not as hypothesized. However, Black students' value orientations (Carter & Helms, 1987) and cognitive styles (Helms & Parham, 1990) have been found to be related to Black racial identity development.

In summary, there is empirical support for the concept of Black Racial Identity Development (BRID) and the stages of BRID have been found to be related to counseling process and outcome variables. Future research will likely shed light on the validity of the revised Cross model and the reconceptualized Helms PCRI model. In the meantime, racial identity development continues to serve as an important variable for recognizing within-group differences among ethnic minority groups.

Minority Identity Development (MID) Model

Although the Black identity development models pertain specifically to the African American experience, we believe that some of the basic tenets of these theories can be generalized and applied to other minority groups, due to their shared experience of oppression. Although each of the ethnic groups discussed in this book has a unique culture (indeed, within these broad groupings are a number of unique cultures), that they have been subjected to various forms of physical, economic, and social discrimination suggests that they share a common experience affecting how they view themselves and others. Several earlier writers (Stonequist, 1937; Berry, 1965) have also observed that minority groups share the same patterns of adjustment to cultural oppression.

Based on views expressed by earlier writers and our own clinical observation that these changes in attitudes and subsequent behavior follow a predictable sequence, we developed a five-stage Minority Identity Development (MID) model. The MID model we describe on the following pages is not presented as a comprehensive theory of personality development, but rather as a schema to help counselors understand minority client attitudes and behaviors within existing personality theories. The model defines five stages of development that oppressed people may experience as they struggle to understand themselves in terms of their own minority culture and the oppressive relationship between the two cultures. Although five distinct stages are presented in the model, the MID is more accurately conceptualized as a continuous process in which one stage blends with another and boundaries between stages are not clear.

It is our observation that not all minority individuals experience the entire range of these stages in their lifetimes. Prior to the turbulent 1960s—a decade in which the transition of many individuals through this process was accelerated and, therefore, made more evident—many people were raised and lived their lives in the first stage. Nor is the developmental process to be interpreted as irreversible. It is our opinion that many minority individuals are socialized by their parents to hold the values associated with level five, but in coming to grips with their own identity, offsprings often move from level five to one of the lower levels. Further, it does not appear that functioning at lower levels of

Table 2.1

Summary of Minority Identity Development Model

Stages of Minority Development Model	Attitudes toward Self	Attitude toward Others of the Same Minority	Attitude toward Others of Different Minority	Attitude toward Dominant Group
Stage 1— Conformity	Self-depreciating	Group-depreciating	Discriminatory	Group-appreciating
Stage 2— Dissonance	Conflict between self-depreciating and appreciating	Conflict between group-depreciating and group-appreciating	Conflict between dominant-held views of minority hierarchy and feelings of shared experience	Conflict between group-appreciating and group-depreciating
Stage 3— Resistance and Immersion	Self-appreciating	Group-appreciating	Conflict between feelings of empathy for other minority experiences and feelings of culturocentrism	Group-depreciating
Stage 4— Introspection	Concern with basis of self-appreciation	Concern with nature of unequivocal appreciation	Concern with ethnocentric basis for judging others	Concern with the basis of group depreciation
Stage 5— Synergetic Articulation and Awareness	Self-appreciating	Group-appreciating	Group-appreciating	Selective appreciation

development is prerequisite to functioning at higher levels. Some people born and raised in a family functioning at level five appear never to experience a level-one sense of identity.

At each level we provide examples of four corresponding attitudes that may assist the counselor to understand behaviors displayed by individuals operating at or near these levels (see table 2.1). Each attitude is believed to be an integral part of any minority person's identity or of how he/she views

(a) self, (b) others of the same minority, (c) others of another minority, and (d) majority individuals. It was not our intention to define a hierarchy with more valued attitudes at higher levels of development. Rather, the model is intended to reflect a process that we have observed in our work with minority clients over the past three decades.

Stage One—Conformity Stage

Minority individuals in the Conformity stage of development are distinguished by their unequivocal preference for dominant cultural values over those of their own culture. Their choices of role models, life-styles, value system, and so forth, follow the lead of the dominant group. Those physical and/or cultural characteristics that single them out as minority persons are a source of pain and are either viewed with disdain or are repressed from consciousness. Their views of self, fellow group members, and other minorities in general are clouded by their identification with the dominant culture. Minorities may perceive the ways of the dominant group as being much more positive, and there is a high desire to "assimilate and acculturate." The attitudes minorities may have about themselves in this stage are ones of devaluation and depreciation on both a conscious and subconscious level. For example, Asian Americans may perceive their own physical features as less desirable and their cultural values and Asian ways as a handicap to successful adaptation in the dominant society. Their attitudes toward members of their own group tend to be highly negative in that they share the dominant culture's belief that Asian Americans are less desirable. Stereotypes portraying Asian Americans as inarticulate, good with numbers, poor managers, and aloof in their personal relationships are accepted. Other minority groups are also viewed according to the dominant group's system of minority stratification (i.e., those minority groups that most closely resemble the dominant group in physical and cultural characteristics are viewed more favorably than those less similar). Attitudes toward members of the dominant group, however, tend to be highly appreciative in that the members are admired, respected, and often viewed as ideal models.

In the Conformity stage of development Asian Americans and other minorities view themselves as deficient in the "desirable" characteristics held up by the dominant society. Feelings of racial self-hatred caused by cultural racism may accompany this type of adjustment (S. Sue & D. W. Sue, 1971).

A. *Attitude toward self: Self-depreciating attitude.* Individuals who acknowledge their distinguishing physical and/or cultural characteristics consciously view them as a source of shame. Individuals who repress awareness of their distinguishing physical and/or cultural characteristics depreciate themselves at a subconscious level.
B. *Attitude toward members of same minority: Group-depreciating attitude.* Other members of the minority group are viewed according to dominant-held beliefs of minority strengths and weaknesses.

C. *Attitude toward members of different minority: Discriminatory attitude.*
Other minorities are viewed according to the dominant group's system of
minority stratification (i.e., those minority groups that most closely
resemble the dominant group in physical and cultural characteristics are
viewed more favorably than those less similar).
D. *Attitude toward members of dominant group: Group-appreciating attitude.*
Members of the dominant group are admired, respected, and often viewed
as ideal models. Cultural values of the dominant society are accepted
without question.

Stage Two—Dissonance Stage

The movement into the Dissonance stage is most often a gradual process but as
Cross (1971) points out, a monumental event such as the assassination of
Martin Luther King, Jr., may propel the Black person into the next stage. Denial
is a major tool used by persons in the Conformity stage; minorities in the
Dissonance stage begin to experience a breakdown in their denial system. A
Latino who may feel ashamed of his/her cultural upbringing may encounter a
Latino who seems proud of his/her cultural heritage. An African American who
may have deceived himself/herself into believing that race problems are due to
laziness, untrustworthiness, or personal inadequacies of his/her group, suddenly
encounters racism on a personal level.

A. *Attitude toward self: Conflict between self-depreciating and self-
appreciating attitudes.* With a growing awareness of minority cultural
strengths comes a faltering sense of pride in self. The individual's attitude
toward distinguishing physical and/or cultural characteristics is typified by
alternating feelings of shame and pride in self.
B. *Attitude toward members of same minority: Conflict between group-
depreciating and group-appreciating attitudes.* Dominant-held views of
minority strengths and weaknesses begin to be questioned, as new,
contradictory information is received. Cultural values of the minority group
begin to have appeal.
C. *Attitude toward members of different minority: Conflict between dominant-
held views of minority hierarchy and feelings of shared experience.* The
individual begins to question the dominant-held system of minority
stratification and experiences a growing sense of comradeship with other
oppressed people. Most of the individual's psychic energy at this level,
however, is devoted to resolving conflicting attitudes toward self, the same
minority, and the dominant group.
D. *Attitude toward members of dominant group: Conflict between group-
appreciating and group-depreciating attitude.* The individual experiences a
growing awareness that not all cultural values of the dominant group are
beneficial to him/her. Members of the dominant group are viewed with
growing suspicion.

Stage Three—Resistance and Immersion Stage

In the Resistance and Immersion stage of development, the minority individual completely endorses minority-held views and rejects the dominant society and culture. Desire to eliminate oppression of the individual's minority group becomes an important motivation of the individual's behavior.

D. W. Sue and D. Sue (1990) believe that movement into this stage seems to occur for two reasons. First, the person begins to resolve many of the conflicts and confusions in the previous stage. As a result, a greater understanding of societal forces (racism, oppression, and discrimination) emerges, along with a realization that he/she has been victimized by it. Second, the individual begins to ask himself/herself the following question: "Why should I feel ashamed of who and what I am?" The answers to that question will evoke both guilt and anger (bordering on rage): guilt that he/she has "sold out" in the past and contributed to his/her own group's oppression and anger at having been oppressed and "brainwashed" by the forces in the dominant society.

A. *Attitude toward self: Self-appreciating attitude.* The minority individual at this stage acts as an explorer and discoverer of his/her history and culture, seeking out information and artifacts that enhance his/her sense of identity and worth. Cultural and physical characteristics that once elicited feelings of shame and disgust at this stage become symbols of pride and honor.

B. *Attitude toward members of same minority: Group-appreciating attitude.* The individual experiences a strong sense of identification with, and commitment to, his/her minority group, as enhancing information about the group is acquired. Members of the group are admired, respected, and often viewed as ideal models. Cultural values of the minority group are accepted without question.

C. *Attitude toward members of different minority: Conflict between feelings of empathy for other minority experiences and feelings of culturocentrism.* The individual experiences a growing sense of camaraderie with persons from other minority groups, to the degree that they are viewed as sharing similar forms of oppression. Alliances with other groups tend to be short-lived, however, when their values come in conflict with those of the individual's minority group. The dominant group's system of minority stratification is replaced by a system which values most those minority groups that are culturally similar to the individual's own group.

D. *Attitude toward members of dominant group: Group-depreciating attitude.* The individual totally rejects the dominant society and culture and experiences a sense of distrust and dislike for all members of the dominant group.

Stage Four—Introspection Stage

In the Introspection stage of development, the minority individual experiences feelings of discontent and discomfort with group views rigidly held in the

Resistance and Immersion stage and diverts attention to notions of greater individual autonomy.

What occurs at this stage is interesting. First, the minority individual may begin to feel progressively more comfortable with his or her own sense of identity. This security allows the person to begin to question some of the rigidly held beliefs of the Resistance stage that all "Whites are bad." There is also a feeling that too much negativism and hatred directed at White society tends to divert energies from more positive exploration of identity questions. This stage is characterized by greater individual autonomy. During this stage the person may begin to experience conflict between notions of responsibility and allegiance to his/her own minority group and notions of personal autonomy. There is now a belief that perhaps not everything in the dominant culture is bad and that there are many positive and negative elements within it.

A. *Attitude toward self: Concern with basis of self-appreciating attitude.* The individual experiences conflict between notions of responsibility and allegiance to minority group and notions of personal autonomy.
B. *Attitude toward members of same minority: Concern with unequivocal nature of group appreciation.* While attitudes of identification are continued from the preceding Resistance and Immersion stages, concern begins to build regarding the issue of group usurpation of individuality.
C. *Attitude toward members of different minority: Concern with ethnocentric basis for judging others.* The individual experiences a growing uneasiness with minority stratification that results from culturocentrism and places a greater value on groups experiencing the same oppression than on those experiencing a different oppression.
D. *Attitude toward members of dominant group: Concern with the basis of group depreciation.* The individual experiences conflict between an attitude of complete distrust for the dominant society and culture and an attitude of selective trust and distrust according to dominant individuals' demonstrated behaviors and attitudes. The individual also recognizes the utility of many dominant cultural elements yet is uncertain whether to incorporate such elements into his/her minority culture.

Stage Five—Synergistic Stage

Minority individuals in the Synergistic stage experience a sense of self-fulfillment with regard to cultural identity. Conflicts and discomforts experienced in the Introspection stage have been resolved, allowing greater individual control and flexibility. Cultural values of other minorities and those of the dominant group are objectively examined and accepted or rejected on the basis of experience gained in earlier stages of identity development. Desire to eliminate *all* forms of oppression becomes an important motivation for the individual's behavior.

A. *Attitude toward self: Self-appreciating attitude.* The individual experiences a strong sense of self-worth, self-confidence, and autonomy as the result of having established his/her identity as an individual, a member of a minority group, and/or a member of the dominant culture.
B. *Attitude toward members of same minority: Group-appreciating attitude.* The individual experiences a strong sense of pride in the group without having to accept group values unequivocally. Strong feelings of empathy with the group experience are coupled with an awareness that each member of the group is an individual.
C. *Attitude toward members of different minority: Group-appreciating attitude.* The individual experiences a strong sense of respect for the group's cultural values coupled with awareness that each member of the group is an individual. The individual also experiences a greater understanding and support for all oppressed people, regardless of their similarity or dissimilarity to the individual's minority group.
D. *Attitude toward members of dominant group: Attitude of selective appreciation.* The individual experiences selective trust and liking for members of the dominant group who seek to eliminate repressive activities of the group. The individual also experiences an openness to the constructive elements of the dominant culture.

Implications of the MID Model for Counseling

As suggested earlier, the MID model is not intended as a comprehensive theory of personality, but rather as a paradigm to help counselors understand minority client attitudes and behaviors. In this respect, the model is intended to sensitize counselors to (1) the role oppression plays in a minority individual's identity development, (2) the differences that can exist between members of the same minority group with respect to their cultural identity, and (3) the potential each minority person has for changing his/her sense of identity. Beyond helping to understand minority client behavior, the model has implications for the counseling process itself.

The general attitudes and behaviors that describe minority individuals at the Conformity stage (e.g., denial of minority problems, strong dependence on and identification with dominant group, etc.) suggest that clients from this stage are unlikely to seek counseling related to their cultural identity. It is more likely that they will perceive problems of cultural identity as problems related to their personal identity. Clients at this stage are more inclined to visit and be influenced by counselors of the dominant group than those of the same minority. Indeed, clients may actively request a White counselor and react negatively toward a minority counselor. Counselors from the dominant group may find the conformist client's need to please and appease a powerful force in the counseling relationship because of the client's strong identification with dominant group members. Attempts to explore cultural identity or to focus on feelings may be threatening to the client. This is because exploration of identity may eventually touch upon feelings of racial self-hatred and challenge the client's self-deception ("I'm not like other minorities"). Clients at the Conformity stage are likely to present problems that are most amenable to problem-solving and goal-oriented counseling approaches.

Minority individuals at the Dissonance stage of development are preoccupied by questions concerning their concept of self, identity, and self-esteem; they are likely to perceive personal problems as related to their cultural identity. Emotional problems develop when these individuals are unable to resolve conflicts that occur between dominant-held views and those of their minority group. Clients in the Dissonance stage are more culturally aware than Conformity clients and are likely to prefer to work with counselors who possess a good knowledge of the client's cultural group. Counseling approaches that involve considerable self-exploration appear to be best-suited for clients at this stage of development.

Minority individuals at the Resistance and Immersion stage are inclined to view all psychological problems (whether personal or social) as a product of their oppression. The likelihood that these clients will seek formal counseling regarding their cultural identity is slim. In those cases when counseling is sought, it will tend to be only an ethnically similar counselor and generally in response to a crisis situation. Therapy for Stage Three clients often takes the form of exposure to, and practice of, the ways and artifacts of their cultures. Clients at this stage who seek counseling are likely to prefer a group setting. In addition, approaches that are more action-oriented and aimed at external change (challenging racism) are well received. D. W. Sue and D. Sue (1990) believe that most counselors find minorities at this stage difficult to work with. A counselor (even if a member of the client's own racial/ethnic group) is often viewed by the culturally different client as a symbol of the oppressive establishment. A great amount of direct anger and distrust may be expressed toward the counselor. The counselor will be frequently tested and challenged as to his/her own racism and role in society.

Clients at the Introspection stage are torn between their preponderant identification with their minority group and their need to exercise greater personal freedom. When these individuals are unable to resolve mounting conflict between these two forces, they often seek counseling. While Introspective clients still prefer to see a counselor from their own cultural group, counselors from other cultures may be viewed as credible sources of help if they share world views similar to those of their clientele and appreciate their cultural dilemmas. Counselors who use a self-exploration and decision-making approach can be most effective with these clients.

Clients at the Synergistic stage of identity development have acquired the internal skills and knowledge necessary to exercise a desired level of personal freedom. Their sense of minority identity is well balanced by an appreciation of other cultures. While discrimination and oppression remain a painful part of their lives, greater psychological resources are at their disposal in actively engaging the problem. Attitudinal similarity between counselor and client becomes a more important determinant of counseling success than membership-group similarity.

Racial/ethnic identity development occurs along many dimensions. While we have focused primarily on the evolution of attitudes, changes also occur in the cognitive (beliefs), affective (feelings), and behavioral domains of the person. These aspects of the human condition may evolve at different rates. For example, it may be possible that a person exhibits the attitudes of the immersion/resistance stage, but that this is not manifest in his or her behavior. The possibility that not all aspects of the person's identity will evolve at an identical rate may be the source of much confusion, especially in situations of assessment. Measures developed to assess the stage of ethnic identification are primarily cognitive and may not adequately tap the affective or behavioral domain.

While the MID model makes good intuitive and clinical sense, it has yet to be adequately tested empirically. Morten and Atkinson (1983) did find evidence of a relationship between level of MID and preference for counselor race among African Americans but we are not aware of any attempt to replicate these results with other racial/ethnic populations. Part of the difficulty is the lack of a racial/ethnic identity development instrument that can be used across various racial/ethnic populations. Helms and Carter (1986) developed a scale that might be useful for this purpose, but information about it has yet to be published in the professional counseling literature.

As authors of the model we are perhaps negligent for not submitting it to empirical verification but each of us has been occupied with research and writing in other areas. However, we hope the model will stimulate much-needed research with regard to minority identity development and that the model will help the reader distinguish and comprehend intragroup differences that are evident in the readings to follow. The development of an instrument that can measure identity development across minority groups would be a major first step to researching the relationship between MID stages and counseling process and outcome. We encourage readers interested in minority identity development to pursue this avenue of research.

Socioeconomic Within-Group Differences

Mental health workers are generally aware of the socioeconomic differences between racial/ethnic groups. For example, over twice as many Blacks (11 percent) were unemployed in 1993 than Whites (5 percent), and those Blacks who were employed full-time earned less money than Whites. The median earnings in 1993 for Blacks who were twenty-five years of age or older, high school graduates, and working full-time was $18,460. This compares to $24,120 for comparable White workers. Similarly, Hispanics and American Indians are more likely to be unemployed than Whites, they have lower incomes on average than Whites, and they are more likely to live below the poverty level than Whites (U.S. Bureau of the Census, 1995).

What tends to get lost, however, is the socioeconomic differences *within* racial/ethnic minority groups. Figures like those listed previously tend to create a stereotype that all members of these racial/ethnic groups are poor or uneducated. This is often reinforced by counseling research that fails to take within-group socioeconomic differences into account as an independent variable. Although current large-scale epidemiological studies involving racial/ethnic minority participants often assess socioeconomic background, most contemporary studies of counseling process and outcome still fail to include socioeconomic status as a variable of interest. In this section we will briefly document the range of economic differences within racial/ethnic groups to dispel the myth that all members of these groups are poor (or, in the case of Asian Americans, well off).

For African Americans, like other racial/ethnic groups, there is a direct relationship between income and educational attainment. In 1993, 73 percent of African Americans twenty-five years and older had at least a high school diploma. The median income for those African Americans who only had a high school education was $18,460. However, approximately 13 percent of African Americans twenty-five years and older had earned at least a bachelor's degree; the median income for those who had at least a bachelor's degree was $32,360. While these figures trail those of European Americans with comparable educational levels, they demonstrate that although an unacceptable percent of African Americans live on incomes below the poverty level, there is a sizable portion of African Americans who live on middle-class incomes (U.S. Bureau of the Census, 1995).

Similar data for Hispanic Americans suggest a wide range of educational and income levels as well. About 47 percent of Hispanics in 1993 had less than a high school education while 9 percent had completed college. For those Hispanic men who were employed full-time in 1992, about 12 percent earned less than $10,000 a year but 6.7 percent earned over $50,000 a year. For Hispanic women, 16.5 percent earned less than $10,000, while about 26.9 percent earned $25,000 or more in 1992 (U.S. Bureau of the Census, 1995).

Although approximately 34 percent of American Indians twenty-five years and over had less than a high school education in 1990, 9 percent had completed a bachelor's degree or higher and over 3 percent had a graduate or professional degree. In 1989, the median income of American Indian married-couple families was $28,287, while the per capita income for American Indians residing on a reservation was $4,478 (U.S. Bureau of the Census, 1995).

The figures for Asian and Pacific Islanders are much different but again suggest a great disparity in socioeconomic backgrounds within the ethnic group. For Asian and Pacific Islanders in 1994, nearly 9 out of 10 men and 8 out of 10 women had at least a high school diploma. Two out of every five Asians and

Pacific Islanders twenty-five years or older in 1994 held at least a bachelor's degree. However, although 88 percent of Japanese Americans had graduated from high school in 1994, only 31 percent of Hmongs had at least a high school diploma. Further, although approximately 58 percent of Asian Indians had earned at least a bachelor's degree, only 6 percent or less of Tongans, Cambodians, Laotians, and Hmongs had graduated from college. Among Asian and Pacific Islanders, it is particularly important to recognize the socioeconomic differences associated with the various Asian ethnic groups. Although Asian and Pacific Islander married-couple families had a median income in 1993 that was higher than comparable non-Hispanic White families ($49,510 compared to $45,240), fully 12.4 percent of Asian and Pacific Islander married-couple families lived below the poverty level (U.S. Bureau of the Census, 1995). On the average, Japanese Americans have the highest median family income level, followed in order by Asian Indian, Filipino, Chinese, Korean, Hawaiian, and Vietnamese.

It is important for psychologists and counselors to recognize the impact of poverty on mental health needs; being poor relates to a number of mental health outcomes. First, low income people experience more stress than do middle-class and high-income people. Also, being poor for ethnic minorities is related to length and type of treatment; being poor is predictive of a fewer number of treatment sessions (Sue, Fujino, Hu, Takeuchi, & Zanbe, 1991). However, it is equally important that psychologists and counselors recognize that not all African Americans, American Indians, and Hispanic Americans are poor and not all Asian Americans are well off. Failure to recognize the educated, middle-income background of an African American, American Indian, or Hispanic American client or the uneducated, low-income background of an Asian American client can be as culturally insensitive as failing to recognize their ethnic background. Psychologists, counselors, and other mental health workers need to be vigilant to stereotypes they may hold of racial/ethnic groups based on knowledge of between-group socioeconomic differences.

Cultural Mistrust

Due to the long history of European American oppression of African Americans in the United States, many African Americans are mistrustful of European Americans. F. Terrell and S. Terrell (1981) labeled the tendency of Blacks to be mistrustful of Whites "cultural mistrust." These authors reviewed the literature on Black attitudes toward Whites and concluded that, in general, Blacks are mistrustful of Whites in four areas: (a) educational and training settings; (b) political and legal system; (c) work and business interactions; and (d) interpersonal or social contexts. F. Terrell and S. Terrell developed the Cultural Mistrust Inventory (CMI) to measure cultural mistrust across these four areas. Cultural mistrust varies among African Americans, therefore it represents a within-group difference that is of considerable interest to psychologists and counselors.

There is some evidence that African American utilization of, and expectations for, counseling services provided by European Americans may be related to cultural mistrust. After a review of theoretical and empirical articles on cultural mistrust, Nickerson, Helms, and Terrell (1994) concluded that "the notion that Blacks' mistrust of Whites seems to serve as a significant barrier to the counseling process has theoretical merit" and "it seems reasonable to speculate that Black students' reluctance to seek counseling might be related to their mistrust of White counselors" (p. 379). Terrell and Terrell (1984) found that Black clients with a high level of cultural mistrust who were seen by a White counselor were more likely to prematurely terminate counseling (i.e., fail to show for a second, scheduled appointment) than were highly mistrustful Black clients seen by a Black counselor. Interestingly, they also found that highly mistrustful Black clients had significantly higher rates of premature termination than their counterparts who were less culturally mistrustful, regardless of the race of counselor. A subsequent study by Watkins and Terrell (1988) found that highly mistrustful Blacks who were assigned to White counselors had lower expectations for counseling than highly mistrustful Blacks assigned to Black counselors. A more recent study found that highly mistrustful Blacks express more negative attitudes toward seeking help and they anticipate less satisfaction with counseling from facilities staffed primarily by White counselors than facilities staffed primarily by Black counselors (Nickerson et al., 1994).

There is also evidence that cultural mistrust may be related to the credibility Black clients will assign a White counselor and their willingness to self-disclose to a White counselor. Watkins, Terrell, Miller, and Terrell (1989) reported that in comparison to Blacks low on mistrust, highly mistrustful Blacks regarded the White counselor as less credible and less able to help them with four problem areas: general anxiety, shyness, inferiority feelings, and dating difficulties. Thompson, Worthington, and Atkinson (1994) found an interaction between counselor ethnicity and cultural mistrust such that less mistrustful Black clients were more self-disclosing with a Black counselor than they were with a White counselor.

These theoretically consistent findings suggest that cultural mistrust is an important variable for distinguishing within-group differences among African Americans, one with important implications for providing counseling services for African American clients. Although the construct appears to have similar relevance for other ethnic minority groups, research extending to cultural mistrust to other populations is lacking.

References

Atkinson, D. R., & Gim, R. H. (1989). Asian-American cultural identity and attitudes toward mental health services. *Journal of Counseling Psychology, 36,* 209–212.

Barona, A., & Miller, J. A. (1994). Short acculturation scale for Hispanic youth (SASH-Y): A preliminary report. *Hispanic Journal of Behavior Sciences, 16,* 155–162.

Berry, B. (1965). *Ethnic and race relations.* Boston: Houghton Mifflin.

Berry, J. W. (1990). Psychology of acculturation: Understanding individuals moving between cultures. In R W. Brislin (Ed.), *Applied cross-cultural psychology* (pp. 232–253). Newbury Park, CA: Sage Publications.

Berry, J. W. (1994). Acculturation and psychological adaptation: An overview. In A. M. Bouvy, F. J. R. vander Vijver, P. Boski, & P. Schmitz (Eds.), *Journeys into cross-cultural psychology.* Amsterdam, Holland: Swets & Zeitlinger.

Berry, J. W., & Kim, U. (1988). Acculturation and mental health. In P. Dasen, J. W. Berry, & N Sartorius (Eds.), *Health and cross-cultural psychology* (pp. 207–236). Newbury Park, CA: Sage Publications.

Berry, J. W., Kim, U., Power, S., Young, M., & Bajaki, M. (1989). Acculturation attitudes in plural societies. *Applied Psychology: An International Review, 38,* 185–206.

Berry, J. W., Trimble, J., & Olmeda, E. (1986). The assessment of acculturation. In W. J. Lonner & J. W. Berry (Eds.), *Field methods in cross-cultural research* (pp. 291–324). Newbury Park, CA: Sage Publications.

Carter, R. T., & Helms, J. E. (1987). The relationship between Black value-orientation and racial identity attitudes. *Measurement and Evaluation in Counseling and Development, 19*(4), 185–195.

Casas, J. M., & Casas, A. (1994). The acculturation process and implications for education and services. In A. C. Watiella (Ed.), *The multicultural challenge in health education* (pp. 23–49). Santa Cruz, CA: ETR Associates.

Cass, V. C. (1979). Homosexual identity formation: A theoretical model. *Journal of Homosexuality, 4,* 219–235.

Cross, W. E., Jr. (1970, April). *The black experience viewed as a process: A crude model for black self-actualization.* Paper presented at the Thirty-fourth Annual Meeting of the Association of Social and Behavioral Scientists, Tallahassee, FL.

Cross, W. E., Jr. (1971). The Negro-to-Black conversion experience: Toward a psychology of Black liberation. *Black World, 20*(9), 13–27.

Cross, W. E., Jr. (1978). The Cross and Thomas models of psychological Nigrescence. *Journal of Black Psychology, 5*(1), 13–19.

Cross, W. E., Jr. (1991). *Shades of Black: Diversity of African-American identity.* Philadelphia, PA: Temple University Press.

Cross, W. E., Jr. (1995). The psychology of Nigrescence: Revising the Cross model. In J. G. Ponterotto, J. M. Casas, L. A. Suzuki, & C. M. Alexander (Eds.), *Handbook of multicultural counseling* (pp. 93–122). Thousand Oaks, CA: Sage Publications.

Cuellar, I., Arnold, B., Maldonado, R. (1995). Acculturation Rating Scale for Mexican Americans-II: A revision of the original ARSMA scale. *Hispanic Journal of Behavioral Sciences, 17,* 275–304.

Cuellar, I., Harris, L. C., & Jasso, R. (1980). An acculturation rating scale for Mexican American normal and clinical populations. *Hispanic Journal of Behavioral Sciences, 2,* 199–217.

de Anda, D. (1984). Bicultural socialization: Factors affecting the minority experience. *Social Work, 29,* 101–107.

Downing, N. E., & Roush, K. L. (1985). From passive acceptance to active commitment: A model of feminist identity development for women. *The Counseling Psychologist, 13,* 695–709.

Ford, R. C. (1987). Cultural awareness and cross-cultural counseling. *International Journal for the Advancement of Counseling, 10*(1), 71–78.

Gay, G. (1984). Implications of selected models of ethnic identity development for educators. *The Journal of Negro Education, 54*(1), 43–52.

Gim, R. H., Atkinson, D. R., & Kim, S. J. (1991). Asian American acculturation, counselor ethnicity and cultural sensitivity, and ratings of counselors. *Journal of Counseling Psychology, 38,* 57–62.

Gim, R. H., Atkinson, D. R., & Whiteley, S. (1990). Asian-American acculturation, severity of concerns, and willingness to see a counselor. *Journal of Counseling Psychology, 37,* 281–285.

Hall, W. S., Cross, W. E., & Freedle, R. (1972). Stages in the development of Black awareness: An exploratory investigation. In R. I. Jones (Ed.), *Black psychology* (pp. 156–165). New York: Harper & Row.

Heath, A. E., Neimeyer, G. J., & Pedersen, P. B. (1988). The future of cross-cultural counseling: A Delphi poll. *Journal of Counseling and Development, 67,* 27–30.

Helms, J. E. (1984). Toward a theoretical explanation of the effects of race on counseling: A Black and White model. *The Counseling Psychologist, 12,* 153–165.

Helms, J. E. (1985). Cultural identity in the treatment process. In P. Pedersen (Ed.), *Handbook of cross-cultural counseling and therapy.* Westport, CT: Greenwood Press.

Helms, J. E. (1990). *Black and White racial identity: Theory, research, and practice.* Westport, CT: Greenwood Press.

Helms, J. E. (1995). An update of Helms's White and people of color racial identity models. In J. G. Ponterotto, J. M. Casas, L. A. Suzuki, and C. M. Alexander (Eds.), *Handbook of Multicultural Counseling* (pp. 181–198). Thousand Oaks, CA: Sage Publications.

Helms, J. E., & Carter, R. T. (1986, August). Manual for the Visible Racial/Ethnic Identity Attitude Scale. *An exploratory investigation into the relationship between career maturity, work role salience, value orientation, and racial identity attitudes.* Paper presented at the ninety-fourth annual convention of the American Psychological Association, Washington, DC.

Helms, J. E., & Parham, T. A. (1990). The relationship between Black racial identity attitudes and cognitive styles. In J. E. Helms (Ed.), *Black and White racial identity: Theory, research, and practice* (pp. 119–131). Westport, CT: Greenwood Press.

Highlen, P. S., Reynolds, A. L., Adams, E. M., Hanley, C. P., Myers, L. J., Cox, C. I., & Speight, S. L. (1988, August). *Self-identity development model of oppressed people: Inclusive model for all?* Paper presented at the meeting of the American Psychological Association, Atlanta, GA.

Ho, D. Y. F. (1995). Internalized culture, culturocentrism, and transcendence. *The Counseling Psychologist, 23,* 4–24.

Jackson, B. (1975). Black identity development. *MEFORM: Journal of Educational Diversity & Innovation, 2,* 19–25.

Keefe, S. E. (1980). Acculturation and the extended family among urban Mexican Americans. In A. M. Padilla (Ed.), *Acculturation: Theory, models and some new findings* (pp. 85–110). Boulder, CO: Westview Press.

Kunkel, M. A. (1990). Expectations about counseling in relation to acculturation in Mexican-American and Anglo-American student samples. *Journal of Counseling Psychology, 37,* 286–292.

Marin, G. (1992). Issues in the measurement of acculturation among Hispanics. In K. F. Geisinger (Ed.), *Psychological testing of Hispanics* (pp. 235–251). Washington, DC: American Psychological Association.

Marin, G., Sabogal, F., Marin, B. V., Otero-Sabogal, R., & Perez-Stable, E. J. (1987). Development of a short acculturation scale for Hispanics. *Hispanic Journal of Behavior Sciences, 9,* 183–205.

Morten, G., & Atkinson, D. R. (1983). Minority identity development and preference for counselor race. *Journal of Negro Education, 52,* 156–161.

Moyerman, D. R., & Forman, D. (1992). Acculturation and adjustment: A metaanalytic study. *Hispanic Journal of Behavioral Sciences, 14,* 163–200.

Myers, L. J., Speight, S. L., Highlen, P. S., Cox, C. I., Reynolds, A. L., Adams, E. M., & Hanley, T. C. (1991). Identity development and world view: Toward an optimal conceptualization. *Journal of Counseling and Development, 70,* 54–63.

Neidert, L. J., & Farley, R. (1985). Assimilation in the United States: An analysis of ethnic and generation differences in status and achievement. *American Sociological Review, 50,* 840–850.

Nickerson, K. J., Helms, J. E., & Terrell, F. (1994). Cultural mistrust, opinions about mental illness, and Black students' attitudes toward seeking psychological help from White counselors. *Journal of Counseling Psychology, 41,* 378–385.

Novak, M. (1972). *The rise of the unmeltable ethnics.* New York: Macmillan.

Oberg, K. (1954). *Culture shock.* Indianapolis, IN: Bobbs-Merril Series in Social Sciences.

Olmedo, E. L. (1979). Acculturation: A psychometric perspective. *American Psychologist, 34,* 1061–1070.

Padilla, A. M. (1980a). *Acculturation: Theory, models and some new findings.* Boulder, CO: Westview Press.

Padilla, A. M. (1980b). The role of cultural awareness and ethnic loyalty in acculturation. In A. M. Padilla (Ed.), *Acculturation: Theory, models and some new findings* (pp. 47–84). Boulder, CO: Westview Press.

Parham, T. A., & Helms, J. E. (1981). The influence of black students' racial identity attitudes on preference for counselor's race. *Journal of Counseling Psychology, 28,* 250–257.

Parham, T. A., & Helms, J. E. (1985a). Attitudes of racial identity and self-esteem of Black students: An exploratory investigation. *Journal of College Student Personnel, 26* (2), 143–146.

Parham, T. A., & Helms, J. E. (1985b). Relation of racial identity attitudes to self-actualization and affective states of Black students. *Journal of Counseling Psychology, 32,* 431–440.

Park, R. E. (1928). Human migration and the marginal man. *American Journal of Sociology, 33,* 881–893.

Park, R. E. (1950). *Race and culture.* Glencoe, IL: The Free Press.

Park, R. E., & Burgess, E. W. (1921). *Introduction to the Science of Sociology.* Chicago: University of Chicago Press.

Phinney, J. S. (1996). When we talk about American ethnic groups, what do we mean? *American Psychologist, 51,* 918–927.

Pomales, J., & Williams, V. (1989). Effects of level of acculturation and counseling style on Hispanic students' perceptions of counselor. *Journal of Counseling Psychology, 36,* 79–83.

Ponterotto, J. G. (1988). Racial consciousness development among White counselor trainees: A stage model. *Journal of Multicultural Counseling and Development, 16,* 146–156.

Ponterotto, J. G., Alexander, C. M., & Hinkston, J. A. (1988). Afro-American preferences for counselor characteristics: A replication and extension. *Journal of Counseling Psychology, 35,* 175–182.

Poston, W. S. C. (1990). The biracial identity development model: A needed addition. *Journal of Counseling and Development, 69,* 152–155.

Redfield, R., Linton, R., & Herskovits, M. (1936). Memorandum on the study of acculturation. *American Anthropologist, 37,* 149–152.

Rogler, L., Cortes, D. E., & Malgady, R. G. (1991). Acculturation and mental health status among Hispanics. *American Psychologist, 467,* 585–597.

Ruiz, A. S. (1990). Ethnic identity: Crisis and resolution. *Journal of Multicultural Counseling and Development, 18,* 29–40.

Sanchez, A. R., & Atkinson, D. R. (1983). Mexican-American cultural commitment, preference for counselor ethnicity, and willingness to use counseling. *Journal of Counseling Psychology, 30,* 215–220.

Smith, E. J. (1991). Ethnic identity development: Toward the development of a theory within the context of majority/minority status. *Journal of Counseling & Development, 70,* 181–188.

Stonequist, E. V. (1937). *The marginal man.* New York: Charles Scribner's Sons.

Stonequist, E. V. (1961). *The marginal man: A study in personality and culture conflict.* New York: Russell & Russell, Inc.

Sue, D. W., & Sue, D. (1990). *Counseling the culturally different: Theory and practice.* New York: John Wiley & Sons.

Sue, S., Chun, C., & Gee, K. (1995). Ethnic minority intervention and treatment research. In J. F. Aponte, R. Young-Rivers, & J. Wohl (Eds.), *Psychological interventions and cultural diversity* (pp. 266–282). Boston: Allyn and Bacon.

Sue, S., Fujino, D. C., Hu, L. T., Takeuchi, D. T., & Zanbe, N. W. S. (1991). Community mental health services for ethnic minority groups: A test of the cultural responsiveness hypothesis. *Journal of Counseling Psychology, 59,* 533–540.

Sue, S., & Sue, D. W. (1971). Chinese-American personality and mental health. *Amerasia Journal, 1,* 36–49.

Suinn, R. M., Rickard-Figueroa, K., Lew, S., & Vigil, P. (1987). The Suinn-Lew Asian Self-Identity Acculturation Scale: An initial report. *Educational and Psychological Measurement, 47,* 401–407.

Szapocznik, J., Kurtines, W., & Fernandez, T. (1980). Bicultural involvement and adjustment in Hispanic-American youths. *International Journal of Intercultural Relations, 4,* 353–365.

Terrell, F., & Terrell, S. (1981). An inventory to measure cultural mistrust among Blacks. *Western Journal of Black Studies, 5,* 180–184.

Terrell, F., & Terrell, S. (1984). Race of the counselor, client sex, cultural mistrust level, and premature termination from counseling among Black clients. *Journal of Counseling Psychology, 31,* 371–375.

Thompson, C. E., Worthington, R., & Atkinson, D. R. (1994). Counselor content orientation, counselor race, and Black women's cultural mistrust and self-disclosures. *Journal of Counseling Psychology, 41,* 155–161.

Troiden, R. R. (1989). The formation of homosexual identities. *Journal of Homosexuality, 17,* 43–73.

U.S. Bureau of the Census (1995). *Population Profile of the United States: 1995,* Current Population Reports, Series P23-189. Washington, DC: U.S. Government Printing Office.

Valentine, C. A. (1971). Deficit, difference, and bicultural models of Afro-American behavior. *Harvard Educational Review, 41,* 137–157.

Vontress, C. E. (1971). Racial differences: Impediments to rapport. *Journal of Counseling Psychology, 18,* 7–13.

Ward, C., & Kennedy, A. (1994). Acculturation strategies, psychological adjustment, and sociocultural competence during cross-cultural transitions. *International Journal of Intercultural Relations, 18,* 329–343.

Watkins, C. E., & Terrell, F. (1988). Mistrust level and its effects on counseling expectations in Black client-White counselor relationships: An analogue study. *Journal of Counseling Psychology, 35,* 194–197.

Watkins, C. E., Terrell, F., Miller, F. S., & Terrell, S. L. (1989). Cultural mistrust and its effects on expectational variables in Black client-White counselor relationships. *Journal of Counseling Psychology, 36,* 447–450.

Winkelman, M. (1994). Cultural shock and adaptation. *Journal of Counseling & Development, 73,* 121–126.

Yoshioka, R. B., Tashima, N., Chew, M., & Maruse, K. (1981). *Mental health services for Pacific/Asian Americans.* San Francisco: Pacific Asian Mental Health Project.

3

Addressing the Mental Health
Needs of Racial/Ethnic Minorities

In chapter 1, we described how the United States is becoming increasingly diverse as a result of the wave of immigrants from Latin America and Asia and the higher birth rate among racial/ethnic minority populations than among the European American population. The diversification of the population suggests that counselors, psychologists, and other mental health practitioners will need to be prepared to work with a variety of racial/ethnic populations as we move toward and into the twenty-first century. In chapter 2, we described the diversity within racial/ethnic minority groups often overlooked by mental health professionals. To work with racial/ethnic minority clients, counselors need to understand the variables that contribute to individual differences within ethnic minority populations. In this chapter, we briefly discuss the mental health needs of ethnic minorities (more specific discussion about the needs within racial/ethnic groups is provided in chapters 4–15), examine what psychology and other mental health professions have done in the past to meet these needs, and critique current efforts to meet the mental health needs of racial/ethnic minorities.

Ethnic Minority Mental Health Needs

Treatment Rate As a Measure of Mental Health Needs

Ethnic minority utilization of mental health services has been one of the most misused and misunderstood concepts in mental health research and practice. Until recently, conclusions about ethnic minority utilization of mental health services have been based largely on inpatient and outpatient treatment rates; mental health records have been examined to see if the proportion of ethnic minority clients being seen for a given psychological problem are comparable to the proportion of European American clients being seen for the same problem (Neighbors, Caldwell, Thompson, & Jackson, 1994). Based on treatment rate comparisons, conclusions have been drawn about whether the ethnic population is underutilizing or overutilizing mental health services for particular disorders or for mental health concerns in general.

Historically, these data comparing mental health treatment rates across ethnic groups have then been used for such disparate purposes as estimating ethnic minority mental health needs, justifying mental health resource allocations, and, in some instances, promoting racist views of ethnic minorities and their culture. An example of the latter use of treatment rate is provided by Williams (1986, cited in Griffith & Gonzalez, 1994), who found data published in the mid-nineteenth century suggesting that Blacks who were freed and living in the northern states had high rates of mental illness. These data were then used to argue that Blacks were incapable of dealing with the stresses of being free and that they were better off in slavery.

On the other hand, low treatment rates for ethnic minorities in the late nineteenth century through the 1970s were interpreted by many mental health service providers as evidence that minorities in general, and Asian Americans and Hispanic Americans, in particular, experienced fewer or less severe mental health problems than European Americans (Jaco, 1959; Jones & Gray, 1986; Leong, Wagner, & Tata, 1995; D. W. Sue, 1994). The conclusion that ethnic minorities had fewer mental health problems was in turn used to justify mental health policies that largely ignored the special psychological needs of ethnic populations (Schwab, 1978, cited in Griffith & Gonzalez, 1994).

By the mid-1970s, however, low treatment rates for minorities were being reinterpreted as evidence that mental health services were not adequately or appropriately addressing the needs of ethnic minority populations. Based on a review of national data, the Special Populations Task Force of the President's Commission on Mental Health concluded in 1978 that racial/ethnic minorities "are clearly underserved or inappropriately served by the current mental health system in this country" (Special Populations, 1978, p. 73).

More recently, researchers have suggested that patterns of utilization (based on treatment rates) differ among ethnic groups, treatment settings, and types of problems and that these patterns of utilization are changing (Leong et al., 1995; S. Sue, Chun, & Gee, 1995). In reviewing research on the relationship between race and use of inpatient mental health services, Snowden and Cheung (1990) found a history of Black overrepresentation in mental hospitals dating back to 1914. They also reviewed 1980 and 1981 survey data from the National Institute of Mental Health and found that African Americans and American Indians are more likely, and Asian Americans/Pacific Islanders less likely, to be hospitalized than Whites. Examining only involuntary psychiatric hospitalization (which constitutes 29 percent of all psychiatric hospitalization), Rosenstein, Milazzo-Sayre, MacAskill, and Manderscheid (1987) found that non-Whites are 3.5 times more likely than Whites to receive involuntary criminal commitment and 2.4 times more likely to receive involuntary noncriminal commitment. African American overrepresentation among involuntary commitments may be particularly acute in public psychiatric hospitals (Cannon & Locke, 1977; Snowden & Cheung). Snowden and Cheung suggest that racial differences in public hospitalization rates may be due to socioeconomic differences, cultural differences in seeking help, and diagnostic biases on the part of referring psychologists and psychiatrists.

Differential treatment rates also have been documented in outpatient settings. Cheung and Snowden (1990) reviewed data from community-based surveys of mental health utilization and concluded that compared to Whites: (1) Asian Americans and Latinos are underrepresented; (2) African Americans are underrepresented in some studies and overrepresented in others; and (3) little is known about Native American utilization rate. In a major study that sampled from over 1.2 million federal employees and their families, Padgett, Patrick, Burns, and Schlesinger (1994) found that Black and Hispanic women were less likely to use outpatient mental health services than White women, even after controlling for socioeconomic and other factors. In his review of research on Asian American use of inpatient and outpatient mental health services, Leong (1994) concluded that "studies of Asian-American clients in both mental health hospitals and community mental health centers have found that they tend to have a lower rate of utilization of mental health services" (p. 83) than other ethnic groups. His study of archival data for a ten-year period from Hawaii's Department of Health confirmed this pattern of underutilization. When racial/ ethnic minorities do make an initial contact with a mental health service, there is evidence that they are less likely to return for subsequent counseling than their European American counterparts (Barnes, 1994). S. Sue, Fujino, Hu, Takeuchi, and Zane (1991), examining data from the Los Angeles County mental health system, found that African Americans average fewer sessions and terminate outpatient services sooner than European Americans.

There is also evidence that racial/ethnic minority students underutilize college counseling services. In a survey of university counseling services across the country, Magoon (1988) found that Black students were underrepresented as clients in 40 percent of the small schools and 46 percent of the large schools. For Hispanic clients, 32 percent of the small schools and 37 percent of the large schools reported underrepresentation. In a separate study of a single campus, only 7 percent of the Mexican American students made use of the counseling services in a one-year period compared to 14 percent of the White students (Sanchez & King, 1986). As a result of data like these, Stone and Archer (1990) concluded that the provision of counseling services to ethnic minority students was one of the major challenges facing college and university counseling centers in the 1990s.

Treatment rate may be a useful measure for comparing utilization across settings or time periods *within* an ethnic population, but it is a misleading index of mental health needs *across* ethnic groups. If ethnic group A and ethnic group B have the same outpatient treatment rates for depression, for example, we might erroneously conclude that the two groups are utilizing mental health services equally and that they have the same level of need (i.e., the same prevalence of depression). However, the actual level of need may be much higher in one group than another. Furthermore, help-seeking behavior may vary across the two ethnic groups. S. Sue et al. (1995) have urged that caution be exercised in interpreting the results of utilization studies because: (a) data from national surveys including untreated minorities may disagree with data from treated samples obtained from community, state, or county mental health facilities; (b) utilization patterns are changing over time and need to be constantly monitored; and (c) prevalence of a disorder within an ethnic group needs to be taken into account as well as comparing use of services by the group to the population at large in determining underutilization and overutilization. Furthermore, need prevalence is only one of many factors affecting help-seeking behavior, which in turn influences treatment rates (Leong et al., 1995).

Neighbors et al. (1994) argue that instead of relying on treatment rate as a measure of utilization parity, researchers should compare data on prevalence of mental health problems from epidemiological surveys of ethnic populations to treatment rate to more accurately determine if these populations are underutilizing or overutilizing mental health services. Adebimpe (1994) also points out the need to formulate operational definitions for determining equity and parity with respect to mental health service provisions.

> For any population unit, the prevalence of mental disorders in the community, adjusted for utilization rates, can be used to calculate an expected prevalence rate in the treated population, which can then be compared with the actual prevalence. The gap between expected and actual rates would be a measure of whether each group is receiving the amount of services it needs. (Adebimpe, 1994, p. 30)

Another important component of utilization is help-seeking behavior. In his review of studies based on ECS data, Adebimpe (1994) found that fewer Blacks than Whites who met diagnostic criteria for depression sought help in the six-month period before the study. Greene, Jackson, and Neighbors (1993) found that older African Americans are more likely than their younger counterparts to not seek any help, either formal or informal, for serious personal problems. Furthermore, they found that a substantial portion of older African Americans were true nonusers of any type of help. "When faced with a serious crisis, they have no access whatsoever to outside sources of assistance" (p. 1297). When racial/ethnic minorities do make an initial contact with a mental health service, there is evidence that they are less likely to return for subsequent counseling than their European American counterparts (Barnes, 1994). S. Sue et al. (1991) found that African Americans average fewer sessions and terminate outpatient services sooner than European Americans.

Thus, it is a mistake to draw conclusions about need and underutilization/overutilization on the basis of treatment rate. Yet that is exactly what researchers did throughout much of the 1970s and 1980s. More recently, researchers have attempted to refine these measures of utilization and need by "partialling out" public from private and inpatient from outpatient mental health treatment rates. However, they have continued to use treatment rate as both a measure of ethnic minority utilization parity and mental health need. Conceptualizing mental health

Table 3.1

Formulas Defining Relationships Between Minority Mental Health Needs, Utilization, and Treatment Rate

Conventional Utilization Formula

Needs = Utilization = f (treatment rate)

Refined Utilization Formulas

Outpatient Needs = Outpatient Utilization Rate = f (public + private outpatient treatment rate)

Inpatient Needs = Inpatient Utilization Rate = f (public + private inpatient treatment rate)

Proposed Utilization Formulas

Public Outpatient Treatment Rate = f (help-seeking behavior and return rate) = f (needs, enabling, and predisposing factors)

Private Outpatient Treatment Rate = f (help-seeking behavior and return rate) = f (needs, enabling, and predisposing factors)

Public Inpatient Treatment Rate = f (help-seeking behavior and return rate) = f (needs factors + referral sources)

Private Inpatient Treatment Rate = f (help-seeking behavior) = f (needs, enabling, and predisposing factors)

---

need as function of treatment rate juxtaposes the true relationship between these two variables. This conventional way of conceptualizing the relationship between need and treatment rate is presented in table 3.1.

Also presented in table 3.1 is an alternative view, one that identifies treatment and utilization rates as functions of n*eed factors, enabling factors,* and *predisposing factors.* Instead of conceptualizing minority mental health needs as a function of treatment rate, this alternative formula suggests that treatment rate equals utilization rate, utilization rate is a function of help-seeking behavior and return rate, and help-seeking behavior and return rate are a function of need moderated by either enabling and predisposing factors or referral sources. According to Anderson and Newman (1973, cited in Barney, 1994), need factors, enabling factors, and predisposing factors all contribute to outpatient mental health utilization patterns:

> Need factors comprise both an objective measure of mental impairment and a subjective measure of "perceived need." This perceived need is an individual's own self-perception or individual judgment about their need for services. . . . Enabling factors include possession of both individual attributes and personal resources that would facilitate use or non-use of needed available services. These include attributes such as knowledge of service availability (i.e., level of education), access to insurance, and financial resources. Predisposing factors are individual characteristics that influence an objective measure of need or an individual's perception of need. These characteristics may include gender, age, social or environmentally induced psychological stress, and level of social or community support. (p. 3)

This schema of factors affecting mental health utilization is a useful one for our purposes, and we will use it later in this chapter when examining factors that affect ethnic minority utilization of mental health services.

Prevalence Rate As a Measure of Mental Health Needs

It is generally assumed that mental disorders, particularly those having a biogenic base, are evenly distributed across the various ethnic groups (Lefley, 1994). Several contemporary reviews of epidemiological research have documented that ethnic minorities experience mental health problems at about the same rate as European Americans.

In the largest and most scientific attempt to date to assess the actual prevalence rate of mental disorders in the United States, the Epidemiologic Catchment Area (ECA) survey assessed prevalence of thirty major psychiatric disorders through standardized interviews with 20,000 Americans in five states. In general, studies and reviews of research based on the ECA data have concluded that African Americans report higher levels of symptoms than European Americans, but symptom differences are not maintained when adjustments are made for sociodemographic differences (Adebimpe, 1994; Jones-Webb & Snowden, 1993; Lefley, 1994). For example, Horwath, Johnson, and Hornig (1994) examined data on 4,287 African Americans and 12,142 White Americans from the ECA survey and concluded that "the lifetime prevalence of panic disorder is similar in white and African-American populations" (p. 60). Similarly, Friedman, Paradis, and Hatch (1994) reported finding that "the presenting symptoms and clinical characteristics of African American and white patients with panic disorder and agoraphobia were very similar" (p. 142). Analyses of ECA data like these lead Lefley to conclude that "although there were significant ethnic differences in prevalence rates for some of these disorders, the differences disappeared when the data were controlled for age, gender, marital status, and most importantly, socioeconomic status" (p. 225).

However, others have reviewed the ECA data and concluded that ethnic minorities may actually experience more mental health problems than do European Americans. For example, Adebimpe (1994) reviewed the ECA data and concluded that "race-related differences were found in rates of alcoholism, phobic disorders, generalized anxiety disorder, and somatization disorder, which were more frequent among blacks, and in obsessive-compulsive disorder, which was less frequent" (p. 27).

Studies and reviews of research based on other data sources also have lead to the conclusion that ethnic minorities disproportionately experience psychological problems (Castaneda, 1994; Leong et al., 1995; Rosenheck & Fontana, 1994). Using data from the 1984 National Alcohol Survey, Jones-Webb and Snowden (1993) found that Blacks who were thirty to thirty-nine-years-old, belonged to nonwestern religious groups, and in the western region of the United States were at greater risk of depression than comparable Whites. On the other hand, "those that were widowed, members of the middle and lower-middle class, and unemployed were at less risk" (p. 240). Fabrega and Miller (1995) reviewed epidemiological studies of adolescent psychopathology and found higher levels of symptoms among Mexican American adolescents than among adolescents of other ethnic groups. Barney (1994) reviewed several studies on the mental health of American Indian elders and found evidence of a higher incidence of clinically significant levels of depressive symptoms than among elderly Whites.

Racial/ethnic minorities experience at least as many mental health problems as do European Americans, and the hypothesis that ethnic minorities underutilize outpatient mental health services and university counseling services because of less need is clearly unjustified.

Factors That Contribute to Ethnic Minority Mental Health Needs

As documented in the preceding section, even if one accepts that biogenic mental disorders are found at similar rates across the various ethnic populations, there is reason to believe that ethnic minorities have greater mental health needs than European Americans. Although it would be a mistake to suggest a cause and effect relationship between race/ethnicity (or culture) and mental health problems, a number of reasons for increased psychological problems among ethnic minorities can be hypothesized. Lefley (1994) points out that "populations suffering harsh economic and/or social pressures may have an equivalent distribution of serious mental disorders in terms of lifetime prevalence, but manifest differences in the frequency of acute psychotic episodes and in the persistence of severe disability" (p. 225).

To the extent that stress leads to mental health problems, it can be hypothesized that the unique or particularly intense sources of stress experienced by ethnic minorities will generate greater mental health problems among these groups than among European Americans. Lefley (1994) has suggested that, for example, "the relatively higher [inpatient] admission rates of African-American and American-Indian patients may reflect greater exposure to environmental stressors such as poverty, unemployment, neighborhood crime and substance abuse, loss of housing, and erosion of traditional support systems" (p. 229). Although Lefley's observation is based on the questionable practice of using treatment rates to infer need, her list of environmental stressors underscores the probability that many members of ethnic minority groups are at risk of stress-induced mental illness.

For those ethnic minorities who immigrate to the United States, immigration can be one source of considerable stress (Cheung, 1987; Esquivel & Keitel, 1990). According to Griffith and Gonzalez (1994), "dislocation of human beings from their own cultural groups has frequently been a contributory element to the emergence of psychopathology in the individual" (p. 1394). For example, several research reviews (Leong, 1986; D. W. Sue & D. Sue, 1990) have found consistent evidence that stress associated with immigration has contributed to the mental health problems of Asian Americans.

Brody (1994) points out that some immigrants migrate voluntarily, some involuntarily. Among involuntary immigrants are economic and political refugees. Political refugees often have experienced the added stress associated with war and violence in their native land (Nguyen & Henkin, 1983; Orley, 1994; Rumbaut, 1995). Since 1975, hundreds of thousands of South East Asians have fled Vietnam and Cambodia, many of them survivors of rape, torture, and battering and many of whom witnessed the murders of loved ones (Mollica, 1994). Similarly, Farias (1994) points out that tens of thousands of people have been displaced by organized repression in South American countries and civil wars in Central America in the 1970s and 1980s. As a result of such experiences, refugees "are at a greatly increased risk for the development of serious psychiatric disorders" (Chung & Lin, 1994, p. 109). For a more extensive discussion of the impact that the refugee experience can have on mental and physical health, the reader is referred to Marsella, Bornemann, Ekblad, and Orley (1994).

In addition to the stress associated with the physical act of relocation and the trauma experienced by economic and political refugees, immigrants may experience stress due to cultural conflict between the culture they are leaving and the U.S. culture. Once they arrive in the United States, immigrants are under constant pressure to acculturate (but not necessarily assimilate). Pressure to acculturate can also create generational conflict within families of immigrants when, for example, values of the dominant U.S. culture undermine the authoritarian role of the father, encourage a more liberated role for the mother, and promote a sense of autonomy and independence in children (Griffith & Gonzalez, 1994). Smart and Smart (1995) argue that Hispanic immigrants (and other immigrants of color) experience more stress as the result of the acculturation process than do immigrants from Northern and Western Europe. As we pointed out in chapter 2, although two metaanalyses (Moyerman & Forman, 1992; Rogler, Cortes, & Malgady, 1991) have failed to unequivocally document the nature of the relationship between acculturation and various mental health problems among Hispanics, a number of studies have reported that the acculturation process is accompanied by adjustment problems. Dona and Berry (1994) have suggested that the outcome of acculturation "depends on a number of factors influencing the relation between acculturation and mental health, among them being acculturation attitudes, cultural maintenance, acculturative experience and values" (p. 60). It may be that other factors, such as level of family income and availability of extended families and support groups, mediate the effects of acculturation. However, the overall evidence is strong that acculturation places stress on many immigrants and that this stress can lead to mental health problems.

Another source of stress experienced by racial/ethnic groups that could account for a higher incidence of mental health problems is the discrimination they experience as minorities (Aponte & Crouch, 1995). Smith (1985) concluded that although differences in psychopathology between Blacks and Whites largely dissipates when investigators control for socioeconomic variables, the prejudice, discrimination, and hostility experienced by African Americans and other racial/ethnic minorities contribute to their mental health problems. According to Carter (1994), "Epidemiological studies of mental illness invariably identify racism as a major contributor to psychopathology" (p. 546).

Poverty is still another source of stress for many ethnic minority people (Barnes, 1994; Castaneda, 1994). There is substantial evidence that psychological disorders are most common and severe among the lowest socioeconomic classes (Korchin, 1980). Ogbu (1987) points out that those racial/ethnic groups that became minorities in the United States involuntarily through slavery, conquest, or colonization (e.g., American Indians, African Americans, native Hawaiians) are among the very lowest socioeconomic groups in this country. The negative effects that have been associated with poverty among ethnic minority populations include anxiety, depression, low self-esteem, aggression, poor school achievement, and loneliness (Canino, Earley, & Rogler, 1980; Chin, 1983; Torres-Matrullo, 1976). In her review of the literature documenting a higher incidence of psychopathology among Blacks than among Whites, Smith (1985) concluded that the higher rate of psychopathology among Blacks largely was due to socioeconomic factors (and, as already noted, racism). Moyerman and Forman (1992) found that socio-economic status was a strong predictor in 7 of 11 areas of adjustment in their meta-review of studies linking mental health indices to Hispanic acculturation.

Factors That Affect Ethnic Minority Mental Health Utilization

If one assumes that ethnic minorities have the same mental health needs as European Americans, then it's clear that at least Asian Americans and Hispanic Americans are not seeking help at parity with other ethnic groups (i.e., they are underutilizing mental health services). If ethnic minorities have even greater mental health needs than European Americans due to the added stresses placed on them, then it is probably safe to assume that African Americans and American Indians also underutilize mental health services (if not across all clinical diagnoses and all treatment settings, at least for a number of specific diagnoses and for voluntary outpatient settings). For example, based on a 1992 telephone survey assessing depression among 1,210 Black participants, Neighbors et al. (1994) concluded that "substantial numbers of African Americans are not obtaining the professional help they need" and that "underutilization is a problem for African Americans, especially when use is viewed in relation to the prevalence of psychiatric morbidity in the general population" (p. 34).

Researchers have used cultural and service delivery factors to explain ethnic minority underutilization of outpatient mental health services (Leong et al., 1995). Using the schema outlined by Anderson and Newman (1973, cited in Barney, 1994), cultural explanations can be included in the category of predisposing factors, while service delivery explanations can be included in the category of enabling factors. In the remaining sections of this chapter we will examine several key predisposing and enabling factors that help account for ethnic minority underutilization of mental health services.

Predisposing Factors

Anderson and Newman (1973, cited in Barney, 1994) identified characteristics such as sex, age, socially or environmentally induced psychological stress, and level of social or community support as factors that predispose an individual to use or not use mental health services. To this list we would add the cultural factors found by Leong et al. (1995) to affect mental health utilization. In particular, we will focus on cultural values and alternative sources of help as two types of predisposing factors.

Cultural Values Inherent in Ethnic Minority Cultures

The review of research by Leong et al. (1995) suggests that values inherent in some traditional cultures may hinder ethnic minority utilization of mental health services. In some cultures there is a stigma against seeking professional help for psychological problems. This stigma has been found among African Americans (Neighbors et al., 1994), Asian Americans (D. W. Sue, 1994), and Hispanic Americans (Leong et al., 1995). For example, Nickerson, Helms, and Terrell (1994) reviewed several studies examining African American opinions about mental illness and found evidence that compared to Whites, Blacks tend to stigmatize and reject those with mental illness, avoid the label of mental illness, and have more negative attitudes about the efficacy of psychotherapy.

The need to preserve family honor is a cultural value that may be a deterrent to seeking professional mental health services for some ethnic minorities. D. W. Sue (1994) points out that:

> In traditional Asian families, much stress is placed upon bringing honor to the family name and maintaining a good reputation through public consumption. . . . Behaviors such as failure in school, delinquency, vocational problems, or mental illness may bring shame, disgrace, and dishonor to the family name. . . . As a result, the family system exerts great pressures to keep such things hidden from public view, and thus may result in the low usage of clinical services. (p. 293)

Similarly, Esquivel and Keitel (1990) noted that "in some cultures it is a dishonor for the family to have a child with an emotional problem" (p. 215).

Lefley (1994) points out that some observers have suggested that Hispanic and Asian families may, as a result of cultural values, keep family members experiencing psychological distress at home longer and "present them for hospitalization at an advanced stage of illness, when they might require longer hospital stays" (p. 226).

Ethnic minority individuals or families may find that the need to express emotions and/or relate intimate information to a mental health practitioner conflicts with their traditional cultural values. In some cultures, the expression of emotions may be considered inappropriate or a sign of unacceptable instability. In these cultures, denial of psychological problems may produce somatic symptoms and/or physical solutions. For example, D. W. Sue (1994) pointed out that:

> the manner of symptom formation and expression among Asians seems influenced by cultural values as well. . . . Asians are more likely to express psychological conflicts somatically and to present their problems in a much more symbolic and circuitous manner than their White counterparts. (p. 293)

Lippincott and Mierzwa (1995) reviewed the research on Asian and Asian American mental health and stated that "a common trait among those studied whose cultural background was Asian appeared to be their tendency, when seeking help, to present somatic complaints in place of psychological complaints" (p. 201). Thus, many traditional ethnic minorities will seek help from medical practitioners when they are experiencing psychological problems.

Traditional beliefs about the causes of, and cures for, psychological problems also may work against the utilization of mental health services. For example, there is some evidence that Asian Americans are more likely than European Americans to attribute mental illness to a biological cause (S. Sue, Wagner, Margullis, & Lew, 1976), thereby suggesting a medical rather than a psychological solution. Similarly, Hispanic Americans attribute many psychological symptoms to physical and metaphysical causes, for which advice or treatment is sought from a folk healer rather than a mental health practitioner (Rivera, 1988). Even when ethnic minorities seek out and attend an initial counseling session with a mental health practitioner, they may not return for additional sessions if they perceive the practitioner to be operating outside their cultural belief system. For example, many traditional Asian Americans feel they can control their mental health by exercising will power and avoiding morbid thoughts (S. Sue et al., 1976). A therapist who asks them to discuss their negative feelings may be challenging traditional beliefs about how problems are cured. Wohl (1995) points out that "if the explanatory models of the clinician and the patient are far apart and the distance between them is not negotiated, treatment will flounder" (p. 81).

Although cultural values within an ethnic minority community may contribute to underutilization of outpatient mental health services, we object to singling out cultural values as the primary cause. A more valid explanation is that values within an ethnic culture may conflict with values inherent in conventional counseling strategies. Instead of blaming the values in the minority culture for underutilization of services, the problem can be reframed as a conflict between values inherent in the counseling process and those inherent in the culture of the client. This hypothesis of conflicting values will be discussed in the section on enabling factors.

Alternative Sources of Help

Some African Americans, American Indians, Asian Americans, and Hispanic Americans make use of informal help and/or folk healers when they experience psychological distress (Adebimpe, 1994; Greene et al., 1993; Koss-Chioino, 1995; Leong et al., 1995; Neighbors & Jackson, 1984). Ethnic minorities may seek alternative sources of help because of some of the cultural values already discussed. However, they may also use alternative sources of help for psychological problems due to lack of trust in conventional mental health services and service providers. For example, Leong et al. (1995) found that African Americans often prefer parents, relatives, neighbors, and friends as sources of help because they distrust professional help sources.

The desire to see a healer who shares their cultural beliefs about the causes of, and cures for, psychological problems is also an important reason that some ethnic minority persons seek out folk healers to address these problems (Esquivel & Keitel, 1990). In her discussion of ethnomedical systems employed by African Americans, American Indians, Asian Americans, and Hispanic Americans, Koss-Chioino (1995) suggested that "all ethnic groups have transferred to the United States many or all of their main beliefs and practices connected to healing" (p. 145). Chung and Lin (1994) reviewed research on refugees from Southeast Asia and concluded that "most Southeast Asian refugees are unfamiliar with Western mental health concepts, and are still deeply influenced by a multitude of indigenous cultural beliefs and practices that significantly affect the symptom presentation, conceptualization, and the help-seeking behavior of this group" (p. 109). In their review of research on help-seeking attitudes among ethnic minorities, Leong et al. (1995) found that Hispanic Americans often prefer family, folk healers, clergy, and general medical providers as alternatives to professional mental health service providers because of shared beliefs about the causes and cures of mental problems.

Although people in all four ethnic groups discussed in this book may make use of folk healers to some extent, there are conflicting data about the proportion that actually see folk healers for physical and/or mental health problems. Rivera (1988) reviewed research on Mexican American use of *curanderos* (folk healers) and found that studies conducted in the 1960s reported use was widespread (20-25 percent actually using curanderos; 50-60 percent believing in them) while studies conducted in the 1970s and 1980s reported very low use (less than 10 percent actually using curanderos). In his own survey of 128 Hispanic women living in the Denver, Colorado area, Rivera found that 23 percent of the respondents had received treatment from a folk healer. He concluded that "Curanderismo is still part of Hispanic health care beliefs and practices, even among people born mostly in the United States and speaking English at home" (p. 239).

As ethnic immigrants acculturate, presumably the likelihood that they will begin seeking help from professional mental health services increases. However, use of alternative sources of help may continue for many generations, despite increasing acculturation among later generations. Based on data from the California Southeast Asian Mental Health Needs Assessment Project, Chung and Lin (1994) concluded that for most ethnic groups from Southeast Asia, "there was a dramatic change from prominently utilizing traditional medicine in their home country to a higher usage of mainstream service in the United States . . . [but] . . . regardless of the significant increase in the use of Western medicine, traditional medicine continued to be important for all five Southeast Asian refugee groups after resettlement" (p. 109).

Interestingly, a study by Snowden and Lieberman (1994) suggests that African Americans are not inclined to use self-help groups as an alternative to professional mental health services. Using data from the Epidemiologic Catchment Area Program, a large multisite study sponsored by the National Institute of Mental Health, these authors found that "African Americans were about one third as likely as Whites to indicate involvement in a self-help group over the course of their lifetime" (p. 57) for a mental health problem, even after accounting for differences in income. Drawing on data from a statewide program for self-help groups in California, Snowden and Lieberman concluded that "African Americans were also underrepresented also (sic) when findings were considered for concerns other than those related to mental health and substance abuse" (p. 58). Given our earlier discussion, African American inclination not to use self-help groups cannot be attributed to less need. The authors speculate that African Americans may prefer to address mental health and lifestyle issues with family, friends, or clergy, rather than members of a self-help group.

Enabling Factors

Factors that enable people to use mental health services, according to Anderson and Newman (1973, cited in Barney, 1994), include individual attributes and personal resources such as knowledge of service availability, access to insurance, and financial resources. Two enabling factors, financial resources and availability of ethnicity-specific mental health services needs, have played a major role in determining ethnic minority utilization of mental health services. We briefly discuss these enabling factors before turning our attention to an examination of the reasons why ethnic minorities have perceived mental health services as irrelevant to their needs in the past.

Financial Resources

Not only does poverty contribute to the prevalence of mental health problems among ethnic minorities, poverty helps explain why many ethnic minority individuals do not obtain mental health services for those problems. According to Rouse, Carter, and Rodriguez-Andrew (1995) ethnic minorities are less likely to earn incomes sufficient to pay for mental health treatment, less likely to have insurance, and more likely to qualify for public assistance than European Americans. Thus, ethnic minorities often have to rely on public (government-sponsored) or nonprofit mental health services to obtain help with their psychological problems. However, Gottesfeld (1995) contends that mental health services also are underutilized by minority clients because:

> public and nonprofit organizations have no financial incentives to retain minority mental patients. Funding does not depend on retention and usually there is a waiting list of patients to replace those who drop out. Incentives for mental health organizations to make changes to retain minority patients do not seem to exist at the present time. (p. 210)

Poverty also helps explain African American overutilization of publicly supported mental health hospitals. Many African Americans (and other ethnic minority individuals) do not have the financial resources needed to obtain outpatient treatment when their psychological distress is still mild or to obtain private inpatient treatment when their mental problems require hospitalization. Thus, Rosenheck and Fontana (1994) reported that:

> Black veterans and Mexican Hispanic veterans were significantly less likely than white veterans to have used non-VA mental health services or self-help groups, after adjusting for health status and other factors. [However,] there were no differences between ethnocultural groups in use of VA mental health services. (p. 685)

This finding suggests that when publicly supported services are made readily available to them, African Americans and Hispanic Americans will make use of them.

During the 1980s and early 1990s, the provision of psychological services became increasingly privatized. Public agencies, like county and community mental health centers, often were faced with diminishing moneys from local, state, and federal governments at a time when severely disabled individuals who were not considered to be a threat to themselves or others were being released from state hospitals. As a result, many community and county mental health agencies, by necessity, have had to restrict their services to providing medication-based and/or crisis-oriented interventions for people with chronic mental disorders. Therefore, ethnic minorities who do not have mental health coverage through an insurance policy, do not have surplus financial resources for mental health services, or do not qualify for Medicare often must go without help.

Availability of Ethnicity-Specific Mental Health Services

That various racial/ethnic minorities are underrepresented in community mental health services, despite the fact that they experience as much or more stress than do nonminorities, suggests these groups may perceive professional mental health services as irrelevant to their needs. A number of authors have cited language differences, western-oriented psychotherapeutic techniques, culturally dissimilar counselors, and culturally insensitive counselors as barriers to ethnic minority utilization of mental health services. S. Sue and Zane (1987) point out that "the single most important explanation for the problems in service delivery (for ethnic minorities) involves the inability of therapists to provide culturally responsive forms of treatment" (p. 37).

However, there is evidence that when ethnicity-specific mental health programs are made available to ethnic minority communities, members of those communities will make use of them. According to Takeuchi, S. Sue, and Yeh (1995):

> ethnicity-specific mental health programs . . . typically involve the recruitment of ethnic personnel, modifications in treatment practices that are presumably more culturally appropriate, and development of an atmosphere in which services are provided in a culturally familiar context. Most are located in communities with relatively large ethnic populations and serve a predominantly ethnic clientele. (p. 638)

To determine if ethnicity-specific mental health programs have more positive effects than mainstream mental health programs for ethnic minority clients, Takeuchi et al. (1995) examined the return rates, total number of treatment sessions, and therapist ratings at termination for African American ($n = 1,516$), Asian American ($n = 1,888$), Mexican Americans ($n = 1306$) and Whites (an unspecified but comparable number) using Los Angeles County Department of Mental Health services over a six-year period ending in 1988. The results indicated that ethnic minority clients involved in ethnicity-specific mental health programs are more likely to continue beyond one session and to stay for more total sessions (length of treatment has been found to be associated with treatment outcome) than those minority clients involved in a mainstream mental health program. Interestingly, culturally appropriate treatment provided in a culturally familiar context was apparently a more important determinant of utilization than having an ethnically similar counselor. For the most part, participation in an ethnicity-specific program produced a higher return rate and more total number of treatments regardless of whether clients were ethnically matched with their therapist.

In reviewing treatment outcome research on ethnic minorities, S. Sue et al. (1995) concluded "the research suggests that interventions involving culturally sensitive approaches produce more positive changes than interventions that do not consider cultural factors" (p. 276) and that "culture-specific treatment should be available to ethnic clients, especially those who are unacculturated or who hold very traditional ethnic values that are discrepant from Western values" (p. 278).

Summary of Factors Affecting Minority Mental Health Utilization

When ethnic minority people have the financial resources to make use of mental health services, and when ethnicity-specific mental health services are made available to them, they will make use of those services. Although cultural values inherent in traditional ethnic minority cultures may play a role in explaining ethnic minority underutilization of mental health services, we believe that the historical lack of culturally relevant mental health services has played an even greater role. In the next section we explore some of the specific reasons why ethnic minorities may perceive past and present mental health services as irrelevant to their needs.

Reasons Why Ethnic Minorities Perceive Mental Health Services As Irrelevant to Their Needs

There are a number of different reasons why ethnic minorities may perceive contemporary mental health services as irrelevant to their mental health needs. We begin our discussion of these reasons by reviewing the history of involvement with ethnic minority issues for two professional psychological organizations.

Lack of Attention to the Mental Health Needs of Ethnic Minorities

Until the late 1960s, the counseling and psychology professions demonstrated little interest in, or concern for, the status of racial/ethnic minority groups (Barnes, 1994). Counseling and guidance, with its traditional focus on the needs of the "average" student, tended to overlook the special needs of individuals who, by virtue of their skin color, physical characteristics, cultural background, or socioeconomic condition, found themselves disadvantaged in a world designed by and for European Americans. Psychologists in private practice, with their clientele primarily limited to middle- and upper-class individuals, also overlooked the needs of ethnic minority populations. Psychotherapy researchers did not address ethnicity as a research variable due to a number of factors, including their own lack of interest in ethnicity, lack of funding for ethnicity-related research topics, and the view that only massive social and political change could address the needs of ethnic minorities (S. Sue et al., 1995).

The social movements of the 1960s probably can be credited with stimulating the American Psychological Association (APA), the American Personnel and Guidance Association (APGA, now called the American Counseling Association—ACA), and other professional mental health organizations to begin addressing the needs of ethnic minorities. ACA and APA have divisions that focus on racial/ethnic minority issues. According to McFadden and Lipscomb (1985), the first formal step toward forming the ACA for Multicultural Counseling and Development (AMCD) was taken in 1969 when the APGA Senate adopted a resolution establishing a salaried National Office of Non-White Concerns as part of the APGA central office. The Association for Non-White Concerns in Personnel and Guidance became a reality in 1972 and was renamed the AMCD in the mid-1980s.

Casas (1984) has documented that APA interest in ethnic minority issues moved from an ad hoc committee level in the 1960s to the granting of divisional status (Division 45) to ethnic psychologists in 1987. The first formal sign of interest in racial/ethnic minority issues within the APA structure was the establishment of an ad hoc committee on equal opportunity in psychology in 1963. The purpose of this committee was to examine problems experienced by racial/ethnic minorities who seek training and employment in psychology. This ad hoc committee was made a standing committee (Committee on Equality of Opportunity in Psychology—CEOP) in 1967 and was charged with the formulation of policy regarding the education, training, employment, and status of minority groups in psychology. In 1970 their charge was broadened to include, among other things, women's issues, advocacy for victims of racism, affirmative action efforts, and Project Impact (the precursor of the Minority Fellowship program).

In 1971 APA established the Board of Social and Ethical Responsibility for Psychology (BSERP) to examine ways in which social responsibility can be integrated as a dominant theme in the science and profession of psychology. The CEOP was one of three Committees assigned to BSERP. The scope of the CEOP was narrowed to focus only on racial/ethnic minority issues in 1974. The APA Office of Cultural and Ethnic Affairs was established in 1978, and the Board of Ethnic Minority Affairs was established in 1980. An important step was taken in 1981 when the APA revised the organization's ethical guidelines and mandated that psychologists receive training in cultural differences. The APA also amended accreditation standards to include the requirement for formal training in cross-cultural issues (Mio & Morris, 1990). The Society of Psychological Study of Ethnic Minority Issues (Division 45) was formally established by APA in January 1987. In 1990, the APA published "Guidelines for providers of psychological services to ethnic, linguistic, and culturally diverse populations" (APA, 1990).

The increased attention to ethnic minority issues within ACA, APA, and other mental health organizations can be attributed in part to the political activities of racial/ethnic minority members and their nonminority supporters. For example, in 1969, the Black Student Psychological Association presented a number of demands to the APA Council of Representatives that directed attention to the underrepresentation of ethnic minorities in professional psychology. Also, advocates for racial/ethnic minority issues were active at the 1973 Vail Conference, the 1975 Austin Conference, and the 1978 Dulles Conference, all of which addressed at some level the need to expand the roles of culturally diverse people in psychology (D. W. Sue, 1990). The establishment of Division 45 was the direct result of an intense lobbying effort by ethnic minority members of APA. Similarly, Carter (1994) credits activism by a small group of African American psychiatrists at the 1969 annual meeting of the American Psychiatric Association for efforts in 1972 and later by the American Psychiatric Association Board of Trustees for increased attention to racism among psychiatrists.

In examining these historical events, it is clear that professional psychology has moved from a position of ignoring the special needs and experiences of racial/ethnic minorities to a position of increased sensitivity and activity. It is also clear, however, that the profession has been largely reactive (to the political pressures of constituent groups) rather than proactive in its response and that many inequities still remain. Furthermore, it remains to be seen whether the policies of these professional organizations will translate into increased and more culturally relevant mental health services for ethnic minorities.

Lack of Bilingual Counselors

Another reason that many ethnic minority individuals do not seek help for psychological problems is the lack of bilingual counselors. The heavy reliance by counselors and other mental health professionals on verbal interaction to build rapport and provide treatment presupposes that the participants in a counseling dialogue are capable of understanding each other. Yet rapport-building and treatment may be impossible when counselors fail to understand the client's language and its nuances (Altarriba & Santiago-Rivera, 1994; Romero, 1985). Furthermore, counselors may incorrectly or negatively interpret statements from clients who speak with an accent or who do not use standard English to express themselves (Padilla, 1991; D. W. Sue & D. Sue, 1990). Scott and Borodovsky (1990) suggest that in cross-cultural counseling, "language differences become barriers when (a) the participants misconstrue the statements of one another, (b) negative prejudgments by participants of one another are based on these differences, and (c) such differences are not experienced or appreciated as expressions of the client's cultural heritage and/or identity" (p. 167).

When language appropriate mental health services are provided, ethnic minority use of these services rises to parity with European American usage (Takeuchi et al., 1995; S. Sue et al., 1995). Ethnic minority utilization of culturally-appropriate mental health services will be discussed in a later section.

Lack of Ethnically Similar Counselors

Theoretically, language and cultural differences would not be an issue if clients always had access to a linguistically and culturally similar counselor. In an extensive review of process and outcome research, Atkinson and Lowe (1995) found that "substantial evidence that treatment outcomes are enhanced by matching therapist and client on the basis of language and ethnicity" (p. 397). Even when language is not an issue, there is overwhelming evidence that ethnic minorities prefer to work with an ethnically similar counselor; Atkinson and Lowe found that "Other things being equal, ethnic minority participants prefer an ethnically similar counselor over an ethnically dissimilar counselor" (p. 392). A study by Blank, Tetrick, Brinkley, Smith, and Doheny (1994) reinforced this conclusion; these researchers found that ethnically-similar case manager and client dyads resulted in more total client visits than did ethnically-dissimilar dyads.

Unfortunately, however, racial/ethnic minorities are severely underrepresented in professional psychology and the chances of achieving parity with European American counselors in the near future is highly unlikely. In the most recent longitudinal study of ethnic minority representation in doctoral training programs, Kohout and Pion (1990) found that between 1977 and 1987 the percentage who were African American actually dropped slightly (3.5 percent to 3.4 percent) while comparable figures for Asian Americans (1.2 percent to 1.7 percent), American Indians (0.3 percent to 0.6 percent), and Hispanic Americans (1.5 percent to 3.5 percent) increased only slightly. A subsequent study reported that African Americans make up 5 percent, Hispanic Americans 5 percent, Asian Americans 4 percent, and American Indians 1 percent of the student enrollment in doctoral psychology programs (Kohout & Wicherski, 1993). Based on data like these, Bernal and Castro (1994) pessimistically (but accurately) observed that "there is clear indication that the need for mental health services and research on ethnic minority populations will increase at a greater rate than will the availability of qualified professionals to address these needs" (p. 798).

The underrepresentation of ethnic minorities among doctoral students in psychology is not surprising given that ethnic minorities are even more underrepresented among psychology faculty and that faculty play a major role in the recruitment and mentoring of ethnic minority students (Atkinson, Brown, & Casas, 1996). Kohout and Wicherski (1993) report that African Americans constitute 5 percent of the faculty in clinical, counseling, and school psychology training programs, while Hispanics, Asian Americans, and American Indians make up 2 percent, 1 percent, and less than 1 percent, respectively. Thus, while ethnic minorities make up approximately 25 percent of the current U.S. population with dramatic increases ahead, they constitute less than 15 percent of the student enrollment and less than 9 percent of the full-time faculty in applied psychology programs (Atkinson et al., 1996).

Training programs will need to actively recruit and support ethnic minority students if ethnic parity is to be achieved in psychology and counseling. However, there is reason to believe that few training programs make any significant effort to systematically recruit and retain ethnic minorities. Moses (1990) reported that APA estimates only fifteen or twenty training programs have been proactive in recruiting and retaining ethnic minority students.

Reliance on Intrapsychic Etiology Model

Although research like that cited earlier has documented that ethnic minority mental health problems are often a function of environmental forces, psychology practitioners continue to rely heavily on an intrapsychic model of problem etiology and continue to base psychological interventions on an intrapsychic model. Counseling in this country has grown out of a philosophy of "rugged individualism" in which people are assumed to be responsible for their own lot in life. Success in society is attributed to outstanding abilities or great effort. Likewise, failures or problems encountered by the person may be attributed to some inner deficiency such as lack of effort or low aptitude (D. W. Sue, 1978). For the minority individual who is the victim of oppression, the person-blame approach tends to deny the existence of external injustices (racism, sexism, age, bias, etc.).

To some extent, the assumption of an internal problem etiology is inherent in all conventional counseling approaches. According to Smith (1985),

> What has become known as the traditional model of counseling is, in reality, a set of principles that has been extracted from various counseling theories and that is seen to cut across theoretical counseling formulations. Such principles tend to stress that (1) clients' problems are located within the individual (intrapsychically based), rather than in the conditions to which minorities adjust; (2) clients' problems should be resolved internally; (3) clients are familiar with the roles of client and counselor; and (4) talk rather than direct action is the more desirable counseling technique. (p. 568)

Katz (1985), Smith (1985), and others urge counselors to acknowledge the extrapsychic causes of client problems and work to change oppressive environments that create mental health problems for members of disfranchised groups, rather than changing individual behavior or helping people to adapt to their stressful living conditions.

Recognizing that ethnic minority clients may not be responsible for *causing* their mental health problems does not mean that counselors should also minimize the responsibility that ethnic minority clients have for *solving* their mental health problems. The models of helping and coping described by Brickman et al. (1982) provide a useful way of conceptualizing this distinction. Briefly, Brickman et al. pointed out that we all make internal and external attributions of responsibility for causing and solving problems experienced by ourselves and others. "Whether or not people are held responsible for causing their problems or whether or not they are held responsible for solving these problems are the factors determining four fundamentally different orientations to the world, each internally coherent, each in some measure incompatible with the other three" (Brickman et al., 1982, p. 369). These four orientations to the world were labeled by Brickman et al. the moral, enlightenment, compensatory, and medical models. In the moral model, high attributions of responsibility for causing and solving the problem are attributed to the individual. In the enlightenment model, the individual is assumed to have a high responsibility for causing the problem but a low responsibility for solving the problem. The inverse is true for the compensatory model; the individual is assumed to have low responsibility for causing the problem but high responsibility for solving the problem. In the medical model, low attributions of responsibility for causing and solving the problem are attributed to the individual.

Some authors have suggested that we do a disservice to ethnic minorities when we apply the medical model, because in doing so counselors relieve their clients of personal responsibility for bringing about change in their lives. Instead, they argue that mental health service providers need to apply either a moral model, a compensatory model, or some combination of the two models. A combination of the moral and compensatory models suggests that clients need to feel a sense of personal responsibility for their behavior, even though it may have initially evolved out of an oppressive environment. Thus, Parham and McDavis (1987) advise counselors to work toward changing oppressive external environments and destructive personal behavior when counseling African American men. These authors point out that:

> restricting intervention to external factors alone, however, implies that Black men have no part in alleviating their predicament as a population at risk and that they lack the mental fortitude to deal effectively with adverse conditions in society. . . . Black men must simultaneously shoulder some of the blame for their predicament and some of the responsibility for developing personal intervention strategies that will ultimately better their condition. Counseling professionals can assist Black men in developing such strategies. (p. 24)

Parham and McDavis' point is well taken; an overemphasis on external causes of mental health problems could lead to a denial of responsibility on the part of clients for either causing or resolving their problems. However, we also feel that because most counselors have been trained to view client problems as having an internal etiology and to treat mental health problems with strategies that assume an intrapsychic cause, the threat of misdiagnosing a problem with an external cause is greater than that of misdiagnosing a problem with an internal cause.

Reliance on Western-Oriented Counseling Theories and Strategies

According to D. W. Sue (1994), "multicultural specialists have repeatedly pointed out that traditional forms of counseling and therapy are Eurocentric and perhaps inappropriate and antagonistic to the lifestyles and cultural values of various minority groups" (p. 293). Clearly, contemporary theories and techniques of counseling have evolved out of a predominantly European and European American belief system applied to the problems experienced by a predominantly European and European American clientele. This recognition provides a strong argument for providing more culturally relevant interventions when working with ethnic minority clients. However, as S. Sue et al. (1995) pointed out, "[our] . . . concept of 'culturally responsive' interventions often consists only of vague notions of being culturally sensitive and knowledgeable about the client's culture" (p. 269). According to Wohl (1995), "culturally specific approaches are psychotherapeutic methods designed to be congruent with the cultural characteristics of a particular ethnic clientele, or for problems believed to be especially prominent in a particular ethnic group or to ethnic groups in general" (p. 76). There is disagreement, however, about how much contemporary psychological theory and techniques need to be tweaked to be congruent with ethnic minority cultures. At one extreme are authors who contend that the constructs from several existing counseling theories and strategies are universally applicable (Fukuyama, 1990; Ho, 1995; Vontress, 1979). At the other extreme are authors who urge counselors to adopt the helping strategies from the client's indigenous culture (Cayleff, 1986; Heinrich, Corbine, & Thomas, 1990; Torrey, 1970). Between these two extremes are a number of other positions, including the views that conventional counseling theories and strategies can be matched with (Majors & Nikelly, 1983; Ponterotto, 1987), adapted to (Ruiz & Casas, 1981; Wohl, 1995), or combined into eclectic approaches compatible with (McDavis, 1978; Stikes, 1972) the client's culture. Wohl argues against discarding altogether conventional theories of counseling and psychotherapy:

> A . . . conclusion sometimes drawn . . . is . . . that so-called traditional therapies cannot be used effectively with cultural minorities and should be replaced by some new "culturally specific" techniques. Culturally specific approaches are psychotherapeutic methods designed to be congruent with the cultural characteristics of a particular ethnic clientele. . . . Although such experimentation to develop more efficacious means of treating ethnic minorities using culturally specific techniques is desirable, these efforts should not be taken to rule out the use of traditional psychotherapies. . . . Any reasonable review of the literature shows no justification for the sweeping conclusion that would dismiss traditional psychotherapies out of hand. . . . Traditional psychotherapies can be used, but they must be adapted and flexibly applied by taking into account social, economic, cultural, ethnic, and political determinants of the patient's situation. (p. 76)

In general, we find ourselves in agreement with Wohl (1995). Counselors and mental health workers need not discount all their knowledge of psychological theory and strategies when working with ethnic minority clients. However, they must adapt these theories and strategies to meet the needs and experiences of their clients, taking into account the within-group variables discussed in chapter 2. In chapter 16 we provide a three-dimensional model of cross-cultural counseling intended to help counselors conceptualize how mental health services need to be adapted to the unique needs and experiences of the ethnic minority client.

Lack of Culturally Sensitive/Knowledgeable/ Skilled Counselors

Given that only minuscule gains are being made in the number of ethnic minorities being trained as psychologists (and other mental health service providers), while the general population is rapidly becoming increasingly diverse, European American counselors will need to play an important role in meeting the mental health needs of ethnic minority clients for the foreseeable future. In an earlier section, we pointed out that professional psychology has been slow in responding to the special needs of racial/ethnic minority populations. Carney and Kahn (1984) suggest that the tendency on the part of White mental health professionals to ignore or minimize the importance of ethnic/cultural differences "is based on the belief that persons who are racially and culturally different are also culturally and/or genetically deficient" (p. 111). Even those psychologists and counselors who consciously try to promote ethnic equality may unconsciously commit racist acts.

There is substantial evidence that European American psychotherapists are biased in their diagnosis and treatment of racial/ethnic minorities. An earlier major review of research by Abramowitz and Murray (1983) revealed that ethnic minorities are diagnosed differently and receive "less preferred" forms of treatment than do European American clients. More recently, Snowden and Cheung (1990) found that African Americans are more likely to be diagnosed as schizophrenic and less likely to be diagnosed as having an affective disorder than are Whites. In their review of research on anxiety disorders among African Americans and non-African Americans, Paradis, Hatch, and Friedman (1994) found that African Americans are underdiagnosed with anxiety disorders and overdiagnosed with schizophrenic disorders. According to Adebimpe (1994), "the evidence of different treatment experiences can no longer be regarded as 'scanty, piecemeal, and inconclusive' or as an artifact of a transient period of heightened research interest in blacks" (p. 30).

Differential diagnoses and treatment of ethnic minorities is presumably a function of stereotypes held by counselors. Analog studies have generally not provided evidence that counselors hold biased views of racial/ethnic minorities, presumably because the purpose of such studies is usually self-evident. However, several studies employing an illusory correlation paradigm have found that counselors hold stereotypic views of racial/ethnic minorities. Atkinson, Casas, and Wampold (1981) found that university counselors tend to group student characteristics into constellations reflective of common ethnic stereotypes. Wampold, Casas and Atkinson, (1982) found that nonminority counselor trainees are more likely to be influenced by stereotypes when assigning characteristics to racial/ethnic groups than are minority counselor trainees.

Clearly, racism takes many forms, ranging from unconscious stereotyping by someone consciously committed to egalitarianism to those individuals who commit acts of violence against racial/ethnic minorities. European American counselors probably represent a range of racist attitudes. Sabnani, Ponterotto, and Borodovsky (1991) point out that White counselor trainees enter training at different levels of White identity development and that a developmental approach is needed to raise their awareness of ethnic issues. We will have more to say about this in chapter 16. For our purposes here, however, we conclude that training programs need to address the conscious and unconscious racist attitudes held by European American counselors.

There is a growing recognition that graduate training programs must not only overcome racism in their students, they must proactively prepare their students to serve racial/ethnic minority clients. Ridley (1985) describes five imperatives for the development of training programs that promote cross-cultural competence. In a position paper that resulted from the APA-sponsored Vail Conference, it was strongly recommended that it be considered unethical for psychologists not trained in cultural diversity to provide services to ethnically diverse groups. Also, both the APA and ACA have incorporated knowledge of cultural diversity into their training standards.

Although the need for culturally knowledgeable and sensitive counselors is reflected in the APA and ACA ethical guidelines, mandated by the APA accreditation requirements, and supported by research, there is evidence that doctoral programs still may not be providing formal training in this area. Mio and Morris (1990) suggest that "there still seems to be much resistance against the inclusion of cross-cultural issues as part of the standard curriculum" (p. 435). Their perception is confirmed by the Committee on Accreditation, which currently cites diversity issues in about 75 percent of its program reviews (Moses, 1990).

Psychology programs are reluctant to change their curricula (Moses, 1990). Cultural influences affecting personality, identity formation, and behavior manifestations frequently are not a part of the training psychologists and counselors receive. When minority group experiences are discussed, they are generally seen and analyzed from the "White, middle-class perspective." Unimodal counseling approaches are perpetuated by graduate programs in counseling that give inadequate treatment to the mental health issues of minorities (Ponterotto & Casas, 1987). As a result, counselors who deal with the mental health problems of minorities often lack understanding and knowledge about cultural differences and their consequent interaction with an oppressive society.

While there is general agreement that training programs must prepare students to work with racial/ethnic minority populations "there is little agreement on what organized psychology can and should do to help programs improve their records in this field" (Moses, 1990). Some authors have suggested that APA, ACA, and other organizations have not been specific enough about the training that counselors and psychologists should receive with respect to culturally diverse groups. As Ponterotto and Casas (1987) suggest, "the [counseling] profession has not yet defined culturally competent training" (p. 433). Others argue that professional organizations have not pushed curriculum change forcefully enough through their accreditation procedures (Wyatt, quoted in Moses, 1990).

Although professional mental health associations have not included specific cultural competencies in their training standards, models of cross-cultural competencies do exist. The APA Division 17 Education and Training Committee developed a position paper identifying cross-cultural counseling competencies that was published in *The Counseling Psychologist* (D. W. Sue, Bernier, Durran, Feinberg, Pedersen, Smith, & Vasquez-Nuttall, 1982). More recently, the Professional Standards Committee of the AMCD developed a position paper than expands on some of the principles put forth in the Division 17 paper. The AMCD paper is reprinted in the Appendix. Models for achieving competence in cross-cultural counseling are also discussed in a number of journal articles (e.g., LaFromboise & Rowe, 1983; Mio & Morris, 1990; S. Sue, Akutsu, & Higashi, 1985). These models will be discussed at greater length in chapter 16.

References

Abramowitz, S. I., & Murray, J. (1983). Race effects in psychotherapy. In J. Murray & P. R. Abramson (Eds.), *Bias in psychotherapy* (pp. 215–255). New York: Praeger.

Adebimpe, V. R. (1994). Race, racism, and epidemiological surveys. *Hospital & Community Psychiatry, 45,* 27–31.

Altarriba, J., & Santiago-Rivera, A. L. (1994). Current perspectives on using linguistic and cultural factors in counseling the Hispanic client. *Professional Psychology: Research and Practice, 25,* 388–397.

American Psychological Association. (1990). *Guidelines for providers of psychological services to ethnic, linguistic, and culturally diverse populations.* Washington, DC: Author.

Aponte, J. F., & Crouch, R. T. (1995). The changing ethnic profile of the United States. In J. F. Aponte, R. Young Rivers, & J. Wohl (Eds.), *Psychological interventions and cultural diversity* (pp. 1–17). Boston: Allyn and Bacon.

Atkinson, D. R., Brown, M. T., & Casas, J. M. (1996). Achieving ethnic parity in counseling psychology. *The Counseling Psychologist, 24,* 230–258.

Atkinson, D. R., Casas, J. M., & Wampold, B. (1981). The categorization of ethnic stereotypes by university counselors. *Hispanic Journal of Behavioral Sciences, 3,* 75–82.

Atkinson, D. R., & Lowe, S. M. (1995). The role of ethnicity, cultural knowledge, and conventional techniques in counseling and psychotherapy. In J. G. Ponterotto, J. M. Casas, L. A. Suzuki, & C. M. Alexander (Eds.), *Handbook of multicultural counseling* (pp. 387–414). Thousand Oaks, CA: Sage Publications.

Barnes, M. (1994). Clinical treatment issues regarding Black African-Americans. In J. L. Ronch, W. Van Ornum, & N. C. Stilwell (Eds.), *The counseling sourcebook: A practical reference on contemporary issues* (pp. 157–164). New York: Crossroad.

Barney, D. D. (1994). Use of mental health services by American Indian and Alaska Native elders. *American Indian and Alaska Native Mental Health Research, 5*(3), 1–14.

Bernal, M. E., & Castro, F. G. (1994). Are clinical psychologists prepared for service and research with ethnic minorities? A report of a decade of progress. *American Psychologist, 49,* 797–805.

Blank, M. B., Tetrick, F. L., Brinkley, D. F., Smith, H. O., & Doheny, V. (1994). Racial matching and service utilization among seriously mentally ill consumers in the rural south. *Community Mental Health Journal, 30,* 271–281.

Brickman, P., Rabinowitz, V. C., Karuza, J., Coates, D., Cohn, E., & Kidder, L. (1982). Models of helping and coping. *American Psychologist, 37,* 368–384.

Brody, E. (1994). The mental health and well-being of refugees: Issues and directions. In A. J. Marsella, T. Bornemann, S. Ekblad, & J. Orley (Eds.), *Amidst peril and pain* (pp. 57–68). Washington, DC: American Psychological Association.

Canino, I. A., Earley, B. F., & Rogler, L. H. (1980). *The Puerto Rican child in New York City: Stress and mental health* (Monograph No. 4). New York: Hispanic Research Center, Fordham University.

Cannon, M. S., & Locke, B. Z. (1977). Being black is detrimental to one's mental health: Myth or reality? *Phylon, 38,* 408–428.

Carney, C. G., & Kahn, K. B. (1984). Building competencies for effective cross-cultural counseling: A developmental view. *The Counseling Psychologist, 12,* 111–119.

Carter, J. H. (1994) Racism's impact on mental health. *Journal of the National Medical Association, 86,* 543–547.

Casas, J. M. (1984). Policy, training, and research in counseling psychology: The racial/ethnic minority perspective. In S. D. Brown & R. W. Lent (Eds.), *Handbook of counseling psychology* (pp. 785–831). New York: John Wiley & Sons.

Castaneda, D. M. (1994). A research agenda for Mexican-American adolescent mental health. *Adolescence, 29*(113), 225–239.

Cayleff, S. E. (1986). Ethical issues in counseling gender, race, and culturally distinct groups. *Journal of Counseling and Development, 64,* 345–347.

Cheung, F. K., & Snowden, L. R. (1990). Community mental health and ethnic minority populations. *Community Mental Health Journal, 26,* 277–291.

Cheung, L. R. L. (1987). *Assessing Asian language performance.* Rockville, MD: Aspen Publishers.

Chin, J. L. (1983). Diagnostic considerations in working with Asian Americans. *American Journal of Orthopsychiatry, 53,* 100–109.

Chung, R. C., & Lin, K. (1994). Help seeking among Southeast Asian refugees. *Journal of Community Psychology, 22,* 109–120.

Dona, G., & Berry, J. W. (1994). Acculturation attitudes and acculturative stress of Central American refugees. *International Journal of Psychology, 29,* 57–70.

Esquivel, G. B., & Keitel, M. A. (1990). Counseling immigrant children in the schools. *Elementary School Guidance & Counseling, 24,* 213–221.

Fabrega, H., Jr., & Miller, B. D. (1995). A cultural analysis of adolescent psychopathology. *Journal of Adolescent Research, 10,* 197–226.

Farias, P. (1994). Central and South American refugees: Some mental health challenges. In A. J. Marsella, T. Bornemann, S. Ekblad, & J. Orley (Eds.), *Amidst peril and pain: The mental health and well-being of the world's refugees* (pp. 101–113). Washington, DC: American Psychological Association.

Friedman, S., Paradis, C. M., & Hatch, M L. (1994). Issues of misdiagnosis in panic disorder with agoraphobia. In S. Friedman (Ed.), *Anxiety disorders in African Americans* (pp. 53–64). New York: Springer Publishing Company.

Fukuyama, M. A. (1990). Taking a universal approach to multicultural counseling. *Counselor Education & Supervision, 30,* 6–17.

Gottesfeld, H. (1995). Community context and the underutilization of mental health services by minority patients. *Psychological Reports, 76,* 207–210.

Greene, R. L., Jackson, J. S., & Neighbors, H. W. (1993). Mental health and help-seeking behavior. In J. S. Jackson, L. M. Chatters, & R. J. Taylor (Eds.), *Aging in Black America* (pp. 185–200). Newbury Park, CA: Sage Publications, Inc.

Griffith, E. E. H., & Gonzalez, C. A. (1994). Essentials of cultural psychiatry. In R. E. Hales, S. C. Yudofsky, & J. A. Talbott (Eds.), *The American Psychiatric Press textbook of psychiatry* (2nd ed., pp. 1379–1404). Washington, DC: American Psychiatric Press.

Heinrich, R. K., Corbine, J. L., Thomas, K. R. (1990). Counseling Native Americans. *Journal of Counseling & Development, 69,* 128–133.

Ho, D. Y. F. (1995). Internalized culture, culturocentrism, and transcendence. *The Counseling Psychologist, 23,* 4–24.

Horwath, E., Johnson, J., & Hornig, C. D. (1994). Epidemiology of panic disorder. In S. Friedman (Ed.), *Anxiety disorders in African Americans* (pp. 53–64). New York: Springer Publishing Company.

Jaco, E. G. (1959). Mental health of Spanish Americans in Texas. In M. F. Opler (Ed.), *Culture and mental health: Cross cultural studies* (pp. 467–485). New York: Macmillan.

Jones, B. E., & Gray, B. A. (1986). Problems in diagnosing schizophrenia and affective disorders among blacks. *Hospital and Community Psychiatry, 37,* 61–65.

Jones-Webb, R. J., & Snowden, L. R. (1993). Symptoms of depression among Blacks and Whites. *American Journal of Public Health, 83,* 240–244.

Katz, J. H. (1985). The sociopolitical nature of counseling. *The Counseling Psychologist, 13,* 615–624.

Kohout, J., & Pion, G. (1990). In G. Stricker, E. Davis-Russell, E. Bourg, E. Duran, W. R. Hammond, H. McHolland, K. Polite, & B. E. Vaughn (Eds.), *Toward ethnic diversification in psychology education and training* (pp. 105–111). Washington, DC: Education Directorate, American Psychological Association.

Kohout, J., & Wicherski, M. (1993). *Characteristics of graduate departments of psychology: 1991–92.* Washington, DC: Education Directorate, American Psychological Association.

Korchin, S. J. (1980). Clinical psychology and minority problems. *American Psychologist, 35,* 262–269.

Koss-Chioino, J. D. (1995). Traditional and folk approaches among ethnic minorities. In J. F. Aponte, R. Young Rivers, & J. Wohl (Eds.), *Psychological interventions and cultural diversity* (pp. 145–163). Boston: Allyn and Bacon.

LaFromboise, T. D., & Rowe, W. (1983). Skills training for bicultural competence: Rationale and application. *Journal of Counseling Psychology, 30,* 589–595.

Lefley, H. P. (1994). Service needs of culturally diverse patients and families. In H. P. Lefley & M. Wasow (Eds.), *Helping families cope with mental illness* (pp. 223–242). Chur, Switzerland: Harwood Academic Publishers.

Leong, F. T. L. (1986). Counseling and psychotherapy with Asian Americans: Review of literature. *Journal of Counseling Psychology, 33,* 196–206.

Leong, F. T. L. (1994). Asian Americans' differential patterns of utilization of inpatient and outpatient public mental health services in Hawaii. *Journal of Community Psychology, 22,* 82–96.

Leong, F. T. L., Wagner, N. S., & Tata, S. P. (1995). Racial and ethnic variations in help-seeking attitudes. In J. G. Ponterotto, J. M. Casas, L. A. Suzuki, & C. M. Alexander (Eds.), *Handbook of multicultural counseling* (pp. 415–438). Thousand Oaks, CA: Sage.

Lippincott, J. A., & Mierzwa, J. A. (1995). Propensity for seeking counseling services: A comparison of Asian and American undergraduates. *Journal of American College Health, 43,* 201–204.

Magoon, T. M. (1988). *1987/88 College and university counseling center data bank.* College Park, MD: University of Maryland Counseling Center.

Majors, R., & Nikelly, A. (1983). Serving the Black community: A new direction for psychotherapy. *Journal of Non-White Concerns in Personnel and Guidance, 11,* 142–151.

Marsella, A. J., Bornemann, T., Ekblad, S., & Orley, J. (1994). *Amidst peril and pain.* Washington, DC: American Psychological Association.

McDavis, R. J. (1978). Counseling Black clients effectively: The eclectic approach. *Journal of Non-White Concerns in Personnel and Guidance, 7,* 41–47.

McFadden, J., & Lipscomb, W. D. (1985). History of the Association for Non-White Concerns in Personnel and Guidance. *Journal of Counseling and Development, 63,* 444–447.

Mio, J. S., & Morris, D. R. (1990). Cross-cultural issues in psychology training programs: An invitation for discussion. *Professional Psychology: Theory and Practice, 21,* 434–441.

Mollica, R. (1994). Southeast Asian refugees: Migration history and mental health issues. In A. J. Marsella, T. Bornemann, S. Ekblad, & J. Orley (Eds.), *Amidst peril and pain* (pp. 83–100). Washington, DC: American Psychological Association.

Moses, S. (1990, December). Sensitivity to culture may be hard to teach: APA approves practice guidelines. *APA Monitor,* p. 39.

Moyerman, D. R., & Forman, B. D. (1992). Acculturation and adjustment: A meta-analytic study. *Hispanic Journal of Behavioral Sciences, 14,* 163–200.

Neighbors, H. W., Caldwell, C. H., Thompson, E., & Jackson, J. S. (1994). Help-seeking behavior and unmet need. In S. Friedman (Ed.), *Disorders in African Americans* (pp. 26–39). New York: Springer Publishing Co.

Neighbors, H. W., & Jackson, J. S. (1984). *American Journal of Community Psychology, 12,* 629–644.

Nguyen, L. T., & Henkin, L. B. (1983). Change among Indochinese refugees. In R. J. Samuda & S. C. Woods (Eds), *Perspectives in immigrant and minority education* (pp. 156–171). New York: University Press of America.

Nickerson, K. J., Helms, J. E., & Terrell, F. (1994). Cultural mistrust, opinions about mental illness, and Black students' attitudes toward seeking psychological help from White counselors. *Journal of Counseling Psychology, 41,* 378–385.

Ogbu, J. U. (1987). Variability in minority school performance: A problem in search of an explanation. *Anthropology and education quarterly, 18,* 312–334.

Orley, J. (1994). Psychological disorders among refugees: Some clinical and epidemiological considerations. In A. J. Marsella, T. Bornemann, S. Ekblad, & J. Orley (Eds.), *Amidst peril and pain: The mental health and well-being of the world's refugees* (pp. 193–206). Washington, DC: American Psychological Association.

Padgett, D. K., Patrick, C., Burns, B. J., & Schlesinger, H. J. (1994). Women and outpatient mental health services: Use by Black, Hispanic, and White women in a national insured population. *Journal of Mental Health Administration, 21,* 347–360.

Padilla, A. M. (1991). On the English-only movement: Reply to Murray. *American Psychologist, 46,* 1091–1092.

Paradis, C. M., Hatch, M., & Friedman, S. (1994). Anxiety disorders in African Americans: An update. *Journal of the National Medical Association, 86,* 609–612.

Parham, T. A., & McDavis, R. J. (1987). Black men, an endangered species: Who's really pulling the trigger? *Journal of Counseling & Development, 66,* 24–27.

Ponterotto, J. G. (1987). Counseling Mexican Americans: A multimodel approach. *Journal of Counseling and Development, 65,* 308–312.

Ponterotto, J. G., & Casas, J. M. (1987). In search of multicultural competence within counselor education programs. *Journal of Counseling and Development, 65,* 430–434.

Ridley, C. R. (1985). Imperatives for ethnic and cultural relevance in psychology training programs. *Professional Psychology: Research and Practice, 16,* 611–622.

Rivera, G. (1988). Hispanic folk medicine utilization in urban Colorado. *Sociology & Social Research, 72,* 237–241.

Rogler, L. H., Cortes, D. E., & Malgady, R. G. (1991). Acculturation and mental health status among Hispanics: Convergence and new directions for research. *American Psychologist, 46,* 585–597.

Romero, D. (1985). Cross-cultural counseling: Brief reactions for the practitioner. *The Counseling Psychologist, 13,* 665–671.

Rosenheck, R., & Fontana, A. (1994). Utilization of mental health services by minority veterans of the Vietnam era. *The Journal of Nervous and Mental Disease, 182,* 685–691.

Rosenstein, M. J., Milazzo-Sayre, L. J., MacAskill, R. L., & Manderscheid, R. W. (1987). Use of inpatient services by special populations. In R. W. Manderscheid & S. A. Barrett (Eds.), *Mental health, United States, 1987* (DHHS Publication No. ADM 87-1518). Washington, DC: U.S. Government Printing Office.

Rouse, B. A., Carter, J. H., & Rodriguez-Andrew, S. (1995). Race/ethnicity and other sociocultural influences on alcoholism treatment for women. *Recent developments in alcoholism, 12,* 343–367.

Ruiz, R. A., & Casas, J. M. (1981). A model of culturally relevant and behavioristic counseling for Chicano college students. In P. Pedersen, J. C. Droguns, W. J. Lonner, C. J. Trimble (Eds.), *Counseling Across Cultures* (pp. 181–202). Honolulu: University of Hawaii Press.

Rumbaut, R. G. (1995). Vietnamese, Laotian, and Cambodian Americans. In Pyong Gap Min (Ed.), *Asian Americans: Contemporary trends and issues* (pp. 232–266). Thousand Oaks, CA: Sage Publications.

Sabnani, H. B, Ponterotto, J. G., & Borodovsky, L. G. (1991). White racial identity development and cross-cultural counselor training: A stage model. *The Counseling Psychologist, 19,* 76–102.

Sanchez, A. R., & King, M. (1986). Mexican Americans' use of counseling services: Cultural and institutional factors. *Journal of College Student Personnel, 27,* 344–349.

Scott, N. E., & Borodovsky, L. G. (1990). Effective use of cultural role taking. *Professional Psychology: Research and Practice, 21,* 167–170.

Smart, J. F., & Smart, D. W. (1995). Acculturative stress of Hispanics: Loss and challenge. *Journal of Counseling & Development, 73,* 390–396.

Smith, E. M. J. (1985). Ethnic minorities: Life stress, social support, and mental health issues. *The Counseling Psychologist, 13,* 537–579.

Snowden, L. R., & Cheung, F. H. (1990). Use of inpatient mental health services by members of ethnic minority groups. *American Psychologist, 45,* 347–355.

Snowden, L. R., & Lieberman, M. A. (1994). African-American participation in self-help groups. In T. J. Powell (Ed.), *Understanding the self-help organization: Framework and finding* (pp. 50–61). Thousand Oaks, CA: Sage Publications.

Special Populations Task Force of the President's Commission on Mental Health. (1978). *Task panel reports submitted to the President's Commission on Mental Health: Vol. 3.* Washington, DC: U.S. Government Printing Office.

Stikes, C. S. (1972). Culturally specific counseling: The Black client. *Journal of Non-White Concerns in Personnel and Guidance, 1,* 15–23.

Stone, G. L., & Archer, J. (1990). College and university counseling centers in the 1990s: Challenges and limits. *The Counseling Psychologist, 18,* 539–607.

Sue, D. W. (1978). Eliminating cultural oppression in counseling: Toward a general theory. *Journal of Counseling Psychology, 25,* 419–428.

Sue, D. W. (1990). Culture-specific strategies in counseling: A conceptual framework. *Professional Psychology: Research and Practice, 21,* 424–433.

Sue, D. W. (1994). Asian-American mental health and help-seeking behavior: Comment on Solberg et al. (1994), Tata and Leong (1994), and Lin (1994). *Journal of Counseling Psychology, 41,* 292–295.

Sue, D. W., & Sue, D. (1990). *Counseling the culturally different: Theory and practice* (2nd ed.). New York: John Wiley & Sons.

Sue, D. W., Bernier, Y., Durran, A., Feinberg, L., Pedersen, P. B., Smith, E. J., & Vasquez-Nuttall, E. (1982). Position paper: Cross-cultural counseling competencies. *The Counseling Psychologist, 10,* 45–52.

Sue, S., Akutsu, P. D., & Higashi, C. (1985). Training issues in conducting therapy with ethnic-minority clients. In P. B. Pedersen (Ed.), *Handbook in cross-cultural counseling and therapy* (pp. 275–280). Westport, CT: Greenwood Press.

Sue, S., Chun, C., & Gee, K. (1995). Ethnic minority intervention and treatment research. In J. F. Aponte, R. Young Rivers, & J. Wohl (Eds.), *Psychological interventions and cultural diversity* (pp. 266–282). Boston: Allyn and Bacon.

Sue, S., Fujino, D. C., Hu, L., Takeuchi, D. T., & Zane, N. W. S. (1991). Community mental health services for ethnic minority groups: A test of the cultural responsiveness hypothesis. *Journal of Consulting and Clinical Psychology, 59,* 533–540.

Sue, S., Wagner, D. J., Margullis, C., & Lew, L. (1976). Conceptions of mental illness among Asian and Caucasian American students. *Psychological Reports, 38,* 703–708.

Sue, S., & Zane, N. (1987). The role of culture and cultural techniques in psychotherapy: A critique and reformulation. *American Psychologist, 42,* 37–45.

Takeuchi, D. T., Sue, S., & Yeh, M. (1995). Return rates and outcomes from ethnicity-specific mental health programs in Los Angeles. *American Journal of Public Health, 85,* 638–643.

Torres-Matrullo, C. (1976). Acculturation and psychopathology among Puerto Rican women in mainland United States. *American Journal of Orthopsychiatry, 46,* 710–719.

Torrey, E. F. (1970). Mental health services for American Indians and Eskimos. *Community Mental Health Journal, 6,* 455–463.

Vontress, C. E. (1979). Cross-cultural counseling: An existential approach. *Personnel and Guidance Journal, 58,* 125–127.

Wampold, B., Casas, J. M., & Atkinson, D. R. (1982). Ethnic bias in counseling: An information-processing approach. *Journal of Counseling Psychology, 28,* 489–503.

Wohl, J. (1995). Traditional individual psychotherapy and ethnic minorities. In J. F. Aponte, R. Young Rivers, & J. Wohl (Eds.), *Psychological interventions and cultural diversity* (pp. 74–91). Boston: Allyn and Bacon.

PART 2

The African American Client

Introduction

For centuries, we have struggled to resolve a basic contradiction in our society, one that espouses the democratic principles of "liberty" and "justice," while denying these rights to African Americans. John Gardner (1968), in the book *No Easy Victories,* wrote:

> The problem of justice for the Negro has gnawed on the national consciousness ever since this nation was founded. It is, in an important sense, the American problem. If any problem is especially and peculiarly ours, with roots in our history and scars in our memory, this is it. No other modern problem touches more profoundly the values we profess to cherish. (p. 17)

Gardner concluded that history handed his generation the task of solving this problem.

Over a quarter of a century later, some are claiming that we have answered the call of history, that the mistreatment of the African American has finally ended. They point to civil rights laws that grant African Americans the same rights as other Americans; to affirmative action programs that give "special privileges" to minorities; and to numerous gains—in education, elected offices, and the general standard of living. Even Hollywood got the message a few years ago and expanded its line-up of African American sitcoms that portray highly affluent and well-educated African American families. Programs such as "The Jeffersons," "The Cosby Show," and "The Fresh Prince of Bel-Air" were so successful that they reached syndicated status. African American sports stars such as Michael Jordan and Shaquille O'Neal were touted for their multimillion dollar contracts, while Bill Cosby and his wife piqued the interests of talk show and tabloid audiences by their donation of $20 million to an African American College.

There is a danger in this imaging (apart from the obvious distortions) that should not be overlooked. In spite of enormous evidence to the contrary, African Americans historically have been viewed and, for the most part, treated in homogeneous terms—poor, lazy, violent, and, more recently, rich. Regardless of whether the label is positive or negative, some segments of the group are always left out. The danger in accepting the exaggerated view of this group as having overcome or as being exceptionally well-off is that the needs of the other segments of the community, such as the disenfranchised poor or the struggling middle class, are often ignored.

There is an even greater danger. We may also come to accept the illusion that African Americans are no longer the target of racial prejudice and discrimination. This is not a new perspective. White liberals and conservatives have been suggesting this since the 1960s (Lemann, 1996). In recent years a small group of neoconservative African Americans has also been accused of holding similar views (Black Perspectives, 1991). Conservatives like Justice

Clarence Thomas, Professor Shelby Steele, and Mr. William Raspberry, who fall within this group, acknowledge that discrimination still exists, but downplay the influence it has over group success. In the article, "The Myth that is Crippling Black America," Raspberry (1990) argues that African Americans have accepted "the myth that racism is the dominant influence in our lives." He asserts that African Americans are not deprived of their rights. "They can vote, live where their money permits them, eat where their appetites dictate, work at jobs for which their skills qualify them. They have their civil rights" (Raspberry, p. 96).

However it is difficult to overlook the negative attitudes and racial violence that have lately emerged. For example, a recent survey found that many of the same stereotypes that White Americans held of Blacks during slavery are still accepted by members of this group. Some 20 percent of the public expressed a belief that Blacks are innately inferior in thinking ability to Whites, 19 percent believed that Blacks have thicker craniums than Whites, and 23.5 percent believed that Blacks have longer arms than Whites (Plous & Williams, 1995). These views are not much different than those recently attributed to professional golfer Jack Nicklaus by D. Hatfield (1996). According to Hatfield, Nicklaus claimed that African American golfers are born with the wrong muscles to play at the highest level in golf (apparently he has never seen Tiger Woods play golf). Similar views were also expressed by Frederick Goodwin, former director of the Alcohol, Drug Abuse, and Mental Health Administration, when he drew an analogy between the behavior of inner-city youth to that of the rhesus monkey. He commented:

> If you look, for example, at male monkeys, especially in the wild, roughly half of them survive to adulthood. The other half die by violence. In fact, there are some interesting evolutionary implications of that because the same hyperaggressive monkeys that kill each other are also hypersexual, so they copulate more. Now, one could say that some of the loss of social structure in this society, and particularly within the high-impact inner city areas, has removed some of the civilizing evolutionary things that we have built up, and that maybe it isn't just a careless use of the word when people call certain areas of certain cities "jungles." (Williams, 1994, p. 95)

There is evidence that these attitudes are associated with racial violence (Hevesi, 1994; "Judge says," 1991; "Man apologizes," 1993; Plous & Williams, 1995). According to a 1994 FBI survey of hate crimes, 5,932 incidents were reported in forty-three states including the District of Columbia. Sixty percent of these were motivated by racial bias. Of the 6,265 known offenders, more than half were White (Landay, 1996). In 1995 and 1996, over forty Black churches were burned in cities throughout the South; racism has been proven or strongly suspected in the majority of these incidents (Reibstein, 1995). Even among the nation's police forces, charged with enforcing the law, incidents of race discrimination is reported. Few can forget the videotaped beating of

Rodney King by Los Angeles police or the Christopher Commission report, which charged that, "Racism in the LA Police Department is as raw as the message sent from one white officer to another regarding the event: 'sounds like monkey-slapping time' " (Harrison et al., 1991, p. 18).

In 1995, the LAPD was again rocked—this time by the infamous Mark Fuhrman tapes, which outlined countless acts of violence by LAPD officers against helpless minority victims (Reibstein, 1995). Police violence is by no means limited to the Los Angeles Police Department. The Congressional Black Caucus became so outraged by the increase in civil rights violations by police, that they asked the U.S. Attorney General to conduct an investigation of seven police departments across the country including Los Angeles; Philadelphia; New York; Prince Georges County, MD; and Miami ("Black Caucus members," 1995).

As much as we would like to believe that we have solved the "race problem" in our generation, examples like these leave little doubt that the problem still exists. Unfortunately, while we continue to debate the question, millions of African American men and women struggle to stay afloat. Bethea, in the first article in this section, "African-American Women and the Male-Female Relationship Dilemma: A Counseling Perspective," offers special insight into the African American male-female relationship from a woman's perspective. She examines contemporary issues that affect Black male identity development, communication, and intimacy. Common myth and stereotypes frequently associated with African American male and female roles are also discussed. Special attention is given to counseling African American women and the management of personal grief and loss, effective communication, and negative stereotypes.

In "Psychosocial Development and Black Male Masculinity: Implications for Counseling Economically Disadvantaged African American Male Adolescents," Harris explores the impact that race, sociocultural, and economic conditions place on members of this subgroup as they move from adolescence to adulthood. She asserts that counselors can play a meaningful role in helping the young adult successfully integrate sex-role tasks and other psychological concerns that are important to becoming a mature adult. Harris also offers a number of culturally sensitive counseling tips and interventions especially suited to this subgroup.

The final article to this section, "Culturally Sensitive Therapy with Black Clients," combines the African American male and female experience under the umbrella of the Black family. Critical issues essential to working with the African American family are outlined and discussed. Basic strategies for heightening counseling effectiveness are also presented.

References

Black Caucus members urge Justice Department probe of racism in nation's police departments. (1995, October 2). *Jet Magazine*, 5.

Black Perspectives. (1991, September 6). *The MacNeil/Lehrer news hour*. New York and Washington, DC: Public Broadcasting Service.

Gardner, J. W. (1968). *No easy victories.* New York: Harper & Row.

Harrison, R., Minerbrook, S., Cooper, M., Johnson, C., Roberts, S. V., & Gest, T. (1991, July 22). Black and White in America. *U.S. News & World Report, 18.*

Hatfield, D. (1996, July/August). The Jack Nicklaus syndrome. *The Humanist,* p. 38.

Hevesi, D. (1994, July 24). Kraft resigns after denying that he made racial remarks. *New York Times,* Section 8, p. 1.

Judge says remarks on "gorillas" may be cited in trial on beating. (1991, June 12). *New York Times,* p. A24.

Landay, J. S. (1996). Rise in hate crimes looms behind church burnings. *The Christian Science Monitor,* p. 4.

Lemann, N. (1996, February/March). The end of racism? *American Heritage,* pp. 93–105.

Man apologizes for gorilla-suited message. (1993, October 9). *New York Times,* Section 1, p. 29.

Plous, S., & Williams, T. (1995). Racial stereotypes from the days of American slavery: a continuing legacy. *Journal of Applied Social Psychology,* 795–817.

Raspberry, W. (1990). The myth that is crippling black America. *Reader's Digest,* pp. 96–98.

Reibstein, L. (1995, March). The Detective's Story. *Newsweek,* p. 57.

Williams, J., (1994). Violence, genes, and prejudice. *Discover,* pp. 92–115.

4

African-American Women and the Male-Female Relationship Dilemma: A Counseling Perspective

Patricia Davis Bethea

Although considerable attention has been given to the socioeconomic crisis of African-American men in this country (Parham & McDavis, 1987; Staples, 1993), relatively little attention has focused on the related crisis between African-American men and African-American women. Although the issues of these two groups are different in many respects, they are also similar in the sense that African-American men and African-American women are inextricably bound in a quest for many common goals. Particular among these goals is the desire for romantic relationships and, ultimately, marriage partners and families. At this juncture, their issues interface and it becomes clear that the dilemmas of African-American men really are the dilemmas of African-American women as well.

This article focuses both on the historical origin of the African-American male-female dilemma and on the contemporary forces that have an impact on the opportunities for intimacy and for marriage among African-American women. Additionally, attention is given to loss as a by-product of relationship and to the problems of communication and negative stereotypes, also from the perspective of African-American women. This is not to suggest that these issues do not affect African-American men or other groups, but to emphasize that the cultural milieu of the African-American woman creates a unique perspective important in the counseling process. Each issue is discussed in conjunction with related counseling strategies and is followed by implications for future counseling practice and research.

Reprinted from *Journal of Multicultural Counseling and Development, 23,* 1995, pp. 87–95. © ACA. Reprinted with permission. No further reproduction authorized without written permission of the American Counseling Association.

Male-Female Relationships

Owing to numerous cultural and historical factors, relationships between African-American men and African-American women have become increasingly complex and tenuous. According to cultural myth, the African-American man is unreliable and lazy and the African-American woman, characterized as too domineering for the good of her man, is viewed as the central figure in his emasculation. To the degree that African-American men and women have accepted these stereotypic views as documented fact of mutual inadequacies, a schism has developed between them that disregards the weight of history.

The Historical Perspective

American society has historically defined manhood and womanhood differently for African-American men and women than for their Caucasian counterparts. During slavery, African-American men were limited in their role as father or husband and essentially removed from positions of power in the family and in the workforce (Staples, 1993). Likewise, if femininity for the White woman was frail, valued, and protected, then "the Black woman had to be released from the chains of the myth of femininity" (Davis. 1973, p.144) and "annulled as woman" (Davis, 1973, p. 145) for slavery to work. Consequently, "the sheer force of things rendered her equal to her man" (Davis, 1973, p. 145) and, in some cases, superior to him in terms of her permission to manipulate the system for the good of her family.

The result of this upheaval has been the social equivalent of what Berne labels "Lets You and Him Fight" (1964), a game that, in this case, can end badly for everyone involved. Such a game maintains the victims in a continual posture of opposition and blaming without ever focusing on the real persecutor, the system that offers unequal access to education and employment as vehicles for success. As a result, African Americans often find that "the tension of living in a racist society filters into their most intimate relationships" (Staples, 1988, p. 189).

Contemporary Issues

A number of variables complicate the prospect of relationships for African-American women, but the majority of difficulties are a direct outgrowth of the African-American male crisis. At the same time that many African-American women are seeking partners, African-American men are confronting increased risk of death by violent crime, more contact with the judicial system, imprisonment, decreased opportunities for educational advancement, unemployment, and underemployment (Parham & McDavis, 1987; Staples, 1993). As a result, some African-American men are unprepared or unable to assume a positive role in the economic structure or in the family. Therefore, the dilemma for many African-American women will be finding marriageable partners among men who are increasingly disenfranchised in the educational system and in the workforce.

Lichter, LeClere, and McLaughlin (1991) concluded that the marital prospects of African-American women are directly linked to the supply of economically attractive Black men and that their "apparent retreat from traditional family structures may be located in the Black man's deteriorating employment circumstances" (p. 865). When these issues of race and gender are compounded by income, African-American men with earnings below the poverty level become the least likely to marry and the most likely to experience the dissolution of their marriages. Conversely, higher levels of education and income among middle-class African-American men correlate with marrying and remaining married, which also has the effect of removing them from the pool of eligible partners (Staples, 1993).

Confronted with the harsh realities of mate selection, African-American women often pursue education as the path to social and economic security (Chapman, 1988). Contrary to popular opinion, the resulting financial resources of these women is less of a hindrance to their ability to marry than is the lack of financial resources of their prospective partners (Lichter et al., 1991). Staples (1988) suggested that financial resources make it possible for some women to seek marriage largely for psychological reasons and that few men are able to meet such intrinsic needs. Moreover, a high level of educational achievement and financial independence often detract from a woman's desirability as a partner, leaving her as the least likely to marry or to remain married (Staples, 1988).

The existing difficulties of mate selection are compounded by an increasing resistance among African-American women to the prospect of marrying beneath their social status or of "marrying down" (Staples, 1985) and the keen competition for acceptable partners. Consequently, African-American women are often pitted against each other, and African-American men may seek to manipulate the situation to their advantage with a resulting increase in the number of polygamous relationships (Braithwaite, 1981). Women often conceptualize this phenomenon as a fear of commitment.

In reality, both African-American men and African-American women may be experiencing a unique vulnerability in relationships compounded by the drive to protect themselves from rejection (Chapman, 1988). Chapman found through informal counseling interviews that both men and women "feel lonely, sad and scared about the lack of stable relationships with the opposite sex" (p. 197). In this scenario, relationships are often "so shaky that they cannot accommodate mutual demands or expectations—not to mention commitment and monogamy. Both sexes invest in playing it safe" (p. 197).

Finally, African-American men are more likely to select a White partner than are African-American women (U.S. Bureau of the Census, 1991). Although a growing number of African-American women are perceiving interracial marriage as an option, 98% of African-American women marry African-American men (Staples, 1993). Interracial relationships between African-American men and White women often generate resentment among

African-American women (Poussaint, 1993) and, more important, further complicate the prospect of marriage for African Americans.

Counseling Issues and Approaches

To be effective, counselors of African-American women will need to facilitate the growth of their clients in several key areas. These areas include processing grief and loss, enhancing effective communication, and confronting negative stereotypes.

Loss

Counselors need to be attuned to the issues of loss and grieving relative to African-American women and male-female relationships for several reasons. First, many African-American women remain in the dating pool until later in life (Staples, 1993), and although this phenomenon affords the opportunity to experience multiple positive relationships, it also makes women more vulnerable to the vicissitudes of the dating experience, especially the processes of loss. Often, ending a dating relationship leads to physical loss of the dating partner, and in a positive relationship this can be a difficult experience. Physical losses can also precipitate symbolic or psychosocial losses (Rando, 1984) such as loss of status or access to "couples" activities. Additionally, even when the dating partner is not lost physically, the relationship will often take on altered dimensions over time, and some interaction will cease to exist. For example, a romantic relationship may become a platonic friendship. Because of the barriers to relationships that African-American women face, these losses are significant.

Second, there are some women for whom quiet despair may mask grieving for the losses of home, husband, and children as expectations they cannot actualize. Schlossberg and Robinson (1993) identified these failed expectations as "non-events" that are often "hidden, unnoticed, and unacknowledged" (p. 22) because women may consider them irrational and because society disregards them. This is not to suggest that all African-American women are interested in marriage and family in a traditional sense. In fact, Davenport and Yurich (1991) pointed out that "one important contribution that the study of African American women can make to the theory . . . is to show that all women may not desire a primary connection to a romantic partner but may, instead, gain a sense of relatedness with children, parents, and other adults" (p. 69). Nevertheless, most African Americans view their single status as a forced choice (Staples, 1993), and for many lower- and middle-class African-American women, the forced choice is based on diminishing opportunities to develop relationships with African-American men.

Schlossberg and Robinson (1993) suggested that individuals need to discover their non-event, name it, and grieve it. They also need to refocus the non-event by releasing old expectations and reshaping goals and visions. To facilitate this process with African-American women, effective counselors will need to understand the historical and the contemporary context of the African-American woman and the dynamics of loss relative to relationships.

Communication

Many African-American men and African-American women are finding communication to be increasingly difficult, and the results of this are devastating. Gary and Berry (1985) found that "one of the best predictors of depression scores for Black men is conflict between Black men and women" (p. 127). The main causes of conflict—stereotyped views and inauthentic communication—often leave African-American men unable to disclose themselves to their partners and leave African-American women frustrated with poor communication and the resulting effects.

Gary and Berry (1985) concluded that "programs designed to build better interpersonal communications between Black men and women will have an important impact on improving the mental health of all people" (p. 128). Specifically, Parker, Berieda, and Sloan (1984) concluded that African-American men and African-American women need growth groups that focus on "individual and group stereotypes; understanding stereotypes as barriers to communication and relationship building" and on "effective communication skills: listening, responding, assertiveness training" (p. 46).

Stereotypes

The negative "individual and group stereotypes" (p. 46) pointed out by Parker, Berieda, and Sloan (1984) have been a source of continuing relational problems for African-American men and African-American women. Regarding African-American men, Staples (1993) concluded that these biases often have their roots in the gender role stereotypes of the larger society and that African-American men cannot avoid the indoctrination of stereotyped roles. Additionally, Norment (1986) suggested that African-American men have tended to internalize the dominant view of African-American women as "undesirable," "domineering," and "second best." More specific to the African-American relationship dilemma, Cazenave (1983) found that middle-class African-American men often view African-American women as having more opportunity than do African-American men. In fact, some African-American men may view themselves as victims of the achievement and independence of African-American women (Staples, 1993) and may displace their racial and economic frustrations onto their relationships with them (Cazenave, 1983). Poussaint (1993) identified a lack of respect, and physical and psychological dominance as the most frequent manifestations of conflict.

Ultimately, the issues of respect and dominance become important in counseling African-American women, who experience the scathing consequences of such negative stereotypes. Young (1993) emphasized that

African-American women do not have to accept unacceptable circumstances to maintain a relationship and added that "the African American woman has an equal responsibility to select a mate/partner who affirms her strengths, capabilities, and potential" (p. 85). Therefore, African-American women are encouraged to select supportive partners and to confront the negative stereotypes that are often evident in relationships.

African-American women have perpetuated stereotyped views of African-American men in two crucial areas. First, according to Staples (cited in Norment, 1986), they have often adopted the cultural stereotypes that African-American men are unreliable and preoccupied with sexual exploitation. Second, they have often accepted a dominant worldview of manhood and, perhaps unfairly at times, held African-American men to that standard. For example, Chapman (1988) has suggested that among middle-class women, a man is unacceptable as a potential mate if he does not exhibit certain physical characteristics, has not achieved a particular professional status, and does not earn a substantial salary. Although many African-American women are able to provide for themselves and actually expect to contribute to the economic base of their families, they may still maintain an image of the ideal mate (Staples, 1993) that some African-American men are not able to fulfill.

Therefore, some women may find themselves in a conundrum of faulty cognitions. Believing, for example, that it would be awful if no marriage partner were found, juxtaposed with the apprehension that it would be horrible if the prospective partner did not fit a given profile might account for more of the resulting frustration and internal conflict experienced by some women than do the actual external circumstances. For the most part, the central issue is the fantasy of male economic superiority colliding with the reality that many African-American women will outearn their potential partners (Lichter, LeClere, & McLaughlin, 1991). Women who conceptualize any compromise at all as "settling," however, may put up significant resistance to alternatives in mate selection.

To some degree, women may be able to reduce the cognitive dissonance by altering the belief system. Using cognitive restructuring, the counselor can help women "to identify long-standing styles of thinking . . . the misapplication of rules or unwavering belief" and dispute them (Kanfer & Goldstein, 1991, p. 372).

Therefore, the counselor may support and facilitate the process of reconceptualizing the meaning of manhood and restructuring the criteria for mate selection to explore previously unacceptable alternatives.

Implications for Counseling and Research

Counselors need to recognize that African-American women are a very heterogeneous group and that differences of age and socioeconomic status may modify their position regarding relationships. For example, Staples (1993) suggested that lower-class and middle-class women have different criteria for an ideal mate based on what they perceive to be realistic expectations and the economic constraints or opportunities of their environments. Additionally, a 1985 Gallup poll (cited in Staples, 1993) found that 56% of African-American women considered marriage and a full-time job to be an ideal lifestyle; however, some women are not interested in marriage or in other romantic relationships (Davenport & Yurich, 1991). Therefore, African-American women cover the spectrum in terms of their pursuit of traditional and nontraditional lifestyles.

Also, counselors need to assess their readiness to serve African-American women. Smith (1985) identified the problem of counseling African-American women as being one that is ultimately "linked to counselors' lack of awareness, sensitivity, and knowledge of black women's history, culture, and life concerns" (p. 185). For many counselors, this means continued training through courses and workshops as well as continued openness to experiencing the world of the client in the counseling relationship.

There is also a need for more empirical research on African-American women and relationships. Topics might include the effect of adjusting a criteria for the ideal mate, or the impact of grief and loss. Davenport and Yurich (1991) have suggested that African-American women, although very capable, sometimes resent African-American men for being what they consider to be poor marriage partners. Such an idea could greatly illuminate the conflict between African-American men and African-American women if investigated further. Overall, the counseling profession needs to take assertive leadership in exploring the issues of African-American women and in making information available to practitioners in the field.

Finally, there is a need to integrate the research on African-American men with the research on African-American women so that their related issues can be investigated from a single perspective. Two examples of this focus are the barriers to communication and the impact of stereotypic thinking (Parker, et al., 1984). These issues are especially important considering that African-American men and African-American women are the basic unit of the African-American family, and further research could contribute significantly to the effectiveness of their relationships.

References

Berne, E. (1964). *Games people play.* Secaucus, NJ: Castle Books.
Braithwaite, R. L. (1981). Interpersonal relations between Black males and Black females. In L. E. Gary (Ed.), *Black men* (pp. 83–97). Newbury Park, CA: Sage.
Cazenave, N. A. (1983). Black male-Black female relationships: The perceptions of 155 middle-class Black men. *Family Relations, 32,* 341–350.
Chapman, A. B. (1988). Male-female relations: How the past affects the present. In H. P. McAdoo (Ed.). *Black families* (pp. 190–200). Newbury Park, CA: Sage.

Davenport, D. S., & Yurich, J. M. (1991). Multicultural gender issues. *Journal of Counseling & Development, 70,* 64–71.

Davis, A. (1973). Reflections on the Black woman's role in the community of slaves. In R. Chrisman & N. Hare (Eds.), *Contemporary Black thought* (pp. 138–157). New York: Bobbs-Merrill.

Gary, L. E., & Berry, G. L. (1985). Depressive symptomatology among Black men. *Journal of Multicultural Counseling and Development, 13,* 121–128.

Kanfer, F. H., & Goldstein, A. P. (1991). *Helping people change.* New York: Pergamon.

Lichter, D. T., LeClere, F. B., & McLaughlin, D. K. (1991). *American Journal of Sociology, 96,* 843–867.

Norment, L. (1986, August). The cure: Resolve tensions between Black men and women. *Ebony, 41,* 153–156.

Parham, T. A., & McDavis, R. J. (1987). Black men, an endangered species: Who's really pulling the trigger. *Journal of Counseling and Development, 66,* 24–27.

Parker, W. M., Berieda, M., & Sloan, D. (1984). Exploring male-female relations among Black college students: A survey. *Journal of Non-White Concerns, 12,* 40–47.

Poussaint, A. F. (1993, February). Enough already! Stop the male-bashing and infighting. *Ebony, 48,* 86–89.

Rando, T. A. (1984). *Grief, dying, and death: Clinical interventions for caregivers.* Champaign, IL: Research Press Company.

Schlossberg, N. K., & Robinson, S. P. (1993, Fall). Non-events: Another name for heartbreak. *American Counselor, 2,* 21–25.

Smith, E. M. (1985). Counseling Black women. In P. Pedersen (Ed.), *Handbook of cross cultural counseling and therapy* (pp.181–187). Westport, CT: Greenwood Press.

Staples, R. (1985). Changes in the Black family structure: The conflict between family ideology and structural conditions. *Journal of Marriage and Family, 47,* 1005–1013.

Staples, R. (1988). An overview of race and marital status. In H. P. McAdoo (Ed.), *Black families* (pp. 189–200). Newbury Park, CA: Sage.

Staples, R. (1993). Black families at the crossroads. San Francisco, CA: Jossey-Bass.

U.S. Bureau of the Census, (1991). *Statistical abstracts of the United States: 1991* (111th ed.). Washington, DC: U.S. Government Printing Office.

Young, C. (1993). Psychodynamics of coping and survival of the African-American female in a changing world. In D. R. Atkinson, G. Morten, & D. W. Sue (Eds.), *Counseling American minorities* (pp. 75–87). Dubuque, IA: Brown & Benchmark.

5

Psychosocial Development and Black Male Masculinity: Implications for Counseling Economically Disadvantaged African American Male Adolescents

Shanette M. Harris

Over the last 20 years, the number of studies conducted on the counseling process related to African Americans has shown a dramatic increase. Articles, books, monographs, and theoretical reviews related to training issues (Arredondo-Dowd & Gonsalves, 1980; Casas, Ponterotto, & Gutierrez, 1986; Copeland, 1983; Mio, 1989; Pederson, 1988), characteristics of African American culture (Carter, 1991; Cheatham, 1990; Helms, 1984), cross-cultural models (Helms, 1984; Parham & Helms, 1981), clients' preferences for counselors' race (Parham & Helms, 1981; Pomales, Claiborn, & LaFromboise, 1986), and the use of counseling services are some of the many topics that have been investigated (June, 1986; Larrabee, 1986). Nevertheless, within this domain of empirical and theoretical research, few articles have been published that provide information about sex-role and devolopmental issues and how to conceptualize these concerns to guide counselors with subgroups of the African American population. Because counseling researchers have rarely considered subgroups within the African American population, only a small percentage of the literature focuses on African American male adolescents.

Several reasons exist for why counselors should explore ways to assist this

Reprinted from *Journal of Counseling & Development, 73*, 1995, pp. 279–287. © ACA. Reprinted with permission. No further reproduction authorized without written permission of the American Counseling Association.

population. These youth are faced with sociocultural (Gibbs, 1984, 1988; Hendricks & Montgomery, 1984; Pierce, 1986), academic (Gibbs, 1984, 1985; Hahn, 1987; Rumberger, 1983; Smith, 1982), and economic dilemmas (Leonard, 1985; Sessions, 1988; Thomas, 1985), and the consequences of not eradicating such problems present physical and psychological obstacles for accomplishing the goals of later life stages (Davis, 1981; Gary & Berry, 1985; Gibbs, 1984, 1988; Palinkas & Colcord, 1985; Snowden & Cheung, 1990; Warfield & Marvin, 1985; Watts & Wright, 1985). These concerns adversely affect members of the African American community, creating a myriad of issues that generalize to society overall. In addition, the complex nature of the interactions among masculinity, social class, developmental tasks, and cultural factors make this population likely to receive short-term and long-term gains from counseling. To understand the traumatic outcomes that are often associated with young adulthood for African American boys, it is important to examine the role of masculinity in the adolescent stage of development. As stated by Bowman (1989): "Among high risk Black men, chronic role strains and related psychosocial problems do not just occur at a point in time. Rather, they evolve out of interactions between past role experiences, immediate role barriers, and adaptive efforts" (p. 142).

The purpose of this article is to discuss the relationship between tasks of psychosocial development and expressions of masculinity, examine the effects of this relationship on African American male adolescents' response to counseling, and identify specific ways by which counselors can assist this population with its psychoemotional and social well-being.

Black Masculinity: Alternative Norms

Several authors have discussed the roles of African American men (Cazenave, 1984; Clark, 1965; Curtis, 1974, Hannerz, 1969; Liebow, 1967; Miller, 1958; Perkins, 1975; Pettigrew, 1964; Washington, 1987) in attempts to explain and understand their economic, social, and interpersonal difficulties. The behaviors of a minority of this population may seem outrageous and unbelievable to some who cannot comprehend and integrate the numerous factors that impinge upon these men and the reactions and coping strategies that have evolved to ensure personal survival. Because of this perception, some previous authors conceptualized the problems faced by these men from a "blame the victim" or environmental perspective. Recently, an expressive style of interacting has been described that considers structural conditions and responses to these conditions. This style focuses primarily on impression management and involves an aggressive assertion of masculinity (Harris, 1992; Majors, 1989; Majors & Billson, 1992; Oliver, 1989; Staples, 1982; Wilson, 1991). According to Blackwell (1975), "Two kinds of forces have always been at work in the black community: (1) centripetal forces—those elements that draw members of a minority toward their group, and (2) centrifugal forces—those elements that magnetize minority group members in the direction of the dominant group's cultural values, societal norms, and institutional arrangements" (p. 282). Pressures to meet European American standards of manhood as provider, protector, and disciplinarian are representative of such a dilemma for African American men. Although most African American men have internalized and accepted these standards of manhood (Cazenave, 1984; Staples, 1982), inequities in earning potential and employment and limited access to educational opportunities prevent the expression of these behaviors.

In general, the African American community is diverse, and numerous factors influence male responses to issues of masculinity (Hunter & Davis, 1992). For those who are unable to meet traditional standards of masculinity, manhood has been redefined to be consistent with their alienation from mainstream values and institutions. This alternative definition also differs from that adhered to by low-income European American men because of historical and ongoing racial discrimination and prejudice.

To compensate for feelings of powerlessness, guilt, and shame that result from the inability to enact traditional masculine roles, some African American male youth of low-income social status have redefined masculinity to emphasize sexual promiscuity, toughness, thrill seeking, and the use of violence in interpersonal interactions. Observable mannerisms characteristic of this set of alternative masculine behaviors include physical posture, style of clothing, content and rhythm of speech, walking style, standing, form of greeting, and overall demeanor. Less frequently described but nevertheless relevant cognitive and affective components involve suppressed emotions (other than anger), distrust of organizations and authority, need for approval and support from peers, disdain for feminine qualities, predominant heterosexual focus, and denial of vulnerability. These attitudes, interests, and mannerisms constitute a unique way of defining manhood and have been referred to as "compulsory masculinity," "cool pose," "exaggerated masculinity," "black male masculinity," "reactionary masculinity," and "the compulsive masculine alternative" (Franklin, 1984; Harris, 1992; Kochman, 1981; Majors, 1989; Majors & Billson, 1992; Oliver, 1989; Wilson, 1991).

Majors (1989) used the term *cool pose* to refer to African American men and boys' concern with roles, values, presentation of self, and situationally constructed and performance-oriented behaviors. Franklin (1984) described Black male masculinity as "an emphasis on physical strength, an expectation of both submissiveness and strength in women, angry and impulsive behavior, functional (and often violent) relationships between men and between men and women, and strong male bonding" (pp. 60–61). Other theorists have attempted to identify patterns of masculine behaviors and have described these constellations as "sexual conquest" and "thrill seeking" (Perkins, 1975; Staples,

1982). Oliver (1989) proposed that the alternative masculine behaviors adopted by African American men and boys represent distinct cultural adaptations to structural constraints and consist of two primary orientations: "tough guy" and "player of women."

Black male masculinity has both costs and benefits. Alternative masculine behaviors moderate stressful conditions and provide a basis for personal achievement and self-respect (Harris, 1992; Harris & Majors, 1993; Majors, 1989; Majors & Billson, 1992; Wilson, 1991); however, these behaviors have been hypothesized to lead to even more negative consequences than those linked with the traditional European American male role (David & Brannon, 1976; Doyle, 1983, 1989; Fasteau, 1975; O'Neil, 1982; Pleck, 1981).

Expectations for African American men to adhere to incompatible masculine norms exacerbate conflicts related to manhood. Afrocentric values that emphasize "collectivism" over individualism, "spirituality" over materialism, and "oneness with nature" are at odds with values associated with the alternative behaviors adopted by a significant proportion of economically disadvantaged African American men. Alternative masculine behaviors and Afrocentric values also differ from traditional European American standards of manhood. Thus, the masculine role of African American men can best be understood by invoking a sex-role strain explanation (Pleck, 1981)—that is, ambivalence and confusion stem from conflicting norms and standards of masculinity, eventually resulting in psychological distress and maladaptive coping strategies.

Forming a masculine identity in the face of conflicting norms and values can be especially stressful for African American male youth. Although many African American young men successfully resolve demands specific to this stage, those with less resilience may compensate with inappropriate patterns of behavior. Consequently, a successful passage into adulthood requires that competing masculine norms are sufficiently integrated with other adolescent tasks.

Psychosocial Tasks and Black Male Masculinity

Several tasks must be completed by adolescents as they move from one stage in the life cycle to the next. Farnsworth (1966), Chickering (1976), and Erikson (1966) have discussed the following psychosocial tasks, including separation and emancipation from family; formation of a sense of self; consolidation of ethical and moral values; and selection of a career, occupation, or work role. Additional tasks pertain to the need to establish a satisfactory sexual identity, form intimate relationships, and to find a place in a community that engenders a sense of belonging. Nevertheless, an alternative masculine sex-role identity can be formed at the expense of resolving other tasks because of the salience of masculinity for this age group.

Separation-Individuation

Although the process of adolescent separation and individuation has been conceptualized in numerous ways (Blos, 1962, 1979; Grotevant & Cooper, 1985; Josselson, 1988), the need to differentiate from the family and yet maintain some degree of relatedness is a principal theme of adolescence. Successful resolution of this task contributes to the formation of an identity and is central to adjustment (Blos, 1962). Theoretically, successful negotiation of the transition from adolescence to adulthood depends on how issues are handled surrounding individuation (Moore, 1987). Several factors, however, influence the degree to which African American male adolescents successfully complete this task.

As contrasted with middle-class youth, who begin to conform to peer group norms during middle childhood and show a rise in attachment during the late elementary school years, low-income African American male youth separate from the family and align with and show greater dependence on peers for support and approval at earlier ages (Kunjufu, 1986; Silverstein & Krate, 1975). Family characteristics and parenting strategies contribute to the earlier gravitation of African American boys toward the peer culture. Father-absent homes in which no other male figures are available (Wilkinson, 1974), the presence of several siblings, and parents who show little affection and use restrictive and punitive types of discipline (Silverstein & Krate, 1975) are associated with boys' greater and earlier reliance on peers. Premature disengagement from the family may also stem from dysfunctional family dynamics that neglect young male family members' needs and prevent close familial bonds. Thus, actual and perceived parental rejection can influence youth's involvement in the peer group (Gray-Ray & Ray, 1990). This early transition away from the family prohibits the development of a secure attachment necessary for healthy separation and the formation of subsequent stable relationships (Josselson, 1988). Although African American male youth display earlier behavioral indications of independence, emotional states are less definitive. They may experience feelings of resentment and anxiety because of early separation, although observable behaviors are indicative of independence. For example, exchanges of insults among some low-income male youth that involve criticisms of female parents' appearance, sexuality, femininity, and economic status (e.g., "your momma wears combat boots") sever existing ties to the mother, while simultaneously validating feelings of manliness (Silverstein & Krate, 1975). Ambivalent feelings toward the family and a desire for approval and support maximize the significance of the rewards offered by peers, making it difficult to negotiate a balance between emotional and behavioral independence and dependence.

Belonging and Security

The achievement of positive interpersonal relations with same-sex peers is a significant determinant of adult interpersonal competence. Youth acquire skills in communicating, cooperating, and managing relationships that generalize to other situations. The peer group also provides opportunities for participation in activities that offer public recognition and visibility. Successes within the peer group increase self-esteem and validate the well-being of participants. Some peer groups emphasize school activities so that academic performance is valued and those who excel in these areas are held in high regard, but others offer rewards to those who disrupt class, fight, and share stories about sexual escapades. Some peer groups also reward interpersonal and property violence, theft, drug use, and incarceration as representations of manhood (Harris, 1992). Additionally, athletic peer groups meet needs for esteem and security, although academic prerequisites expand the range of behaviors acceptable as masculine (Lapchick, 1988; Messner & Sabo, 1990). Because of unmet needs for security and belonging, African American male youth are especially vulnerable to the demands of any of these same-sex groups. This overdependence on the peer group, however, results in diminished capacities for independent decision making, producing major obstacles for those who adhere to group norms that conflict with societal mores.

The African-American male peer culture usually involves extensive ties with large groups that focus on combative and competitive interactions rather than affection and sharing of feelings (Farrell, 1986). According to Kunjufu (1986), as early as the third grade, success in athletics, fighting, and risk-taking are perceived as "manly." The ability to outsmart peers by "sounding" or "playing the dozens" (a competitive ritual characterized by an exchange of verbal insults related to the participants or members of the participants' families) and the strength to accept taunts and teasing about appearance, skill, or family background also become symbols of manhood.

Boys who exhibit skill in the expression of alternative behaviors acquire group status and recognition as decision makers and leaders. Those who show competence in fighting, participating in sports, teasing, and reporting actual or contrived sexual conquests are bestowed with greater privileges than those perceived as less adequate in these areas (Harris, 1992). Thus, even boys from families that promote educational achievement, gender equity, a strong work orientation, and appropriate interpersonal ethics may internalize opposing values—those characteristic of the same-sex peer culture (Steinberg, Dornbusch, & Brown, 1992). Low-income African American boys who are less capable of expressing behaviors and interests compatible with these standards are likely to be ridiculed and rejected by peers, leading to negative feelings about the self and social isolation.

Selection of a Career

The adolescent's perspective of the future is influenced by past interactions between personal characteristics and the opportunities and demands of the surrounding environment. Personal competence, feelings of mastery, and the understanding of the immediate and mainstream environment influence the process of planning and purposeful behavior necessary to select and commit to a specific career. Although research results are contradictory, the findings suggest that African American boys' vocational and educational aspirations are not lower than those of their European American peers (Gibbs, 1985; Smith, 1982; Steinberg et al., 1992); however, low-income African American male youth do report an incongruence between aspirations and career and educational expectations. The career progress of this population is also characterized by early labor force participation, unrelated work experiences, and episodic employment (Leonard, 1985).

Structural factors and cultural issues contribute to these adolescents' lower levels of optimism and proactive vocational efforts. Most African American boys are unlikely to belong to families that are able to provide role models and guidance to assist with career awareness and selection. Career and employment choices are also narrowed because of school difficulties that arise from contextual and stylistic interactions based on fundamental differences in cultural values. An absence of relationships with adult male role models who take pride in intellectual pursuits and media images that portray African American males as athletic competitors and comedians also discourage the pursuit of academic goals.

Many academic problems originate from the repudiation of stereotypical feminine qualities. Although adolescent boys in general disparage feminine qualities, the intensity of this disdain appears to have a greater impact upon the completion of tasks that are essential for African American male youth's adjustment to adult roles. Unlike their European American counterparts, African American male adolescents are more likely to deny, devalue, and actually forgo intellectual interests to avoid the ridicule and shame that arise from academic success (Fordham & Ogbu, 1986; Harris & Majors, 1993; Mickelson, 1990). Consequently, the peer group's emphasis on physicality and the rejection of behaviors that deviate from the Black masculine alternative have been shown to have deleterious consequences for African American male youth (Gibson & Ogbu, 1991; Mickelson, 1990). Observations of only a small percentage of same-race males who commit to intellectual pursuits and expectations that academic achievement will result in alienation from peers and the community give rise to behaviors that deemphasize vocational and academic goals.

Although some youth completely reject academics, others create additional roles (e.g., class clown, class bully) to compensate for poor academic performance. Many African American male adolescents conceal evidence of academic competence and interests by monitoring and varying their behavior across settings (e.g., hide books, withhold truth about grades). Still others manage to openly engage in intellectual pursuits with peer approval and acceptance by engaging in extreme alternative masculine behaviors that override any suggestion of a lack of manliness (e.g., drug dealing, gang leader). Definitions of manhood which hold that certain occupations (e.g, white collar versus blue collar) are more manly than others coupled with a fear of being perceived as White also compound ambivalence toward vocational pursuits (Fordham & Ogbu, 1986).

Counselors' neglect to realistically impart vocational and career information also limits the vocational perspective of adolescent males. The failure to offer guidance in career and job interests, however, is intricately related to structural factors, such as the allotment of state resources based on the location and racial composition of schools and imbalances in student-to-counselor ratios in economically disadvantaged districts. Even for districts with relatively stable resources, a scarcity of qualified and committed counselors exists because of inadequate academic preparation to meet the needs of racially and ethnically diverse student groups.

Furthermore, structural and staffing changes in the composition of new job opportunities combine with deficits in vocational education to pose economic hardships for this population (Sum & Fogg, 1990). Federal reductions in the number of male youth needed for branches of the military and increased test score standards for enlisted recruits also restrict opportunities for male adolescents (Parham & McDavis, 1987) who view military service as a chance to be employed without sacrificing the "tough guy" image. Together, these circumstances encourage vocational identity foreclosure early in adolescence. Resulting joblessness predisposes African American male youth for community crime and family disruption in later years (Sampson, 1987). These conditions, in turn, perpetuate a cycle in which alternative masculine behaviors are enacted to protect the self from the pain that emerges in response to perceived and actual academic and employment barriers.

Identity Formation

The process of achieving an identity, which results in defining who one is and hopes to be, involves examining social systems and institutions and committing to those that have offered the greatest opportunities for mastery. Although this process continues throughout life, the adolescent identity becomes an integration of the selves that have evolved in each context in relation to feedback from peers and the adult world. Researchers suggest that boys primarily forge an identity characterized by autonomy, achievement concerns, mastery, competency, and the development of an ideology (Blos, 1962; Chodorow, 1978; Erikson, 1968; Gilligan, 1982; LaVoie, 1976; Stoller, 1964; Wainrib, 1992), but this pathway to identity seems limited in its application to the identity development of low-income, African American male youth.

First, these youth must reconcile several different identities, namely those specific to mainstream masculine requirements, alternative masculine standards, and Afrocentric norms. Second, African American boys have been reported to be less autonomous than same-race girls (Gibbs, 1985; Smith, 1982) and seem to value relatedness as evidenced by an extreme reliance on the peer group

(Franklin, 1984; Silverstein & Krate, 1975). Finally, structural factors of racism and discrimination constrain the domains over which mastery can actually be achieved. The complex intersection of these influences make identity development a more complicated process than suggested by identity research conducted with European American male youth.

For example, limited opportunities for academic mastery are evidenced in African American boys' disproportionate placement in remedial and special education courses, lower grades, more frequent and severe forms of discipline, and a greater number of expulsions and suspensions than their female counterparts (Gibbs, 1988; Irvine, 1991; Taylor & Foster, 1986). An absence of positive feedback from the academic environment and the media combine with frequent observations of violence and the incarceration of friends to generate a pervasive sense of pessimism toward the future. Even for male youth who show academic competence, experiences with mainstream institutions often lead to the conclusion that mastery can never actually be attained because of a "glass ceiling" based on racial background (Zweigenhaft & Domhoff, 1991). Therefore, it is imperative that counselors address the direct and indirect effects of masculine behaviors and attitudes on the developmental progress of adolescent African American males.

Proposals for Counseling African American Male Adolescents

The perspective on counseling proposed here maintains that African-American male adolescents are both creators of and created by influences that emanate from complex interactions among cultural, structural, personal, and contextual factors. Overt behaviors can be viewed as attempts to regulate the self in response to perceptions of demands created by interpretations of social cues filtered through a framework of alternative Black masculine values and beliefs.

Consistent with this perspective, the task of the counselor is to establish a positive bond with the adolescent and to use this connection to assess conflicts between masculinity and psychosocial tasks. To successfully integrate sex-role tasks with other psychosocial concerns, counseling should focus on empowering these youth to produce desired outcomes (McWhirter, 1991; Pinderhughes, 1983). As used in the assessment and intervention phases of counseling, empowerment would emphasize an awareness of skills and abilities that have been learned and are expressed with the purpose of controlling the self. To encourage change in African American male adolescents' personal power, specific counseling interventions would involve the following: (a) increasing competency in interpreting social cues; (b) differentiating among situations and individuals; (c) developing a repertoire of alternative responses; (d) evaluating and selecting situation- and person-appropriate responses; and (e) enacting the chosen chain of behaviors with accuracy.

Assessment and Intervention: A Structural-Cultural Framework

The counselor should determine the client's perceptions of those responsible for his presence in counseling. Because many African American male adolescents appear in counseling at the suggestion of other agents, it is important to elicit the adolescent's perception of how the decision for a counseling referral was made. Focusing on this matter provides information about the client's emotional and cognitive response to counseling and provides feedback about his perception of how others view him. This line of inquiry also assists in the development of rapport and the acquisition of information about the adolescent's perception of his behavior in relation to the behavior of others. Mistrust and skepticism can also be reduced by clarifying the limits of confidentiality and explaining the present and future relationship (if any) between the counselor and referral source. A distinction between the role of counselor and external agents should also be made as clear as possible. For some of these adolescents, the roles of counselors, law enforcement officials, social service personnel, and educational employees may be ambiguous, leading to resistance because of previous negative interactions.

The impact of masculinity on personal, social, and familial relationships should also be carefully determined. The primary goal of counseling with this population is to assist them to integrate various facets of masculinity with other developmental tasks. To move toward this goal, the counselor should recognize the ease with which these youth adapt. Low-income male adolescents learn to adjust to numerous social environments characterized by different sets of masculine norms and standards. The counselor should therefore seek to increase awareness of how these standards differ across settings and the degree to which the adolescent feels pressure to conform. This information can assist with targeting appropriate levels of intervention and selecting the most effective intervention strategies.

When assessment data indicate that masculine concerns are related to self-defeating patterns that interfere with developmental progress, assessment should focus on acquiring detailed information. A functional analysis of the internal and external cues that elicit, mediate, and maintain alternative masculine behaviors such as emotional inexpressiveness, physical aggression, or aloof and withdrawn postures should be carefully assessed. Additionally, the counselor needs to obtain insight into the adolescent's awareness of his behaviors and the outcomes.

Implications for Treatment

Interventions should be evaluated in relation to the cultural realities and contextual characteristics of the adolescent's daily life. Because the selection of an intervention can be contaminated by cultural and theoretical biases, resulting in the exclusion of appropriate alternatives, counselors need to differentiate between the skills required to successfully adapt to specific contexts. Assuming that a single standard of behavior is appropriate across settings can have serious implications for these adolescents. In some instances, the counselor's preferred treatment strategy may be antagonistic to the adolescent's family, social group, or neighborhood situation. For example, many African American male adolescents experience frustration during interactions with teachers, which often result in punishment based on teachers' perceptions of verbal aggression. In these cases, a counselor's consideration of assertiveness training might be a plausible intervention. However, cultural and contextual issues such as whether behavior is aggressive or assertive when after-school survival depends on the use of verbal maneuvers to distance and protect the self from physical harm must be considered in the assessment phase. If selected, this intervention should be modified with relevant situational concerns in mind (e.g., type and degree of assertiveness required for peers, family, neighborhood, school).

Counselors must also be aware of the structural pressures that exist for African American male youth as a function of discrimination. This awareness should be translated into supportive behaviors that acknowledge and validate feelings of anger, powerlessness, and, to some extent, a certain degree of skepticism and caution when faced with interpersonal, employment-career, and educational decisions. Therefore, counselors must be knowledgeable of the psychosocial and emotional costs that adherence to masculine norms can lead to for this population. The secondary gains of a tough guy or player of women image must also be considered. Counseling strategies that focus on assisting male adolescents to understand and differentiate among the norms of mainstream, peer, and African American cultural situations and institutions and on how to use subtle social factors as cues for the expression of behaviors consistent with these situations can be extremely valuable. This approach enhances personal power and provides a cognitive framework for the adolescent to view himself as an active agent in his experiences. Thus, counseling should be geared towards promoting confidence, self-esteem, and a sense of personal power and responsibility required to successfully cope with educational, interpersonal, and social challenges.

Specific interventions that have been found to be effective with this population include group assertiveness training, expressive group therapy, and self-instructional techniques. Group assertiveness training delivered by peers and counselors has been found to reduce classroom displays of aggression (Huey & Rank, 1984). Expressive group psychotherapy also appears to have some positive effects for latency-age male youth, although a similar treatment has not been reported with older boys (Lothstein, 1985). Self-instructional techniques have also been found to modify African American male youth's behavioral risks for Acquired Immunodeficiency Syndrome (AIDS; Schinke, Gordon, & Weston, 1990).

Counseling Responses to the Tasks of Psychosocial Development

In working with African American male adolescents, counselors need to attend to the specific tasks of the developmental stages discussed earlier.

Separation-Individuation

Counselors should be prepared to assess and intervene in ways that promote the adolescent's sense of self without severing the interdependence that is often characteristic of African American families (Boyd-Franklin, 1989; Hines & Boyd-Franklin, 1982). Recognition of how characteristics of the family have influenced the adolescent, including his feelings toward each parent (whether present or absent), siblings, and extended family members is essential. Researchers report that the absence of male involvement in the rearing of boys is associated with engaging in violence and avoiding behaviors traditionally associated with femininity, such as displaying empathy and sensitivity (Miedzian, 1991). Consequently, a relevant line of inquiry for this population relates to information about the presence of male figures with whom they identify.

Because boundaries in some African American families are less rigidly defined than those of European American families (Boyd-Franklin, 1989), the roles and associated tasks and responsibilities of the adolescent in the family system and ambivalence toward those roles should also be addressed. In particular, the behaviors prescribed for males and strategies used within the family to encourage manhood need to be examined. For example, household rules and privileges that differentiate male and female sex-roles and disciplinary practices (if any) that are used to encourage adherence to these norms should be discussed. The degree to which present masculine attitudes and behaviors are linked to historical patterns and recent cultural shifts in values can be assessed by employing strategies that clarify the intergenerational transmission of sex-role behaviors (e.g., a family genogram that focuses on masculinity). These results can be used to gauge male-role flexibility and changes in masculine styles as a function of family stressors.

Value differences between the adolescent and family members should be elicited, and techniques should be used to clarify beliefs about the role of masculinity in his life. Differences in values among family members can lead to ambivalence that is reflected in numerous ways. For example, value differences may appear as inconsistent academic performance or consistent patterns of under- or overachievement. Adolescents who are dysfunctionally attached to the family may experience distress in attempts to make choices that are incompatible with traditional family norms and values. Thus, self-defeating behaviors may be enacted to maintain closeness when rigid systems prevail (e.g., leaving high school because other family members did not graduate). Counselors can help adolescents by presenting alternatives that allow them to maintain a sense of self, yet remain attached to the family.

Specific efforts should also be made to understand the adolescent's thoughts, fantasies, and feelings about family relatedness and separateness as a young adult. Concerns such as how much closeness is desirable and how much closeness is acceptable should be discussed in relation to family values and customs. Cultural and personal needs for relatedness can also be discussed in relation to mainstream expectations for evidence of autonomy. The adolescent should be guided in differentiating between family values and customs that are beneficial and those that reduce personal effectiveness and responsibility.

Belonging and Security

Although family, neighborhood, and school are the most important communities in the lives of African American male youth, factors specific to the larger macrosystem also influence their sense of security. As mentioned earlier, discomfort experienced within various social settings usually contributes to reliance on the same-sex peer culture. This limited sphere of safety, however, maximizes separateness and emphasizes these youth's minority status within the greater society. Counselors should aim to assist these young men to feel more secure from a psychoemotional and environmental standpoint. Thoughts and feelings about each social setting should be explored and adolescents' strengths used to modify circumstances that contribute to isolation. From an empowerment perspective, however, the counselor needs to move beyond the individual level and incorporate the involvement of external agents and institutions into the treatment program.

A systems approach offers an understanding of the varied factors that impinge on these adolescents and provides a global perspective of transactions that occur between the adolescent and the environment. Resources from relevant external systems should be included in the intervention program to assist the adolescent with meeting needs for support and security. Thus, the family, peer group, school, and community represent important dimensions for assessment and intervention. Parents can be invited to participate in the boys' treatment programs and encouraged to meet with teachers when academic concerns are the focus of counseling. Efforts to include siblings, parents, and extended family can also be made to target tensions that contribute to the youths' concerns. Similarly, issues that pertain specifically to in-school behaviors can be handled in small-group sessions with male adolescents, teachers, or peers to help the youths feel less isolated and alienated from the academic environment.

An understanding of the neighborhood and available community resources can assist with the design of activities that are of interest and benefit to adolescents. For example, research has shown that involvement in church and other meaningful instrumental activities reduce high-risk behavior for students who drop out of school (Zimmerman & Maton, 1992). Teachers and ministers in the community can be contacted to assist with the development and promotion of group-oriented services that involve these male adolescents.

Additionally, counselors can engage in more proactive efforts for this population by advocating the design and implementation of culturally based programs and services geared toward meeting belonging and security needs (e.g., rites of passage activities).

Selection of a Career

Career awareness, exploration, and preparation are crucial to helping these young men integrate conflicting masculine norms. Counselors should examine the existing beliefs, values, and perceptions of these youth as related to work. A careful assessment of how masculine standards influence vocational values and academic commitment are also prerequisites to intervening in this area. The initial focus should be on delineating the skills and abilities that each youth brings to the world of work. In particular, level of self-confidence and the ability to interpret social cues are important.

For young men who express resistance because of inconsistencies between masculine standards and career concerns, the counselor should reframe career exploration and selection within an Afrocentric and African American cultural values perspective. The value of working together to assist current and future generations, the spiritual importance of offering assistance to others, and the need to acquire employment to help family and friends can be presented in a non-threatening way. Adolescents' employment uncertainties can be modified with awareness activities that focus on role-play exercises, work-site trips, simulated job interviews, visits from employed and unemployed African American men, and school-based programs that emphasize career mentorship and intern or apprentice training. Counselors should also make a special effort to examine adolescents' feelings about work in relation to the types of employment habits observed among family members and neighbors. These discussions should access ambivalent feelings about certain career choices because of loyalty to cultural traditions and peer group members. Alternatives should be offered that address effective ways to maintain connectedness with the peer group and community without forgoing a desired career choice.

Conceptually, this task requires counselors to have insight into the relation between the adolescent and the community. For some, the belief that familiar ways of relating and behaving have to be sacrificed to acquire a career or employment will lead to the rejection of this aspect of identity. Inviting African American male adults with behavioral qualities acceptable as masculine but who have managed to meet the work expectations of mainstream institutions to interact with these youth or to serve as mentors can be valuable (Perry & Locke, 1985). Peers who are employed part-time and show competence in academics and the peer culture should also be invited to address work concerns. The internal fortitude and verbal skill that allow these young men to accept taunts from the peer group can be presented as a method to cope with the responses of peers when life choices and decisions are made that differ from those of other group members.

Identity Formation

The primary goal for counseling these youth is to assist with the negotiation of different identities so that conflicts that give rise to self-defeating outcomes are minimized. Integrating the collective African American group identity with a masculine identity and educating the adolescent about the norms and standards of European American institutions are included in this endeavor. To move adolescents to integrate conflicting aspects of the self that arise from culture, peer group, and mainstream expectations, the counselor should be familiar with the similarities and differences among these sets of influences. Additionally, the counselor must recognize the individuality of each adolescent.

For example, many adolescents lack insight into the structural and cultural pressures that affect their attitudes and behaviors. These youth accept and prefer the Black masculine norms described earlier and hold this set of behaviors to be of greater worth than the masculine characteristics of other African American men or European American men. As a result, some can be expected to react in a defensive manner when presented with a structural-cultural conceptualization of their behaviors. A denial of the importance of these factors and the desire to discuss more relevant concerns are other possible reactions. To avoid overwhelming them with this perspective, the counselor should allow an adolescent to set the pace without intervening until the boy's level of insight has been determined. The counselor can enhance the effectiveness of the integrative work by making inquiries related to this theme and empathetically responding to the adolescent's communications. Encouraging the interaction with comments that convey the idea that behaviors stem from internal and external demands can elicit responses that reveal the adolescent's stage of awareness. Assessing the primary and secondary gains of alternative masculine behaviors and gently exposing the costs of these behaviors in a direct but nonconfrontational manner is likely to be most effective. Given a positive emotional alliance, the adolescent will begin to see the connection between his behaviors and the existing contextual and social conditions.

Some male adolescents come to the counselor with higher levels of awareness regarding the influence of these factors. For these youth, counselors should be prepared to hear and channel feelings of anger and shame into assisting adolescents to form an ideology about their lives as African American young men. These feelings should be validated and promoted as resources for personal power to assist in changing surrounding systems and altering the self. These adolescents may also be more willing to relinquish some maladaptive masculine behaviors and to engage in activities designed to increase emotional expressiveness, assertiveness, and anger control. Nevertheless, they are still likely to be unaware of inconsistencies in cognitions and behaviors because of a need for affirmation and security offered by peers. In addition, ambivalence about feelings of closeness toward counselors may surface. Counselors can assist with integrating these thoughts and feelings by engaging the youth in an exploration of alternative methods to acquire affirmation from peers, family, and mainstream institutions.

Group interactions may be quite beneficial in this regard. African American boys are more likely to experience safety interacting with other youth who share similar fears and anxieties. Early tasks of the group should concentrate on establishing a bond among members and the counselor. The counselor should serve as a leader only until group members are prepared to take this role. Allowing each member to serve as leader provides an appropriate outlet for expressions of power and control. The need to belong to a group can also be used to enhance cooperation and social skills. Both structured and unstructured activities should be employed to enhance awareness of feelings toward African American culture, same-race men and boys, and European American society. An emphasis on conflict resolution, anger control, and emotional expression should also be encouraged during group meetings.

Some male youth arrive for counseling with a more in-depth awareness of the relation among overt behaviors used to cope with cultural, structural, and personal pressures than these other two groups. These youth may already feel attached to the African American community and hold cultural teachings in high regard. Additionally, they may feel connected to school, church, and other social institutions. Yet, issues related to more subtle themes such as homophobia and effeminacy can prevent them from embracing an image of masculinity that incorporates African American cultural values, Afrocentric norms, and mainstream values. For these males, it would seem valuable to impart educational information about homosexuality as a sexual preference, effeminacy, and gender identity issues. Homosexuality and bisexuality should be openly addressed with a particular focus on clarifying myths and encouraging acceptance and tolerance as traditional responses of the African and African American communities. This line of discussion should also emphasize commonalities among African American men irrespective of sexual preference. Perceptions of how structural and historical factors such as slavery have influenced the masculinity of African American men should also be explored. Strengths of African American men and women that have allowed for group survival and success (e.g., sex-role flexibility) should also be integrated into this educational approach. The goal is to encourage an African American masculine ideology that includes respect for gender, sexual and cultural value differences, and genuine bonds among African Americans based on a collective group identity.

Conclusion

Both the extent and nature of problems specific to African American male adolescents suggest the need for creative counseling interventions and expanded roles of counselors. Although defining and targeting the most appropriate level of intervention can be difficult, the detrimental effects of these problems and the possible advantages of counseling favor intervention.

The nature of the difficulties encountered by this population and the number of developmental concerns that can generalize beyond the adolescent years suggest that a variety of counseling strategies may be beneficial. Likewise, a broader spectrum of counseling goals is required than has traditionally been promoted by counselors. Psychological and educational counseling that employs diverse strategies and objectives in relation to the developmental and sociocultural needs of these adolescents are likely to be of value.

If, as the literature indicates, African American male adolescents are at risk for severe and long-standing problems, the primary question is, How do we reach this population? One suggestion is that researchers apply the findings from the many studies on counseling African Americans to counseling African American male adolescents. Creative techniques for each stage of psychosocial development should be designed to increase the likelihood that these adolescents will voluntarily initiate and engage in therapeutic work. Examining relationships among stereotypical behavioral, cognitive, and affective dimensions of masculinity, specific counseling interventions and counselor behaviors will also promote knowledge in the area of counseling effectiveness for African American male adolescents. An increasing rise in suicide rates; intraracial, interpersonal, and gang violence; continued discrimination; and data indicating that male peer groups are important agents of adolescent socialization substantiate the significance of counseling research specifically directed to this population.

References

Arredondo-Dowd, P. M., & Gonsalves, J. (1980). Preparing culturally effective counselors. *The Personnel and Guidance Journal, 58,* 657–661.

Blackwell, J. E. (1975). *The Black community: Diversity and unity.* New York: University of Massachusetts.

Blos, P. (1962). *On adolescence.* New York: Free Press.

Blos, P. (1979). *The adolescence passage.* New York: International Universities Press.

Bowman, P. J. (1989). Research perspectives on Black men: Role strain and adaptation across the adult lifecycle. In R. L. Jones (Ed.), *Black adult development and aging* (pp. 117–150). Berkeley, CA: Cobb & Henry.

Boyd-Franklin, N. (1989). *Black families in therapy: A multisystems approach.* New York: Guilford.

Carter, R. T. (1991). Cultural values: A review of empirical research and implications for counseling. *Journal of Counseling and Development, 70,* 164–173.

Casas, J. M., Ponterotto, J. G., & Gutierrez, J. M. (1986). An ethical indictment of counseling research and training: The cross-cultural perspective. *Journal of Counseling and Development, 64,* 347–349.

Cazenave, N. A. (1984). Race, socioeconomic status, and age: The social context of American masculinity. *Sex Roles, 11,* 639–656.

Cheatham, H. E. (1990). Africentricity and career development of African-Americans. *Career Development Quarterly, 38,* 334–346.

Chickering, A. W. (1976). *Education and identity.* San Francisco: Jossey-Bass.

Chodorow, N. (1978). *The reproduction of mothering.* Berkeley: University of California.

Clark, K. (1965). *Dark ghetto: Dilemmas of social power.* New York: Harper & Row.

Copeland, E. J. (1983). Cross-cultural counseling and psychotherapy: A historical perspective; implications for research and training. *The Personnel and Guidance Journal, 62,* 10–15.

Curtis, L. A. (1974). *Criminal violence.* Lexington, MA: Lexington Books.

David, D. S., & Brannon, R. (Eds.). (1976). *The forty-nine percent majority: The male sex role.* Reading, MA: Addison-Wesley.

Davis, R. (1981). A demographic analysis of suicide. In L. E. Gary (Ed.), *Black men* (pp. 179–195). Newbury Park, CA: Sage.

Doyle, J. A. (1983). *The male experience.* Dubuque, IA: Brown.

Doyle, J. A. (1989). *The male experience* (2nd ed.). Dubuque, IA: Brown.

Erikson, D. L (1966). *Childhood and society.* New York: Norton.

Erikson, E. (1968). *Identity: Youth and crises.* New York: Norton.

Farnsworth, D. L. (1966). *Psychiatry, education and the young adult.* Springfield, IL: Thomas.

Farrell, M. P. (1986). Friendship between men. *Marriage and Family Review, 9,* 163–197.

Fasteau, M. F. (1975). *The male experience.* New York: Dell.

Fordham, S., & Ogbu, J. M. (1986). Black students' school success: Coping with the burden of "acting White." *Urban Review, 18,* 176–206.

Franklin, C. (1984). Black male–black female conflict: Individually caused and culturally nurtured. *Journal of Black Studies, 15,* 139–154.

Gary, L. E., & Berry, G. L. (1985). Depressive symptomatology among black men. *Journal of Multicultural Counseling and Development, 13,* 121–129.

Gibbs, J. T. (1984). Black adolescents and youth: An endangered species. *American Journal of Orthopsychiatry, 54,* 6–21.

Gibbs, J. T. (1985). City girls: Psychosocial adjustment of urban black adolescent females. *SAGE: A Scholarly Journal on Black Women, 2,* 2–36.

Gibbs, J. T. (1988). *Young, black and male in America: An endangered species.* Dover, MA: Auburn House.

Gibson, M. A., & Ogbu. J. U. (1991). *Minority status and schooling: Immigrant vs. nonimmigrant.* New York: Garland.

Gilligan, C. (1982). *In a different voice.* Cambridge, MA: Harvard University.

Gray-Ray, P., & Ray, M. C. (1990). Juvenile delinquency in the black community. *Youth and Society, 22,* 67–84.

Grotevant, H., & Cooper, C. (1985). Patterns of interaction in family relationships and the development of identity exploration in adolescence. *Child Development, 56,* 424–428.

Hahn, A. (1987, December). Reaching out to America's dropouts: What to do? *Phi Delta Kappan,* pp. 256–263.

Hannerz, U. (1969). *Soulside: Inquiries into ghetto culture and community.* New York: Columbia University.

Harris, S. M. (1992). Black male masculinity and same sex friendships. *The Western Journal of Black Studies, 16*(2), 744–781.

Harris, S. M., & Majors, R. (1993). Cultural value differences: Implications for the experiences of African-American men. *Journal of Men's Studies, 1*(3), 227–238.

Helms, J. E. (1984). Toward a theoretical explanation of the effects of race on counseling: A Black and White model. *The Counseling Psychologist, 12,* 153–165.

Hendricks, L. E., & Montgomery, T. A (1984). Educational achievement and locus of control among black adolescent fathers. *Journal of Negro Education, 53,* 182–188.

Hines, P. M., & Boyd-Franklin, N. (1982). Black families. In M. McGoldrick, J. K. Pearce, & J. Giordano (Eds.), *Ethnicity and family therapy* (pp. 84–107). New York: Guilford.

Huey, W. C., & Rank, R. C. (1984). Effects of counselor and peer-led group assertive training on black adolescent aggression. *Journal of Counseling Psychology, 35,* 603–623,

Hunter, A. G., & Davis, J. E. (1992). Constructing gender: An exploration of Afro-American men's conceptualization of manhood. *Gender & Society, 6*(3), 464–479.

Irvine, J. J. (1991). *Black students and school failure.* New York: Praeger.

Josselson, R. (1988). The embedded self: I and thou revisited. In D. K. Lapsley & F. C. Power (Eds.), *Self, ego and identity: Integration approaches* (pp. 91–108). New York: Springer.

June. L. N. (1986). Enhancing the delivery of mental health and counseling services to black males: Critical agency and provider responsibilities. *Journal of Multicultural Counseling and Development, 14,* 39–45.

Kochman, T. (1981). *Black and white styles in conflict.* Chicago: The University of Chicago.

Kunjufu, F. (1986). *Countering the conspiracy to destroy black boys* (Vol. 2). Chicago: African American Images.

Lapchick, R. E. (1988). The high school athlete as the future college student-athlete. *Journal of Sport and Social Issues, 11,* 104–124.

Larrabee, M. J. (1986). Helping reluctant black males: An affirmation approach. *Journal of Multicultural Counseling and Development, 14,* 25–38.

LaVoie, J. (1976). Ego identity formation in middle adolescence. *Journal of Youth and Adolescence, 5,* 371–385.

Leonard, P. Y. (1985). Vocational theory and the vocational behavior of black males: An analysis. *Journal of Multicultural Counseling and Development, 13,* 91–105.

Liebow, E. (1967). *Talley's corner.* Boston: Little, Brown.

Lothstein, L. (1985). Group therapy for latency age black males: Unplanned interventions, setting, and racial transference as catalysts for change. *International Journal of Group Psychotherapy, 35,* 603–623.

Majors, R. (1989). Cool pose: The proud signature of black survival. In M. S. Kimmel & M. A. Messner (Eds.), *Men's lives* (pp. 83–87). New York: Macmillan.

Majors, R., & Billson, J. M. (1992). *Cool pose: The dilemmas of black manhood in America.* New York: Lexington.

McWhirter, E. H. (1991). Empowerment in counseling. *Journal of Counseling & Development, 69,* 222–227.

Messner, M. A., & Sabo, D. (1990). *Sport, men, and the gender order: Critical feminist perspectives.* Champaign, IL: Human Kinetics.

Mickelson, R. A. (1990). The attitude-achievement paradox among black adolescents. *Sociology of Education, 63,* 56–59.

Miedzian, M. (1991). *Boys will be boys: Breaking the link between masculinity and violence.* New York: Doubleday.

Miller, W. (1958). Lower-class culture as a generating milieu of gang delinquency. *Journal of Social Issues, 14,* 5–l9.

Mio, J. S. (1989). Experiential involvement as an adjunct to teaching cultural sensitivity. *Journal of Multicultural Counseling and Development, 17,* 38–46.

Moore, D. (1987). Parent-adolescent separation: The construction of adulthood by late adolescents. *Developmental Psychology, 23,* 298–307.

Oliver, W. (1989). Sexual conquest and patterns of black-on-black violence: A structural-cultural perspective. *Violence and Victims, 4,* 257–273.

O'Neil, J. M. (1982). Gender-role conflict and strain in men's lives: Implications for psychiatrists, psychologists. and other human-service providers, In K. Solomon & N. B. Levy (Eds.), *Men in transition: Changing male roles, theory and therapy* (pp. 5–44). New York: Plenum.

Palinkas, L., & Colcord, C. (1985). Health risks among enlisted males in the U.S. Navy: Race and ethnicity as correlates of disease incidence. S*ocial Science and Medicine, 20,* 1129–1141.

Parham, T. A., & Helms, J. E. (1981). The influence of Black students' racial identity attitudes on preferences for counselors' race. *Journal of Counseling Psychology, 28,* 250–257.

Parham, T. A., & McDavis, R. (1987). Black men, an endangered species: Who's pulling the trigger? *Journal of Counseling and Development, 66,* 24–27.

Pederson, P. B. (1988). *A handbook for developing multicultural awareness.* Alexandria, VA: American Association for Counseling and Development.

Perkins, E. (1975). *Home is a dirty street: The social oppression of black children.* Chicago: Third World.

Perry, J. L., & Locke, D. C. (1985). Career development of black men: Implications for school guidance services. *Journal of Multicultural Counseling and Development, 13,* 106–111.

Pettigrew, T. (1964). *A profile of the American Negro.* Princeton, NJ: Van Nostrand.

Pierce, H. P. (1986). Blacks and law enforcement: Toward police brutality reduction. *The Black Scholar, 17,* 49–54.

Pinderhughes, E. B. (1983). Empowerment for our clients and for ourselves. *Social Casework, 64*(6), 331-338.

Pleck, J. H. (1981). *The myth of masculinity.* Cambridge: MIT.

Pomales, J., Claiborn, C. D., & LaFromboise, T. D. (1986). Effects of black students' racial identity on perceptions of white counselors varying in cultural sensitivity. *Journal of Counseling Psychology, 33,* 57–61.

Rumberger, R.W. (1983). Dropping out of high school: The influence of race, sex, and family background. *American Educational Research Journal, 20,* 199–220.

Sampson, R. J. (1987). Urban black violence: The effect of male joblessness and family disruption. *American Journal of Sociology, 93,* 348–382.

Schinke, S. P., Gordon, A. N., & Weston, R. E. (1990). Self-instruction to prevent HIV infection among African-American and Hispanic-American adolescents. *Journal of Consulting and Clinical Psychology, 58,* 432–436.

Sessions, W. B. (1988). *Crime in the United States.* Washington, D.C.: Department of Justice.

Silverstein, B., & Krate, R. (1975). *Children of the dark ghetto: A developmental psychology.* New York: Praeger.

Smith, E. J. (1982). The black female adolescent: A review of the educational career and psychological literature. *Psychology of Women Quarterly, 6,* 261–288.

Snowden, L. R., & Cheung, F. K. (1990). Use of inpatient mental health services by members of ethnic minority groups. *American Psychologist, 45,* 347–355.

Staples, R. (1982). *Black masculinity: The Black males' role in American society.* San Francisco: Black Scholar.

Steinberg, L., Dornbusch, S. M., & Brown, B. B. (1992). Ethnic differences in adolescent achievement: An ecological perspective. *American Psychologist, 47,* 723–729.

Stoller, R. J. (1964). A contribution to the study of gender identity. *International Journal of Psychoanalysis, 45,* 220–226.

Sum, A., & Fogg, N. (1990, January/February). The changing economic fortunes of young black men in America. *The Black Scholar,* 47–55.

Taylor, M. C., & Foster, G. A. (1986). Bad boys and school suspension: Public policy implications for Black males. *Sociological Inquiry, 56,* 498–506.

Thomas, C. W. (1985). A view from counseling of adult Afro-American males. *Journal of Non-White Concerns in Personnel and Guidance, 13,* 43–53.

Wainrib, B. R. (1992). *Gender issues across the lifecycle.* New York: Springer.

Warfield, J. L., & Marvin, R. L. (1985). Counseling the black male. *Journal of Non-White Concerns in Personnel and Guidance, 13,* 54–71.

Washington, C. S. (1987). Counseling black men. In M. Scher, M. Stevens, G. Good, & G. A. Eichenfield (Eds.), *Handbook of counseling & psychotherapy with men* (pp. 192–202). Newbury Park, CA: Sage.

Watts, T. D., & Wright, R. (1985). Some notes on black alcoholism prevention. *Journal of Alcohol and Drug Education, 30,* 1–3.

Wilkinson, K. (1974). The broken family and juvenile delinquency: Scientific explanation or ideology? *Social Problems, 21,* 726–739.

Wilson, A. N. (1991). *Understanding black adolescent male violence: Its prevention and remediation.* New York: Afrikan World InfoSystems.

Zimmerman, M. A., & Maton, K. I. (1992). Life-style and substance use among male African-American urban adolescents: A cluster analytic approach. *American Journal of Community Psychology, 20,* 121–138.

Zweigenhaft, R. L., & Domhoff, G. W. (1991). *Blacks in the white establishment? A study of race and class in America.* New Haven, CT: Yale University.

6
Culturally Sensitive Therapy with Black Clients

Laurie L. Wilson and Sandra M. Stith

A heritage of chattel slavery, segregation, and racial prejudice provides obstacles that have burdened Black Americans and affected the development of Black American families. In addition to continuous pressures of racism and oppression, Black American families face contemporary threats to family stability. Such threats include poverty, widespread drug abuse, teenage pregnancy, communicable diseases, and violent crimes. Traditional values and coping mechanisms of Black American families may not be adequate to deal with these contemporary threats to family stability. In fact, the U.S. Bureau of the Census (1983) reported that two out of three Black marriages will eventually dissolve and that in 1982 only one-half of all Black families included parents of both sexes.

More recent research, however, suggests that despite racism and its concomitant poverty, the Black family is strong. For instance, although college-educated Black men earn less than White male high school dropouts, approximately 90 percent of them are married and living with their spouses (Staples, 1985). Another example of the strength of the Black family is the fact that, contrary to popular opinion, 69 percent of Black families are not poor (Wilson, 1989).

The other 31 percent of Black families struggle for their daily survival. Ironically, they are often dependent on government and social service institutions that they "often perceive as non-supportive and exploitive" (Hayes & Mindel, 1973, p. 52). It is a serious social contradiction when a family cannot trust those who are charged to help them.

This article, focusing only on the mental health needs of Black families, describes the importance of a systemic theoretical orientation and delineates five critical issues that therapists must consider in working with Black families. Throughout this article we speak of Black families as though they are a

Reprinted from *Journal of Multicultural Counseling and Development, 19,* 1991, 32–43. © ACA. No further reproduction authorized without written permission of American Counseling Association.

homogeneous group, yet many variations exist. In spite of these variations, the historical and current experiences of racism and prejudice seem to be an organizing and universal experience that link Black American families and that demands our attention. Without understanding the experience of the Black family, it is not possible to meet the needs of these families.

Black Families and Therapy

Previous literature (Terrell & Terrell, 1984; Thompson & Cimbolic, 1978) has suggested that Black clients are frequently reticent to seek counseling and when they do seek therapy they frequently terminate after one session. This is not surprising given the lack of attention that has been given to understanding and treating non-White families.

There are other reasons why therapists may not be meeting the needs of their Black clients. First, White therapists and many Black therapists, who have been primarily trained in White institutions studying research based on White families, may lack a basic historical perspective on the Black family. Second, they may have stereotypical views regarding Black Americans and may not understand the unique strengths and problems faced by Black families seeking treatment. They may have basic value differences and communication difficulties with clients who are different from them. Finally, they may not recognize or understand the effect of racism on their interaction with Black families. Thus, lacking that understanding, they may interpret the Black family's reluctance to trust as resistance or noncompliance. Additionally, therapeutic theories and interventions, which primarily have been developed by White therapists and used with White clients, may not always be directly applicable to Black clients.

However, we believe that Black American families needing mental health assistance can greatly benefit from culturally sensitive family therapy. This is suggested by previous research that shows the greatest source of life satisfaction among Black Americans is their family life (Gary, Beatty, & Price, 1983). Family therapists believe that the dominant forces in personality development are located externally in current interactions in the family system. In fact, the fundamental premise of family therapy is that "people are products of their social context, and that any attempt to understand them must include an appreciation of their families" (Nichols, 1984, p. 80). In addition, family therapy may be particularly appropriate for Black families because it addresses the family in its larger social context: historical, political, institutional, and environmental factors that affect the family as a unit as well as individual family members (Minuchin, 1974).

Even though Black American families in trouble may benefit from effective family therapy, they are often reluctant to seek these services. Many Black Americans have responded to racism, oppression, and discrimination by refusing to trust persons differing from them in color, life-style, and class values

(Boyd-Franklin, 1989). Hines and Boyd-Franklin (1982) pointed out that this suspiciousness is frequently a direct-learned survival response. Suspicion extends particularly to "White institutions," as most clinics and mental health centers are perceived to be. Therefore, if family therapists expect to meet the needs of Black families and to encourage them to feel comfortable using family therapy, they need to develop culturally sensitive attitudes and skills. These attitudes and skills include awareness of the therapist's own cultural background, values, and biases, as well as acknowledgment of and comfort with the client's cultural differences (Pomales, Claiburn, & LaFromboise, 1986).

Five Critical Issues

Therapy with Black Americans must be consistent with their worldview, must be respectful of their history, and must be nonracist. There are at least five major issues that a culturally sensitive therapist needs to consider in working with Black families: (a) historical perspectives on the experience of Black American families, (b) the current and historical social support system of the Black American family, (c) the unique characteristics of the value systems of Black American families, (d) communication barriers that may hinder the development of trust between the Black client and a non-Black therapist, and (e) strategies for providing effective systems-based family therapy to Black clients.

Historic Perspectives of Black American Families

The family is the primary source from which individuals extract a sense of self (Minuchin, 1974). All families impart values and ways of understanding life to new members. Family therapy is based on the idea that to help individuals change their behavior, the therapist must understand the context from which the individual developed and in which the individual lives. Although family therapists emphasize the importance of treating the individual in context, many focus so intensely on the here-and-now that they forget to look at the historical context from which the family developed. This blind spot may hamper the effort of the therapist (both Black and White) in working with Black families. Black families in America have a unique history. Slavery and postslavery segregation have impeded their development of a strong ethnic identity, cohesion, and direction necessary for the successful development of Black communities. During slavery Black families were separated, and extended families were discouraged. The development of Black ethnic identity, confidence, and direction was limited (Jones, 1982).

The oppression of Black Americans continued into the postslavery era, in which continuing racist actions against individuals and families only intensified remaining psychological scars. Wilson (1969) identified obstacles facing Black Americans in the postslavery era as a series of struggles: the struggles for survival, expression, participation, meaning, and fulfillment. These struggles included physical and psychological struggles; struggles to overcome negative stereotypes; struggles to develop appropriate methods for expressing anger, distress, and pain; struggles to develop a clear ethnic identity, heritage sense of self, and reason for human existence for the Black American.

Historical evidence suggests that strong family ties bound Black Americans together during the confusion that followed the Civil War. To adapt to pressures of slavery and discrimination, Black families developed the ability to persevere, organize, and succeed despite odds. Gary, Beatty, and Price (1983) reported that Black Americans continue to cite their family life as the source of most satisfaction. Hence, "traditional family life remains the one viable option for Black Americans on all socioeconomic strata because it is less subject to the vagaries of race than any other institution in American life" (Staples, 1985, p. 1011).

Without a historical perspective of the Black family, any approach to treatment of these families may fail. McAdoo (1983) emphasized that although Black families share many problems with White families, "a racist environment changes and intensifies the meaning and impact of these normative and catastrophic sources of stress" (p. 179). Although some family therapy models (e.g., Haley, 1976; Stuart, 1980) encourage therapists to avoid discussing the past with families, it seems critical that family therapists study Black history and begin to have some sense of the meaning and impact of racism on their Black clients.

In addition to difficulties that can emerge from family therapy models that encourage therapists to disregard that past, difficulties may emerge from applying family therapy models that emphasize gathering and reworking historical material (e.g., Bowen, 1978). When Black families are asked to investigate historical patterns of replication and compensation by discovering patterns in past generations, their historical experiences of slavery, separation of family members, disruption of family bonds from African ancestors, and so forth may lead them to feel incomplete or uncomfortable with their lack of historical knowledge. A historical approach, however, that focuses on more recent family patterns can be very useful in working with Black families after initial trust has been established.

Social Support Systems

Black Americans face unique psychological, environmental, and economic stresses caused by racism and oppression. Additionally, they may face problems common to many other American families, such as marital problems or parenting problems. Strong social support systems may distinguish those Black family members who are able to cope with these various problems from those who are unable to cope (Lyles & Carter, 1982). A social support system is defined as "a set of personal contacts through which the individual maintains [his or her] social identity and receives emotional support, material aid and services, information and new social contact" (Walker, MacBride, & Vachon, as cited in Malson, 1982, p. 37).

Although the Black American family has many support systems, the two primary ones throughout history have been the church and the kin network (Comer, 1972; Malson, 1982). The importance of church and kin is consistent with the African values of sharing, affiliation, and spirituality.

The Black church is the root of social support for the Black family (Comer, 1972; Lyles & Carter, 1982; Mayes, 1938). Its members are respected and able to excel in the struggle for survival, expression, participation, meaning, and fulfillment. It helps to maintain family solidarity while also allowing for the expression of anger, distress, and pain (Lyles & Carter, 1982).

Additionally, the Black church has provided a deep sense of spirituality to Black Americans. The church and spirituality provide support plus an adaptive mechanism for coping with stress that must be recognized and incorporated into the therapeutic process (Boyd-Franklin, 1989).

Therapists should be aware that extended family relationships, including fictive or adoptive kin, provide a second important source of support for Black American families. Black co-workers may also be considered part of the extended family. These relationships may be especially important when co-workers experience prejudice on the job. Their mutual support provides a buffer to the psychological stresses of their work world. This extended support system needs to be considered in helping Black families.

Other support systems are governmental and social service agencies. Although the original intent was for these services to be auxiliary, too many families become dependent on them for day-to-day survival. A family therapist may be able to help these families renegotiate and clarify their relationship with these agencies so that they become an enhancing support, rather than a debilitating crutch.

Whether therapists choose to work with only one person in the room or with the entire family, it is important that all those considered influential in the family's lives be included in the therapist's conceptualizing and implementing treatment plans. Omitting important sub-systems may reduce the effectiveness of therapy interventions.

Contrasts in Values of Black Americans and White Americans

In addition to examining the historical influences on the Black family and their current social support network, culturally sensitive therapists must make an effort to understand similarities and dissimilarities between Black American and White American values. Whereas many similarities exist, researchers have noted that Black families emphasize values different from those of White families. For example, Pinderhughes (1982) reported that White Americans place greater emphasis on independence, achievement, material assets, planning, youth, and power; Black Americans put greater emphasis on sharing, obedience to authority, spirituality, and respect for elders and heritage.

Contemporary Black Americans ascribe to three value systems: African, American, and Victim (Pinderhughes, 1982). Within Black American families, the experience of oppression and racism (i.e., victimization) may discourage a strong sense of self-esteem and, therefore, encourage doubtful responses in communities, families, and individuals. For example, obstacles that block opportunities for education limit opportunities for advancement and employment. This in turn may lead to stress and victimization. Victim system values are a result of adaptation to racism and oppression in which individuals isolate themselves as a defense against the stresses that hinder them.

Black Americans have adapted to these systems, and although this requires great expenditure of energy and may lead to identity confusion, some Black families have been able to remain particularly clear about their identity and values. Successful adaptation varies from family to family depending on the degree of racism, poverty, and oppression and methods of social support. This accounts for the diversity in values, behaviors, and family structures in Black American families. These multiple values constitute the Black American cultural system. It is important that therapists examine these competing value systems and begin to assess the impact that each system has had on the unique stressors and coping mechanisms with which each family comes to therapy.

Class and value issues are especially important with the lower-class Black client who is primarily concerned with day-to-day survival. With these clients, long-range therapy goals must be put aside until immediate problems of daily functioning are resolved.

Allen (1978) summarized three theoretical positions that are often used to examine Black American families. The "cultural equivalent" position suggests that Black American families may be compared with White American families because their cultures are similar. The "cultural deviant" suggests that Black American families are deviations from the norms represented by White American middle-class families. The "cultural variant" suggests that there are differences in Black American family norms due to natural adaptation to stress. With the cultural variant position, Black American family norms are seen as strengths, not weaknesses as suggested in the first two positions, which either deny differences or view the Black American family as abnormal.

To work effectively with Black families, therapists using the cultural variant model would be sensitive to the influence that racism and prejudice have on Black families. Culturally sensitive family therapists would look at Black values as strengths rather than as weaknesses. When assessing Black families, "normal" family functioning would be viewed from a Black rather than a White perspective. For example, a structural family therapist (Minuchin, 1974) assesses family boundaries along a continuum of extremes: enmeshment or over-involvement to extreme disengagement or emotional cutoffs. Boyd-Franklin (1989) emphasizes that "the vast majority of families fall within the normal range while the cultural norm among Black families tends to fall more within the enmeshed range. Normal, functional Black families often have very close relationships" (p. 123). Thus, therapists must be sensitive to assess Black family functioning according to Black, not White people's norms.

Overcoming Communication Barriers When Counseling Black Clients

Effective verbal and nonverbal communication for both the therapist and the client is important in successful therapy (Sue & Sue, 1977). A premature termination of therapy may result when there is miscommunication between a therapist and client due to "cultural variations in communication." This miscommunication "may lead to alienation and/or an inability to develop trust and rapport" (Sue & Sue, 1977, p. 420).

Although there is a mixture of cultures and classes in America, for verbal communication our society still recognizes "standard English" as the norm. Black Americans using Black English may be viewed negatively by White therapists. For the lower-class or ghetto Black, it may be difficult to communicate feelings, behaviors, and thoughts in standard English. Thus, "a counselee may be seen as uncooperative, sullen, negative, nonverbal, or repressed on the basis of language expression alone" (Sue & Sue, 1977, p. 422).

In discussing nonverbal communication among Blacks, Nancy Boyd-Franklin (1989) used the terms *vibes* as follows:

> Black people, because of the often extremely subtle ways in which racism manifests itself socially, are particularly attuned to very fine distinctions among such variables in all interactions. . . . Because of this, many Black People have been socialized to pay attention to all of the nuances of behavior and not just to the verbal message. The term most often applied to this multilevel perception on Black culture is "vibes." (p. 97)

Boyd-Franklin emphasized the importance of clinicians being aware that every Black client and family member is " 'checking out' him or her in terms of appearance, race, skin color, clothing, perceived social class, language, and a range of more subtle clues such as warmth, genuineness, sincerity, respect for the client, willingness to hear the client's side, patronizing attitudes, condescension, judgments, and human connectedness" (p. 96). She noted that Black families will leave treatment very quickly in the initial stage if this connection is not made with each family member.

Strategies for Providing Effective Therapy to Black Clients

Family therapy as it is traditionally practiced takes place in private practice or in community facilities. A problem-solving model of family therapy (Haley,

1976) includes several stages in the first interview: (a) social or joining stage, (b) problem stage, (c) interaction stage, and (d) goal-setting stage. Each stage is affected by the family's historical experiences, social support network, value systems, and means of communicating. In the joining stage the family is greeted by the therapist, developing trust and rapport vital to continued therapy. Without good communication, clients feel alienated and misunderstood. This, together with historical and current mistrust of White institutions, may lead to premature termination.

Both the problem stage, in which the therapist gathers information about the presenting problem, and the goal-setting stage are affected by the values of the family and the therapist. McAdoo (1988) suggested that "whether a phenomenon is viewed as a problem or solution may not be objective reality at all but may be determined by the observer's values" (p. 265). The personal values of the therapist determine both the questions asked in therapy and the way the answers are perceived (Allen, 1978).

In the interaction stage the family is asked to talk to one another while the therapist studies the family process. This stage of therapy may not be successful because (a) the therapy session usually takes place in an unfamiliar setting and (b) many Black families are affected by numerous systems such as welfare, courts, schools, public housing, extended family, and the church. The therapist who has not included the other systems in the interaction stage will not understand the influence these other systems have on the family's interaction process. Seeing Black clients in their own environment (e.g., community centers, homes, or churches) may help them participate more fully in therapy.

One early study found Black clients either passive or aggressive during the onset of therapy (Clark, 1972). This passive or aggressive behavior was seen as an expression of anger and frustration that could be easily displaced toward the therapist. The therapist should realize that the family's behavior may reflect not only their mistrust of the therapist but also their mistrust of the therapeutic process (Ho, 1987). During the onset of therapy many Blacks exhibit "healthy cultural paranoia" and refuse to develop rapport and trust with therapists from different ethnic, cultural, and value backgrounds (Orier & Cobbs, 1968; Ho, 1987). Thus, certain strategies, such as those listed as follows, may help the family therapist to provide effective culturally sensitive systematic therapy to Black clients:

1. Become aware of the historical and current experience of being Black in America.

2. Consider value and cultural differences between Black Americans and other American ethnic groups and how your own personal values influence the way you conduct therapy.

3. Consider the way your personal values influence the way you view both the presenting problem and the goals for therapy.

4. Include the value system of the client in the goal-setting process. Be sensitive to spiritual values and the value of the family and the church.

5. Be sensitive to variations in Black family norms due to normal adaptations to stress, and be flexible enough to accept these variations.

6. Be aware of how ineffective verbal and nonverbal communication due to cultural variation in communication can lead to premature termination of therapy. Become familiar with nonstandard or Black English, and accept its use by clients.

7. Consider the client's problem in the large context. Include the extended family, other significant individuals, and larger systems in your thinking, if not in the therapy session.

8. Be aware of your client's racial identification, and do not feel threatened by your client's cultural identification with his or her own race.

9. Learn to acknowledge and to be comfortable with your client's cultural differences.

10. Consider the appropriateness of specific therapeutic models or interventions to specific Black families. Do not apply interventions without considering unique aspects of each family.

11. Consider each Black family and each Black family member you treat as unique. Do not generalize the findings of any study or group of studies on Black families to all Black clients. Use the studies to help you find your way, not to categorize individuals.

Conclusion

The concept of family therapy is new to most Black families and, therefore, must be first accepted as another form of social support. "Within the Western framework, counseling is a White, middle class activity that holds many values and characteristics different from third world groups" (Sue & Sue, 1977, p. 421).

As long as racism and oppression maintain the victim system, family treatment must enable the family to cope constructively with those stresses and to counteract their pervasive influence. "Treatment must be directed toward strengthening family structure, enhancing flexibility, and reinforcing the ability of friends, community, and the larger social system to offer effective and appropriate support" (Pinderhughes, 1982, pp. 114–115). "The real challenge in therapy is to aid the Black family in rediscovering those strengths that historically have buttressed them from pervasive racism and provided them with needed support systems unavailable from other institutions" (Lyles & Carter, 1982, pp. 1122–1123).

References

Allen, W. (1978). The search for applicable theories of Black family life. *Journal of Marriage and the Family, 40,* 117–130.
Bowen, M. (1978). *Family therapy in clinical practice.* New York: Aronson.

Boyd-Franklin, N. (1989). *Black families in therapy: A multisystems approach.* New York: Guilford Press.

Clark, C. (1972). Black studies or the study of Black people. In R. Jones (Ed.), *Black psychology.* New York: Harper & Row.

Comer, J. (1972). *Beyond Black and White.* New York: Quandrangle Books.

Gary, L., Beatty, L., & Price, M. (1983). *Stable Black families.* Final report, Institute for Urban Affairs and Research, Howard University, Washington, DC.

Grier, W., & Cobbs, P. (1968). *Black rage.* New York: Basic Books.

Haley, J. (1976). *Problem-solving therapy.* New York: Harper & Row.

Hayes, W., & Mindel, C. (1973). Extended kinship relations in Black and White families. *Journal of Marriage and the Family, 35,* 51–57.

Hines, P., & Boyd-Franklin, N. (1982). Black families. In M. McGoldrick, J. Pearce, & J. Giordano (Eds.), *Ethnicity and family therapy* (pp. 84–107). New York: Guilford.

Ho, M. K. (1987). *Family therapy with ethnic minorities.* Beverly Hills, CA: Sage.

Jones, J. (1982). "My mother was much of a woman": Black women, work, and the family under slavery. *Feminist Studies, 8*(2). 235–269.

Lyles, M., & Carter, J. (1982). Myths and strengths of the Black family: A historical and sociological contribution to family therapy. *Journal of The National Medical Association, 74*(11), 1119–1123.

Malson, M. (1982). The social support system of Black families. *Marriage and Family Review, 5*(4), 37–57.

Mayes, B. (1938). *The negro's god as reflected in his literature.* Boston: Chapman & Grimes.

McAdoo, H. (1983). Societal stress: The Black family. In H. McCubbin & C. Figley (Eds.), *Stress and the family: Coping with normative transitions* (pp. 178–187). New York: Brunner/Mazel.

McAdoo, H. (1988). The study of ethnic minority families: Implications for practitioners and policymakers. *Family Relations, 37,* 265–267.

Minuchin, S. (1974). *Families and family therapy.* Cambridge, MA: Harvard University Press.

Nichols, M. (1984). *Family therapy: Concepts and methods.* New York: Gardner Press.

Pinderhughes, E. (1982). Afro-American families and the victim system. In M. McGoldrick, J. K. Pearce, & J. Giordano (Eds.), *Ethnicity and family therapy* (pp. 109–122). New York: Guilford Press.

Pomales, J., Claiburn, C., & LaFromboise, T. (I 986). Effects of Black students' racial identity on perceptions of White counselors varying in cultural sensitivity. *Journal of Counseling Psychology, 33,* 57–61.

Staples, R. (1985). Changes in Black family structure: The conflict between family ideology and structural conditions. *Journal of Marriage and the Family, 47,* 1005–1013.

Stuart, R. (1980). *Helping couples change: A social learning approach to marital therapy.* New York: Guilford.

Sue, D., & Sue, D. (1977). Barriers to effective cross-cultural counseling. *Journal of Counseling Psychology, 24,* 420–429.

Terrell, F., & Terrell, S. (1984). Race of counselor, client sex, cultural mistrust level, and premature termination from counseling among Black clients. *Journal of Counseling Psychology, 31*(3), 371–375.

Thompson, R., & Cimbolic, P. (1978). Black students' counselor preference and attitudes toward counseling center use. *Journal of Counseling Psychology. 25,* 570–575.

U.S. Bureau of the Census. (1983). *America's Black population, 1970–1982: A statistical view, July 1983* (Series P10/P0P83). Washington, DC: U.S. Government Printing Office.

Wilson, F. (1969). An interpretation of Afro-American history. *Social Progress, 60,* 13–23.

Wilson, N. (1989). Child development in the context of the Black extended family, *American Psychologist, 44,* 380–385.

The African American Client
Cases and Questions

1. You are a counselor in the counseling center on a predominantly European American college campus. You were just asked to meet with an African American student who walked in without an appointment. The student is upset over recent racial incidents on the campus: Black students have complained of being racially singled out in the classroom by White teachers, overhearing Black racial jokes told by White students, and finding racial graffiti. Your client has experienced each of these incidents. As a counselor, your client is asking for help in stopping the racial violence.

    a) How would you respond?
    b) How would you help your client deal with her immediate stress associated with her negative experiences?
    c) What information, knowledge, or experience would you draw on in relating to the student's ethnicity or her problem?
    d) In what way, if any, would your thoughts or feelings about the racial incidents have been different, if the student had approached you as a friend outside of a counseling relationship?

2. You are a counselor in a local high school. One of your many responsibilities is to provide counseling to the campus football team. The team's star running back, who is African American, has stopped by to discuss a personal problem. He has disclosed to you that he is gay and that he is tired of hiding this part of his life from family and friends.

    a) What are your personal thoughts and feelings about homosexuality and your own sexual orientation and how might these affect your work with the student?
    b) What cultural/ethnic issues should you be aware of in helping this student?
    c) What information, knowledge, or experience would you draw on in relating to the student's ethnicity, sexual orientation, or his decision to come out?

3. You have just been hired by a social service agency that has contracted to provide home-liaison services between the local schools and the parents of students attending these schools. Although a large number of the students are African American (approximately 35 percent), your agency to date has hired only one Black home-liaison counselor (of a staff of twelve

counselors). As a home-liaison counselor, your responsibilities include home visits to acquaint parents with community services available to them and to establish rapport between the parents and the schools.

a. What expectations would you have for your first home visit with an African American family?

b. What are some examples of "small talk" you might use to "break the ice" with the parents of a fourteen-year-old African American student who is consistently truant from school?

c. Assuming none exists when you are hired, what courses and experiences related to African culture would you recommend that the school district offer to students?

4. You have just accepted a counseling position in a correctional facility where a large number of African American inmates are incarcerated, most of whom come from nearby urban centers.

a. What expectations do you have for your own performance as a counselor in this setting?

b. Do you anticipate African American inmates will avail themselves of your services as a counselor? Why?

c. What psychological needs can you anticipate African American inmates may have that you as a counselor might attempt to fulfill? How will you attempt to fulfill them?

5. You are a counselor in a small midwestern college that is predominantly European American but recruits African American athletes. One of the Black athletes (Bill) has been dating a White cheerleader (Mary) you have seen before for counseling. Mary, seeing you alone, has just informed you that Bill has moved in with her and she fears her parents will disown her when they find out. She has also asked you if she may bring Bill for an appointment the next day.

a. How do you feel about Mary and Bill's cross-racial living arrangement?

b. What are some of the issues you will want to explore with Mary and Bill when they come to see you together?

c. What do you suppose Mary and Bill each want to get out of meeting with a counselor?

The African American Client
Role Playing Exercise

Divide into groups of four or five. Assign each group member to a role and the responsibilities associated with the role as follows:

Role	Responsibility
1. Counselor	1. Assume role as a counselor or mental health worker who is assigned an African American client. Attempt to build rapport with the client.
2. Client	2. Assume role of an African American client. To play this role effectively, it will be necessary for the student to (a) identify cultural values of African Americans, (b) identify sociopolitical factors that may interfere with counseling, and (c) portray these aspects in the counseling session. It is best to select a few powerful variables in the role play. It is important for you to be sincere in your role and your reactions to the counselor.
3. Observers	3. Observe interaction and offer comments during feedback session.

This exercise is most effective in a racially and ethnically mixed group. For example, an African American student can be asked to play the client role. However, this is probably not possible in most cases. Thus, students who play the client role will need to thoroughly read the articles for the group they are portraying.

Identifying the barriers that could interfere with counseling is an important aspect of this exercise. We recommend that a list be made of the group's cultural values and sociopolitical influences prior to the role playing.

Role playing may go on for a period of five to fifteen minutes, but the time limit should be determined prior to the activity. Allow ten to fifteen minutes for a feedback session in which all participants discuss (within the group) how they felt in their respective roles, how appropriate were the counselor responses, what else they might have done in that situation, and so forth.

Rotate and role play the same situation with another counselor trainee *or* another African American client with different issues, concerns, and problems. In the former case, the group may feel that a particular issue is of sufficient importance to warrant reenactment. This allows students to see the effects of other counseling responses and approaches. In the latter case, the new exposure will allow students to get a broader view of barriers to counseling.

If videotaping equipment is available, we recommend that the session be taped and processed in a replay at the end. We have found this to be a powerful means of providing feedback to participants.

PART 3

The American Indian Client

Introduction

W e are not free. We do not make choices. Our choices are made for us; we are the poor. For those of us who live on reservations these choices are made by federal administrators, bureaucrats, and their "yes men," euphemistically called tribal governments. Those of us who live in non-reservation areas have our lives controlled by local white power elites. We have many rulers. They are called social workers, "cops," school teachers, churches, etc. . . . (Warrior, 1967, p. 72).

The depth of feeling, anger and resentment expressed by this quote extends to mental health workers as well and portends a world view faced by the helping professional who works with American Indian clients. For nearly 500 years, American Indians have been fighting a defensive war for their right to freedom, their lands, their organizations, their traditions and beliefs, their way of life, and their very lives. They have experienced massacres by the U.S. Army, have seen the Bureau of Indian Affairs systematically destroy their leadership and way of life, have known broken promises, have had their land taken from them, and have watched their children die because of inadequate health care, poverty, and suicide. By almost every measure of impoverishment and deprivation, the American Indian is the poorest of the poor. The American Indian population has been decimated due to contact with Euro-American wars (declared and undeclared) waged against them and through diseases brought by the early settlers. By the end of the eighteenth century, the Indian population declined to only 10 percent of its numbers and still has not reached its historical peak.

While this decline halted and the population increased by 21.6 percent in the 1980s (now at 2.2 million—less than 1 percent of the U.S. population), cultural genocide continues to rear its ugly head in the form of institutional racism. The common practice of systematically removing young children from their homes and literally raising them in boarding schools; instituting relocation acts for the expressed purpose of assimilation; and passing numerous local, state, and federal laws aimed at breaking up the experience of tribal family life strikes at the very heart of the American Indian world view and the extended family, which they hold to be sacred; a way of life that emphasizes the interconnectedness of family and mother earth. The negative impact of these racist policies and practices on American Indians has devastated their standard of living and created major cultural conflicts: (a) death from alcoholism is six times greater than the general population, terminal liver cirrhosis is fourteen times greater among them than the non-Indian population; (b) suicide rates are twice that of the national average, with adolescence to adulthood as the time of greatest risk; (c) average income is some 75 percent less than Whites; (d) unemployment is ten times the national average; (e) infant mortality after the first three months of life is three times the national average; (f) drop out rates from school are higher and their educational levels are the lowest of any ethnic group; and (g) delinquency and mental illness far surpasses most groups in society.

It is ironic that many of the Whites who created these problems refer to them as "Indian problems" and have tried a variety of White-imposed solutions; policies and practices that attempted to force assimilation and acculturation, literally an attempt to turn the American Indian into a White person! The U.S. government has also seen fit to impose a legal definition of Indian identity as well: An individual must have an Indian blood quantum of 25 percent to be considered an Indian. This arbitrary definition has caused problems in and out of the community. Such attempts are not only manifestations of cultural oppression, they have marked a failure on the part of Whites to understand that the twenty-five hundred years of Indian histories and cultures have little in common with European-based cultures.

In the opening chapter of part 3, LaFromboise has updated an earlier article entitled "American Indian Mental Health Policy." This chapter provides us with valuable demographic data concerning American Indian status and adjustment to U.S. culture. We are reminded that American Indians form a highly heterogeneous group comprised of approximately 530 distinct tribes of which some 478 are recognized by the U.S. government. Of these, 280 have a land base or reservation and the tribes vary in customs, language, and type of family structure. Given the importance of balancing tribal differences and similarities, the author provides us with insights into the types of mental distress suffered by many American Indians, how the current mental health services are inappropriate, and the need for understanding the traditional healing of Indian culture in the development of relevant services. The author makes concrete recommendations for individual, professional, and institutional change in the treatment of the American Indian.

Throughout this text, we have given examples of how traditional therapeutic approaches may be antagonistic to the life experiences and cultural values of minority populations. In "Counseling Intervention and American Indian Tradition: An Integrative Approach," LaFromboise, Trimble, and Mohatt advocate moving away from such approaches toward the use of culturally sensitive methods more consistent with native values and beliefs. The authors discuss three types of psychological interventions—social learning, behavioral, and network therapy, which may prove helpful in working with American Indians. Above all, they strongly indicate that the weakening or dissolution of the extended family system is a key element in the disruption of healthy family functioning. In view of the importance of the extended family, therapeutic approaches that are family oriented may produce more satisfactory results.

Our final selection, "The Path of Good Medicine: Understanding and Counseling Native American Indians" by Garrett and Garrett, provides an excellent overview of Native American cultural beliefs and practices concerning the tribe, elders, family, and spirituality. The latter two are especially important for counselors to understand. Central to American Indian life is the concept of extended family, which is the primary unit of socialization emphasizing interdependency, reciprocity, and mutual obligation; it is the single most important survival mechanism in their culture. Basic to American Indian belief and manifested in traditional healing methods is the concept that wellness is harmony and that unwellness is disharmony in spirit, mind, and body. Specific suggestions are given to the helping professional for working with Native Americans. The authors take us through a journey that suggests that counselors should "walk the path of good medicine" by honoring native values and customs.

7

American Indian Mental Health Policy

Teresa LaFromboise

The American Indian population is culturally heterogenous, geographically dispersed, and remarkably young. There are 200 tribal languages still spoken today. The diversity found in some 317 Indian entities in the 48 contiguous states and 226 Native entities in Alaska defies distinct categorizations (Bureau of Indian Affairs, 1993). The 1990 census indicated that the American Indian population numbered approximately 1.96 million (U.S. Bureau of the Census, 1993b). It also verified that the trend toward increased urbanization occurring among American Indians in the 1970s and 1980s for subsistence and for gainful employment has slowed down (Snipp, 1996). In 1990 22 percent of American Indians lived on reservations and 60 percent in urban areas. The 26.7 year median age of American Indians is significantly younger than the median age of the U.S. population in general (33 years).

Recently Indian people have been affected by national economic cycles. Between 1980 and 1990 their unemployment rate increased 12.6 percent. This rate hovers at about 46 percent and ranges from a high of over 80 percent on some reservations to a low of 0 percent in the case of more prosperous tribes (Kaufman & Joseph-Fox, 1996; U.S. Bureau of the Census, 1993a).

By almost all economic indicators of poverty American Indians can be classified as "poorest of the poor" in this country. Poverty and prolonged unemployment have combined with substandard housing, malnutrition, inadequate health care, shortened life expectancy, and high suicide rates to affect and limit opportunities for educational attainment. 4.7 percent of American Indian adults have less than 5 years of formal education. Indian students appear to be staying enrolled in school somewhat longer than in 1980, yet they are more likely to be behind in school (Indian Nations at Risk Task Force, 1991). 34.5 percent of American Indians have less than 12 years of school. This is below the 22.1 percent high school attainment rate of Whites. In 1990 only 2.1 percent of American Indian 18–to–24 year olds completed an undergraduate degree, compared to 8.6 percent of their White counterparts (Ward, 1993, 1995). This can undoubtedly be attributed to the stressful pressures American Indian students have experienced in the dominant White culture of higher education institutions (Deyhle, 1992; Reyhner, 1992).

Although American Indians have shown impressive reservoirs of strength and coping mechanisms in the face of these environmental realities (Special Populations Subpanel on Mental Health of American Indians and Alaska Natives, 1978), they experience high rates of mental health disorders associated with marginalization, discrimination, and stress. For example, overall rates of alcohol and drug abuse are high (Walker et al., 1996). A congressional hearing on Indian juvenile alcoholism and drug abuse reported that 52 percent of urban and 80 percent of reservation Indian adolescents engaged in moderate to heavy alcohol or drug use as compared to 23 percent of their urban, non-Indian counterparts (U.S. Senate Select Committee on Indian Affairs, 1985). The hearing revealed that in some Indian communities, children as young as four years of age can be found drinking and using inhalants. However, prevalence varies tremendously from tribe to tribe and by age within tribes.

Delinquency and arrest rates of American Indians are among the highest of ethnic minority groups in this nation (U.S. Department of Justice, 1990). American Indians in urban areas are often taken into police custody for violations committed under the influence of drugs or alcohol. American Indians have a homicide rate (9.6 percent per 100,000) that is nearly double that of Whites (4.5 percent) (Bachman, 1992). The problem of domestic violence in Indian country has become increasingly acknowledged. As many as 34.4 percent of American Indian children are at risk of becoming victims of abuse or neglect with the majority of the cases going unreported (National Indian Justice Center, 1990).

American Indians have been characterized as "aliens in their own land" for the past 100 years. Cultural epidemiologists claim that forced acculturation to urban living increases individuals' vulnerability for developing psychological problems (Boyce & Boyce, 1983; Spindler & Spindler, 1978). Barter and Barter (1974) noted the heightened stress involved when Indians adapt to the dominant culture and at the same time are forced by their choice of residency into relinquishing their sovereign rights to health, education, and welfare on reservation land.

Psychological disturbance is often primarily a reaction to life conditions, and mental illness can be a tragic manifestation of unsatisfactory adjustment to a social psychological environment that provides few satisfactory options for human action (DeLeon, 1977). There is a severe imbalance in favor of studies that focus on pathological disorders of American Indians to the neglect of investigations of milder transient problems and of research on familial or sociocultural antecedents of psychopathology. The most glaring gap, however, is the failure to examine the effective strategies currently employed by American Indians for coping with numerous stressors.

Only three community-wide American Indian epidemiological studies of psychopathology exist. The prevalence rates of psychological dysfunction range from a low of 1 percent per 2,000 to a high of 37 percent per 1,000; depression and adjustment reactions are the most prevalent problems (Roy, Chaudhuri, & Irvine, 1970; Sampath, 1974; Shore, Kinzie, Thompson, & Pattison, 1973). The National Center for American Indian and Alaska Native Mental Health Research is conducting community-wide epidemiological studies on a reservation in the Northern Plains area and the Southwest area of the country. These studies involve 4,000 15–54 year olds and a subsample of 55–85 year olds using DSM-III-R and DSM-IV diagnostic criteria (J. Beals, personal communication, September 30, 1996).

Other studies have reported the prevalence of depression within select Indian communities to be four to six times higher than that in the research noted previously (Manson, Shore, & Bloom, 1985). Media attention to American Indian suicide finally stimulated national concern over a problem emphasized by service providers and researchers for quite some time ("Suicides of Young Indians," 1985). In the years between 1989 and 1991 the suicide rate for American Indians was 16.5 as compared to the 11.5 per 100,000 for the rest of the United States (Indian Health Service, 1994). The suicide rate among American Indian school-aged children is three times greater than that of the American White majority (DuClos & Manson, 1994; U.S. Congress, Office of Technology Assessment, 1986).

Given the magnitude of these social and psychological problems, what mental health services are currently available to American Indians?

Available Psychological Service Providers

In 1976 there was only one psychologist of any ethnic background for every 43,000 American Indian people (Welch, 1976). One survey of psychological personnel reported that 110 American Indians hold doctoral degrees in psychology (American Psychological Association, 1991) boosting the personnel rate to one American Indian psychologist for every 18,182 Indian people. This rate compares most unfavorably to the current availability of one psychologist for every 2,780 people in the general population.[1] These figures suggest that American Indian underrepresentation in fields of applied psychology continues to be a serious concern.

Few Indian students seriously consider university training in psychology because there are so few American Indian psychologists as role models and so few psychologists serve American Indians on reservations. For example, there are currently only two American Indian fellows in the American Psychological Association (APA) Minority Fellowship Program despite extensive continuous efforts to recruit applicants. Moreover, tribal efforts at career development have

[1] This figure was arrived at by dividing the 1990 U.S. population of 227,757,000 by APA's (1996) estimate of 81,839 available licensed-eligible psychologists.

placed priority on training in the medical and legal professions since the early 1970s. Finally, there are few programs like the Indians into Psychology Doctoral Education Program at the University of North Dakota recruiting Indian students to psychology at the high school or tribal college level (McDonald, 1994).

There are only nine American Indian psychologists employed by the Indian Health Service (IHS) to deliver direct services to mental health programs in Indian country (S. Nelson, personal communication, September 23, 1996). There are only four American Indians employed by the National Institute of Mental Health (U. Davis, personal communication, October 3, 1996) and two by the APA (Y. Butler, personal communication, September 30, 1996). Few American Indian psychologists are involved in mental health legislative decision making beyond the provision of testimonial support (P. DeLeon, personal communication, September 23, 1996).

The Society of Indian Psychologists (LaFromboise, 1987) and the National Indian Counselors Association, the two professional organizations that have emerged to articulate the need for more Indian psychologists in Indian communities, also try to counteract the high turnover rate of mental health service providers in the IHS and provide support for mental health workers who must often cope with undesirable working conditions. Members have found it advantageous to have a professional forum to articulate American Indian philosophical underpinnings within psychology and share strategies for the coordination of coexisting conventional and traditional Indian psychological service delivery. Members of these organizations frequently express difficulty in delivering psychological services to Indian clients, even to those who may come from their own tribe. Too often, educators assume that because a person is of American Indian descent, that person knows how to organize, support, and develop indigenous community resources.

Utilization of Psychological Services

The U.S. government initiated mental health programs for American Indians and Alaska Natives in 1965. By 1977, 40 reservation mental health programs were supported by the federal IHS. In that same year, there were 60,000 visits by American Indian and Alaska Native clients to outpatient facilities (Beiser & Attneave, 1978). In 1980 Rhodes et al. (1980) reported that 40 percent of all clients who utilize the IHS mental health programs were treated for depression, anxiety, and adjustment reactions. An unpublished summary of a random sample of patient caseloads in three urban health clinics indicated that 30 percent of the presenting complaints were attributable to mental health problems (American Indian Health Care Association, 1978). In 1995, only 4.2 percent of clients seen on an outpatient basis at IHS facilities were assigned a mental health or substance abuse diagnosis; likewise only 4.2 percent of IHS clients seen on an inpatient basis were given a mental health or substance abuse diagnosis

(S. Nelson, personal communication, September 23, 1996). The disparity between American Indians in need and those who use psychological services has been attributed to a difference in values and expectations among practitioners and clients, but it is also due to neglect by representatives of the U.S. government and the profession of psychology in promoting adequate mental health services or health maintenance activities (Liberman & Knegge, 1979).

A number of surveys suggest that American Indians in need of help are less aware of the psychological services available to them than are most Americans (Dinges, Trimble, Manson, & Pasquale, 1981; Trimble, Manson, Dinges, & Medicine, 1984). Even those aware of available services underutilize them because of perceptions that the existing services are unresponsive to their needs (Barter & Barter, 1974). Dukepoo (1980) identified fear, mistrust, and insensitivity as major barriers to mental health service utilization in the Southwest. Manson and Trimble (1982) further suggested that underutilization is the result of negative attitudes toward non-Indian psychologists who are presumably insensitive to the cultural complexities of Indian problems. In some cases, tribal judges and school administrators have considered bussing Indian children in need of psychological assessment as far as 2,044 miles to assure that American Indian psychometricians could conduct the evaluation (R. LaFromboise, personal communication, July 10, 1980). Alternatives proposed for these situations often represent attempts to link traditional community-based practices with relevant modern approaches to mental health. Realistically, however, there are many obstacles to the implementation of more effective delivery systems.

Delivery of Services

The Indian Health Service

The largest single provider of mental health services to American Indians is the IHS in the Department of Health and Human Services. The IHS annually provides inpatient and outpatient care to more than 1.3 million urban and rural American Indians and their family members through direct care or contract services. The IHS Mental Health/Social Services Program headquarters in Albuquerque, New Mexico administers programs in 12 regional areas through 76 service units, 42 hospitals, 66 health centers, 4 school health centers, and 53 health stations. The IHS also pays private specialists and hospitals for care provided to IHS beneficiaries on a limited and preapproved basis (Kaufman & Joseph-Fox, 1996).

The total operating budget for the IHS is $2,300,000,000. Funds appropriated for mental health services within the IHS budget for the fiscal year 1996 amounted to $36.8 million (1.6 percent of the total budget). Funds for substance abuse services amounted to 4.1 percent of the total budget (S. Nelson, personal communication, September 23, 1996).

More services are delivered by paraprofessionals and social workers in the

IHS system than by psychologists, psychiatrists, or psychiatric nurses. The stark absence of psychologists in many IHS service centers is of less concern to tribal leaders than the need for physicians, registered nurses, dentists, optometrists, audiologists, and pharmacists. The standard rationale for mental health prevention efforts that from 60 percent to 70 percent of medical office visits among the U.S. general population are for problems primarily psychological rather than physical (Cummings, Pallak, & Cummings, 1996) falls on deaf ears. Also, response of a wide range of problems for which Indian people seek services, including alcohol misuse, anxiety, depression, cultural conflict and suicide attempts, often are overlooked (Neligh, 1990).

Bureau of Indian Affairs

In addition to the IHS, the Department of the Interior's Bureau of Indian Affairs (BIA) maintains 83 agencies across 12 geographic areas, serving 555 tribes with a population count in 1993 of approximately 1,001,441. Its community service division coordinates educational and social service branches where social services, casework, and counseling related services are available. The education branch is charged with consultant, advisory, and administrative responsibility for programs with American Indian youth and adults. These programs are supported by tribal and state contracts and conducted in BIA educational and vocational guidance centers and federal boarding schools. The BIA social service branch provides child, family, and community services, including help with problems such as family disintegration and emotional instability. Most of these services (approximately 90 percent) are administered by tribes (B. Tippeconie, personal communication, October 3, 1996). Unfortunately, diagnostic observations are seldom a matter of formal record keeping in the BIA.

Urban Indian Health Care Programs

In the early 1970s, American Indian communities began to assume more direct control of the management and provision of health services. In 1972 the IHS began funding urban programs through its community development branch under the general authority of the Snyder Act (1921). This small program represents less than 1 percent of the IHS budget. It grants contracts to thirty-four nonprofit Indian organizations in urban areas to operate health education programs, referrals, and outpatient health care. This program operates twenty-eight health clinics and six referral centers. An example of one of the more innovative programs is the Seattle Indian Health Board's seminar series on traditional medicine, tribal beliefs and mental health, culture conflict, and self-awareness for service providers (Putnam, 1982). It is difficult to determine whether the most innovative programs are found on or off Indian reservations because urban Indian mental health programs receive more attention than reservation programs among those interested in contract care services.

State and Local Mental Health Services

The extent to which Indians use private or public mental health services is unknown. Relatively few Indians seek private care given the availability of services provided by other institutions, but cases do exist where American Indians travel substantial distances to seek services from therapists known to be effective by the Indian community. Many urban and reservation Indians are served by city, county, or state mental health facilities. The points of entry into these facilities are diverse—state hospitals, Veterans Administration hospitals, day treatment centers, other programs such as the Job Training Partnership Act Program, and families (Manson & Trimble, 1982). Referral activities to acquaint potential clients with the mental health services in the surrounding area are conducted by Indian centers and Indian social service programs. Unfortunately, record keeping in these service delivery agencies is also uncoordinated, complicating an assessment of client satisfaction with services or utilization patterns.

University Counseling Centers

The extent to which American Indian university students seek psychological services during their academic training ebbs and flows depending upon the cultural mistrust of students toward non-Indian service providers, their degree of cultural identification, and the extent to which traditional healing practices are available (Simms, 1995). Most university students indicate that they would seek help from family members before seeking psychological services were they living in their home area. University environments typically reinforce formal methods of seeking help. More progressive universities employ American Indian psychologists and allow them to be involved in outreach activities geared toward strengthening of resources within the Indian campus community. Haskell Indian Junior College reported a direct referral rate of less than 30 percent for personal counseling, alcohol-related problems, and campus violations (B. Smith, personal communication, September 23, 1996). American Indian women in university settings report satisfaction when using support groups facilitated by staff from university counseling centers (LaFromboise, 1986). Effective and accessible campus psychological services can help offset the challenges of competitive educational arenas. These services can also provide an excellent opportunity to demonstrate the benefits of psychological interventions because the clientele will likely return to their communities upon completion of a degree.

Tribally Based Mental Health Care Programs

American Indian tribes residing on reservations were empowered with freedom to design a wide range of services including mental health care, through the Indian Self-Determination and Education Assistance Act of 1975 (PL 93-638).

As of 1988 there were sixty-one different tribal health programs under contract to the IHS, but fewer than half of these programs had a mental health component.

The use of traditional healers who help and heal remains a priority over all other forms of clinical treatment in several tribally based mental health care programs (e.g., Swinomish Tribal Mental Health Project, 1991). In recent years there appears to have been a renaissance and revitalization of traditional healing practices (Attneave, 1974; Mohatt, 1985). A research and intervention project on the Rosebud Reservation in South Dakota was designed by Sioux medicine men in collaboration with Western psychologists and was entitled "Identity Through Traditional Lakota Methods." The psychological interventions employed were deemed successful by community members because they reinforced traditional ways of life (Mohatt & Blue, 1982). Attneave (1974) reported a successful two-way referral system between IHS staff and traditional healers in an Eskimo village. The first director of the IHS mental health program also reported recurring evidence of successful collaboration with Navajo healers and the establishment of a school for traditional healers (Bergman, 1974).

Not all attempts at collaboration with traditional healers are considered successful. In fact, Dinges, Trimble, Manson, and Pasquale (1981) asserted that most attempts by psychologists to establish working relationships with healers failed due to confusion regarding credibility, fee for service, professional efficacy, technical explanations, and patient expectations. Traditional community and kinship networks of support may be the most effective delivery agencies.

American Indian communities on and off reservations have traditionally practiced informal caregiving through the extended family. Even though diverse Indian families have transformed over time because of geographic movements and intertribal marriages, relational values have remained intact, and extended family networks provide extensive psychological support (Mohatt, McDiarmid, & Montoya, 1988). Carolyn Attneave (1969) saw the need to make more explicit the ongoing reciprocal support of Indian extended families with urban Indians through "network therapy." This support was necessary because their residence within the dominant culture constrained cultural activities that normally sustained network exchanges. In network therapy the focus of help giving is to mobilize the family, relatives, and friends into a socially interdependent force that can be attentive and responsive to emotional distress within the family to counteract the depersonalizing atmosphere of urban life. Red Horse (1982) applied the cultural network model in Minneapolis with Indian adolescents in a family-as-treatment model entitled the Wido-Ako-Dade-Win Program. Another form of community intervention is Indian Alcoholics Anonymous (AA) groups, which function in a culturally modified manner. National Association of Native American Children of Alcoholics (NANACOA) groups provide annual conferences and local community-based networking to address the needs of American Indian adult children of alcoholics. Political organizations also represent an important source of support. Over two hundred Indian political organizations exist in the United States that provide psychological and social support, and support for advocacy within various levels of the government to bring about changes in everything from the treatment of American Indians in history books to increased funds for the economic development of American Indian resources. The actions of these networks and political organizations reflect general American Indian value systems and beliefs, and particular notions concerning health.

Assumptions American Indians Hold About Psychology

American Indian communities are distinguished by many ties among tribal members and strong group cohesion, particularly in times of crisis. Indian people have concerns about psychological concepts such as "mental health," "personality," and "self" because of the absence of naturalistic or holistic concepts in the design and implementation of therapeutic processes. Mental health translates in the Lakota (Sioux) language as *ta-un* (a state of well-being). *Ta-un* requires certain categories of action and introspection prior to engagement in social relations or group collective actions (Medicine, 1982). Among the Hopi a person in a state of wellbeing is peaceful and exudes strength through self-control and adherence to the universal American Indian values of wisdom, intelligence, poise, tranquility, cooperation, unselfishness, responsibility, kindness, and protectiveness toward all life forms (Trimble, 1981).

Further guidance in understanding American Indian assumptions about psychology emerges from an analysis of the work of traditional healers who have challenged Western psychologists for centuries not to separate cultural ideals and practice (Dell, 1980). Primeaux (1977) stated that traditional medicine potentially embraces a broad spectrum of forces that are interwoven in all aspects of being. Carl Gorman stated that a traditional healer is actually a doctor, counselor, priest, and historian (Greenberg & Greenberg, 1984). Additionally, a healer is viewed as a safekeeper of ancient stories, maintained through the power of the spoken word. The healer uses the wisdom of spiritual legends for insight into human behavior and to explain emotional and behavioral problems (Powers, 1982).

Many American Indians believe that mental illness is a justifiable outcome of human weakness or the result of avoiding the discipline necessary for the maintenance of cultural values and community respect. The Coyote stories, for example, contain a theme of danger associated with excessively individualistic behavior (e.g., greed, envy, trickery). Individualization of responsibility is emphasized as a means of achieving community solidarity rather than a mechanism for personal achievement. Thus, the focus on maintaining cultural values is one way of controlling individuals' preoccupation with themselves and their personal symptoms.

American Indian psychologists generally describe only a few culturally-specific categories of disease causation (Trimble, Manson, Dinges, & Medicine, 1984) and tend to attach diagnostic labels to clients less frequently than non-Indian psychologists (Horowitz, 1982; Kelso & Attneave, 1981). When problems arise in Indian communities, they become not only problems of the individual but also problems of the community. The family, kin, and friends coalesce into a network to observe the individual, find reasons for the individual's behavior, and draw the person out of isolation and back into the social life of the group. The strong social and symbolic bonds among the extended family network maintain a disturbed individual within the community with minimal coercion.

In some cases the tribe has ritually adopted the individual suffering from mental disorders into a new clan group (Fox, 1964). Disturbed individuals in certain tribes are encouraged to attend peyote meetings that involve confession of a ritualized rather than personal nature and end with collective discussions (see Wallace, 1958, for specific examples). The cure may involve confession, atonement, restoration into the good graces of family and tribe, and intercession with the spirit world. Treatment usually involves a greater number of individuals than simply the client and healer, often the client's significant others and community members are included.

The informal resources and reciprocal exchanges of goods and services in American Indian communities diminish the impact of troubled individuals on group functions. This system allows typically autonomous individuals sanctioned opportunities to unite in the social control of disruptive behavior. Thus, the collective treatment of psychologically troubled individuals in tribal groups not only serves to heal the individual but also to reaffirm the norms of the entire group (Kaplan & Johnson, 1964). The goal of therapy is not to strengthen the client's ego but to encourage the client to transcend the ego by experiencing the self as embedded in and expressive of community (Katz & Rolde, 1981). Inner motivations and unique experiences involving repression, self-ambivalence, or insight are ignored, and symptoms are transformed into elements of social categories rather than personal states. New solutions to problems or new ways to see old problems become possible through interconnectedness with the community.

American Indians who engage in individual therapy often express concern about how conventional Western psychology superimposes biases onto American Indian problems and shapes the behavior of the client in a direction that conflicts with Indian cultural life-style orientations and preferences. The incompatibility between conventional counseling approaches and indigenous approaches has been discussed by numerous writers (Duran & Duran, 1995; Jilek-Aall 1976; Trimble, 1982; Trimble & LaFromboise, 1985). Many

American Indians recognize the need for professional assistance only when informal community-helping networks are unavailable.

Assumptions Psychology Holds About American Indians

Psychologists have sought to describe, measure, and understand tribal social phenomena; discover cultural patterns; and explain the practices of diverse American Indian groups for numerous decades. Unfortunately, little has been done regarding their psychological problems other than to document them (LaFromboise & Plake, 1983). Most psychological interventions have been culturally myopic and have not accepted assumptions or procedures that could be helpful to Indian clients. Treatment reports rarely account for the functional aspects of American Indian problems, nor do they recognize the efficacy of coping interventions that have been used for centuries.

A primary difference between Western and American Indian psychology involves a difference of values. Beginning with the work of Freud, psychologists have tried to conduct therapy within a "value-free" framework. Even though the accepted view is that many of the central targets of therapy (e.g., matters of work, marriage, and adjustment) are value laden, most psychologists choose to adopt a quasi-medical, value-free position to avoid the diverse social and religious values of Western society (Rappaport & Rappaport, 1981). In contrast, however, many well-intentioned psychologists believe that they could best help American Indians by helping them adjust to Western value systems or create a more personal value system of their own. As noted earlier, the American Indian approach to psychology assigns importance to healers and therapists as value keepers of the tribe. Much of the work of American Indian therapy centers around the process of deciphering traditional American Indian values that come into conflict with the values espoused by the dominant culture (Trimble, 1981).

The current U.S. mental health care system operates primarily on a scarcity paradigm regarding mental health resources, with university-trained specialists being considered the only valid healers (Katz, 1986). This paradigm still holds even though professionals have argued persuasively that communities can play a vital role in promoting mental health (e.g., Jung, 1972; Rappaport, 1981; Sarason, 1977). Unfortunately, the same psychologists trained during the progressive social era of the 1960s now appear aligned with fiscal conservatives who emphasize the cost ineffectiveness of helping grass-roots institutions involved in therapeutic efforts (Rappaport, 1981). As psychology becomes increasingly more guild oriented, its members attend to pronouncements of the zero-sum gain and restrict mental health delivery to those individuals and agencies who are properly licensed and accredited (i.e., those that are reimbursable by insurance or are supported by grants or by established social agencies).

The Euro-American tradition, on which contemporary psychology (Spence, 1985) is based, espouses an Aristotelian worldview that promotes dualisms, weakens community, and diminishes a sense of rootedness in time and place. The dominant cultural emphasis on personal agency has fostered material prosperity, freedom, and autonomy for the privileged classes. However, the consequences include alienation and narcissistic self-absorption (Bellah, Madsen, Sullivan, Swidler, & Tipton 1985).

Psychology also maintains a distinction between scientific and alternative therapeutic styles (Torrey, 1972). Psychologists believe that working-class clients rely on superstitious or physical explanations of personality problems rather than insight-oriented therapies. Paraprofessionals, traditional healers, and community mental health representatives who run essential programs in American Indian communities are not considered to be bona fide professionals and are often subjected to excessive scrutiny (Kahn, Lejero, Antone, Francisco, & Manuel, 1988). The profession assesses techniques used by Western, licensed therapists with Ph.D.'s as scientific, whereas practices of paraprofessional and indigenous healers are considered to be "largely magical" (Hippler, 1975, p. 24).

Even the process of prevention is different between Western psychologists and American Indians (Fleming, 1994; LaFromboise & Howard-Pitney, 1995; Robbins, 1982). Western psychologists often select high-risk clients and offer them prepackaged programs to teach them how to adjust to circumstances (Rappaport, 1981). Thus, prevention efforts maintain a self-serving aloof flavor unlike the transforming intention of American Indian prevention ceremonies. Further evidence of the individualistic orientation of psychology involves a reluctance to combine therapies despite that consumers make pragmatic decisions to do so, often blending theoretically conflicting psychological interventions (Katz & Rolde, 1981). American Indian clients experience little, if any, conflict about integrating traditional and "modern" conventional psychological approaches (LaFromboise, Trimble, & Mohatt, 1990). These distinctions must be considered in light of American Indian approaches that emanate from a holistic, community-involved perspective that implies a spiritual dimension as well (Katz, 1986; Mohatt, 1985).

Even recently trained psychologists are quick to develop a "clinical mentality" that emphasizes action and a sense of responsibility to individual clients and professional colleagues over a service orientation to the larger community (Goldstein & Donaldson, 1979). Therapy as currently practiced by American Indians is often seen by non-Indian professionals as having comparative insignificance within an overall system of health care delivery. These professionals view the perceptions of the community as unimportant and focus on the therapeutic process between the client and the therapist. This therapeutic enterprise is individualistic. It emphasizes immediate experiencing, intrapsychic processes, and individual motivation rather than community-oriented social causes of illnesses and issues of cohesiveness. Psychologists help clients develop the ego or defenses to mediate between the influences of significant others and the larger society (Frank, 1973). Psychologists also tend to use the strategies common in most theoretical orientations to provide clients with new, corrective experiences and offer them direct feedback to somehow change their psychological and emotional lives (Schofield, 1964, p. 994).

Psychologists are trained within a university model that emphasizes lecture-dominated and cognitive-centered pedagogy. Training has conceptually changed little despite the recommendations of the Vail and Dulles conferences (Boll, 1985; Dulles Conference Task Force, 1978). Trimble (1991) has described this model as leaving students dramatically lacking in the necessary skills for work in unique cultural settings. A typical program in counseling and clinical psychology, for example, involves technical training in everything from principles of psychopathology to research methods; but it rarely includes training in community consultation and social change intervention or alternatives to individual intervention (Atkinson, Thompson, & Grant, 1993). Courses on culturally distinct clients are relegated "to the periphery of the curriculum where they have been subject to the vagaries of faculty politics, budgetary constraints, and student activism or apathy" (Gibbs, 1985, p. 426). Sandwiched in the program are clinical practicums, supervised instruction and internships, and some sort of resident practicum, often devoid of professional character development in areas such as empowerment, transformation, and synergy paradigms. Following the completion of course work and successful defense of a dissertation or thesis, the trainee is granted a degree (usually the doctorate). The trainee subsequently may seek a state license to practice his or her chosen profession. Such a situation, whether intentional or not, tends to inhibit the student from pursuing multicultural interests and subtly influences the student's socialization more solidly into the mainstream profession of psychology.

If non-Indian professionals are to be trained in American Indian cultural styles of healing, it is necessary to understand the process by which Indians become competent as healers. The process begins with the search to find a master teacher or healer willing to accept the student as an apprentice. The decision of who is trained by whom is solely decided by the two people involved. The apprenticeship process can begin as early as adolescence, and the apprenticeship can last for the full duration of training. The healer decides what tasks an apprentice is ready to perform (Bergman, 1974). The interaction of student and healer combines elements of course work, supervision, therapy, and scholarship. Although apprentices receive formal education, the main structure of their education is determined by needs apparent in the apprenticeship. Classes, laboratories, and other university trappings are regarded as adjuncts, not the essence of education.

Recommendations for Policy and Action

Recruitment, Education, and Training

1. Academic institutions should make every effort to acquaint American Indians with the benefits of pursuing careers in psychology and increase

and expedite the recruitment of American Indian students to psychological training programs.

2. Psychological training programs should revise their curriculum to include the impact of cultural environment and contextual effects on American Indian behavior (Duran, Guillory, & Villanueva, 1990; Trimble, 1991).

Course work should begin with a non-Western point of departure, relying on the history of past practice to remind students to analyze indigenous methods and learn from them prior to developing psychological interventions. The sociopolitical history that American Indians have undergone and the present impact of that history should be reviewed. Topics on social influence variables such as trustworthiness (LaFromboise & Dixon, 1981), interpersonal dynamics (LaFromboise, 1992), styles of therapeutic communication (Dauphinais, Dauphinais, & Rowe, 1981), and the personal attributes of a psychologist (Bennet & BigFoot-Sipes, 1991; BigFoot-Sipes, Dauphinais, LaFromboise, Bennett, & Rowe, 1992) should be included.

3. The training of psychologists should include community-based practicum and internships in order that psychologists develop a sensitivity to the effects of their own worldviews on American Indian clients.

Students must learn how American Indian communities are organized, supported, and developed, in order to use networking skills with them. A tribally-based community internship year consisting of intense exposure to American Indian religious and transcendental values and experiences is essential. Interns would study interactions among the therapist, the client, and the client's culture and learn to use individuals and families as brokers, interpreters, and supporters for clients. American Indians would witness the potential of psychology to improve American Indian mental health as they interact with interns endeavoring to integrate cultural healing beliefs and psychotherapy practices (Mohatt, 1985).

4. Mental health service providers should build on clients' strengths while helping clients maintain vital membership in social networks and remain in natural communities in the least restrictive environment. The empowerment of American Indians relies on diagnostic methods that evaluate the functioning of an individual's natural support system, examines the established linkages between natural support systems and professional caregiving systems, and maintains respect for privacy and general collaboration. In a community-empowerment model, the community functions as the locus for services, mechanism for the development of professional and lay helping networks, foundation for the development of community-relevant mental health programming, and means of client involvement (Swinomish Tribal Mental Health Project, 1991).

Rappaport and Rappaport (1981) recommended a two-stage process that focuses on different aspects of the disturbance process. Psychologists would treat symptoms, and traditional support systems would function to manage secondary anxiety or existential value-laden issues. The coordination of psychologists with resources in the Indian community (e.g., community volunteers, indigenous helpers, extended family resources, and other nonprofesssional sources) in help-giving activities enhances organizational effectiveness. By working with already established channels of communication and power structures, psychologists could more easily increase their social influence (Kiesler, 1980). Katz (1983-1984) recommended community empowerment through the expansion of community healing resources. He advocated a process of transformation that involves linking individuals and organizations so that disparate groups might create agreement on how to manage central issues. To operate within a transformational system or an empowerment system, the psychologist needs to emphasize developmental processes rather than treatment processes.

Political-Organizations Involvement

5. American Indian tribal governments must assume a more active stance in regulating the quality of psychological service provision.

McShane (1987) recently encouraged American Indian tribes to assume a more active role in the provision of mental health services through regulatory authority of the Indian Self-Determination and Education Assistance Act of 1975. They exhorted tribes to require tribal licensure in addition to state licensure for psychologists who practice within reservations or within American Indian programs in urban areas. This procedure has already been employed, with researchers conducting investigations on reservations in the form of "scientific ordinances" (Efrat & Mitchell, 1974).

Tribal licensure would allow Indian communities the control necessary to set their own priorities for development and their own criteria for competence in service provision. Presumably, tribal governments would try their best to recruit American Indian and non-Indian psychologists who meet the highest available standards, who are eligible for licensure in the surrounding vicinity, and who can move freely in bicultural professional circles surrounding the reservation. It has been suggested that requirements for tribal licensure include prior course work or supervised experience in American Indian studies and in cross-cultural psychology. It is hoped that this approach to demonstrate firm guidance and concern by tribal governments would attract more psychological professionals to work in American Indian communities.

6. Those interested in improving the status of American Indians within psychology should become actively involved in all levels of professional

and governmental organizations. Increased American Indian involvement in policy-making arenas will sensitize professionals to their needs and allow opportunities for American Indians to use their skills and knowledge in advocating for appropriate actions to redress their mental health needs. Professionals can add relevance to social policy matters by fostering coalitions between grass roots representatives and professional associations.

The formulation of mental health policy should begin with affected people articulating to officials what social policies and programs are necessary (Elmore, 1979). By mobilizing efforts and funding resources for improvement in these critical areas, psychologists can practice their ethical responsibility to use their clinical skills and academic knowledge to work for change in eliminating social and racial inequality.

References

American Indian Health Care Association. (1978). *Six studies concerning the assessment of mental health needs in the Minneapolis-St. Paul area: A summary.* Unpublished manuscript, American Indian Health Care Association, Minneapolis, MN.

American Psychological Association. (1991). *APA directory survey, and new member updates for 1990 and 1991.* Washington, DC: Author.

Atkinson, D. R., Thompson, C. E., & Grant, S. K. (1993). A three-dimensional model for counseling racial/ethnic minorities. *The Counseling Psychologist, 21,* 257–277.

Attneave, C. L. (1969). Therapy in tribal settings and urban network intervention. *Family Process, 8,* 192–210.

Attneave, C. L. (1974). Medicine men and psychiatrists in the Indian Health Service. *Psychiatric Annals, 4*(11), 49–55.

Bachman, R. (1992). *Death and violence on the reservation: Homicide, family violence, and suicide in American Indian populations.* Westport, CT: Auburn House.

Barter, E. R., & Barter, J. T. (1974). Urban Indians and mental health problems. *Psychiatric Annals, 4,* 37–43.

Beiser, M., & Attneave, C. (1978). Mental health services for American Indians: Neither feast nor famine. *White Cloud Journal, 1,* 3–10.

Bellah, R. N., Madsen, R., Sullivan, W. M., Swidler, A., & Tipton, S. M. (1985). *Habits of the heart.* Berkeley, CA: University of California Press.

Bennett, S. K., & BigFoot-Sipes, D. S. (1991). American Indian and White college student preference for counselor characteristics. *Journal of Counseling Psychology, 38,* 440–445.

Bergman, R. L. (1974). The medicine men of the future—Reuniting the learned professions. In A. B. Tulipan, C. L. Attneave, & E. Kingston (Eds.), *Beyond clinic walls* (pp. 131–143). University, AL: University of Alabama Press.

BigFoot-Sipes, D., Dauphinais, P., LaFromboise, T., Bennett, S., & Rowe, W. (1992). American Indian secondary school students' preference for counselors. *Journal of Multicultural Counseling and Development, 20,* 113–122.

Boll, T. J. (1985). Graduate education in psychology: Time for change? *American Psychologist, 40,* 1029–1030.

Boyce, W., & Boyce, T. (1983). Acculturation and changes in health among Navajo boarding school students. *Social Science and Medicine, 17,* 219–226.

Bureau of Indian Affairs (1993, October 21). Indian entities recognized and eligible to receive services from the United States Bureau of Indian Affairs. *Federal Register* (58 FR 54364).

Cummings, N.A., Pallak, M.S., & Cummings, J.L. (1996). *Surviving the demise of solo practice: Mental health practitioners prospering in the era of managed care.* Madison, CT: Psychosocial Press.

Dauphinais, P., Dauphinais, L., & Rowe, W. (1981). Effects of race and communication style on Indian perceptions of counselor effectiveness. *Counselor Education and Supervision, 21,* 72–80.

DeLeon, P. H. (1977). Psychology and the Carter administration. *American Psychologist, 32,* 750–751.

Dell, P. F. (1980). The Hopi family therapist and the Aristotelian parents. *Journal of Marital and Family Therapy, 6,* 123–130.

Deyhle, D. (1992). Constructing failure and maintaining cultural identity: Navajo and Ute school leavers. *Journal of American Indian Education, 31*(2), 24–47.

Dinges, N., Trimble, J., Manson, S., & Pasquale, F. (1981). The social ecology of counseling and psychotherapy with American Indians and Alaska Natives. In A. Marsella & P. Pedersen (Eds.), *Cross-cultural counseling and psychotherapy* (pp. 243–276). New York: Pergamon Press.

DuClos, C. W., & Manson, S. M. (Eds.). (1994). Calling from the rim: Suicidal behavior among American Indian and Alaska Native adolescents [Special issue]. *American and Alaska Native Mental Health Research; The Journal of the National Center Monograph Series, 4.*

Dukepoo, P. C. (1980). *The elder American Indian.* San Diego, CA: Campanile.

Dulles Conference Task Force. (1978, June). *Expanding the roles of culturally diverse peoples in the profession of psychology.* (Report submitted to the Board of Directors of the American Psychological Association). Washington, DC: American Psychological Association.

Duran, E., & Duran, B. (1995). *Native American postcolonial psychology.* Albany, NY: State University of New York Press.

Duran, E., Guillory, B., & Villanueva, M. (1990). Third and fourth world concerns: Toward a liberation psychology. *Toward ethnic diversification in psychology education and training* (pp. 211–217). Washington, DC: American Psychological Association.

Efrat, B., & Mitchell, M. (1974). The Indian and the social scientist: Contemporary contractual arrangements on the Pacific Northwest coast. *Human Organization, 33,* 405–407.

Elmore, R. F. (1979). Backward mapping: Implementation research and policy decisions. *Political Science Quarterly, 80,* 601–612.

Fleming, C. M. (1994). The Blue Bay Healing Center: Community development and healing as prevention [Monograph]. *American Indian and Alaska Native Mental Health Research, 4,* 98–121.

Fox, J. R. (1964). Witchcraft and clanship in Cochiti therapy. In A. Kiev (Ed.), *Magic, faith, and healing: Studies in primitive psychiatry today* (pp. 174–200). New York: Free Press.

Frank, J. D. (1973). *Persuasion and healing: A comparative study of psychotherapy* (2nd ed.). Baltimore, MD: Johns Hopkins University Press.

Gibbs, J. T. (1985). Can we continue to be color-blind and class-bound? *The Counseling Psychologist, 13,* 426–435.

Goldstein, M. S., & Donaldson, D. J. (1979). Exporting professionalism: A case study of medical education. *Journal of Health and Social Behavior, 20,* 322–337.

Greenberg, H., & Greenberg, G. (1984). *Carl Gorman's world.* Albuquerque: University of New Mexico Press.

Hippler, A. E. (1975). Thawing out some magic. *Mental Hygiene, 59,* 20–24.

Horowitz, A. V. (1982). *The social control of mental illness.* New York: Academic Press.

Indian Health Service. (1994). *Trends in Indian health.* Rockville, MD: U.S. Department of Health and Human Services.

Indian Nations at Risk Task Force. (1991). *Indian nations at risk: An educational strategy for action.* Washington, DC: U.S. Department of Education.

Jilek-Aall, L. (1976). The western psychiatrist and his non-western clientele. *Canadian Psychiatric Association Journal, 21,* 353–359.

Jung, C. (1972). *Two essays on analytical psychology.* Princeton, NJ: Princeton University Press.

Kahn, M.W., Lejero, L., Antone, M., Francisco, D., & Manuel, J. (1988). An indigenous community mental health service on the Tohono O'odham (Papago) Indian reservation: Seventeen years later. *American Journal of Community Psychology, 16,* 369–379.

Kaplan, B., & Johnson, D. (1964). The social meaning of Navajo psychopathology and psychotherapy. In A. Kiev (Ed.), *Magic, faith, and healing* (pp. 203–229), New York: Free Press.

Katz, R. (1983-1984). Employment and synergy: Expanding the community's healing resources [Special issue]. *Prevention in Human Services, 3,* 201–225.

Katz, R. (1986). Healing and transformation: Perspectives on development, education and community. In M. White & S. Pollak (Eds.), *The cultural transition: Human experience and social transformation in the Third World and Japan* (pp. 41–64). London: Routledge and Kegan Paul.

Katz, R., & Rolde, E. (1981). Community alternatives to psychotherapy. *Psychotherapy: Theory, Research and Practice, 18,* 365–374.

Kaufman, J. A., & Joseph-Fox, Y. K. (1996). American Indian and Alaska Native women. In M. Bayne-Smith (Ed.), *Race, gender, and health* (pp. 68–93). Thousand Oaks, CA: Sage.

Kelso, D., & Attneave, C. (1981). *Bibliography of North American Indian mental health.* Westport, CT: Greenwood Press.

Kiesler, C.A. (1980). Mental health policy as a field of inquiry for psychology. *American Psychologist, 35,* 1066–1080.

LaFromboise, T. (1986, June). *Bicultural competence for American Indian self-determination.* Paper presented at the Thirteenth Annual McDaniel Conference, Stanford, CA.

LaFromboise, T. (1987). Special commentary from the Society of Indian Psychologists. *American Indian Alaska Native Mental Health Research, 1,* 51–53.

LaFromboise, T. D. (1992). An interpersonal analysis of affinity, clarification, and helpful responses with American Indians. *Professional Psychology: Research and Practice, 23,* 281–286.

LaFromboise, T., & Dixon, D. (1981). American Indian perceptions of trustworthiness in a counseling interview. *Journal of Counseling Psychology, 28,* 135–139.

LaFromboise, T., & Howard-Pitney, B. (1995). The Zuni Life Skills Development Curriculum: Description and evaluation of a suicide prevention program. *Journal of Counseling Psychology, 42,* 486–497.

LaFromboise, T., & Plake, B. (1983). Toward meeting the educational research needs of American Indians. *Harvard Educational Review, 53,* 45–51.

LaFromboise, T. D., Trimble, J. E., & Mohatt, G. (1990). Counseling intervention and American Indian tradition: An integrative approach. *The Counseling Psychologist, 18,* 628–654.

Liberman, D., & Knegge, R. (1979). Health care provider-consumer communication in the Miccosukee Indian community. *White Cloud Journal, 1,* 5–13.

Manson, S., Shore, J., & Bloom, J. (1985). The depressive experience in American Indian communities. A challenge for psychiatric theory and diagnosis. In A. Kleinmen & B. Good (Eds.), *Culture and depression* (pp. 331–368). Berkeley: University of California Press.

Manson, S. M., & Trimble, J. E. (1982). American Indian and Alaska Native communities: Past efforts, future inquiries. In L. R. Snowden (Ed.), *Reaching the underserved: Mental health needs of neglected populations* (pp. 143–163). Beverly Hills, CA: Sage.

McDonald, J.D. (1994). New frontiers in clinical training: The UND Indians Into Psychology Doctoral Education Program. *American Indian and Alaska Native Mental Health Research: The Journal of the National Center, 5,* 52–56.

McShane, D. (1987). Mental health and North American Indian/Native communities: Cultural transactions, education, and regulation. *American Journal of Community Psychology, 15,* 95–116.

Medicine, B. (1982). New roads to coping—Siouan sobriety. In S. Manson (Ed.), *New directions in prevention among American Indian and Alaska Native communities* (pp. 189–212). Portland, OR: National Center for American Indian and Alaska Native Mental Health Research.

Mohatt, G. V. (1985, August). *Cross-cultural perspectives on prevention and training: The healer and prevention.* Paper presented at the meeting of the American Psychological Association, Los Angeles, CA.

Mohatt, G. V., & Blue, A. W. (1982). Primary prevention as it relates to traditionality and empirical measures of social deviance. In S. M. Manson (Ed.), *New directions in prevention among American Indian and Alaska Native communities* (pp. 91–116). Portland, OR: National Center for American Indian and Alaska Native Mental Health Research.

Mohatt, G., McDiarmid, G., & Montoya, B. (1988). Societies, families, and change: The Alaskan example [Monograph]. *American Indian and Alaska Native Mental Health Research, 1,* 325–365.

National Indian Justice Center. (1990). *Child abuse and neglect in American Indian and Alaska Native communities and the role of the Indian Health Service.* (Unpublished final report, U.S. Department of Health and Human Services, Indian Health Service Contract #282-90-036).

Neligh, G. (Ed.). (1990). Mental health programs for American Indians: Their logic, structure and function [Special issue]. *American and Alaska Native Mental Health Research, 3.*

Powers, W. K. (1982). *Yuwipi, vision and experience in Oglala ritual.* Lincoln: University of Nebraska Press.

Primeaux, M. H. (1977). American Indian health care practices: A cross-cultural perspective. *Nursing Clinics of North America, 12,* 55–65.

Putnam, J. S. (1982). *Indian and Alaska Native mental health seminars: Summarized proceedings.* Seattle, WA: Seattle Indian Health Board.

Rappaport, H., & Rappaport, M. (1981). The integration of scientific and traditional healing. *American Psychologist, 36,* 774–781.

Rappaport, J. (1981). In praise of paradox: A social policy of empowerment over prevention. *American Journal of Community Psychology, 9,* 1–25.

Red Horse, Y. (1982). A cultural network model: Perspectives for adolescent services and paraprofessional training. In S. M. Manson (Ed.), *New directions in prevention among American Indian and Alaska Native communities* (pp. 173–185). Portland, OR: National Center for American Indian and Alaska Native Mental Health Research.

Reyhner, J. (1992). American Indians out of school: A review of school-based causes and solutions. *Journal of American Indian Education, 31*(2), 37–56.

Rhodes, E. R., Marshal, M., Attneave, C. L., Echohawk, M., Bjork, J., & Beiser, M. (1980). Mental health problems of American Indians seen in outpatient facilities of the Indian Health Service. *Public Health Reports, 96,* 329–335.

Robbins, M. (1982). Project *Nak-nu-we-sha:* A preventive intervention in child abuse and neglect among a Pacific Northwest Indian community. In S. M. Manson (Ed.), *New directions in prevention among American Indians and Alaska Native communities* (pp. 233–248). Portland: Oregon Health Sciences University.

Roy, C., Chaudhuri, A., & Irvine, O. (1970). The prevalence of mental disorders among Saskatchewan Indians. *Journal of Cross-Cultural Psychology, 1,* 383–392.

Sampath, B. M. (1974). Prevalence of psychiatric disorders in a southern Baffin Island Eskimo settlement. *Canadian Psychiatric Association Journal, 19,* 363–367.

Sarason, S. (1977). *The psychological sense of community: Prospects for a community psychology.* San Francisco, CA: Jossey-Bass.

Schofield, W. (1964). *Psychotherapy: The purchase of friendship.* Englewood Cliffs, NJ: Prentice-Hall.

Shore, J. H., Kinzie, J. D., Thompson, D., & Pattison, E. M. (1973). Psychiatric epidemiology of an Indian village. *Psychiatry, 36,* 70–81.

Simms, W.F. (1995). Cultural identification and cultural mistrust: A study among Native American Indian college students (Doctoral dissertation, Oklahoma State University, 1995). *Dissertation Abstracts International, 57,* 02A,0592.

Snipp, C.M. (1996). The size and distribution of the American Indian population: Fertility, mortality, residence, and migration. In G. Sandefur, R. Rondfuss, & B. Cohen (Eds.), *Changing numbers, changing needs: American Indian demography and public health* (pp. 17–52). Washington, D.C.: National Academy Press.

Special Populations Subpanel on Mental Health of American Indians and Alaska Natives. (1978). *A good day to live for one million Indians.* Washington, DC: U.S. Government Printing Office.

Spence, J. T. (1985). Achievement American style: The rewards and costs of individualism. *American Psychologist, 40,* 1285–1295.

Spindler, G. D., & Spindler, L. S. (1978). Identity, militancy, and cultural congruence: The Menomonee and Kainai. *Annals of the American Academy, 436,* 73–85.

Suicides of Young Indians called epidemic. (1985, October 6). *New York Times,* p. 4.

Swinomish Tribal Mental Health Project. (1991). *A gathering of wisdoms: Tribal mental health. A cultural perspective.* Mount Vernon, WA: Veda Vangarde.

Torrey, E. F. (1972). What western psychotherapists can learn from witch doctors. *American Journal of Orthopsychiatry, 42,* 69–76.

Trimble, J. E. (1981). Value differentials and their importance in counseling American Indians. In P. Pedersen, J. Draguns, W. Lonner, & J. Trimble (Eds.), *Counseling across cultures* (pp. 203–226). Honolulu: University Press of Hawaii.

Trimble, J. E. (1982). American Indian mental health and the role of training for prevention. In S. M. Manson (Ed.), *New directions in prevention among American Indian and Alaska Native communities* (pp. 147–168). Portland: Oregon Health Sciences University.

Trimble, J. E. (1991). The mental health service and training needs of American Indians. In H. Myers, P. Wohlford, L. P. Guzman, & R. J. Echemendia (Eds.), *Ethnic minority perspectives on clinical training and services in psychology* (pp. 43–48). Washington, DC: American Psychological Association.

Trimble, J. E., & LaFromboise, T. (1985). American Indians and the counseling process: Culture, adaptation, and style. In P. Pedersen (Ed.), *Handbook of cross-cultural mental health services* (pp. 127–134). Beverly Hills, CA: Sage.

Trimble, J. E., Manson, S. M., Dinges, N. G., & Medicine, B. (1984). American Indian concepts of mental health: Reflections and directions. In P. Pedersen, N. Sartorius, & A. Marsella (Eds.), *Mental health services: The cross-cultural context* (pp. 199–220). Beverly Hills, CA: Sage.

U.S. Bureau of the Census. (1993a). *1990 Social and economic characteristics, United States.* Washington, DC: Government Printing Office.

U.S. Bureau of the Census. (1993b). *We the first Americans.* Washington, DC: Racial Statistics Branch, Population Division.

U.S. Committee on Interior and Insular Affairs. (1985). R*eauthorizing and amending the Indian Health Care Improvement Act.* (House of Representatives Report No. 99-94). Washington, DC: U.S. Government Printing Office.

U.S. Congress, Office of Technology Assessment. (1986). *Indian health care* (OTA-H-290). Washington, DC: U.S. Government Printing Office.

U.S. Department of Justice, Federal Bureau of Investigation. (1990). *Uniform crime reports.* Washington, DC: U.S. Government Printing Office.

U.S. Senate Select Committee on Indian Affairs. (1985). *Indian juvenile alcoholism and eligibility for BIA schools* (Senate Hearing 99-286). Washington, DC: U.S. Government Printing Office.

Walker, R. D., Lambert, M. D., Walker, P. S., Kivlahan, D. R., Donovan, D. M., & Howard, M. O. (1996). Alcohol abuse in urban Indian adolescents and women: A longitudinal study for assessment and risk evaluation. *American Indian and Alaska Native Mental Health Research, 7*(1), 1–47.

Wallace, A. (1958). Dreams and wishes of the soul: A type of psychoanalytic theory among seventeenth century Iroquois. *American Anthropologist, 60,* 234–248.

Ward, C. J. (1993). Explaining gender differences in Native American high school dropout rates: A case study of the Northern Cheyenne school patterns. *Family Perspective, 27*(4), 415–444.

Ward, C. J. (1995, May). *Recent trends in educational attainment and employment among American Indians and Alaska Natives.* Paper presented at the workshop on Demography of American Indians, National Research Council, Washington, DC.

Welch, W. (1976, April). Wanted: An American Indian psychologist. *Behavior Today,* pp. 2, 3.

8

Counseling Intervention and American Indian Tradition: An Integrative Approach

Teresa D. LaFromboise, Joseph E. Trimble,
and Gerald V. Mohatt

One need not be a historian to federal Indian policy to detect movement in Indian Health Service mental health policy away from conventional psychological thought toward the recognition of culturally sensitive mental health approaches that maintain Indian community values (Nelson, 1988). Development of new service delivery approaches may have implications for the education and training of counseling psychologists and is likely to occur in the wake of this new policy.

This article outlines the process of helping from an American Indian traditional healing perspective and describes beliefs associated with efforts toward maintaining wellness and overcoming psychological disturbance. Studies addressing social influence variables that contribute to cultural clashes associated with individual and group counseling are reviewed along with research that supports the efficacy of selected counseling interventions with Indian clients. Considerations for the employment of culturally unique and conventional psychological interventions to advance the goal of Indian empowerment are enumerated. Tribal diversity and structural similarities are suggested in case material illustrating typical case presentations found in service delivery settings with American Indians. Finally, future directions in counseling and research training to prepare counseling psychologists to integrate conventional counseling interventions with American Indian tradition are provided.

Reprinted from *The Counseling Psychologist, 18*(4), 628–654. © Sage Publications, Inc. Reprinted by permission of Sage Publications, Inc.

American Indians and the Helping Process

Traditional American Indian tribal groups have unique perspectives on both the process and theory of counseling and therapy (LaFromboise, 1988). These views differ considerably from those of the dominant society. Knowledge of and respect for an Indian worldview and value system—which varies according to the client's tribe, level of acculturation, and other personal characteristics—is fundamental not only for creating the trusting counselor-client relationship vital to the helping process but also for defining the counseling style or approach most appropriate for each client.

In general, American Indians, especially more traditional or "nativistic" ones, believe that "mental health" is much more spiritual and holistic in nature than conventional psychological definitions would suggest (Locust, 1988; Trimble, Manson, Dinges, & Medicine, 1984). The term "medicine" for many Indians refers to a practice not limited to treating bodily disorders such as disease and injury. In addition, it represents a healing system based on the belief that the "forces of good and evil are interwoven in all aspects of the physical, social, psychological and spiritual being and it is difficult to isolate one aspect for discussion (Primeaux, 1977, p. 55)." According to certain traditional Indian views, a person and his/her psychological welfare must be considered in the context of the community (cf. Trimble & Hayes, 1984).

When problems arise in Indian communities, they become not only problems of the individual but problems of the community. The family, kin, and friends coalesce into an interlocking network to observe the individual, and find comprehensible reasons for the individual's behavior, draw the individual out of isolation, and integrate the individual back into the social life of the group (LaFromboise, 1988). The strong social and symbolic bonds among the extended family network surface to maintain a disturbed member within the community with minimal coercion (Dinges, Trimble, Manson, & Pasquale, 1981).

Many American Indians attribute their psychological or physical problems to human weakness and the propensity to avoid the personal discipline necessary for the maintenance of cultural values and community respect. American Indian psychologists seemingly adhere to these spiritual attributions. They tend to attach diagnostic labels to clients less frequently than do non-Indian psychologists, and they generally describe only a few culturally specific categories of disease causation (Kelso & Attneave, 1981; Neliegh, 1988; Trimble et al., 1984). According to the few small community-based studies of American Indians and Alaska Natives that have been completed, the most prevalent psychological diagnoses associated with weaknesses and neglect within these populations involve depression, anxiety, adjustment reactions, and psychoses. Drug and alcohol abuse are often associated with these disorders (Manson, Walker, & Kivlahan, 1987; Rhoades et al., 1980; Roy, Chaudhuri, & Irvine, 1970; Sampath, 1974; Shore, Kinzie, Hampson, & Pattison, 1973; Trimble, Padilla, & Bell, 1987).

Traditional ceremonies reinforce personal adherence to cultural values and remind participants of the importance of strengthening and revitalizing family and community networks. The sweat lodge ceremony and the peyote meetings practiced through the Native American church by some tribes involve self-disclosure and confessions on the part of those seeking guidance. These and other indigenous healing practices facilitate purification and prayer.

Ceremonial rituals have been of interest to social scientists and non-Indian interveners since early contact. Depending on philosophy, non-Indians saw these practices either as anthropologically interesting or as a major hindrance to their attempts to civilize native people. This latter perspective prevailed and led to laws that outlawed religious healing practices of Indian people and put intense pressure on local people not to attend healing ceremonies. In spite of this pressure, medicine men continued their practices.

Only in the late 1960s and 1970s did the *Zeilgeist* change. In 1978, the American Indian Religious Freedom Act (PL 95–134) affirmed that traditional religious ceremonies could be practiced with the same protection offered all religions under the Constitution. Priests now attend ceremonies, physicians and nurses meet with medicine men, psychologists and medicine men meet in case conferences, and rituals such as the sun dance are held publicly (Mohatt, 1978). The numbers of indigenous people attending such ceremonies have increased dramatically and now involve not only traditional people but also more acculturated tribal members.

This Indian traditional healing process, however, unlike conventional psychological interventions, usually involves more than the client and therapist or healer. The client's significant others and community members often are asked to participate (cf. LaBarre, 1964; Wallace, 1958). The "cure" may require more than therapeutic agents and can also include confession, acts of atonement, restoration into the good graces of family and tribe, and intercession with the spirit world. Thus the collective treatment of psychologically troubled individuals in tribal groups not only serves to heal the individual, but also to reaffirm the norms of the entire group (Kaplan & Johnson, 1964).

Medicine men and women organize a complex set of rituals that serve not only to treat but to prevent illness of a psychological or physical nature. These rituals involve a type of gift exchange that commits the seeker (the client) to attending future ceremonies, thereby becoming immersed in a way of life. Finally, through participation in ceremonial life, a worldview, in which the universe is seen as a complex balance among transcendental forces, human beings, and the natural environment, is revealed (Hammerschlag, 1988). These forces are mutually compatible as long as people respect the natural laws of governing how transactions are to be organized (e.g., respect for taboos such as incest, for an animal's spirit when it is hunted and killed, for ways to speak to others).

The goal of therapy from a traditional healing perspective, then, is not to strengthen the client's ego but to encourage the client to transcend the ego by experiencing self as embedded in and expressive of community (Katz & Rolde, 1981). Inner motivations and unique experiences involving repression, self-esteem, ambivalence, or insight are downplayed, and the experience of symptoms is transformed into elements of social categories rather than being a personal state of mental health. New solutions to problems or new ways to see old problems become possible through interconnectedness, creativity, and wisdom within the ceremonial life of the community (see Powers, 1982; Sandner, 1978; and Walker, 1980 for further information on traditional ceremonies in Indian life). Therefore, prevention and intervention always have a religious and cosmological framework; the medicine man both prays and doctors. Religion and psychology intertwine.

Cultural Clash with Conventional Counseling

Traditionally oriented therapy (e.g., behavioral, person-centered, psychodynamic) clearly takes a different tack than one typically expected by many Indian clients. Psychological training as it is conducted today fosters a "clinical mentality" that emphasizes action and a sense of responsibility to individual clients and professional colleagues over a service orientation to the larger community (Goldstein & Donaldson, 1979). It views as less important the perceptions of the community and focuses instead on the therapeutic process between the client and the therapist. The incompatibility between conventional counseling approaches and indigenous approaches has been discussed by numerous writers (Jilek-Aall, 1976; Manson & Trimble, 1982; Trimble, 1981; Trimble & LaFromboise, 1985; Wax & Thomas, 1961). The self-focus of most conventional counseling emphasizes immediate experience and intrapsychic process for personal change rather than consideration of social causes of illnesses and issues of community cohesion.

There is considerable evidence to support the view that counseling services designed around a conventional individual therapy regime are indeed inappropriate for service deliveries in Indian communities. Several recent studies suggest that American Indian clients' expectations, goals, and attitudes toward therapy may differ significantly from those of the non-Indian client (see Trimble & Fleming, 1989).

The extreme mistreatment of American Indians by the U.S. government including broken treaties, unwarranted violence, and attempted genocide has clearly fostered a good deal of mistrust of the government and non-Indians on the part of Indian people (Lockhart, 1981; Trimble, 1987a). Coupled with racism invoked by non-Indians, Indian clients may perceive all non-Indian (including a non-Indian counselor) as potentially racist and interfering until they prove themselves otherwise (cf. Trimble, 1988). American Indian clients and potential referral sources often hold a number of negative expectations or perceptions regarding counselors and the counseling process that could prevent them from developing a trusting relationship with the counselor and engaging in successful therapy (LaFromboise, Dauphinais, & Lujan, 1981; Schoenfeld, Lyerly, & Miller, 1971).

Unfortunately, problems caused by even a few ignorant or malicious non-Indians can erode potential trust or rapport between "outsiders" and Indian communities. A recent tragedy on the Hopi reservation in Northern Arizona provides an extreme example of this phenomenon. It was discovered that a trusted and well-respected White schoolteacher had sexually abused 94 of his students during his nine years at the reservation school ("Molester Put Lasting Scars," 1987; "Assault on the Peaceful," 1988). Since the incident, life on the reservation has been disrupted by the effects of the teacher's crimes. Sadly, tribal leaders assert that they can no longer trust outsiders' presence within the community.

Besides the open oppression or racism practiced against many Indian people, there are other, more subtle forms of oppression leveled even by those Whites and non-Indians who are "trying to help" Indians. Patronizing attitudes and "missionary zeal" on the part of majority group members are but two kinds of insensitivity experienced by a number of Indians. Both create significant barriers to trust and communication, especially in the context of a counseling relationship. A patronizing attitude is often shown in the counselor's lowering of expectations for minority clients (Bishop & Richards, 1987). Missionary zeal is characterized by the counselor's over-interest or obsession with the minority's culture and customs (LaFromboise, 1983; Trimble & Hayes, 1984). Both maneuvers serve to undermine estimations of the counselor's empathy, trustworthiness, or respect for the client.

In addition to experiencing anxiety regarding patronizing attitudes and missionary zeal, Indian clients may also fear that the counselor—as a member of the dominant culture—will try to influence American Indian value structures rather than help Indians solve their problems, and thereby alienate them from their own people and traditions. In fact, those American Indians who do engage in individual therapy often express concern about the extent to which the majority culture and conventional western psychology superimpose their biases onto American Indian problems. They also express concern about the shaping of their behavior in a way that conflicts with Indian culture life-style orientations and preferences. Although conventional psychological approaches have attempted to avoid the problem of clients' cultural diversity by attempting to conduct therapy in a value-free counseling environment, the evidence suggests that the problems with this practice are twofold.

First, as mentioned earlier, it is clear that the role of therapy in traditional American Indian society has been to reaffirm cultural values and consider the individual in the context of the community. For at least some Indians seeking assistance from a therapist, a value-free environment is not appropriate to their expectations or needs. Instead, they may want someone to help them to assert their traditional value system and define the problem within the context of that network.

Secondly, psychological therapy programs—in both theory and practice—are derived from and serve to affirm the values of American culture. They are not value-free but are infused with the individualistic philosophy and priorities of the dominant culture. These biases must be recognized and corrected in order to create a fair and effective counseling environment for minorities who do not wish to change their values to match those of the dominant culture (Katz & Rolde, 1981).

There is also some concern that certain counseling orientations, such as those emphasizing intrapsychic adjustment, involve processes that can serve to pacify and eliminate legitimate anger and political initiative—that therapy may reinforce ignoring or smoothing over serious problems rather than creating necessary social and personal change (Bulhan, 1985). Furthermore, the perceived lack of privacy of social service agency information within close-knit communities may also be a strong deterrent to seeking and continuing treatment at local clinics (Solomon, Heisberger, & Winer, 1981). Prospective clients may fear the stigma of seeking psychological help should anyone discover their participation in therapy (A. Blue, personal communication, August 26, 1985; G. France, personal communication, November 10, 1980).

Despite these pitfalls, Indian adolescent clients hold positive expectations for the therapist and the counseling process. They hold hope that a counselor will be someone who is an expert and therefore knowledgeable enough to give them concrete, practical advice about their problems (LaFromboise, Dauphinais, & Rowe, 1980). They have indicated that counselor trustworthiness is crucial to effective counseling (Dauphinais, LaFromboise, & Row, 1980; LaFromboise & Dixon, 1981). Given historical and contemporary oppression and cultural clashes associated with the act of seeking help, trustworthiness probably is more important for Indians than it is for non-Indians seeking psychological assistance. Increased knowledge of other relevant social influence variables might facilitate badly needed reform in these areas.

Studies Support Cultural Uniqueness

Several studies in the last decade have attempted to define the role of particular counselor qualities and/or skills that promote successful therapy with American Indian adults and schoolchildren. Other studies have tried to assess the reasons for seeking counseling in these people's lives. Some of the research exploring whether conventional counseling should be modified to better accommodate Indian expectations of counseling will be outlined in this section. First, it has been found that—in addition to trustworthiness—an understanding of the client's cultural values and the willingness to engage in outreach activities in the community are qualities that American Indians expect from an effective counselor (Dauphinais et al., 1980).

Although Indian youth report that counselors need not be of Indian background in order to be helpful as long as they are trustworthy (LaFromboise & Dixon, 1981), the question of counselor-client racial/ethnic similarity has yielded conflicting results until the introduction of methodological innovations by Donald Atkinson and his colleagues. Recent findings now indicate that racial or ethnic similarity appears to be less important than counselor educational level or attitudinal similarity for African Americans (Atkinson, Furlong, & Poston, 1986), Asian Americans and Hispanic Americans (Atkinson, Poston, Furlong, & Mercado, 1989). However, Ponterotto's useful replication (Ponterotto, Alexander, & Hinkston, 1988) seems to suggest that, to the extent that minority students lack access to ethnic contacts and are isolated in the society of the dominant culture, the more important it becomes to have a counselor of similar race or ethnicity. A preliminary report (Bennett, BigFoot, & Thurman, 1989) using this investigative model with Native American clients, appears to show the importance of ethnic similarity to be generally consistent with that described for other minorities. However, this investigation is attempting to verify unique within-group preferences related to cultural identity or commitment and is still in progress.

The success of psychological interventions for Indian clients, however, may be affected by the type of communication style a counselor elects to use. Dauphinais, Dauphinais, and Rowe (1981) found that American Indian students rated both non-Indian and Indian counselors as more credible when they used a culturally relevant counseling style than when these counselors used a nondirective counseling style.[1] In fact, the neo-Rogerian, "facilitative communication" verbal response style—the preferred means of establishing rapport and trust with clients that is taught in many counselor training programs—was found counterproductive not just for Indians, but was considered questionably effective for most American ethnic minorities as well (Atkinson, Morton, & Sue, 1989).

One help-seeking factor (type of client problem) has been found to vary among Indian and non-Indian populations. For instance, female American Indian students reported a strong preference for a female counselor if the problem was personal rather than an educational or vocational concern (Littrell & Littrell, 1982). To find significant differences regarding the type of problems reported and the type of individuals students would confide in about these problems, Dauphinais, LaFromboise, and Rowe (1980) surveyed Oklahoma American Indian and non-Indian high school students. Differences were found not only between Indians and non-Indians but also between Indians from rural areas and those from boarding and metropolitan public schools. Indian boarding school students, for example, nominated problems associated with depression more frequently than did rural or metropolitan students. Indian students differed from non-Indian students in indicating several types of problems that they would not talk to anyone about (e.g., getting along with friends or not caring). In addition, Indian students from boarding and metropolitan schools, but not those from rural areas or non-Indian students, reported a reluctance to talk with anyone about problems involving parents and family members, whether or not to stay in school, and making a decision.

Indian university students often indicate that they would typically seek help from family members before seeking psychological services if they were in their home environment (LaFromboise, 1988). Evidence suggests, however, that

Indian college students who do seek counseling may do so over different concerns than those of their high school counterparts. A study of 1,100 American Indian and Alaskan Native college students from five major universities reports that the most common stressful events in this population were school related: personal pressure to get good grades, fear of failure, fear of losing financial aid, difficulties in receiving financial aid, pressure to succeed, and fear of failure to meet family expectations (U.S. Congress, 1990). Furthermore, it has been reported that an increasing number of American Indian university students are seeking counseling to cope with problems that arise during their academic training, especially when there are American Indian counselors available (B. Smith, personal communication, July 8, 1986). The findings of research on reasons that Indians seek counseling and counselor attributes they view as most salient can aid in the reform of counseling services in educational settings. However, current cultural reforms within Indian communities must not be overlooked when considering services that are either educationally or community-based.

Some Considerations for Psychological Intervention

Several conventional forms of psychological intervention have been and still are in use in American Indian communities. Before briefly discussing the basic theory and practice of these orientations and then assessing their strengths and weaknesses within the context of counseling American Indian clients, the issue of Indian empowerment through retraditionalization and biculturalism must be considered.

Empowerment "refers to the development of skills enabling the person of color to implement interpersonal influence, improve role performance, and develop an effective support system" (Leigh, 1982, p. 10). The term "empowerment" is important because it embodies a way of thinking about social issues that transcends the rights/needs paradigm and the search for simple, one-sided, uniform solutions to complex sociopolitical problems (Rappaport, 1981, 1987).

The goal of empowerment is to do whatever possible so that clients can control their own lives; the underlying assumption is that people are capable of taking control but are unable to do so because of social forces and institutions that are hindering their efforts. A needs-based perspective, on the other hand, depicts people as powerless, helpless or child-like, dependent on the government or social institutions for help and support. In therapy, the interventionist strategies used to help the client gain empowerment include raising self-esteem, educating people about the ways in which an oppressive system operates and what its effects are on the individual (e.g., use of standardized tests such as the Graduate Record Exam to determine admission to institutions of higher education), mobilizing the client's interpersonal and material resources, creating or strengthening familial and extrafamilial support systems, and informing people about their tribal as well as societal rights and entitlements (LaFromboise & LaFromboise, 1982; LaFromboise & Rowe, 1983; Leigh, 1982; Lum, 1986).

For the last 20 years, many Indians have been "consumed with the tasks of revitalizing their culture, languages, and religions which are the heart of tribalism" (Fixico, 1985, p. 33) to revive Indian community empowerment. Indian scholars have labeled this movement retraditionalization. Retraditionalization relies on the use of cultural beliefs, customs, and rituals as a means of overcoming problems and achieving Indian self-determination. Tribal customs and traditions are used as sources of strength that provide culturally consistent coping mechanisms. For example, an honoring ceremony performed for a student graduating from high school might be recalled by that student to cope with an academic setback and persevere in university training.

Maintaining some traditional customs and roles, however, does not necessitate a return to all the "old ways." Many Indian women, for example, have undertaken a retraditionalization of their former roles as caretakers and transmitters of cultural knowledge in contemporary Indian life. According to Green:

> Contrary to standard feminist calls for revolutionary change, Indian women insist on taking their traditional places as healers, legal specialists, and tribal governors. Their call is for a return to forms which, they insist, involve women and men in complementary, mutual roles. (Green, 1983, p. 14)

The structure of the cultural system remains intact, but the specific jobs have been updated and modernized in accordance with societal change. Green (1983) and Allen (1986) further suggest that a complete return to the traditional roles and customs would not be desirable to all Indian women but that awareness and discussion in regard to the retraditionalization paradigm would facilitate more balanced, culturally appropriate research on Indian women. Clearly, the issue of retraditionalization of roles should be considered and addressed in effective therapy with American Indian clients.

Indians vary according to tribal and band affiliation, residential patterns, and also to the extent to which they are committed to maintaining their tribal heritage. In their classic study among the Menomini of Wisconsin, Spindler and Spindler (1958) identified five categories of "Indianness," using degree of acculturation as a reference: Native-oriented, peyote cult, transitional, lower status acculturated, and elite acculturated. Loye and Robert Ryan (1982) modified the Spindler scheme as follows:

1. *Traditional*—These individuals generally speak and think in their native language and know little English. They observe "old-time" traditions and values.
2. *Transitional*—These individuals generally speak both English and the Native language in the home. They question basic traditionalism and religion, yet cannot fully accept dominant culture and values.
3. *Marginal*—These people may be defensively Indian, but are unable either to live the cultural heritage of their tribal group or to identify with the

dominant society. This group tends to have the most difficulty in coping with social problems due to their ethnicity.

4. *Assimilated*—Within their group are the people who, for the most part, have been accepted by the dominant society. They generally have embraced dominant culture and values.

5. *Bicultural*—(Referred to in Ryan and Ryan, 1982, as transcendental)— Within their group are those who are, for the most part, accepted by the dominant society. Yet they also know and accept their tribal traditions and culture. They can thus move in either direction, from traditional society to dominant society, with ease. (pp. 6–7)

Both the retraditionalization movement and increased Indian biculturism have facilitated Indian community empowerment. American Indians have often been portrayed as people stranded between two worlds in conflict over personal preferences and cultural expectations (Hallowell, 1950). More recently, biculturalism—the ability to function effectively and be seen as competent in both worlds—is said to lead to greater cognitive functioning, and self-actualization (Akao, 1984; McCarty, 1985; McFee, 1968; Polgar, 1960). Many Indians believe that the strength of their knowledge of tribal culture augments their bicultural success.

Moses and Wilson (1985) recently stated that it might be better to suggest that Indians live in a complex world of multiple loyalties—a world that challenges, sustains, and sometimes destroys them, but seldom removes their Indianness. Awareness of these various cultural bases will help the counselor to be better prepared to assist Indian clients in coping with various life situations and efforts toward reaching full life potential. Issues associated with retraditionalization or biculturalism can be more or less readily incorporated into various theoretical perspectives underlying counseling. In order for that to occur, counseling theories must be reviewed for their facility in empowering Indian individuals and Indian communities. Person-centered, social learning, behavioral, and network theories were selected for comment in this article. Similar analysis of other counseling theories might improve decisions concerning appropriate treatment approaches with Indians.

Person-Centered

Although Rogerian therapy's on internal values and autonomy is broadly consistent with traditional American Indian values, several process-oriented aspects of this form of intervention create barriers for effective counseling of American Indian clients. The first difficulty arises from the extreme importance and centrality of the client-therapist relationship. There is certainly doubt as to whether this sort of isolated one-on-one interaction, outside the context of family and community, is a valid and/or pragmatic means of dealing with an Indian client's problems (Dauphinais et al., 1981).

This type of process focuses on the client individually, without taking into account the role that the client may perform within the family or community system and the effect of the client's attitudes and behavior on those in his or her environment. It stresses the potential for growth without considering the social issues involved. The effectiveness of the therapy also depends on the length and quality of the client-counselor relationship. Considering the high attrition rate of Indian clients that Sue, Allen, and Conaway (1978) found and the problems involved with developing trust and rapport in Indian client-counselor relations, the type of relationship necessary for successful Rogerian therapy seems unlikely.

In addition, the actual counselor-client communication style essential to this form of therapy is poorly suited for the American Indian population in general. Counselor communication emphasizes minimal encouragers, summarization, restatement, and reflection of feeling and is thus of limited use to reticent clients and those not comfortable expressing feelings. Not only are many American Indians considered "quiet" or untalkative, but a high value is placed on the restraint of emotions and the acceptance of suffering in American Indian culture (Basso, 1970; Bryde, 1971). In fact, Indians in more traditional contexts may be considered "weak" for expressing hurt feelings.

Social Learning

One counseling orientation based on social learning theory that appears to deal with diverse cultural norms better than Rogerian therapy is the skills-training paradigm. Social skills training focuses on teaching appropriate everyday skills and behavior to clients chiefly through the use of modeling and rehearsing activities. Recently, culturally tailored skills training has been successfully applied with Indian adolescents in the reduction of drinking behavior (Bobo, Cvetkovich, Trimble, Gilchrist, & Schinke, 1987; Carpenter, Lyons, & Miller, 1985; Schinke et al., 1988) and tobacco use (Schinke, Moncher, Holden, Botvin, & Orlandi, 1989); and to improve Indian parenting skills (BigFoot, 1989), professionalizing skills (LaFromboise, 1989), and bicultural competence (LaFromboise, 1983; LaFromboise & Rowe, 1983). David (1976) describes its utility in preventing intercultural adjustment problems, and further research is underway using the social skills training approach to prevent Indian adolescent suicide (Belgarde & LaFromboise, 1988).

This type of intervention has several strengths in terms of its use in American Indian populations. First, it is less culturally biased. It allows the community to define the community-level target problems to be solved (e.g., substance abuse, child neglect) and the type of behaviors appropriate for each situation (e.g., culturally appropriate assertiveness, parenting skills). Thus there is less concern on the part of the client and the community that the standards and values of the dominant culture will be imposed on the person through therapy (Bach & Bornstein, 1981). Social skills therapy also lends itself to prevention efforts in that it can address potential problems before they develop (Schinke, Schilling, Palleja, & Zayas, 1987). In addition, a major advantage of skills training for American Indian clients is its extensive use of modeling techniques. Role modeling is a major source of learning in Indian culture, so this form of therapy is both consistent with and reinforcing of that extended family tradition.

Behavioral

A third form of psychological intervention implemented in American Indian communities involves the use of behavior therapy (Penistone & Burman, 1978). This form of therapy assumes that most social behavior is learned via direct experiences through the overt and verbal reactions of others. A strength of behavioral therapy is its action-oriented focus on the present, rather than on the past. The focus is consistent with American Indian cultural worldviews (Trimble, 1981). Another positive aspect of this type of intervention is that many behavior therapy techniques lend themselves to paraprofessional implementation (Conrad, Delk, & Williams, 1974) and prevention interventions (Schinke et al., 1987).

A problem with behavior therapy, and with social skills training, can be its potential misuse through a narrow or inappropriate focus, such as when the goals of the client are not the goals targeted for change in therapy, or when behavior change processes are controlled by professionals who not respect the client's goals. A crucial issue in the ethics of behavior therapy concerns the locus of control over definitions of environment and reinforcers. Those Indian clients who are suspicious of manipulation and the imposition of conforming behavior by the dominant culture may be less willing to participate in such therapy. However, if the client's goals are the ones addressed in therapy, if the reinforcers employed are culturally appropriate and effective, and if the reinforcers outside of therapy (both within and beyond the Indian community) are realistically planned for, behavioral approaches can be effective and powerful in achieving desired change with Indians.

Network

A growing awareness of these cultural concerns has led to efforts to integrate traditional American Indian values and existing indigenous problem-solving mechanisms into the therapy process. Network therapy is one progressive form of counseling intervention that operates on a model similar to and consistent with the more traditional Indian community-oriented guidance system discussed earlier.

In the network approach, a clan or group of family, relatives, and friends is organized and mobilized to form a social force or network that works to combat the depersonalizing aspects of contemporary life patterns especially prevalent in urban environments. The role of the counselor is that of a "catalyst." He or she helps to conduct the process, but it is the social support system which works to deal with the crisis or bring the person out of isolation (Attneave, 1969; Reuveni, 1979).

The client and his or her problem are considered and treated within the context of a larger family and community social system. In this sense, network therapy can be seen as an application of the systems theory conceptual framework to the counseling process. A systems theory perspective on psychological problems offers a way of thinking about symptoms in terms of several characteristics including their functional roles or consequences within a given system (e.g., workplace, family, community).

Network therapy is practical in process as well as in theory. It has a decidedly informal, nonprofessional approach, is conducted in the home, and sometimes involves from 40 to 70 people at one time (Speck & Attneave, 1973). Clearly, this process seems to be a more natural and less intimidating problem-solving alternative than a one-on-one client-counselor office interaction to American Indians who have been raised in a culture that has historically relied on group consensus to prevent and deal with community and tribal problems. All things considered, network therapy does seem to be a viable, culturally consistent approach for preventing and dealing with psychiatric problems in Indian communities (Schoenfeld, Halevy-Martini, Hemley-Van der Velden, & Ruhf, 1985).

Thus far we have outlined three basic strategies for effective transcultural therapy with American Indians. First, making traditional treatments more accessible to Indian clients; second, selecting culturally appropriate therapy techniques and orientations; and third, integrating traditional healing methods with culturally appropriate therapy to develop a progressive yet culturally consistent therapeutic process (Rogler, Malgady, Constantino, & Blumenthal, 1987). Of the interventions reviewed, social learning and network therapy approaches appear to have greater potential for enhancing a client's interaction with others and involvement in empowerment issues. It is assumed that increased interpersonal support brought about through these interventions will ensure more lasting changes outside the context of the counseling relationship.

Indian Diversity and Mental Health Intervention

The geographic location of American Indian mental health centers also shapes the types of counseling and clinical interventions available to clients. Centers located in urban and metropolitan areas are likely to be more oriented to Indian clients representing diverse tribal orientations with varying degrees of acculturative status. Some clients are highly acculturated and have little or no knowledge about traditions, customs, and belief systems of their relatives on the reservation or in the native village. Others, usually mobile between reservation and various urban areas in search of employment or contact with extended family members, are less familiar with the demands and life-style orientations in urban areas. Often these clients are highly traditional and nativistic and, consequently, have quite different expectations from the more urbanized Indians about the role of counselors linked to urban Indian mental health clinics.

Reservation and village mental health clinics tend to be set up to respond to tribally specific customs and practices. Mental health staff and counselors are usually well known in the community and, in many cases may be related to the client through an extended family network. But, in addition to the existence of reservation and village clinics, tribal members often have access to the traditional healing systems outlined earlier, which are often preferred over the clinics. Occasionally, clients will receive services from the two entities in the hope of balancing the effectiveness of the "treatment" orientations, thus assuring that the traditional approach will cure a part of the problem not accessible by the conventional counselor.

To assist one in understanding the complexities of urban and reservation mental health services, material was obtained from Ryan and Ryan (1982) describing the circumstances one is likely to find in certain settings. These descriptions are highly condensed and are provided with the understanding that both traditional and conventional services will vary considerably from one community to the next depending, of course, on a multitude of circumstances.

The following cases describe types of Indian mental health clients and the kinds of situations that may give counselors problems. Furthermore, the following cases represent two of the acculturative styles. The first case illustrates reactive depression not directly related to culture; the second illustrates existential anxiety that only cultural knowledge can illuminate.

Client one was a fifty-six-year-old Ojibwa Indian woman who first came to an urban Indian mental health clinic in 1980. She was categorized as assimilated according to acculturation criteria because she was born on an Ojibwa reservation, but moved to an urban area with her family while she was still in high school. In November 1979, her father died of cancer, and she and her son moved to the city to help care for her elderly mother. In January 1980, her daughter was permanently disabled in an automobile accident that also claimed the life of her nephew. In March 1980, her eighteen-year-old son committed suicide. At the time of her first visit, she had been a widow for six years. The client suffered so much grief that she was hospitalized for reactive depression for five days at a crisis unit and was subsequently referred to a mental health clinic.

The two-year therapeutic intervention included antidepressant medication and grief therapy to help her deal with the multiple tragedies in her family. Social cognitive therapy was used to assist her acceptance and understanding of the facts that her daughter was not going to get better and that she was not responsible for her son's suicide. The next level of therapy involved behavioral and social skills training, to assist her in reentering the social sphere and receiving available community support for self-esteem enhancement. At the time of the report she had been working full time for approximately eight months and was functioning very well in the community. Her prognosis was excellent.

Client two was a twenty-eight-year-old Lakota Sioux woman who was born and lived on a reservation until she was nine years old, when she went to an off-reservation elementary boarding school for three years. She is the oldest of seven children. Her mother is an alcoholic, and the seven siblings have different fathers. From the time the client was four years old, she had been sexually abused by her mother's boyfriends. She lived with her grandparents for brief periods with some of her other siblings. When she was thirteen years of age, her mother moved the family to the city. The client married a White man who had a stable position in county government.

When the client returned to her reservation to attend her grandfather's memorial she was ridiculed by her relatives as being "White." She came to the IHS clinic and asked a physician for tranquilizers because she was afraid she was going to have a breakdown. She told the doctor that her biggest problem was not understanding why her relatives would not accept her and why they considered her White. Her newly ascribed marginal acculturation status haunted her.

The non-Indian physician could not understand how being considered White was her major concern when her other problems seemed much more overwhelming to him. The client in this instance needed to be accepted by the Indian community because she rarely felt accepted by the dominant society. Network therapy could have been employed to help her relatives realize how being called White diminished the client's dignity and ethnic identity at a particularly vulnerable time. Until she encounters a counselor willing to work through various stages of her identity confusion (preferably with the help of social systems strategies), this client's prognosis is very grim.

Both culturally appropriate and inappropriate interventions commonly used in counseling Indians have been highlighted here. In the first case a combination of cognitive and behavioral therapies were employed with concern for the client's social system noted throughout treatment. Knowledge of Ojibwa beliefs about death and the grieving process was essential for the grief therapy to be effective (Densmore, 1979). In the second case treatment did not take place because of the lack of sensitivity over the importance of Indian identity and community acceptance (Trimble, 1987b) on the part of the physician. Had rapport been established during the initial hospital contact, the need for network or family therapy might have been determined. Collaboration with an elder or community leader could have sped the process along. Certainly, talk therapy alone concerning the client's identity and community acceptance, or behavior therapy alone over her reentry into the Siouan community is contraindicated.

Factors such as these can be highlighted in case material analyzed within a cultural framework. Huang and Gibbs (1989) suggest the need to first determine cultural and familial attitudes toward the problem and toward help-seeking behavior and services. They encourage counselors to consider the adaptiveness of the presenting behavior in the ecological environment and to assess the cultural congruity among the client, the family, and the community. Possible identity conflicts in culturally dissonant contexts should be assessed. Finally, the appropriateness of differential diagnostic criteria and counseling interventions within a cultural context must be explored. Further case material on American

Indians can be found in Beiser (1985), Jewell (1952), LaFromboise and Low (1989), Trimble and Fleming (1989), and Tyler and Thompson (1965).

Implications for Counseling Training

These issues, although vitally important to the education and training of effective Indian helpers, and the implementation of mental health programs within Indian communities, are only beginning to be addressed in the counseling literature. Although some widely used counseling psychology texts and training manuals (e.g., Ivey, Ivey, & Simek-Downing, 1987) do discuss cross-cultural counseling questions and themes, the overwhelming majority do not. Instead, students are directed to cross-cultural compilation texts (e.g., Atkinson, Morton, & Sue, 1989; Pedersen, 1985; Pedersen, Draguns, Lonner, & Trimble, 1989) and courses with meager coverage of American Indian mental health material. And although the current American Psychological Association (APA) accreditation manual advises that approved doctoral programs should educate students regarding cultural and racial diversity (APA, 1986), there is no mention of a procedure for assessing doctoral candidates' cross-cultural competence or requiring particular bicultural skills and knowledge for doctoral licensure.

Often, clinicians and educators point out that they have little or no contact with American Indians. Many believe that the problems we continue to point out are germane to areas of the country where there are large Indian population concentrations. Often, East Coast practitioners are quick to note that their counterparts "in the West" should be mindful of the myriad of concerns and problems facing Indian clients. "After all," they maintain, "most of the Indians tend to live 'out west'." To an extent they are correct, for most Indian people do indeed live west of the Mississippi River. However, American Indians can be found in virtually every state, although the numbers may be small in some instances (e.g., Kentucky, Indiana, Vermont, Rhode Island, and West Virginia).

Over the years, we have found that many graduates of counseling psychology programs are thrust into settings where they occasionally are faced with Indian clients. Both urban and reservation American Indians form a sociocultural group greatly in need of specially trained psychologists who have a broad understanding of cultural and social phenomena not found in most textbooks and usually beyond the scope of most training programs. Because of their lack of sensitivity and training, few psychologists are able to work effectively with the Indian client. Consequently, the would-be client, aware of the insensitivity, fails to return, and preconceived notions about trust and apathy are needlessly reinforced. Such occasions are sufficiently numerous that many Indian clients flatly refuse to enter a counseling relationship regardless of the degree of their presenting problem. This is partly due to their previous experiences and to the word-of-mouth stories that circulate in Indian enclaves.

The integration of conventional counseling and American Indian traditional interventions raises some important questions for training programs in counseling psychology. First, how does one define community work and revive communities in terms of networks and empowerment? The way that health and psychological cure is organized among certain tribes suggests that "western" professionals must seriously look at how communities and families can organize themselves synergistically. Sarason (1972) begins to delineate the importance of a sense of community for psychologists. However, much of the current research and practice in counseling psychology among minority groups is specific to certain problems such as suicide prevention, prevention of cardiovascular and other diseases, gerontology, and so forth.

A psychologist within a native community or urban Indian community must discover the indigenous definition of community. This definition will serve as a guide for how to structure intervention within the goal of building community. Courses for psychology graduate students, then, need to examine what community means, how it is organized across diverse cultural groups, and how counseling interventions can facilitate community empowerment. Additionally, practical and internships within Indian communities are critical if professionals are to learn how Indian communities are organized, supported, and developed. Merely being of Indian descent does not in itself equip a student with such knowledge. Programs must face the need for Indian, and non-Indian, students and supervisors to experience native community life. Such an interplay between local university supervisors, students, and the Indian community will enrich all involved and challenge their expertise.

Second, how does a counseling psychologist intervene yet wait for choice? If choice is most central, then many of the anglo techniques that involve manipulation and persuasion without prior individual choice are culturally flawed. Although difficult to facilitate, collaboration with elders, medicine men and women, and other community leaders would be integral in the design of prevention and treatment activities. An ongoing relationship with these leaders would provide interns with an opportunity to create their role as interveners who find or develop choice. Such a process takes much time because the initial request for participation in developing interventions usually leads to stereotypic descriptions of needs without delineation of how to proceed and knowledge of what the community wants. An internship would provide the time.

Third, what is the role of religion in the structure of a community? In any discussion of healing and prevention in a Sioux community, for example, the issues of spirits, religion, and transcendence will arise. Within a native context, helping and health always have a religious dimension. If counseling psychology is to make an impact on native communities or train students to become competent psychologists in such communities, then they must look at religious and transcendental ways of understanding the world. Practitioners must learn to accept these understandings on their own terms rather than reduce them to psychology or physiology. An internship could provide intense exposure to religious and transcendental explanations. Supervisors must recognize such explanations as another system rather than as primitive witchcraft. A corollary concern is the need for training programs to consider seriously the requirement for students to further develop their character and "transform" themselves.

Fourth, when do cultural behaviors occur that "Western" programs misinterpret? Throughout this article, the importance of balance within communities and within helping transactions between healers and helpers has been emphasized. Such a balance always involves "gift" exchange. When one completes a ceremony of any type on the Rosebud reservation, for example, one provides a gift *(woheyaka)* to the healer, such as money, a blanket, food, artifacts, and so forth, and thus balance is created. If supervisors don't understand this custom and prohibit students from engaging in gift exchange, things go awry. Alienation results.

Fifth, what further research is needed to advance the integration of counseling psychology and American Indian tradition? Despite statistics documenting the underuse of mental health programs by American Indians that point to serious problems with the system as it exists today, there is a dearth of controlled research regarding the effectiveness of the various intervention approaches. A starting point for counseling research with American Indians is simply more descriptive research with designs adequate to separate "reservation" from "rural" from "social-class" from "acculturation" factors. Epidemiological research is needed to ascertain use rates in private, state, local, and federal agencies other than the Indian Health Service and the Bureau of Indian Affairs. Cross-tribal studies are almost nonexistent for major Indian mental health problems.

Research typically conducted by counseling psychologists could shed light on a number of important issues. Consistent findings concerning Indian preference for same-race counselors have yet to be found. A clearer articulation of the culturally relevant Indian counseling style operationalized by Dauphinais (1981) would be helpful. There is also a strong need for research on the process of social support (or lack of it) among urban Indians of various ages and backgrounds. Longitudinal studies would be particularly useful in beginning to identify the antecedents of social isolation and the potency of various sources of cultural and social support for Indian clients and their families. Also, attention to the coping styles and life-styles of biculturally competent Indians is necessary for a shift in focus away from deficit hypotheses to the design of interventions that build on the "natural" strengths of Indian people and communities.

Implications and Conclusions

Throughout this article we have provided a good deal of information concerning the counseling process and related issues that focus on the first American—the American Indian. Our main intent was to draw attention to the many problems facing would-be (Indian) clients as they might exist in a variety of settings. The problems remain and are likely to continue well into the future.

Many of the points we raise in this article are not exclusive to American Indians. Counseling-related articles written about Asian-, African-, and

Hispanic/Latino-Americans often raise many of the same points we do (cf. Atkinson, Morton, & Sue, 1989; Pedersen, 1985). From an educational and training perspective, it makes sense to include material about Indians if for no other reason than to expand a prospective counselor's knowledge about an often overlooked and sometimes ignored segment of our overall population. Moreover, a good deal of positive transfer can occur when one compares and contrasts counseling information about one culture to another. The field of counseling psychology stands to gain a great deal when the culturally unique characteristics of a population are reflected against current wisdom and conventional forms of counseling styles.

Our recommendation to expand the knowledge of counselor educators and practitioners is a modest one. We also recognize that the status of current research addresses some important concerns, and much more empirical study is clearly necessary. It is, admittedly, a somewhat difficult task to control for all the variables and contingencies within the mental health networks of Indian people in order to come up with firm conclusions about what works and what does not. We believe, however, that we have provided a framework that can serve as a guide for those keenly interested in pursuing work in this area.

Reference Note

1. In this study a culturally relevant counseling style consisted primarily of direct guidance and approval/reassurance responses with incidental use of restatements and open questions according to the Hill Counselor Response Category System (Hill, 1978).

References

Akao, S. F. (1984). Biculturalism and barriers to learning among Michigan Indian adult students. (Doctoral dissertation. Michigan State University, 1984). *Dissertation Abstracts International, 44,* 3572A.

Allen, P. G. (1986). *The sacred hoop; Recovering the feminine in American Indian traditions.* Boston, MA: Beacon.

American Psychological Association (1986). *Accreditation handbook.* Washington, DC: American Psychological Association Committee on Accreditation and Accreditation Office.

Assault on the peaceful: Indian child abuse. (1988, December 26). *Newsweek,* p. 31.

Atkinson, D. R., Furlong, M. J., & Poston, W. C. (1986). Afro American preferences for counselor characteristics. *Journal of Counseling Psychology, 33,* 326–330.

Atkinson, D. R., Morton, G., & Sue, D. W. (1989). *Counseling American minorities* (3rd ed.). Dubuque, IA: William C. Brown.

Atkinson, D. R., Poston, W. C., Furlong, M. J., & Mercado, P. (1989). Ethnic group preferences for counselor characteristics. *Journal of Counseling Psychology, 36,* 68–72.

Attneave, C. L. (1969). Therapy in tribal settings and urban network intervention. *Family Process, 8,* 192–210.

Bach, P. J., & Bornstein, P. H. (1981). A social learning rationale and suggestions for behavioral treatment with American Indian alcohol abusers. *Addictive Behaviors, 6,* 75–81.

Basso, K. (1970). "To give up on words": Silence in western Apache culture. *Southwestern Journal of Anthropology, 26,* 213–230.

Beiser, M. (1985). The grieving witch: A framework for applying principles of cultural psychiatry to clinical practice. *Canadian Journal of Psychiatry, 30,* 130–141.

Belgarde, M., & LaFromboise, P. (1988, April). Zuni adolescent suicide prevention project. In K. Swisher (Chair). *Sociocultural parameters affecting program development in American Indian/Alaskan Native schools.* Symposium conducted at the meeting of the American Educational Research Association, New Orleans, LA.

Bennett, S. K., BigFoot, D. S., & Thurman, P. J. (1989, August). *American Indian client preference for counselor attributes.* Paper presented at the meeting of the American Psychological Association, New Orleans, LA.

BigFoot, D. S. (1989). *Parent training for American Indian families.* Unpublished doctoral dissertation, University of Oklahoma, Norman, OK.

Bishop, J. B., & Richards, T. F. (1987). Counselor intake judgments about White and Black clients in a university counseling center. *Journal of Counseling Psychology, 34,* 96–98.

Bobo, J. K., Cvetkovich, G., Trimble, J. E., Gilchrist, L. D., & Schinke, S. (1987). Cross-cultural service delivery to minority communities. *Journal of Community Psychology, 15,* 501–514.

Bryde, J. (1971). *Indian students and guidance.* Boston, MA: Houghton Mifflin.

Bulhan, H. A. (1985). *Frantz Fanon and the psychology of oppression.* New York: Plenum.

Carpenter, A., Lyons, C., & Miller, W. (1985). Peer-managed self-control program for prevention of alcohol abuse in American Indian high school students: A pilot evaluation study. *International Journal of the Addictions, 20,* 299–310.

Conrad, R. D., Delk, J. I., & Williams, C. (1974). Use of stimulus fading procedures in the treatment of situation specific mutism: A case study. *Journal of Behavior Therapy and Experimental Psychiatry, 5,* 99–100.

Dauphinais, P. (1981). *Effects of counselor race and counselor response style of American Indian youths' perception of counselor effectiveness.* Unpublished doctoral dissertation, University of Oklahoma, Norman, OK.

Dauphinais, P., Dauphinais, I., & Rowe, W. (1981). Effects of race and communication style of Indian perceptions of counselor effectiveness. *Counselor Education and Supervision, 20,* 37–46.

Dauphinais, P., LaFromboise, T., & Rowe, W. (1980) Perceived problems and sources of help for American Indian students. *Counselor Education and Supervision, 21,* 31–46.

David, K. (1976). The use of social learning theory in preventing intercultural adjustment problems. In P. Pedersen, W. Lonner, & J. Draguns (Eds.). *Counseling across cultures* (pp. 123–138). Honolulu: University Press of Hawaii.

Densmore, F. (1979). *Chippewa customs.* Minneapolis: Minnesota Historical Society.

Dinges, N., Trimble, J., Manson, S., & Pasquale, F. (1981). Counseling and psychotherapy with American Indians and Alaskan Natives. In A. Marsella & P. Pedersen (eds.), *Cross-cultural counseling and psychotherapy* (pp. 243–276). New York: Pergamon.

Fixico, M. (1985). The road to middle class Indian America. In C. E. Trafzer (Ed.), *American Indian identity: Today's changing perspectives* (pp. 29–37). Sacramento, CA: Sierra Oaks Publishing Company.

Goldstein, M. S., & Donaldson, D. J. (1979). Exporting professionalism: A case study of medical education. *Journal of Health and Social Behavior, 20,* 322–337.

Green, R. (1983). *Native American women: A contextual bibliography.* Bloomington: Indiana University Press.

Hallowell, A. I. (1950). Values, acculturation and mental health. *American Journal of Orthopsychiatry, 20,* 732–743.

Hammerschlag, C. A. (1988). *The dancing healers: A doctor's journey of healing with Native Americans.* San Francisco: Harper & Row.

Hill, C. E. (1978). Development of a counselor verbal response category system. *Journal of Counseling Psychology, 25,* 461–468.

Huang, L. N., & Gibbs, J. T. (1989). Multicultural perspectives on two clinical cases. In J. T. Gibbs & L. N. Huang (Eds.) *Children of color: Psychological intervention with minority youth* (pp. 351–374). San Francisco: Jossey-Bass.

Ivey, A., Ivey, M. B., & Simek-Downing, L. (1987). *Counseling and psychotherapy: Integrating skills, theory, and practice* (2nd ed.) Englewood Cliffs, NJ: Prentice-Hall.

Jewell, D. P. (1952). A case of a "psychotic" Navaho Indian male. *Human Organization, 11,* 32–36.

Jilek-Aall, L. (1976). The western psychiatrist and his non-western clientele. *Canadian Psychiatric Association Journal, 21,* 353–359.

Kaplan, B., & Johnson, D. (1964). The social meaning of Navajo psychopathology and psychotherapy. In A. Kiev (Ed.), *Magic, Faith. and healing* (pp. 203–229). New York: Free Press.

Katz, R., & Rolde, E. (1981). Community alternatives to psychotherapy. *Psychotherapy, Theory, Research and Practice, 18,* 365–374.

Kelso, D. R., & Attneave, C. L. (1981). *Bibliography of North American Indian mental health.* Westport, CT: Greenwood.

LaBarre, W. (1964). Confessions as cathartic therapy in American Indian tribes. In A. Kiev (Ed.) *Magic, faith, and healing* (pp. 36–49). New York: Free Press.

LaFromboise, T. D. (1983). *Assertion training with American Indians.* Las Cruces, NM: ERIC Clearinghouse on Rural Education and Small Schools.

LaFromboise, T. D. (1988). American Indian mental health policy. *American Psychologist, 43,* 388–397.

LaFromboise, T. D. (1989). *Circle of women: Professional skills training with American Indian women.* Newton, MA: Women's Educational Equity Act Publishing Center.

LaFromboise, T., Dauphinais, P., & Lujan, P. (1981). Verbal indicators of insincerity as perceived by American Indians. *Journal of Non-White Concerns, 9,* 94–97.

LaFromboise, T., Dauphinais, P., & Rowe, W. (1980). Indian students' perceptions of positive helper attributes. *Journal of American Indian Education, 19,* 11–16.

LaFromboise, T., & Dixon, D. (1981). American Indian perceptions of trustworthiness in a counseling interview. *Journal of Counseling Psychology, 28,* 135–139.

LaFromboise, T., & LaFromboise, R. (1982). Critical legal and social responsibilities facing Native Americans. In I. French (Ed.). *Indians and criminal justice* (pp. 21–38). Totowa, NJ: Allanheld, Osmun & Company.

LaFromboise, T. D., & Low, K. G. (1989). American Indian children and adolescents. In J. T. Gibbs & L. N. Huang (Eds.) *Children of color: Psychological interventions with minority youth* (pp. 114–147). San Francisco: Jossey-Bass.

LaFromboise, T., & Rowe, W. (1983). Skills training for bicultural competence: Rationale and application. *Journal of Counseling Psychology, 30,* 589–595.

Leigh, J. W. (1982). *Empowerment as a process.* Unpublished manuscript, University of Washington School of Social Work. Seattle.

Littrell, J., & Liettrell, M. (1982). American Indian and Caucasian students preferences for counselors: Effects of counselor dress and sex. J*ournal of Counseling Psychology, 29,* 48–57.

Lockhart, B. (1981). Historic distrust and the counseling of American Indian and Alaska Natives. *White Cloud Journal, 2,* 31–34.

Locust, C. (1988). Wounding the spirit: Discrimination and traditional American Indian belief systems. *Harvard Educational Review, 58,* 315–330.

Lum, D. (1986). *Social work practice and people of color: A process-stage approach.* Monterey, CA: Brooks/Cole.

Manson, S., Dinges, N., Lujan, C., Piño, M., Wright, B., Pepion, K., & Montoya, V, (1989). *Stress and coping among American Indian and Alaska Native college students.* Unpublished manuscript. University of Colorado, National center for American Indian and Alaska Native Mental Health Research. Denver.

Manson, S. M., & Trimble, J. E. (1982). American Indian and Alaska Native communities: Past efforts, future inquiries. In L. Snowden (Ed.). *Reaching the underserved: Mental health needs of neglected populations* (pp. 143–164). Beverly Hills, CA: Sage.

Manson, S. M., Walker, R. D., & Kivlahan, D. R. (1987). Psychiatric assessment and treatment of American Indian and Alaska Native youth. *Hospital and Community Psychology, 38,* 165–173.

McCarty, T. L. (1985). Bilingual-bicultural education in a Navajo community. (Doctoral dissertation, Arizona State University). *Dissertation Abstracts International, 45,* 3534A.

McFee, M. (1968). The 150% man, a product of Blackfeet acculturation. *American Anthropologist, 70,* 1096–1107.

Mohatt, G. V. (1978, Spring). Rosebud medicine men and associates. *Wassaja.*

Molester put lasting scars on Hopi tribe. (1987, June 1). *Arizona Republic,* p. 1.

Moses, L. G., & Wilson, R. (1985). *Indian lives: Essays on nineteenth- and twentieth-century Native American leaders.* Albuquerque, NM: University of New Mexico Press.

Neliegh, G. (1988). Major mental disorders and behavior among American Indians and Alaska Natives. *Behavioral Health Issues among American Indians and Alaska Natives: Explorations of the Frontiers of the Biobehavioral Sciences, 1*(1), 116–150.

Nelson, S. (1988). *A national plan for Native American mental health services.* Rockville, MD: Indian Health Service. Office of Health Promotion. Mental Health Planning Branch.

Pedersen, P. (Ed.) (1985). *Handbook of cross-cultural counseling and psychotherapy.* Westport, CT: Greenwood.

Pedersen, P. B., Draguns, J. G., Lonner, W. J., & Trimble, J. E. (Eds.) (1989). *Counseling across cultures* (3rd ed.). Honolulu: University Press of Hawaii.

Penistone, E., & Burman, W. (1978). Relaxation and assertive training as treatment for a psychosomatic American Indian patient. *White Cloud Journal, 1*(1), 7–10.

Polgar, S. (1960). Biculturation of Mesquakie teenage boys. *American Anthropologist, 62,* 217–235.

Ponterotto, J. G., Alexander, C., & Hinkston, J. (1988). Afro American preferences for counselor characteristics: A replication and extension. *Journal of Counseling Psychology, 35,* 175–182.

Powers, W. K. (1982). *Yuwipi. vision and experience in Oglala ritual.* Lincoln: University of Nebraska Press.

Primeaux, M. H. (1977). American Indian health care practices: A cross-cultural perspective. *Nursing Clinics of North America, 12,* 55–65.

Rappaport, J. (1981). In praise of paradox: A social policy of empowerment over prevention. *American Journal of Community Psychology, 9,* 1–25.

Rappaport, J. (1987). Terms of empowerment/examples of prevention: Towards a theory of community psychology. *American Journal of Community Psychology, 15,* 121–147.

Reuveni, U. (1979). *Networking families in crisis.* New York: Human Sciences Press.

Rhoades, E. R., Marshall, M., Attneave, C., Fchohawk, M., Bjork, J., & Beiser, M. (1980). Mental health problems of American Indians seen in outpatient facilities of the Indian Health Services, 1975. *Public Health Reports, 95*(4), 329–335.

Rogler, L., Malgady, R., Constantino, G., & Blumenthal, R. (1987). What do culturally sensitive mental health services mean? The case of Hispanics. *American Psychologist, 42,* 565–570.

Roy, C., Chaudhuri, A., & Irvine, O. (1970). The prevalence of mental disorders among Saskatchewan Indians. *Journal of Cross-Cultural Psychology, 1,* 383–392.

Ryan, L., & Ryan, R. (1982). *Mental health and the urban Indian.* Unpublished manuscript.

Sampath, B. M. (1974). Prevalence of psychiatric disorders in a southern Baffin Island Eskimo settlement. *Canadian Psychiatric Association Journal, 19,* 363–367.

Sandner, D. F. (1978). Navajo medicine. *Human Nature, 1,* 54–62.

Sarason, S. (1972). *The creation of settings and future societies.* San Francisco: Jossey-Bass.

Schinke, S. P., Moncher, M. S., Holden, G. W., Botvin, G. J., & Orlandi, M. A. (1989). American Indian youth and substance abuse: Tobacco use problems, risk factors and preventive interventions. *Health Education Research, Theory and Practice, 4,* 137–144.

Schinke, S. P., Orlandi, M. A., Botvin, G. J., Gilchrist, L. D., Trimble, J. E., & Locklear, V. S. (1988). Preventing substance abuse among American Indian adolescents: A bicultural competence skills approach. *Journal of Counseling Psychology, 35,* 87–90.

Schinke, S. P., Schilling, R. F., Palleja, J., & Zayas, L. H. (1987). Prevention research among ethnic-racial minority group adolescents. *Behavior Therapist, 10,* 151–155.

Schoenfeld, P., Halevy-Martini, J., Hemley-Van der Velden, E., & Ruhf, L. (1985). Network therapy: An outcome study of twelve social networks. *Journal of Community Psychology, 13,* 281–287.

Schoenfeld, L. S., Lyerly, R. J., & Miller, S. I. (1971). We like us. *Mental Hygiene, 55,* 171–173.

Shore, J. H., Kinzie, J. D., Hampson, D., & Pattison, E. M. (1973). Psychiatric epidemiology of an Indian village. *Psychiatry, 36,* 70–81.

Solomon, G., Heisberger, J., & Winer, J. L. (1981). Confidentiality issues in rural community mental health. *Journal of Rural Community Psychology, 2*(1), 17–31.

Speck, R., & Attneave, C. (1973). *Family networks: Retribalization and healing*. New York: Random House.

Spindler, L., & Spindler, G. (1958). Male and female adaptations in culture change. *American Anthropologist, 60,* 217–233.

Sue, S., Allen, D. B., & Conaway, L. (1978). The responsiveness and equality of mental health care to Chicanos and Native Americans. *American Journal of Community Psychiatry, 6,* 137–146.

Trimble, J. E. (1981). Value differentials and their importance in counseling American Indians. In P. Pedersen, J. Draguns, W. Lonner, & J. Trimble (Eds.) *Counseling across cultures* (2nd ed., pp. 203–226). Honolulu: University Press of Hawaii.

Trimble, J. E. (1987a). American Indians and interethnic conflict. In J. Boucher, D. Landis, & K. Clark (Eds.) *Ethnic conflict: International perspectives* (pp. 208–230). Newbury Park, CA: Sage.

Trimble, J. E. (1987b). Self-perception and perceived alienation among American Indians. *Journal of Community Psychology, 15,* 316–333.

Trimble, J. E. (1988). Stereotypic images. American Indians and prejudice. In P. Katz & D. Taylor (Eds.), *Eliminating racism and prejudice* (pp. 210–236). New York: Pergamon.

Trimble, J. E., & Fleming, C. (1989). Providing counseling services for Native American Indians: Client, counselor, and community characteristics. In P. Pedersen, I. Draguns, W. Lonner, & J. Trimble (Eds.). *Counseling across cultures* (3rd ed., pp. 145–168). Honolulu: University Press of Hawaii.

Trimble, J. E., & Hayes, S. (1984), Mental health intervention in the psychosocial contexts of American Indian communities. In W. O'Conner & B. Lubin (Eds.), *Ecological approaches to clinical and community psychology* (pp. 293–321). New York: Wiley.

Trimble, J. E., & LaFromboise, T. D. (1985). American Indians and the counseling process: Culture, adaptation, and style. In P. Pedersen (Ed.), *Handbook of cross-cultural mental health services* (pp. 127–134). Beverly Hills, CA: Sage.

Trimble, J. E., Manson, S. M., Dinges, N. G., & Medicine, B. (1984). American Indian conceptions of mental health: Reflections and directions. In P. Pedersen, N. Sartorius, & A. Marsella (Eds.), *Mental health services: The cross cultural context* (pp. l99–220). Beverly Hills, CA: Sage.

Trimble, J. E., Padilla, A., & Bell, C. (Eds.). (1987). *Drug abuse among ethnic minorities* (DHHS Publication No. ADM 87-1474). Rockville, MD: National Institute on Drug Abuse.

Tyler, I. M., & Thompson, S. D. (1965). Cultural factors in casework treatment of a Navajo mental patient. *Social Casework, 46,* 215–220.

U.S. Congress. Office of Technology Assessment. (1990). *Indian adolescent mental health* (OTA-H-446). Washington, DC: U.S. Government Printing Office.

Walker, J. R. (1980) *Lakota belief and ritual*. Lincoln: University of Nebraska Press.

Wallace, A. (1958). Dreams and wishes of the soul: A type of psychoanalytic theory among seventeenth century Iroquois. *American Anthropologist, 60,* 234–248.

Wax, R. H., & Thomas, R. K. (1961). American Indians and White people. *Phylon, 22,* 305–317.

9

The Path of Good Medicine: Understanding and Counseling Native American Indians

J. T. Garrett and Michael Walkingstick Garrett

This article presents a brief overview of Native American cultural values, beliefs, and practices concerning the tribe, elders, family, and spirituality. Native American Indian communication style, humor, and cultural commitment are briefly discussed and recommendations are given for counseling with Native American Indians.

"While walking in the Smoky Mountains one brisk fall day, an Elder Medicine Man came upon a young Indian man sitting on the ground. He asked the young man, 'Why is it that you are sitting here like this?' sensing that the young man was troubled by something. 'I am sitting here because I do not know which way to go,' answered the young man. 'You do know the path of the Sun,' replied the Elder. 'Yes,' said the young man, 'but I do not know which direction I am to follow.'

"The Elder Medicine Man sat with the young Indian man and reminded him of the lessons offered by each of the Four Directions. He suggested that the young man spend four days and four nights fasting in order to seek the lessons in each of the different directions, one for each night. On the morning of the fifth day, the young man was to nourish his body and resume his journey in the direction that seemed best as revealed in his vision. 'How will I know if I am moving in the right direction?' asked the young man. 'Home is wherever you are,' said the Elder, smiling. 'Stay in harmony and balance in your life's journey, and may the spirits guide you as you walk the path of Good Medicine.'" Story told by J. T. Garrett, Medicine Elder of the Eastern Band of Cherokee.

Reprinted from *Journal of Multicultural Counseling and Development, 22,* 1994, 134–144.

Over 2.3 million Native American Indians live in the United States and the population is steadily growing (U.S. Bureau of the Census, 1991). Native American Indians account for only about 1% of the total U.S. population, yet they have been described as representing "fifty percent of the diversity" that exists in this country (Hodgkinson. 1990). This diversity is illustrated by 252 languages, 505 federally recognized tribes, and 365 state recognized tribes (Herring, 1990; Thomason, 1991). The diversity is also seen in varying levels of cultural commitment among the members of a given tribe or nation based on variances in value orientation (Johnson & Lashley, 1989; LaFromboise, Trimble, & Mohatt, 1990). Nevertheless, a prevailing sense of "Indianness" based on a common worldview seems to bind Native American Indians together as a people of many peoples.

Native American Indian Values

Through value consensus, traditional Native American Indians have consistently resisted acculturation into mainstream society, possibly more than any other ethnic minority group (Herring, 1990; Sanders, 1987). Generally, Native American Indian traditional values consist of sharing, cooperation, being, the group and extended family, noninterference, harmony with nature, a time orientation toward living in the present, preference for explanation of natural phenomena according to the supernatural, and a deep respect for elders (DuBray, 1985; Pedigo, 1983; Sanders, 1987; Trimble, 1981). By contrast, mainstream values (i.e.. European American values) emphasize saving, domination, competition and aggression, doing, individualism and the nuclear family, mastery over nature, a time orientation toward living for the future, a preference for scientific explanations of everything, as well as "clock-watching," winning as much as possible, and reverence of youth (DuBray, 1985; Sanders, 1987). Thus, a diametrical opposition between some very basic ways of living becomes apparent.

Many of the problems facing Native American Indians today result from a vast cultural conflict between Native American Indians and mainstream American culture. Many Native American Indians experience conflict when they either try to internalize unfamiliar values of the dominant society or to practice the traditional roles necessary for the preservation of traditional values and practices. The chasm that exists between mainstream expectations and the cultural values of Native American Indians can be referred to as "cultural discontinuity." This conflict leaves many Native American Indian people "not knowing which way to go."

For example, a cultural conflict is seen in the concept of cooperation and sharing. Cultural views concerning property accentuate the Native American Indian belief that whatever belongs to the individual also belongs to the group. Native American Indian people frequently share or give their possessions away. They also participate well in group activities that emphasize cooperation and group harmony. Competition for the sake of "beating" others or "showing others up" is highly frowned on. The idea of seeking group harmony through cooperation and sharing takes precedence above all else.

Another value conflict is found in areas of modesty. Individual praise is welcomed if it has been earned, but this praise must come from someone else, usually in the presence of the group. Self-serving behaviors (e.g., loud behavior or boasting) are discouraged. An individual who is singled out or "put on the spot" will usually drop the head and eyes as a sign of respect for any elder or honored person. Culturally insensitive counselors and educators generally regard this behavior as being disrespectful and rude or as having something to hide.

Native American Indian culture also emphasizes *being* over *doing* (Garrett & Garrett, 1993). The concept of being says, "It's enough just to be; our purpose in life is to develop the inner self." Meanwhile, the concept of doing advocates "Be active; work hard, apply yourself fully and your efforts will be rewarded" (Kluckhohn & Strodtbeck, 1961; Pedersen, 1988). Whereas mainstream culture asks, "What do you do for a living?" as an indicator of who someone is, Native American Indian culture asks simply, "Where do you come from, who's your family?" Native American Indians tend "to choose being over doing, which implies that intrinsic worth is more important than education, status, power, or wealth" (DuBray, 1985, p. 35).

The concept of being is also imbedded in the Native American Indian's time orientation. Native American Indians are very present oriented—living in the now (DuBray, 1985). They do not live by the clock as people do in mainstream U.S. society. So-called "Indian time" says that things begin when everyone has arrived and are ready, and things end when they are finished.

The Tribe

Native American Indians experience a unique relationship between the tribe and themselves. The extended family (at least three generations) and tribal group take precedence over all else. The tribe is an inter-dependent system of people who perceive themselves as parts of the greater whole rather than as a whole consisting of individual parts. Likewise, Native American Indians judge themselves and their actions according to whether or not they are benefitting the tribe and its continued harmonious functioning.

Among tribal members, a strong sense of belonging relies on cultural values, social relationships, as well as a sacred sense of connection with one's ancestry and tribal history. In mainstream society, worth and status are based on what you do or what you have achieved. For Native American Indians, who you are is where you come from. Native American Indians essentially believe that "If you know my family, clan, tribe, then you know me" (Iron Eye Dudley, 1992). As a result, many who are asked to describe themselves will most likely describe some aspect of their family or tribal heritage and affiliation.

The Importance of Elders

Elders are honored and respected because of the lifetime's worth of wisdom they have acquired. Elders have always played a vital role in the continuance of tribal community by functioning as parent, teacher, community leader, and spiritual guide. Traditionally, the primary responsibility of grandparents is to rear children and that of the parents is to provide economic support. The Native American Indian family is based on a multigenerational support system of interdependence that provides cultural continuity for all.

For mainstream society, one's worth is measured according to ambition and accomplishment. The inactivity associated with old age has coincided with a general devaluing of elders in this society. Currently, many Native American Indian children are influenced, among other things, by mainstream attitudes promoting the worthlessness of elders. Essentially, Native American Indian children learn to perceive elders, the keepers of the sacred ways, as being useless or "all washed up." The effects of mainstream views of elder people have, in many cases, split the Native American Indian multigenerational support system by removing elders from their roles as honored persons in the community.

The Meaning of Family

One of the most important sources of connection and intrinsic worth is the family. Because Native American Indian culture is one in which survival of the individual is synonymous with that of the community, the family holds a prominent place in the lives of Native American Indians. Family relationships include much more than the biological connections of the nuclear family. For example, the claiming of nonblood relatives or "fictive kin" as family members is commonly practiced (Iron Eye Dudley, 1992). Also, a Native American Indian child may live in several different households at various times. Grandparents, aunts, uncles, and community members are all responsible for rearing the children.

Native American Indian perceptions of family are universal. Family extends well beyond one's immediate relatives to extended relatives through the second cousin, clan members, community members, all living creatures in this world, nature as a whole, and the universe itself. The entire universe is thought of as a family with each member serving a useful and necessary function.

Animals are thought of as our four-legged brothers and sisters; the Earth is our Mother; the sky, Father; the Moon, Grandmother; and the Sun, Grandfather to all living creatures. Native American Indians believe the connection we have with others (not just people) can be considered nothing short of sacred. For Native American Indians, *relation* is something that extends beyond that of biological connection to one of a more spiritual nature. For Native American Indians, family symbolizes a unique approach to the entire process of living.

Spirituality

Native American Indians look on all things as having life, as having spiritual energy and importance. A fundamental belief is that all things are connected. The universe consists of a balance among all of these things and a continuous flow or cycling of this energy. Native American Indians believe that we have a sacred relationship with the universe that is to be honored. All things are connected, all things have life, and all things are worthy of respect and reverence.

Spirituality focuses on the harmony that comes from our connection with all parts of the universe in which everything has the purpose and value exemplary of "personhood" including plants (e.g., "tree people"), animals ("our four-legged brothers and sisters"), rocks and minerals ("rock people"), the land ("Mother Earth"), the winds ("the Four powers"), "Father Sky," "Grandfather Sun," "Grandmother Moon," "The Red Thunder Boys" (Garrett & Garrett, 1993). Within this view lies the truest sense of belonging and respect for "all of our relations."

Spiritual being essentially requires only that we seek our place in the universe; everything else will follow in good time. Because everyone and everything was created with a specific purpose to fulfill, no one should have the power to interfere or to impose on others the best path to follow.

Harmony and Balance

The circle, as a sacred symbol, reminds us that what we often see as progression or growth is, indeed, circular in nature or rather, cyclical. The entire universe moves and works in circles. Nature progresses only as long as the many ongoing and contingent cycles that permit the process of life continue in such an extraordinary and intricately balanced fashion.

At the very heart of Native American Indian worldview is the Circle of Life, represented by the Medicine Wheel. The components of the Circle of Life—spirit, nature, body, and mind—constitute the Four Directions represented in this wheel. The Circle of Life symbolizes the innumerable circles that surround us, that exist within us, and of which we are all a part. It shows us the sacred relationship we have to all living things—to life itself.

Medicine refers to "the way of things," or a way of life. We each have our own Medicine or way of life wherein we choose which of the Four Directions to focus most of our energy and how we seek our balance. The Medicine Wheel symbolizes the way of things as represented in the Four Directions, each of which stands for one aspect of living: East for spiritual, South for natural, West for physical, and North for mental. In seeking our Medicine, we are seeking a balance between these Four Directions, between ourselves and the universe. Being in harmony means being in step with the universe; being in disharmony means being out of step with the universe.

Implications for Counseling Practice

The culturally sensitive counselor or helping professional will integrate aspects of Native American Indian cultural heritage within a traditional theoretical orientation. In addition to those values and worldviews already presented, several other important considerations must be made when working with Native American Indian clients.

Cultural Commitment

Native American Indians differ greatly in their commitment to traditional values and customs. A great diversity exists not only between members of different tribes but also among members within a single tribe. Cultural commitment among Native American Indians has been described in the following four ways (adapted from LaFromboise et al., 1990, p. 638):

1. *Traditional*—those who generally speak and think in their native language; they practice only traditional beliefs and values.
2. *Transitional*—those who generally speak both native language and English; they do not fully accept the cultural heritage of their tribal group nor identify completely with mainstream culture.
3. *Bicultural*—those who are generally accepted by dominant society; they are simultaneously able to know, accept, and practice both mainstream values and traditional values and beliefs.
4. *Assimilated*—those who are generally accepted by dominant society; they embrace only mainstream culture.

Keeping this in mind, counselors and educators working with Native American Indians must ascertain the following: (a) degree of cultural commitment; (b) whether the person comes from a reservation, rural, or urban setting; and (c) tribal structure, customs, and beliefs that are relevant to the situation.

View of Illness

Locust (1985) described the Native American Indian view of illness in the following manner:

> Native American Indians believe that each individual chooses to make himself well or to make himself unwell. If one stays in harmony, keeps all the tribal laws and all the sacred laws, one's spirit will be so strong that negativity will be unable to affect it. If one chooses to let anger or jealousy or self-pity control him, he has created disharmony for himself. Being in control of one's emotional responses is necessary if one is to remain in harmony. Once harmony is broken, however, the spiritual self is weakened and one becomes vulnerable to physical illness, mental and/or emotional upsets, and the disharmony projected by others. (p. 14)

When Native American Indians go to the Medicine Man (or Medicine Woman) for healing, they may just sit together and talk for awhile. Together, they decide exactly what the problem is, and the Medicine Man will either suggest ways of dealing with it or simply ask that the person do something (e.g., a specific task). Two very important things the Medicine Man will include as part of the healing process are (a) a support system for the person (i.e., family, friends, or other trusted persons); and (b) some type of ceremony or ritual that helps restore the person to harmony and balance with the environment.

Garrett (1991) described the unique system of health service practiced by the Cherokee Native American Indian hospital in North Carolina:

> Anybody in the hospital who wanted to go to a medicine man, or have a medicine man visit them, could do so, as long as the mode of treatment didn't interfere with the treatment modality used by the clinicians in the hospital. And if it did, then the patient could sign a waiver, or release themselves from the care of the hospital physicians. That way they could make a clear choice about which medicine pathway they wanted to follow. That was the whole idea. There was no judgment made about the way they were going. It gave the choice back to them, so that they could become apart of their own care. (p. 171)

Acceptance

Acceptance includes both the client's acceptance of the process and the counselor's acceptance of the client. It is important for the counselor to demonstrate sincere interest and respect for the client. It is not the counselor's responsibility to judge or act on preconceived notions.

Trustworthiness and Respect

Establishing trustworthiness means being attentive and responsive to the client, giving structure and direction to the process, and displaying respect for culturally relevant values and beliefs (LaFromboise & Dixon, 1981). Showing respect could also mean suggesting the possibility of consultation with a traditional healer. In fact, linking services could prove to be very effective. This process would be a clear demonstration of respect for traditional ways while providing a more comprehensive service.

Another way of demonstrating respect is to encourage extended family members to participate in the healing process. Working in the presence of a group, giving people a choice about the best way to proceed with the process, and encouraging the participation of family members and friends are all natural components of the traditional healing way.

Communication Style

Native American Indians emphasize a nonverbal communication style. Moderation in speech and avoidance of direct eye contact are nonverbal communicators of respect by the listener, especially for respected elders or authority figures. Traditional Native American Indian people are not rewarded for asking questions or verbally analyzing situations. Rather, they are expected to learn through patience and observation.

Native American Indians usually speak softly (if at all) and take ample time to reflect before responding. Therefore, many Native American Indians who are interacting in culturally appropriate ways may be labeled as "slow," "passive," "withdrawn," "uncooperative," "lazy," or "unassertive" by members of mainstream society. Direct confrontation is avoided because it disrupts the harmony and balance that are essential to being. Most Native American Indians will experience great discomfort with what is perceived as intrusive questioning or the demand of self-disclosure (Good Tracks, 1973). A counselor must demonstrate patience exemplified by not offering advice or interpretation without being invited. Possibilities must be described and solutions suggested with the realization that the client knows what is best to do.

In terms of the counselor-client nonverbal interaction, the counselor should attend to and subtly match the client's intonation, pace of speech, and degree of eye contact (LaFromboise et al., 1990; Thomason, 1991). Assessments of cultural commitment and tribal structure, customs, and beliefs will provide useful information on how to proceed. In any case, every Native American Indian client should be approached as an individual first.

Silence, restatement, and general lead tend to be most effective with Native American Indian clients because these methods are the least intrusive and allow plenty of room for clarification (Herring, 1990; Richardson, 1981). Because Native American Indians are taught from a very early age the importance of learning through observation, modeling and role-play are also invaluable methods.

Humor

Contrary to the stereotypical belief that Native American Indian people are solemn, stoic figures poised against a backdrop of tepees, tomahawks, and headdresses, the fact is that Native American Indian people love to laugh and display a dry sense of humor. After all, laughter relieves stress and creates an atmosphere of sharing and connectedness. Laughter is healing.

The use of exaggeration, especially in groups, is a prominent feature of Native American Indian humor. It is not uncommon for Native American Indians to leave themselves open to being teased because it serves the purpose of keeping everyone humble and a part of the group. Humor serves the purpose of reaffirming and enhancing the sense of connectedness experienced in being part of the group.

Additional Recommendations for Counseling

The following are a few additional recommendations:

- Ask permission whenever possible and always give thanks.
- Never interrupt—allow sufficient time for completion of thoughts.

- Be patient.
- Use silence whenever it seems appropriate (or even when it does not).
- Use descriptive statements rather than questioning.
- Model self-disclosure through anecdotes or short stories.
- Make use of metaphors and imagery when appropriate.

Most important, do not separate the person from the spirituality or from affiliation with the tribal group. These aspects may very well be central to how Native American Indian clients view themselves and define their world. Honor that sacred relationship by being open and respectful.

Finally, it is always important to recognize the relative nature of value judgments such as right or wrong and good or bad. "The 'correctness' of behavior can only be evaluated in terms of the particular sociocultural context in which it occurs" (Little Soldier, 1985, p. 191).

If counselors come first as students, and second, as professionals, they might be surprised at how much growth would take place by members of both worlds. Native American Indians view the "respected person" as one who acts in the most friendly, generous, considerate, and modest way (Lewis & Gingerich, 1980). We all want to "walk the path of Good Medicine," and we can always use a little help.

References

DuBray, W. H. (1985). American Indian values: Critical factor in casework. *Social Casework, 66,* 30–37.

Garrett, J. T. (1991). Where the medicine wheel meets medical science. In S. McFadden (Ed.), *Profiles in wisdom: Native elders speak about the earth* (pp. 167–179). Santa Fe, NM: Bear & Company.

Garrett, M. Walkingstick, & Garrett, J. T. (1993). *Full circle: Harmony, balance, and the healing-way.* Manuscript submitted for publication. University of North Carolina at Greensboro.

Good Tracks, J. G. (1973). Native American non-interference. *Social Work, 18,* 30–34.

Herring, R. D. (1990). Understanding Native American values: Process and content concerns for counselors. *Counseling and Values, 34,* 134–137.

Hodgkinson, H. L. (1990). *The demographics of Native Americans: One percent of the people: fifty percent of the diversity.* Washington, DC: Institute for Educational Leadership.

Iron Eye Dudley, J. (1992). *Choteau Creek: A Sioux reminiscence.* Lincoln, NE: University of Nebraska Press.

Johnson, M. E., & Lashley, K. H. (1989). Influence of Native Americans' cultural commitment on preferences for counselor ethnicity and expectations about counseling. *Journal of Multicultural Counseling and Development, 17,* 115–122.

Kluckhohn, F. R., & Strodtbeck, F. L. (1961). *Variations in value orientations.* Evanston, IL: Row, Patterson, & Co.

LaFromboise, T. D., & Dixon, D. N. (1981). American Indian perceptions of trustworthiness in a counseling interview. *Journal of Counseling Psychology, 28,* 135–139.

LaFromboise, T. D., Trimble, J. E., & Mohatt, G. V. (1990). Counseling intervention and American Indian tradition: An integrative approach. *The Counseling Psychologist, 18,* 628–654.

Lewis, R. G., & Gingerich, W. (1980). Leadership characteristics: Views of Native American and non-Native American Indian students. *Social Casework, 61,* 494–497.

Little Soldier, L. (1985). To soar with the eagles: Enculturation and acculturation of Native American Indian children. *Childhood Education,* 185–191.

Locust, C. (1985). *Native American Indian beliefs concerning health and unwellness.* (Native American Research and Training Center Monograph). Flagstaff, AZ: University of Arizona Press.

Pedersen, P. (1988). *A handbook for developing multicultural awareness.* Alexandria, VA: American Association for Counseling and Development.

Pedigo, J. (1983). Finding the meaning of Native American substance abuse: Implications for community prevention. *Personnel and Guidance Journal, 61,* 273–277.

Richardson, E. H. (1981). Cultural and historical perspectives in counseling American Indians. In D. W. Sue (Ed.), *Counseling the culturally different.* New York: Wiley.

Sanders, D. (1987). Cultural conflicts: An important factor in the academic failures of American Indian students. *Journal of Multicultural Counseling and Development, 15,* 81–90.

Thomason, T. C. (1991). Counseling Native Americans: An introduction for non-Native American counselors. *Journal of Counseling and Development, 69,* 321–327.

Trimble, J. E. (1981). Value differentials and their importance in counseling American Indians. In P. Pedersen, J. Draguns, W. Lonner, & J. Trimble, (Eds.), *Counseling across cultures* (2nd ed., pp. 203–226). Honolulu, HI: University Press of Hawaii.

U.S. Bureau of the Census. (1991). *1990 Census counts of American Indians, Eskimos, or Aleuts and American Indian and Alaska Native areas.* Washington, DC: Author.

The American Indian Client
Cases and Questions

1. While working as a counselor in a predominantly European American high school, a female teacher seeks your advice concerning two of her American Indian students. Both appear disinterested in course work, participate minimally in class discussions, never raise their hands to answer questions, and appear withdrawn. They are also doing poor in their course work and seem to have most difficulty with competitive activities such as "debates" and "spelling bees," favorite teaching ploys used by the teacher. The teacher grades on student participation and performance in the classroom, therefore she is concerned that they will get failing grades.

    a) What American Indian cultural values might account for the classroom behavior of the two students? For example, in reading the three chapters, can you pick out cultural assumptions that might be antagonistic to the methods being employed by the teacher?
    b) Communication style differences might offer an additional method of analysis for this case. What hidden assumptions are associated with debates and spelling bees? (Hint: European American teaching methods tend to place a high premium on individual competition.)
    c) It may prove challenging, but can you think of how you would create a learning environment for the two American Indian students that would be culturally consistent with Native values and learning styles?

2. You are working at a mental health clinic near an American Indian community. For the first time in your career, a young American Indian, Johnny Lonetree, comes to you for help. He appears depressed, lonely, and admits to abusing alcohol. You have seen him for three sessions, but find the process of counseling slow and time consuming. Johnny has difficulty self-disclosing, is relatively nonverbal, and makes you uncomfortable with his long periods of silence. You are becoming increasingly impatient with his "resistance to counseling" and are considering taking a more confrontive approach.

    a) What unwarranted assumptions might you be making about Johnny that could be explained through an understanding of American Indian culture and communication styles?
    b) Knowing that premature termination rates are high among many American Indian clients, how might a "confrontive" approach be seen in Native culture? Why?

c) If you lack knowledge and understanding of American Indians, should
    you be working with this population? Although we can never hope to
    understand or have experience with the various diverse groups in our
    society, what might counselors do if they are in a counseling
    relationship without proper knowledge or expertise of the population?

3. You are a community social worker employed by the BIA to work with
    reservation Indian families in which one or both of the parents have a
    history of chronic alcoholism.

    a) What are some of the factors you believe may contribute to alcoholism
        among American Indians, and how would your assumptions about the
        etiology of alcoholism affect your role as a social worker?
    b) What personal and professional qualities that you possess would be
        helpful in your work with American Indians? What qualities might be
        detrimental?
    c) Would you attempt to work with several families at once through
        group counseling? If so, how would you structure the group experience
        and why?

4. You are an elementary school counselor for several rural elementary
    schools that enroll about twelve American Indian students each year
    (approximately 5 percent of the total enrollment). Although the American
    Indian children perform as well as the European American children in
    kindergarten, by fourth grade it is clear they are less advanced in reading,
    writing, and computational skills. The school district is quite poor, and you
    are one of the few specialists available to supplement the resources of the
    classroom teacher.

    a) Upon entering a teacher's lounge in one school, you hear the English
        teacher, in conversation with several other teachers, relate the
        American Indian students' poor performance to their family/cultural
        background in rather uncomplimentary terms. How would you react?
    b) What responsibility, if any, would you accept for attempting to offset
        the deficiencies in academic skills these Native American students
        have?
    c) What response would you expect to receive from American Indian
        students and their parents to your attempts to improve the students'
        academic performance (assuming you accept responsibility for doing
        this)?

5. You are a counselor in an urban high school that enrolls a small number of
    Native American students whose parents have left reservation life for the
    employment opportunities of a big city. George BigFeather, an artistically
    gifted junior who regularly makes the honor roll, has just informed you that

he is contemplating returning to the reservation to live with his grandparents. George knows that for practical purposes this will mean an end to his scholastic education, but he is intensely interested in being immersed in the tribal culture, specifically tribal artwork.

a)   How can you best assist George in his decision-making process?
b)   How might some of your own values affect how you proceed with George?
c)   What are some of the social pressures (from administrators, colleagues, George's parents) that are likely to be exerted upon you and George if he decides to return to the reservation?

The American Indian Client
Role Playing Exercise

Divide into groups of four or five. Assign each group member to a role and the responsibilities associated with the role as follows:

Role	**Responsibility**
1. Counselor	1. Assume role as a counselor or mental health worker who is assigned an American Indian client. Attempt to build rapport with the client.
2. Client	2. Assume role of an American Indian client. To play this role effectively, it will be necessary for the student to (a) identify cultural values of American Indians, (b) identify sociopolitical factors that may interfere with counseling, and (c) portray these aspects in the counseling session. It is best to select a few powerful variables in the role play. You may or may not be initially antagonistic to the counselor, but it is important for you to be sincere in your role and your reactions to the counselor.
3. Observers	3. Observe interaction and offer comments during feedback session.

This exercise is most effective in a racially and ethnically mixed group. For example, an American Indian student can be asked to play the client role. However, this is probably not possible in most cases. Thus, students who play the client role will need to thoroughly read the articles for the group they are portraying.

Identifying the barriers that could interfere with counseling is an important aspect of this exercise. We recommend that a list be made of the group's cultural values and sociopolitical influences prior to the role playing.

Role playing may go on for a period of five to fifteen minutes, but the time limit should be determined prior to the activity. Allow ten to fifteen minutes for a feedback session in which all participants discuss (within the group) how they felt in their respective roles, how appropriate were the counselor responses, what else they might have done in that situation, and so forth.

Rotate and role play the same situation with another counselor trainee *or* another American Indian client with different issues, concerns, and problems. In the former case, the group may feel that a particular issue is of sufficient importance to warrant reenactment. This allows students to see the effects of other counseling responses and approaches. In the latter case, the new exposure will allow students to get a broader view of barriers to counseling.

If videotaping equipment is available, we recommend that the session be taped and processed in a replay at the end. We have found this to be a powerful means of providing feedback to participants.

PART 4

The Asian American Client

Introduction

While the Asian American population stands at only 10 million (3 percent), it is the fastest growing visible racial/ethnic minority in the United States and is expected to double by the year 2010, reaching 10 percent by the year 2050 (LEAP & UCLA, 1993). In the 1980s, the Asian American population increased by an astounding 108 percent. The large increase of Asian Americans is due to (a) the 1965 changes in immigration laws and the entry of large numbers of Indo-Chinese refugees since 1975 (in 1984, over 282,000 Asians entered the United States) and (b) the differential birthrates between White Americans and their Asian counterparts. The large Asian immigration has resulted in radical changes in characteristics of the Asian American population. Japanese Americans, which constituted the largest group in the United States (approximately 11.6 percent), has dropped to third place behind Filipinos (approximately 19.3 percent) and Chinese (approximately 22.6 percent). Demographers predict that Filipinos will be the largest group followed by Chinese, Koreans, Vietnamese, Asian Indians, and Japanese (U.S. Census Bureau, 1992). There has also been increased attention paid to Pacific Islanders (Native Hawaiians, Samoans, and other groups indigenous to the islands) who are demanding recognition for their unique concerns. Indeed, the term "Asian Pacific American" as opposed to the more frequent usage of "Asian American" is being increasingly seen in the literature. Except for Japanese Americans and the indigenous Pacific Island groups, all the other Asian American constituencies are now comprised primarily of those born overseas (i.e., 60 percent of Chinese Americans are recent immigrants). The term "Asian American" masks the great between-group differences among the Asian population. As of this writing, 29–32 distinct subgroups differing in language, religion, and values have been officially identified in the United States. Most of our psychological knowledge base originated from studies on the Chinese and Japanese, therefore multicultural psychologists are beginning to question the appropriateness of contemporary formulations, which fail to take into account the complexity of the Asian Pacific American population. Despite these facts, Asians continue to be perceived by many as possessing similar characteristics and encountering few problems.

One of the most prevalent and contemporary images of Asian Americans, for example, is that of a highly successful minority group who has "made it" in society. There is a common misconception that they are not oppressed and have somehow been immune to prejudice and racism. It is not uncommon for the popular press to play up the "Asian American success myth" with titles such as "Asian Americans: Outwhiting Whites" or "Asian Americans: A Model Minority." The view that Asian Americans are a successful minority is because of the following: (a) higher educational attainment, (b) higher per family income, (c) well represented among technical/professional levels, and

(d) favorable social/personal functioning statistics—lower divorce, delinquency, and mental illness.

A closer analysis of the status and treatment of Asian Americans does not support their success story. Assaulted, murdered, denied ownership of land, denied rights of citizenship, and placed in concentration camps during World War II, Asian Americans have been subjected to some of the most flagrant forms of discrimination ever perpetrated against an immigrant group. The statistics on educational attainment are misleading because they hide a bimodal distribution where high levels of education are attained by some, while a large number remain undereducated (Vietnamese, Laotian, Cambodian, Hmong, and many Pacific Islanders). Reference to higher medium income does not take into account (a) a higher percentage of more than one wage earner in the family; (b) an equal incidence of poverty despite the higher median income; and (c) lower poverty assistance and welfare than the general population. While Asians are well represented in the technical/professional fields, they are underrepresented in middle- and upper-management positions where they encounter a glass ceiling, make salaries not commensurate with their educational levels (low salaries despite higher educational level), and must have greater qualifications than their White counterparts to be promoted to comparable positions. In addition, it is becoming clear that favorable mental health and family statistics may not be due to "better mental health" nor "happier families" but to cultural factors inhibiting self-referral and/or biased institutional policies and practices. For example, traditional Asian culture often associates shame and disgrace with admitting to emotional problems, engaging in a public divorce, or acknowledging delinquency problems with their children. As a result, they will do everything possible to prevent such social emotional difficulties from becoming public.

The persistence of these images and stereotypes has puzzled the Asian American community. Asian American leaders are sensitive to the "model minority" myth because it seems to serve three detrimental functions. First, if it can be shown that one minority group has made it in our society, then it reaffirms that "any minority group" can make it in our society "if they work hard enough." It validates the United States as a land of opportunity, therefore it allows us to "blame the victims" for their failure to achieve. Second, the myth has created "hard feelings," conflicts, and antagonisms between Asian Americans, who are seen as a privileged group, and other communities of color. They are often used as examples to other groups: "Why can't you be more like them?" The Los Angeles riots and the conflicts played up by the press between the Korean American and African American communities are prime examples. Some see the perpetuation of the Asian American myth of success as a political ploy that acts as a "divide and conquer" strategy. Third, such a belief has allowed institutions and policy makers to consider Asian Americans as not in need of special programs and policies. Chinatowns, Little Saigons,

Manilatowns, and Japantowns are seen as tourist attractions, not communities with high unemployment, poverty, delinquency, and health problems.

In a revised and updated lead article, "The Interplay of Sociocultural Factors on the Psychological Development of Asians in America," D. Sue traces the psychological development of several Asian groups in America. He reveals that the Asian experience in America has been the history of prejudice and discrimination. Especially valuable is his description of how the unique experience and cultural values of Asians in America have affected the development of personality traits, academic abilities, and vocational interests. This basic foundation is invaluable information for counselors who work with Asian American clients.

It is now recognized that traditional counseling approaches must be modified to fit the life experiences of minority clients. In an invited article "Facilitating Psychotherapy With Asian American Clients," M. Root takes us on a therapeutic journey that helps us understand how one must take into account such factors as cultural values and experiences of racism to modify traditional counseling/therapy approaches. Her article is rich with case studies illustrating many of her points.

In addition to differences in cultural values and minority group status in the United States, Southeast Asian Americans may experience sources of stress unique to them as America's newest immigrant group. In their article "Psychotherapy with Southeast Asian American Clients," Nishio and Bilmes provide specific information that counselors need to understand problems of dislocation and forced immigration. Indo-Chinese refugees perceive therapy differently from our culture, and cultural clashes may arise in the treatment process. Like Root, the authors provide case studies and practical suggestions for a culturally sensitive approach to therapy.

References

LEAP and UCLA Asian American Studies Center. (1993). *The State of Asian Pacific America: Policy Issues to the Year 2020.* Los Angeles: Author.
U.S. Bureau of the Census. (1992). *Statistical abstract of the United States. The national data book (112th ed.).* Washington, DC: Bureau of the Census.

10

The Interplay of Sociocultural Factors on the Psychological Development of Asians in America

David Sue

As the population of Asian Americans increases in the United States, greater attention is being placed on the impact of culture conflicts between Asian and European values and the role of racism on the psychological development of Asian Americans. The knowledge base that has accumulated on this group, however, is often fragmented and lacks a conceptual framework for understanding the Asian American experience. Most studies that focus on the effects of culture on Asian Americans, for example, tend to be highly compartmentalized. One can find research investigating the relationship of Asian culture to: (a) personality characteristics (Abbot, 1970; Cook & Chi, 1984; Fong & Peskin, 1969; Meredith, 1966; D. Sue, Ino, & Sue, 1983; D. Sue, Sue, & Ino, 1990; Zare, S. Sue, Hu, & Kwon, 1991); (b) child-rearing practices (Bollin, 1989; DeVos & Abbot, 1966; Dornbusch, Ritter, Leiderman, Roberts, & Fraleigh, 1987); (c) the manifestation of behavior disorders (Chung & Singer, 1995; Clarke, Sack, & Goff, 1993; Westermeyer, 1988); (d) effectiveness of psychotherapy (Kenney, 1994; Kinze, 1985; D. W. Sue & D. Sue, 1990; Yeh, Eastman, & Cheung, 1994); and (e) acculturation (Huang, 1994; Kitano, 1989; Nisdorf, 1985). Few have attempted to integrate these findings into a global description of how culture influences the sociopsychological functioning of the "whole" person.

Cultural impact is clearly demonstrated in the study of Asian and Pacific Island Americans, where Asian cultural values collide with European American values. The historical meeting of these two cultures and their consequent interaction in a racist society have fundamental importance in understanding the personality characteristics, academic abilities, and vocational interests of Asians in America.

Asian Cultural Values

A discussion of Asian cultural values is difficult because Asian and Pacific Islanders are made up of over twenty-nine distinct groups each with differences in language, religion, and customs. In addition, it must be remembered that large within group differences occur in terms of generation in the United States and acculturation levels. However, there appears to be a number of areas of similarity in Asian cultural values (Fong, 1994; Ho, 1995; Shon & Ja, 1982; D. W. Sue & D. Sue, 1990).

1. Allegiance to the parents or filial piety is a strong value. The sense of obligation to the parents is strong, especially among the male offspring. This obligation is to be maintained even when they are married. Not only do parents come first, but the values upon the extended family are much different than that of Euro-Americans. Conflicts often arise when Asian and Pacific Island Americans are exposed to the U.S. societal emphasis on the nuclear family with its primary allegiance to the spouse.

2. The roles of family members are highly interdependent. The focus is on the importance of familial and not independent needs, reflecting the collectivistic nature of the culture. The family structure is so arranged that conflicts within the family are minimized; each member has his or her own role to play. If a person has feelings that might disrupt family peace and harmony, he/she is expected to hide them. Restraint of potentially disruptive emotions is strongly emphasized in the development of the Asian character.

3. Asian and Pacific Island families are traditionally patriarchal with communication and authority flowing from top to bottom. The father's behavior in relationship to other family members is generally dignified, authoritarian, remote, and aloof. Sons are generally highly valued. Asian women are expected to carry on the domestic duties; to marry; to become obedient helpers of their mothers-in-law; and to bear children, especially males. This structure is in marked contrast to the egalitarian relationships of contemporary Euro-American families.

4. The inculcation of guilt and shame are techniques used by parents to control the behavior of family members. The children's obligation to the family is emphasized. If they act contrary to the wishes of the parents, they are considered selfish and inconsiderate and are not showing gratitude for all that has been done for them. The behavior of individual members of an Asian family is expected to reflect credit on the whole family. Problems that arise among Asian Americans such as failure in school, disobedience, juvenile delinquency, mental illness, and so forth, are sources of great shame. On the other hand, outstanding achievement in some aspect of life (especially educational and occupational success) is a source of great pride for the entire family.

In summary, traditional Asian values emphasize reserve and formality in social relationships, restraint and inhibition of strong feelings, obedience to authority, obligation to the family, high academic and occupational achievement, and the use of shame and guilt to control behavior. These cultural values have a significant impact on the psychological characteristics of Asians in America.

Historical Experience

Asian Americans have been the object of much prejudice and discrimination, which may have impacted their behaviors and values as well. Ironically, the American public is unaware that no higher walls of prejudice have been raised, historically around any other ethnic minorities. The first Chinese immigrants came to the United States during the 1840s. Their immigration from China was encouraged by social and economic unrest in the country and overpopulation in certain provinces. During this period, there was a great demand for the Chinese to help build the transcontinental railroad. They were welcomed into the labor force because of the need for cheap labor. However, a diminishing labor market and fear of the "yellow peril" made the Chinese immigrants no longer welcome. Their pronounced racial and cultural differences from the White majority made them conspicuous, and they served as scapegoats for the resentment of White workers. Although Daniels (1971) mainly discusses the economic aspect for the hostility expressed against the Chinese, he points out that the anti-Chinese movement soon developed into an ideology of White supremacy. Chinese were seen as "subhuman" or "heathens" and their mode of living was seen as undesirable and detrimental to the well-being of America. Laws were passed to harass the Chinese. They were denied the rights of citizenship, ownership of land, the right to marriage, and so forth. At the height of the anti-Chinese movement, many Chinese were assaulted and killed by mobs of Whites. This anti-Chinese sentiment culminated in the passing of the Federal Chinese Exclusion Act of 1882, the first exclusion act against any ethnic group, and was not repealed until 1943.

Likewise, the Japanese in America faced severe hostility and discrimination from White citizens. Japanese began immigrating to the United States during the 1890s when anti-Chinese sentiment was great. As a result, they shared in the pervasive anti-Asian feeling. Originally brought in to fill the demand for cheap agricultural labor, many eventually became engaged in this field (Kitano, 1969). Their success in the agricultural occupations, coupled with a racist climate, enraged many White citizens. Legislation similar to the anti-Chinese acts were passed against the Japanese, and individual-mob violence repeated itself. Such cries as "The Japs must go" were frequently echoed by the mass media, labor, and political leaders. Within this environment, it became relatively easy to accept the relocation of 110,000 Japanese Americans into camps during World War II. There is no doubt that cultural racism has been practiced against the Chinese and Japanese. Likewise, the influx of Southeast Asian immigrants and refugees beginning in the 1960s has spawned a high anti-Asian sentiment most strongly manifested in welfare reform legislation and anti-immigration policies. Ironically, many people would argue that, today, Asian Americans face no such obstacles. The myth that Asians represent a "model minority" and are successful and functioning well in society is a popular belief.

Culture Conflict

Jones (1972) believes that many forms of culture conflict are really manifestations of cultural racism. Although there is nothing inherently wrong in acculturation and assimilation, he believes that ". . . when it is forced by a powerful group on a less powerful one, it constitutes a restriction of choice: hence, it is no longer subject to the values of natural order" (p. 166). This occurs when the values of ethnic minorities are evaluated through that of the dominant culture. For example, values of filial piety, modesty, and restraint of emotions are important to Asian groups. However, the dominant culture, which values independence and assertiveness, often views Asian values negatively and as deficits (Chin, 1983).

When an ethnic minority becomes increasingly exposed to the values and standards of the dominant host culture, there is progressive inculcation of these norms. As Asians become Westernized, many begin to view the majority culture's values as more desirable. Unfortunately, hostility to a person's minority cultural background may cause Asians to turn their hostility inward. Asian American children often express more negative feelings about their physical appearance than do Caucasian comparison groups (Liu, Campbell, & Condie, 1995; Pang, Mizokawa, Morishima, & Olstad, 1985). Kitano and Maki (1996) believe that the clash between Western and traditional Asian values can produce four different dimensions of acculturation: (1) High Assimilation, Low Ethnic Identity. Individuals in this group identify primarily with Western values and have little identification with their ethnic culture; (2) Low Assimilation, Low Ethnic Identity. These individuals are truly marginal. They do not have a sense of identity with either culture and tend to be dysfunctional; (3) High Assimilation, High Ethnic Identity. Biculturalism or the ability to accept both cultural systems is characteristic of individuals in this group; and (4) Low Assimilation, High Ethnic Identity. Many recent immigrants and refugees are in this category. They want to stick with traditional values and keep contact with outsiders at a minimum. The conflicting demands on the different sets of values will continue to have an impact on Asian Americans.

Psychological Characteristics of Asian Americans

The historical and continuing forces of White racism have left their mark on the life-styles of Asian Americans. Although it is difficult to impute a direct cause-effect relationship between these forces and the psychological characteristics of

Asian Americans, the following descriptions certainly seem consistent with their past background. The remaining sections will focus on the personality traits, academic abilities, and vocational interests of Asian Americans.

Personality Characteristics

The large majority of studies done examining personality characteristics have involved Chinese and Japanese American populations, and we must be careful in generalizing the findings to other Asian American populations. Chinese and Japanese American students demonstrate a tendency to evaluate ideas on the basis of their immediate practical application and to avoid an abstract, reflexive, and theoretical orientation. They tend to be more intolerant of ambiguities and to feel more comfortable in well-structured situations because of their practical and applied approach to life problems. They also appear to be less autonomous and less independent from parental controls and authority figures. They are more obedient, conservative, conforming, and restrained. In interpersonal relationships, they tend to be cautious in directly expressing their feelings. In comparison to Caucasian norms, Asian American students appear more socially introverted and will more often withdraw from social contacts and responsibilities (D.W. Sue & Kirk, 1973). Other researchers report that Asians have more difficulty with assertion (Fukuyama & Greenfield, 1983; D. Sue, Ino, & D.M. Sue, 1983) and score lower on dominance and aggression (Fenz & Arkoff, 1962; Johnson & Marsella, 1978) and higher in introversion, passivity, and self-restraint (Bourne, 1975; Conner, 1975; Meredith & Meredith, 1966).

Cultural values that emphasize restraint of strong feelings, obedience, dependence upon the family, and formality in interpersonal relations are reflected in the responses of Asians on personality inventories. These values are in sharp contrast to the Western emphasis on spontaneity, assertiveness, and informality. Although the results of personality measures on Asian Americans appear to be consistent, and fit Asian cultural values, several considerations have to be made. First, most of the studies were done on college samples, involving relative small numbers, and involving primarily Japanese and Chinese subjects. Second, the paper and pencil measures may not have cross-cultural validity. For example, several studies (D. Sue, Ino, & D. M. Sue, 1983; D. Sue, D. M. Sue, & Ino, 1990) have found discrepancies between self reports of anxiety and the ability to perform assertively in role-play situations. We need to determine if response on personality measures mean the same for Asian populations as for Caucasian groups. Third, as Chin (1983) points out, differences in personality are interpreted from a Western perspective. Behaviors and values that may be esteemed in one culture may be viewed negatively in another.

Academic Abilities

The major Asian American groups have done very well academically in the United States (Brandon, 1991). A greater number of Asian and Pacific Islanders complete high school than that found in the total U.S. population (74.8 percent versus 66.5 percent) and twice as many complete four years of college (32.9 percent versus 16.2 percent) (U. S. Census Bureau, 1988). Nearly one third of Asian students taking the California Achievement Test scored at or over the 90th percentile in math (McLeod, 1986). However, Asian Americans do show consistently lower verbal scores on aptitude tests than do Whites (S. Sue & Okazaki, 1990).

Although attention is placed on Asian American achievement, many groups are undereducated. Only 2.9 percent of Hmong, 5.6 percent of Cambodians, and 12.9 percent of Vietnamese have graduated from college (Wang, 1993). Certain groups of Asian and Pacific Islanders show a less than 50 percent completion of high school (Hmong, 22.3 percent; Laotian, 31.4 percent; Cambodians, 42.6 percent) (U.S. Census Bureau, 1993).

Vocational Interests

Most educators, pupil personnel workers, and counselors throughout the West and East coasts have frequently remarked on the abundance of Asian students entering the physical sciences. This pattern is reflected in their overrepresentation in the science and engineering fields (Leong & Chou, 1994). On a vocational measure, Asian females and males scored higher in the investigative (scientist, mathematician, architect) and conventional (clerks, secretaries, financial analysts) categories and lower in social categories (Park & Harrison, 1995). Reasons for the greater interest in these areas may involve cultural and societal factors. Personality tests have indicated that Asians prefer structured rather than ambiguous tasks and occupations that require verbal assertion may conflict with the value of restraint in expression. In addition, discrimination and prejudice may also play a part. Occupations requiring people contact are more likely to put individuals at risk for exposure to racism. Career plans need to be carefully explored with Asian Americans to not limit their choices.

Conclusions

The psychological characteristics exhibited by Asian Americans are related to their culture and interaction with Western society. Although personality differences have been found, these have been interpreted from the Western perspective and often viewed negatively. Acculturational forces have also had an impact on the psychosocial development of Asian Americans. The degree of influence varies from different Asian American groups, their generational status, and response to acculturation. Women and children appear to acculturate more quickly than do older males. Although Asian cultural values can be identified, it is not clear how they have been shaped or altered by societal forces.

References

Abbott, K. A. (1970). *Harmony and individualism*. Taipei: Orient Cultural Press.

Alva, S. A. (1993). Differential patterns of achievement among Asian-American adolescents. *Journal of Youth and Adolescence, 22*, 407–423.

Bollin, G. G. (1989). Ethnic differences in attitudes towards discipline among day care providers: Implications for training. *Child and Youth Care Quarterly, 18*, 111–117.

Bourne, P. G. (1975). The Chinese student: Acculturation and mental illness. *Psychiatry, 38*, 269–277.

Brandon, P. R. (1991). Gender differences in young Asian Americans' educational attainments. *Sex Roles, 25*, 45–61.

Chin, J. L. (1983). Diagnostic considerations in working with Asian Americans. *American Journal of Orthopsychiatry, 53*, 100–108.

Chung, R. C., & Singer, M. K. (1995). Interpretation of symptom presentation and distress: A southeast Asian refugee example. *Journal of Nervous & Mental Disease, 183*, 639–648.

Clarke, G., Sack, W. H., & Goff, B. (1993). Three forms of stress in Cambodian adolescent refugees. *Journal of Abnormal Child Psychology, 21*, 65–77.

Conner, J. W. (1975). Value changes in third generation Japanese Americans. *Journal of Personality Assessment, 39*, 597–600.

Cook, H., & Chi, C. (1984). Cooperative behavior and locus of control among American and Chinese American Boys. *Journal of Psychology, 118*, 169–177.

Daniels, R. (1971). *Concentration camps USA: Japanese Americans and World War II*. New York: Holt, Rinehart & Winston.

DeVos, G., & Abbot, K. (1966). *The Chinese family in San Francisco*. Unpublished master's thesis, University of California, Berkeley.

Dornbusch, S. M., Ritter, P. L., Leiderman, P. H., Roberts, D. F., & Fraleigh, D. (1987). The relation of parenting style to adolescent school performance. *Child Development, 58*, 1244–1257.

Fenz, W., & Arkoff, A. (1962). Comparative need patterns of five ancestry groups in Hawaii. *Journal of Social Psychology, 58*, 67–89.

Fong, R. (1994). Family preservation. Making it work for Asians. *Child Welfare*, LXXIII, 331–333.

Fong, S. L. M., & Peskin, H. (1969). Sex-role strain and personality adjustment of China-born students in America: A pilot study. *Journal of Abnormal Psychology, 74*, 563–567.

Fukuyama, M. A., & Greenfield, T. K. (1983). Dimensions of assertiveness in an Asian-American population. *Journal of Counseling Psychology, 30*, 429–432.

Ho, D. Y. F. (1995). Selfhood and identity in Confucianism, Taoism, Buddhism, and Hinduism: Contrasts with the West. *Journal for the Theory of Social Behaviour, 25*, 115–139.

Huang, L. N. (1994). An integrative approach to clinical assessment and intervention with Asian-American adolescents. *Journal of Clinical Child Psychology, 23*, 21–31.

Johnson, R. A., & Marsella, A. (1978). Differential attitudes toward verbal behavior in students of Japanese and European ancestry. *Genetic Psychology Monographs, 97*, 43–76.

Jones, J. M. (1972). *Prejudice and racism*. Reading, MA.: Addison-Wesley.

Kenney, G. E. (1994). Multicultural investigation of counseling expectations and preferences. *Journal of College Student Psychotherapy, 9,* 21–39.

Kinze, J. D. (1985). Overview of clinical issues in the treatment of Southeast Asian refugees. In T. C. Owan (Ed.), *Southeast Asian Mental Health* (pp. 91–112). Rockville, MD: National Institute of Mental Health.

Kitano, H. H. L. (1969). *Japanese-Americans: The evolution of a subculture.* Englewood Cliffs, NJ: Prentice-Hall.

Kitano, H. H. L. (1989). A model for counseling Asian Americans. In P. B. Pedersen, J. G. Draguns, W. J. Lonner, J. E. Trimble (Eds.), *Counseling across cultures* (pp. 139–152). Honolulu: University of Hawaii Press.

Kitano, H. H. L., & Maki, M. (1996). Continuity, change, and diversity: Counseling Asian Americans. In P. B. Pedersen, J. G. Draguns, W. J. Lonner, & J. E. Trimble (Eds.). *Counseling across cultures* (4th ed.), (pp. 124–144). Honolulu: University of Hawaii Press.

Leong, F. T. L., & Chou, E. L. (1994). The role of ethnic identity and acculturation in the vocational behavior of Asian Americans: An integrative review. *Journal of Vocational Behavior, 44,* 155–172.

Liu, J. H., Campbell, S. M., & Condie, H. (1995). Ethnocentrism in dating preferences for an American sample: the ingroup bias in social context. *European Journal of Social Psychology, 25,* 95–115.

McLeod, B. (1986). The Oriental express. *Psychology Today, 20,* 48–52.

Meredith, G. M. (1966). Amae and acculturation among Japanese-American college students in Hawaii. *Journal of Social Psychology, 70,* 171–178.

Meredith, G. M., & Meredith, C. W. (1966). Acculturation and personality among Japanese-American college students in Hawaii. *Journal of Social Psychology, 68,* 175–182.

Nisdorf, J. F. (1985). Mental health and refugee youths: A model for diagnostic training. In T. C. Owan (Ed.), *Southeast Asian Mental Health* (pp. 391–430). Rockville, MD: National Institute of Mental Health.

Pang, V. O., Mizokawa, D. T., Morishima, J. K., & Olstad, R. G. (1985). Self-concept of Japanese-American children. *Journal of Cross-Cultural Psychology, 16,* 99–103.

Park, S. E., & Harrison, A. A. (1995). Career-related interests and values, perceived control, and acculturation of Asian-American and Caucasian-American college students. *Journal of Applied Social Psychology, 25,* 1184–1203.

Shon, S. P., & Ja, D. Y. (1982). Asian families. In M. McGoldrick, J. K. Pearce, & J. Giordano (Eds.), *Ethnicity and family therapy* (pp. 208–228). New York: Guilford Press.

Sue, D., Ino, S., & Sue, D. M. (1983). Nonassertiveness of Asian Americans: An inaccurate assumption? *Journal of Counseling Psychology, 30,* 581–583.

Sue, D., Sue, D. M., & Ino, S. (1990). Assertiveness and social anxiety in Chinese American women. *Journal of Psychology, 123,* 155–163.

Sue, D. W., & Kirk, B. A. (1973). Differential characteristics of Japanese-American and Chinese-American college students. *Journal of Counseling Psychology, 20,* 142–148.

Sue, D. W., & Sue, D. (1990). *Counseling the culturally different.* New York: John Wiley & Sons.

Sue, S. & Okazaki, S. (1990). Asian-American educational achievements: A phenomenon in search of an explanation. *American Psychologist, 45,* 913–920.

U.S. Bureau of the Census. (1988). *We, the Asian Pacific Islander Americans.* Washington, D.C.: Government Printing Office.

U.S. Bureau of the Census. (1993). *Statistical Abstracts of the United States: 1993* (13th ed.). Washington, D.C.: Government Printing Office.

Wang, L. L-C. (1993). Trends in admissions for Asian Americans in colleges and universities: Higher education policy. In *The state of Asian Pacific America* (pp. 49–60). Los Angeles, CA.: LEAP Asian Pacific Public Policy Institute and UCLA Asian American Studies Center.

Westermeyer, J. (1988). DSM III psychiatric disorders among Hmong refugees in the United States: A point prevalence study. *American Journal of Psychiatry, 145,* 197–202.

Yeh, M., Eastman, K., & Cheung, M. K. (1994). Children and adolescents in community health centers: Does the ethnicity or the language of the therapist matter? *Journal of Community Psychology, 22,* 153–163.

Zare, N. W., Sue, S., Hu, L., & Kwon, J. (1991). Asian-American assertion: A social learning analysis of cultural differences. *Journal of Counseling Psychology, 38,* 63–70.

11

Facilitating Psychotherapy with Asian American Clients

Maria P. P. Root

With the rapidly increasing size of the Asian American population in the United States there will undoubtedly be an increase in their numbers seeking mental health services in public and private sectors. Regardless of the source of psychological health care, Asian American clients may experience many obstacles that may influence their willingness to seek services or return for continuity of care. This article outlines obstacles that may exist in therapy and provides guidelines for structuring therapy to be meaningful to clients. These guidelines expand my earlier suggestions (Root, 1985) and are consistent with the American Psychological Association's *Guidelines for Providers of Psychological Services to Ethnic, Linguistic, and Culturally Diverse Populations* (Pine et al., 1990).

Background

A change in discriminatory immigration laws in 1965 and more recent ones in 1990 (Min, 1995) coupled with unstable or impoverished economic conditions of different Asian countries, largely explain the population surge witnessed among Asian Americans. In contrast to Japan and Thailand with stronger economies and low economic incentive to immigrate, other countries like the Philippines, Vietnam, and South Korea were characterized by political and economic turmoils. In addition, Hong Kong Chinese have emigrated at an accelerated rate because of potential economic and political instability as it reverts back to Chinese control in 1997. In the last ten years, the immigrant population from Vietnam, Laos, and Cambodia has contributed to the diversity of Asian America as these countries still struggle with economic recovery after the Vietnam War. South Asians (from India, Pakistan, Bangladesh, and Sri Lanka) seeking a new life in the United States have also increased their rates of immigration.

The U.S. involvement in the Vietnam War has created another means by which the Asian American population has diversified and grown. Since 1975, over 1 million people in three waves of refugees from Vietnam, then Cambodia and Laos arrived in the United States (Rumbaut, 1995). Many Cambodians and Laotians did not plan to come to the United States, but as refugees subjected to the Pol Pot regime of the 1970s, they accepted asylum where it was offered. Their experience has been much more traumatic than their immigrant counterparts from Cambodia, Laos, and Vietnam in the last ten years who have sought a better life.

These economic factors provide only a small window into the sociopolitical and historical factors that catalyze an individual or family's emigration to the United States. Difficulty making ends meet with no immediate hope for improved conditions leads many persons, particularly parents—or parents to be—to sacrifice kinship ties, social status, and loyalty to their homeland for the prospect of providing better opportunities for their children, and thus, generations after them. These sacrifices are in line with the paramount importance and duty to family and children. This willingness to leave what is familiar, to leave a social and kinship network, to tolerate underemployment, to assume a lower social status, to face racial and economic discrimination, and to struggle with a foreign language may be for the sake of future generations.

Despite the stressors of immigration, racial and ethnic discrimination, and economic disadvantage, Asian Americans have historically underutilized the public sector of mental health services compared to their numbers in the population (Durvasula & S. Sue, 1996; S. Sue, Fujino, Hu, Takeuchi, & Zane, 1991; S. Sue & McKinney, 1975). Some Asian American psychologists (S. Sue, D. W. Sue, & Takeuchi, 1995) caution against using these statistics to conclude that Asian Americans have less need for mental health services. These authors suggest that the data taken from studies of the mental health of users of community health systems (Durvasula & S. Sue, 1996; S. Sue et al., 1991; S. Sue & McKinney, 1975), student counseling services focusing on Chinese Americans (S. Sue & Frank 1973; S. Sue & Zane, 1985), Southeast Asian refugees (Kinzie et al., 1990; Mollica, Wyshak, & Lavelle, 1987), and San Francisco Chinatown (Loo, Tong, & True, 1989) lead to the conclusion that they may suffer more psychological distress compared to the general population. The therapeutic questions thus become, what barriers stand in the way of Asian American help-seeking behavior and *how do mental health professionals overcome these obstacles?*

Obstacles to Treatment

Once services are geographically convenient and ethnic matches and personnel who are culturally sensitive are available, several obstacles to therapy may still be present for many Asian Americans. Various researchers and clinicians have offered explanations of underutilization patterns among Asian Americans and cultural barriers to the willingness to seek mental health services (Kitano, 1989; Leong, 1986; Root, 1985; D. W. Sue & D. Sue, 1990; S. Sue, 1977; and S. Sue

& Zane, 1987). Many of these explanations include not only cultural factors dictating against use of traditional mental health services, but institutional and therapist biases. Before we discuss these obstacles in depth, however, therapists need to be cognizant of several important factors.

What the mental health professional needs to guard against is the tendency to view Asian Americans as a homogenous group (Furuto, Biswas, Chung, Murase, & Ross-Sheriff, 1992; D. W. Sue, 1981; D. W. Sue & D. Sue, 1990; S. Sue & Morishima, 1982). Understanding Chinese families will not automatically mean that one will understand Vietnamese families or Japanese families. In an analysis of intragroup differences among Asian Americans seeking services in Seattle-King County from 1983–1988, it was found that compared to White clients, when Asian Americans were distilled into a single group, they functioned at a higher level (Uehara, Takeuchi, & Smukler, 1994). However, when the Asian Americans are broken down into their ethnic groups only the Chinese support this conclusion. Cambodian, Filipino, Laotian, and Vietnamese clients served during this period had lower levels of functioning compared to Chinese and White clients.

If there is one striking overarching similarity between and among Asian American groups of different ethnicities, however, it is their collectivistic family orientation. This difference is likely to continue for generations after immigration, though the consistency with which it is applied becomes more variable between individuals. The next level of loyalty for many individuals is the ethnic community. In a survey of Chinese, Hawaiian, Japanese, Filipino, and Samoan ethnic groups in Hawaii it was found that people sought help from family first, followed by the cultural community (priests) and then public sources (psychiatrists) (Prizzia & Villaneuva-King, 1977) . Thus, the family's approval, reputation of family in the community, and respect for elders may all be influential factors in when and if and from whom someone seeks assistance. Thus, throughout this discussion of obstacles to treatment, family influence figures prominently.

Conceptual Frameworks of Distress and Healing

The conceptual system for understanding distress to some degree shapes symptom expression. Health care givers have found Asian Americans more likely to express stress psychosomatically (Morishima, 1975): headaches, intestinal problems, changes in appetite, sleep difficulties. These symptoms may also be part of the picture of anxiety and depression. Under stress, existing physical disorders may be exacerbated, for example, allergies, arthritis, ulcers. Given that stress effects the immune system, the somatic expression of distress should not be construed as a less valid expression of distress.

Many traditional Asian medical conceptualizations of health locate emotional distress in certain systems and organs of the body. For example, grief may show up in respiratory problems. Considered an alternative framework for health, it may be the prevailing conceptual system, though intuitive, for some of the clients therapists will encounter. Among refugees of Vietnamese, Chinese-Vietnamese, Cambodian, Lao, and Hmong ethnicity, once in the United States, Cambodians utilized mainstream services the most and Hmong the least (Chung, 1994). Although all four groups showed an increased tendency to use Western medicine once they were in the United States, this trend did not indicate a replacement of traditional beliefs and conceptual models of illness and health. All five groups continued significant reliance upon traditional medicine and healers for help. Both because the somatopsyche system is less distinctly divided in Eastern v. Western medicine *and* because psychotherapy and therapists may not fit into existing conceptual schemes of health, many persons turn to their primary healers for help when they do not feel good. Healers may include: primary care physicians, religious and spiritual leaders, naturalistic healers such as herbalists, and/or spiritual healers (Lee, Oh, & Mountcastle, 1992). For example, a client expressed frustration that a relative who she thought was diabetic refused to see the doctor and instead wanted to go to the psychic healer esteemed in his community. Through discussion in therapy, this client was subsequently able to support her relative to use both health care systems rather than replace one system with the other. An individual might only be referred to or taken to a counselor when their family perceives their behavior to be intolerable or their physician feels ineffective in treating their problems (Root, 1985).

It is also not surprising that somatic symptoms may prevail during times of stress when one considers that many different cultural groups of Asians consider emotional distress a sign of weakness, lack of discipline or willpower, or the result of morbid thoughts. This conceptual framework is not that different from current conceptual bases of cognitive behavioral therapy that suggests that certain thoughts will cause distress and one must learn to either block them out (willpower and discipline) or replace them with more realistic thoughts (discipline to avoid or challenge morbid thoughts). This need is still compatible with psychotherapy (Tsai, Teng, & S. Sue, 1980). Asian American students of Chinese, Japanese, and Filipino descent tended to believe that good mental health was supported by the avoidance of morbid thoughts (S. Sue, 1976). Lum (cited in S. Sue & Morishima, 1982) found similar results in a survey study of Chinese American residents of San Francisco's Chinatown. Not only was the avoidance of bad thoughts deemed preventive, willpower was also seen as a primary form of intervention. Furthermore, if certain forms of distress are perceived as weakness or lack of discipline, to expose this weakness means more than simply obtaining help with a symptom; it is a reflection on character. Subsequently, it may be important and meaningful to the individual to be able to solve their problems privately and on their own (Loo, Tong, & True, 1989).

D. W. Sue, Ivey, and Pederson (1996) propose a Multicultural Counseling and Therapy model (MCT) that respects cultural relativism. Within this model they support other persons who suggest that valid healers of emotional distress extend beyond the conventional psychotherapists. Lee et al. (1992) observed that non-Western healers utilize more often the following resources: 1) community networks such as family and friends; 2) spiritual and religious sources and personnel; and 3) traditional healers. U.S. training in psychology sees the therapy role as a professional rather than a "friendship" one, deemphasizes the spiritual dimension of healing, and provides a constricted view of who is a qualified healer.

Orientation and Value Systems

Traditional Asian values and orientation to life are quite different from Euro-American values and beliefs. When a conceptual or value systems mismatch occurs between therapist and client, the potential for misdiagnosis may result in underpathologizing or overpathologizing a presenting concern or problem (D. Sue & S. Sue, 1987; Zane, Enomoto, & Chun, 1994). In working with Asian Americans, therapists are more likely to be credible and effective if they have a sense of the importance of family and the attendant values that maintain family reputation in the community and harmonious interpersonal relationships. The therapist can guide families and clients to their own awareness of what their values are and how acculturation may impact the generations differently. Furthermore, the culturally competent and credible therapist may help family members determine which values must be ultimately retained and in what contexts to serve the survival of family ties and relations from the values that are necessarily affected by acculturation. Some of the more important ones are briefly discussed.

1. Ethnicity

Service providers need to have knowledge of the individual's culture and level of acculturation to make an assessment of normal versus abnormal functioning (Kleinman, Eisenberg, & Good, 1978). It can be assumed that as one's level of acculturation increases, the influences of cultural heritage may be more indirect and less obvious, but nevertheless are present. While presenting problems may not be unique to Asian or Pacific American clients, orientation to cultural values and systems of beliefs as part of ethnicity does play a role in the etiology of the problem, the symptoms, help-seeking behavior, and acceptance of the treatment plan (D.W. Sue, 1981). Kitano (1989) observes four orientations derived from the four combinations that arise in a 2 x 2 matrix of assimilation (high, low) and ethnic identity (high, low). Guided by this model, when an individual seeks help, the therapist must attend to the orientation and values of the overarching American culture that influences the client and the culture of his or her specific ethnic group. This latter orientation may be further influenced by a generation culture gap, particularly between first and second generation. As mentioned before, the individual's problems and plans for treatment need to be evaluated in context, specifically, culture and family. The therapist must maintain an awareness of how their ethnic and racial identity and the social and political process, which inform these personal identities and orientations, may influence the way in which they perceive and react to their client.

A study of domestic violence illustrates some of the previous points (Ho, 1990). A focus group methodology was used to study attitudes toward domestic violence in Chinese and three Southeast Asian groups, Laotian, Khmer, and Vietnamese in Seattle. Although the diversity of values represented among these groups is homogenized and distilled to the label Asian American on a national level, significant differences were found. For example, Laotian and Khmer groups related and accepted more overt power differences between men and women compared to Chinese and Vietnamese. This single difference has great implications for expectations of domestic violence, which is distinctly tied to power differences cross-culturally.

2. Family

One of the powerful value systems that may differentiate Asian Americans from what is represented as Euro-American, resides in the relational system. This system places the family at the center of life and as the reference point for almost all aspects of an individual's functioning. This orientation guides intense loyalty to family and kin, underscores the importance of interdependence, and models a hierarchical system of respect for authority. Thus, the family's needs take precedent over the individual's needs. This collectivist orientation conflicts with the individualistic ones, which value autonomy and independence from the family (D. W. Sue et al., 1996; D. W. Sue & D. Sue, 1990). The Asian worldview is reflected in the value placed on harmony, sharing of expenses, living with parents longer, and submergence of the self for the collective good. These values, beliefs, and behaviors may be unfamiliar and even pathologized by a therapist who has little knowledge of Asians and Asian Americans. A 28-year-old Cambodian man, earning a good income and who lives with his parents is not unusual. It does not necessarily reflect enmeshment, difficulty in individuating, or family pathology. In contrast, a 19-year-old trying to move out of his parents' home to live with friends in an apartment may encounter conflict with the core values prized by Asian families; the parents may wonder what is wrong with their child—he could save money living at home and still have friends over. The family may experience the son's desires as an insult, a disavowal of the importance of family and parental sacrifice, or a failure to learn to place the family at the center of life.

A culture gap, particularly between first and second generation, arises often in the obligations parents expect their children to fulfill in their sickness and older age. The implicit system of obligations seems to provide a balance of fairness across the lifespan. However, the second generation's exposure to the prevailing individualism abundantly taught and displayed in American society opens up a critical analysis of this system, particularly when it is inconvenient. Resentments build from younger generation to older generation and vice versa.

The older generation may repeatedly remind their children of how much they have sacrificed for them as a reminder of their children's indebtedness to them. The children in turn, in the context of living in this country may experience these reminders as manipulative and guilt inducing; they attribute motives to their parents behavior that are far afield from their parents' motives. Other adult children have implicity absorbed certain values. For example, children are expected to fulfill the obligation of taking care of their parents. This implicit understanding while acceptable to the adult child may be a source of conflict in a subsequent cross-cultural and interracial marriage. The orientation to the family and the attendant values that maintain family relations are so strong, that terms and language exist in Asian languages to reflect this important difference. The concepts associated with appropriate social behavior in native Asian languages, whether they be Tagalog, Japanese, Vietnamese, and so forth, reflect a system of reciprocal obligation among family members and a responsibility to reflect the ability to put one's needs aside for the collective (e.g., Bradshaw, 1990; Marcelino, 1990). Loyalty to family members and the family name may override a willingness to criticize one's parents or other family members before the client has determined the credibility and competency of the therapist to help them. Furthermore, criticism of one's family is not to be displayed in public. This creates some problems in therapy because the therapist, a stranger to the client, may represent the public, despite the therapist's regard for therapy as private.

3. Gender

Alice, a 20-year-old Cambodian woman, was very hurt and furious that her twin brother had it easier than she. Her parents had helped him buy a car, but would not help her buy hers until she had saved some money. When she challenged them about the inequitable treatment, they simply said it's because her brother is a boy. When her brother was sick, her mother not only catered to him, but insisted that Alice and her other sister be more sensitive to her brother's needs. The reverse was not practiced for her. When there were leftovers, though not enough for everyone to have seconds, her brother was offered those first after her father. Alice was torn. She implicitly understood that boys and men were valued more than girls, but understanding that this was the cultural way did not make sense and did not sit well. The accumulation of unfair treatment over the years has left Alice hurt and angry.

In general, Asian American families place a higher value on males and this knowledge may help in understanding many decisions made by individuals within the family constellation. With the exception of some matrilineal cultural origins in the Philippines (Agbayani-Siewert & Revilla, 1995), and evidence of some women-dominated families in areas of China (Yung, 1995), Asian and Asian American culture tend to be very patriarchal, patrilocal, and patrilineal resulting in entitlements for being male. This hierarchical structuring of gender impacts privileges and distribution of resources.

True (1990) provides guidelines for therapeutic approaches to working with Asian American women given a variety of sociocultural values, economic factors, sources of stress, and history. It is important that the therapist has an understanding of the conflict that might ensue for the individual client when an individualistic and women-centered approach is offered. This is not a reason to discourage education and interventions that come from feminist approaches. Rather, the therapist must cautiously determine how and in what contexts interventions are used and how to make them fit within some aspect of the cultural or emerging bicultural understanding of the client's life. Sometimes, bibliotherapy, a cornerstone of feminist therapy, might be useful. For example, Agtuca (1993) provides a short, easy-to-read book on understanding and responding to domestic violence as a Filipina American. Other texts for the lay reader are being developed and in the primary languages of the first generation immigrants. Ethnic specific agencies may provide groups for women in which members share similar experiences living in male-dominated systems. In these groups, women may come up with solutions that are culturally viable.

Understanding the role gender plays in a therapy session is crucial to maintaining credibility with Asian American clients or families. For example, if the therapist is dealing with a traditional Asian family in counseling, it may be important to address the husband/father first as a means of recognizing the patriarchical system. Likewise, a female therapist may elicit negative gender role reactions from an Asian male client, especially if the client is much older. Therapists may need to modify their approaches when gender impacts the cultural context of therapy.

4. Sex and Sexuality

Sexuality in terms of performance and orientation and/or sexual identity may be difficult to discuss in therapy for Asian American clients (Chan, 1994). These are subjects considered private and for intimate and personal expression. Being also associated with emotion, it is expected that displays of affection and sexuality are restrained in public (Hirayama & Hirayama, 1996). This restrained public expression of sexuality may also make it more difficult to sort out sexual identity and orientation (Chan). The result is that the individual needing to talk about sex or sexuality is restrained by the value placed on a taboo topic and the lack of public displays of sexual affection or behavior. Jumping into this topic, without the client's initiation, shortly after the start of therapy, may communicate a lack of understanding of cultural rules. However, it is also important not to stereotype Asian Americans of any generation around issues of sexuality.

5. Intersecting Values

A combination of values related to privacy about sexual relationships, family loyalty, male entitlement, respect for elders in a hierarchical system of relationships, obligation to parents, value on harmony, and concern for the collective over individual welfare make it difficult to reveal family secrets such as sexual abuse, domestic violence, or physical abuse. Asking about the occurrence of these violations in therapy may not immediately yield a disclosure. Heras (1992) has written one of the only articles on sexual abuse in the Asian American community. Focusing on a Filipino American family, she discusses the importance of sorting out what is culturally congruent about the context within which the sexual abuse occurred and what is culturally incongruent and pathological. With this discussion and the use of a case study, she highlights the significance of understanding how the family structure impacts the therapist's approach to assessment and intervention. Her observations also have relevance for other forms of violations (Rimonte, 1994). Spousal violence may also be difficult to expose for some women because of how several of the values intersect. Nevertheless, some women may stay with abusive partners out of economic necessity for themselves and their extended family and fear. The need for sexual companionship and the negative value placed on divorce in many Asian cultures, makes divorcing a batterer difficult. In the case of cross-national marriages, fear of deportation threatened by an abusive American spouse is also a deterrent to reporting the violence (Rimonte, 1989, 1994). (Fortunately, legal remedies to help women in violent relationships are emerging.) Child physical abuse will also be difficult to expose and discuss due to the values inherent in the difficulty of disclosure of child sexual abuse. Data from a San Diego outpatient agency serving immigrants and refugees found similar rates of physical abuse for this population compared to the general population (Ima & Hohm, 1991). It also revealed that ethnicity was related to differential rates of maltreatment. Rates were higher among Vietnamese and Samoans than other Southeast Asian, Filipinos, Koreans, and Pacific Islanders.

6. Stigma and Shame

Experiencing psychological distress and changes in the ability to function may lead individuals to feel that they have failed to achieve what their family expects of them. The client may want to avoid involving family members in treatment due to shame or burdensomeness. At a core level, the client may be avoiding certain levels and direction of conflicts, for example, child to parent conflicts. Respect for elders, gender rules, acceptance of disparities in power, obligations to parents may all be violated in some suggested interventions or models of individuation and independence as learned by most therapists. The belief that relief rests in the exercise of willpower may explain the tenacity of a distressed individual who needs support, but does not want the family to be involved. Further disgrace would be called for if the individual were to seek help outside of the family. The case of Ms. Pido illustrates some of these issues.

Ms. Pido, a 36-year-old Filipina, came to the mental health center after discharge from a psychiatric hospital for a suicide attempt by overdose on medication. She was nervous, made little eye contact, and repeatedly asked if she was crazy; parents and relatives were treating her as though she were crazy. She had recently moved from her aunt's house because she could not pay her rent since she had quit working. She was currently living in the basement of a house she had found for her parents. She was distressed that her savings were running out and that her parents were old (recently immigrated) and she was unable to support them. Upon taking her history, she revealed that in the past fourteen months she had been mugged three times by Black males. Two of these occasions had occurred as she left different jobs where she worked as a nurse. Subsequently, Ms. Pido had become increasingly suspicious of Black males and was afraid to walk far from her house by herself. This fear coupled with dizzy spells and severe lapses of concentration made it impossible for her to return to work. She had been given medication by her physician to decrease her posttrauma anxiety. During a time of isolation, feeling hopeless that she would ever feel better, unable to perform her duties as a nurse or daughter, and feeling an embarrassment to her family, she overdosed on her medication. After the first interview, her parents, an aunt, and a family friend, who Ms. Pido felt had supplanted her as a daughter and niece in the family, were asked to come in.

The intervention in Ms. Pido's situation provided a way of adjusting the family system to temporarily care for an adult child, by normalizing the period of adjustment she needed and the decreased level of functioning she would temporarily experience. Parents may not seek services because admitting the need for help with parenting might be viewed as unnatural and even disgraceful that they do not know how to take care of their children. Stigma, shame, or loss of face may ironically result in some Asian Americans seeking services outside geographically convenient public health systems—even culture specific agencies. The reasons for this behavior and the potential stigma or shame are diverse. Several clients have told me that they specifically sought me out because I was not in an agency. They feared gossip about them by the agency therapists and potentially from other clients who might recognize them and spread gossip in the community. This concern is not assuaged by education on confidentiality that practitioners promise to keep even in the agency setting. Sometimes gossip is spread by nonclinical staff. Unfortunately, in some ethnic specific agencies in different parts of the country, tightly knit communities have a difficult time avoiding gossip, even at the professional level. Some persons avoid culture specific agencies because they often have become synonymous with serving low-income populations. Whether or not this is accurate, it reflects some of the concerns and struggles with class among individuals and groups of Asian Americans in this country. There is also a concern that the client might obtain better service outside of a public agency. With the change in health care system toward managed care and the limitations or gatekeeping on these services, service in the private sector may provide more efficient and productive help.

Education to Therapy and the Process of Therapy

In so many ways, therapy is a contrived relationship with implicit and odd rules. Seldom might the therapist question the basic premises of therapy. In working with clients for whom therapy is foreign conceptually and experientially, two aspects of the initial engagement should be highlighted. First, the therapist must find a way to communicate his or her understanding of their distress. Second, the therapist may explicitly explain how therapy works. Toward this end, she or he might outline what they expect for that particular day. Although attention to these processes is important for therapy with anyone, the therapist must keep in mind that not only may Asian American clients be unfamiliar with therapy, but that they may desire greater structure and explicitness. Therapists must consciously integrate the cultural context and possibly historical or political issues that affect family functioning or social location in society. It is important for the therapist to have some knowledge of Asian and Asian American history to understand some situations in which a client might not explain themselves. For example, a 60-year-old Korean American woman did not want to have a Japanese therapist even though this therapist had the most expertise in the agency for the difficulties she was experiencing. Knowledge of Korean history and the bitter sentiments that many older Koreans and Korean Americans hold toward Japanese and Japanese Americans would have provided the therapist with a working hypothesis for understanding this client's adamant stance. The more cultural experience and knowledge the therapist has, the greater chance that the individual or family will continue treatment. Implicit to these observations is that the therapist also needs to know what is normative functioning for the different groups of Asian and Pacific American families. Textbook knowledge must be supplemented with consultation and supervised experience.

The basic skills of an effective therapist remain the same: listening to what the client communicates; respecting the client's perspective and experience; formulating treatment goals that take into account clients' level of functioning, their resources, and their environment; and pacing. However, the content of the problems and the cultural context may be less familiar to some therapists. Therefore, effective therapy may require the therapist to adapt skills and information to the cultural context, something that few training programs in psychology offer on a consistent basis (D. W. Sue et al., 1996). If therapists are overwhelmed by their lack of familiarity with the client's values or the content of the problem, they may suffer credibility difficulties. For example, traditional Indian American parents of a 23-year-old daughter may be upset with their daughter's desire to move out. The daughter seeks therapy for her depression and sense of hopelessness about having any say in her life course. The therapist needs to determine what is healthy for this family compared with other families of similar background and generations in the United States. She or he might explore how this family has responded to this change in the family life cycle in previous generations. Does the culture gap between first and second generation contribute to vastly different meanings attributed to the daughter's desire to leave home? The clinician can help the family as a culture broker if they understand what is normative and culturally valued by different generations. Subtlety arises in knowing that a second generation Indian daughter's leaving causing incredible distress to her family has different meaning than a fourth generation Chinese daughter's attempts to leave home causing distress.

The therapist must keep in mind that most Asian Americans seeking professional help are looking for answers and immediate relief (Root, 1985), thus, solution focused therapies, which also tend to be brief models of therapy, may be more culturally acceptable at first (Berg & Miller, 1992). Thus, if the therapist is not an overtly active participant in the sessions and waits for the individual or family members to initiate the process, the client may become confused or question the competency of the therapist. A balance must be achieved between giving of one's expertise in a way that clients can receive it (S. Sue & Zane, 1987). The cultural markers associated with credibility and expertise, and the cultural concept of "gift giving," which conveys respect and appreciation may orient the therapist to think of what emotional "offerings" they might give to their clients. Providing information on resources, suggestions for reading material at the appropriate level, information on classes, and explanations in appropriate language may be consistent with what the client expects. For example, the presenting symptoms of anxiety may indicate difficulty negotiating transition into a new stage of the life cycle precipitated by immigration, births, separation, marriage, retirement, or death. The therapist might inform the individual or family that symptoms may arise when changes in the life cycle may challenge identity and require changes in roles and relationships (Root, 1985). Exploring the context and rituals that might exist in the country of origin for immigrants and refugees to negotiate these changes may place the current difficulty in context, even normalizing it. Relief may also come from the therapist acknowledging and anticipating what clients may experience during the first appointment including: looking for a solution, affirmation that they are not weak or crazy, embarrassment over having to seek help from a mental health professional, and confusion or puzzlement over how therapy can be helpful (Root).

The structure of brief therapy may be most culturally congruent and still allows the client to maintain some privacy and sense of dependence on self to solve problems (Root, 1985). This is not to say that therapy cannot focus on process, but in the initial sessions, many Asian Americans want content rather than process to obtain symptom relief. Furthermore, process therapy may not only be experienced as extremely foreign, it may reflect cultural insensitivity to the rules of relationships. I view some aspects of process therapy as a more intimate therapy. It is my experience that process focused therapies are more effective once a relationship has been established; this takes more than a few sessions.

Questions of clients should be overtly related to the issues for which they came for help. For example, if someone comes for help with their runaway daughter, focusing on the client's immigration history or isolated social existence, while possibly part of what is going on, may not make sense to the client for the problem at hand. They may not come back for additional help. Communicating respect for the client's desire for change and attempts at problem solving may also be brought out with questions. *Why do you think this happened? What have they tried? How did they come up with this idea?* Additionally, the therapist might acknowledge that it may have been difficult to come for help. Useful assessment questions as a window into the meaning of seeking mental health services might be, *Who knows that they have sought assistance?, What other assistance have they previously sought for this problem?,* and *What meaning does seeking psychotherapy have in relationship to your self-view and view of yourself in relationship to people around you?* The resulting information may provide the therapist with a window into anticipating the difficulties the client might have in returning for a subsequent appointment. These questions also provide a window into assessing the client's conceptual model of distress and resolution (Root, 1985). Finally, the therapist may find value in directly asking, *Is there a time frame in which you expect to have the issues resolved?* Additional assessment questions that are in line with the centrality of the family can be found in Root.

Dealing with Structural Barriers to Treatment

Once the client reaches treatment, additional barriers may contribute to premature termination from therapy. This section addresses the cost of therapy, scheduling of therapy, constraints on the relationship, the length of time of sessions, language, and expressions of appreciation.

Cost. The cost of mental health services may prohibit clients from obtaining treatment. Most public mental health agencies provide set sliding scales for fees or have government subsidized services. Most private practitioners set fees for service that create barriers to seeking mental health for individuals with lower incomes (Owan, cited in Sue & Morishima, 1982). Private practice settings, however, can allow some flexibility. Practitioners can make individual decisions about sliding scale fees, the appropriateness of barter, and pro bono services. Pro bono services can be difficult for some clients to accept. However, barter may allow some sense of payment. Barter systems, though, require the therapist to think carefully about what they are concretely and symbolically exchanging with the client. The American Psychological Association and the American Counseling Association warn against barter in their ethical codes. Many are fearful that it may set up a "dual relationship" that adversely impacts the therapeutic effectiveness. However, both organizations recognize that under certain conditions and with some populations, such practices may be acceptable. In many Southeast Asian countries, bartering (the exchange of goods/services for other services/goods) is a common and accepted practice.

Scheduling and the Length of Therapy Sessions. Clinic or private practice hours may determine whether or not a family can come in even if they are very distressed. It will be difficult for many family members to ask for time off from work and further for them to explain why they need the time off. Time off from work may impact income. Evening hours and weekend hours increase the likelihood that a family will be able to obtain help.

The arbitrary nature of the forty-five to fifty minute therapy hour often does not fit a client's way of relating information particularly if answers are contextually driven. Many traditional Asian Americans rely heavily on subtlety and indirectness in dealing with self disclosure, therefore the Euro-American sense of pacing may create problems. Thus, a question from the therapist may be answered with a five to ten minute story. The therapist constrained by the clock and used to a linear transaction between question and answer may interpret this style pathologically. It might be construed as tangential, evasive, and or rambling. Many therapists unfamiliar with the importance of relating context, particularly when getting acquainted, are at the least frustrated. Subsequently, they may cut the client off, ask in a way that may be construed as patronizing if the client understood the question, or provide nonverbal communication of disapproval or frustration. Ironically, the more a client worries that the therapist might not understand them, the more likely he or she may be to provide narrations that have more detail, which results in more negative signals from the therapist. If the therapist cannot adjust either the length of therapy or their expectations of what is accomplished with each session, the process that will ensue in information gathering will impact a potential therapeutic relationship negatively.

Language and Translators. If the therapist and client have different preferred languages for communication, a cotherapist or a translator may provide a solution. A cotherapist can complement the therapist's lack of experience or skills. At other times, if the therapist's skills are so specific that even with a translator they are deemed the best match for the client, certain cautions should be heeded. Translation has inherent difficulties. Certain concepts do not translate cross-culturally. Certain topics may be emotionally or culturally difficult for the translator. Some translators will censor or edit narrations. Pine et al. (1990) address some of the issues to attend to in working with translators. Some clients who have some proficiency in English may initially decline a translator out of pride or a desire not to inconvenience the therapist. However, if they have difficulty expressing themselves in therapy, this increases their chance of termination.

Psychologists and Social Work. Many families may need help with other social service systems or legal systems with which they are unfamiliar. Many psychologists are not trained to help someone maneuver through the social system. However, major relief from stress might be achieved through assistance with practical strategies for negotiating social systems such as social security, immigration, law enforcement, child welfare, schools, and health care. Helping with the practical matters of living may relieve the client significantly (Yu, 1993). Recognizing that over 60 percent of current Asian Americans are born overseas and immigrants, makes it imperative that helping professionals not rigidly define their roles as confined to an in the office, one-to-one, talk therapy. Systemic intervention must be part of the repertoire of the effective therapist.

Appreciation and Gifts. Most psychologists and therapists are trained to either absolutely refuse to accept gifts or reticently accept gifts. This policy helps to avoid boundary transgressions and inappropriate requests and expectations of clients. However, as mentioned previously, gift giving is often an ingrained aspect of transacting relationships in Asian and Asian American cultures. Refusing a gift could be hurtful and damaging to the therapeutic relationship. It is not unusual for clients, particularly first generation Asian American women, to bring gifts of food they have made or special treats they have come across in the grocery. I have always accepted these gifts with sincere appreciation. While I acknowledge gift giving as a culturally normative transaction to relationship building with many Asian American clients, I still assess whether I have indirectly asked or expected this gift. I also assess whether the gift giving means more than the usual cultural transaction. Thus, sometimes in the process of receiving and inquiring about the gift, we may process the meaning of their giving or my accepting the gift.

In the other direction of the transaction, I look at ways I can offer gifts that facilitate the therapeutic relationship, convey my respect for the individual, and confirm my appreciation of their hard work. I might lend a book, offer tea, or even offer some flowers that have special meaning to the client from my garden outside my office. Again, while I culturally acknowledge this normative transaction, I assess where else my desire to offer a gift might come from and if this offering might place the client in an awkward position. I seldom have offered a gift if I have not been the recipient first.

Anticipating a Failure to Return to Therapy. Sometimes, despite the positive signals a therapist might receive about the progress of therapy or the client's investment in the process, they may be mistaken. One way to reduce this source of misunderstanding is to ask clients what factors might change their mind about returning for their appointment. It is useful to utilize this intervention in a first session if it feels very important for the client to return. The therapist may share concern that if the client feels better after the consultation, he or she may not return to follow-up. The client may subsequently have a high likelihood of a relapse in symptoms in the near future without the individual having had the time to develop the tools to prevent or remedy such a relapse. Opening up a direct conversation about the possibility of failure to return provides a means of understanding more about the client's conceptual framework for therapy.

Traps to Avoid

Several traps that impair either the client's receptivity to therapy or the therapist's credibility and sensitivity are outlined in this section. These traps are derived from my consultation with different therapists and my own mistakes. They typically arise from lack of cultural knowledge, overeagerness due to a desire to connect or be accepted by the client (countertransference, insecurity, or anxiety), or insensitivity to one's internal racism.

Credibility and Irrelevant References

Sometimes in an attempt to communicate understanding to Asian American clients, therapists may unwittingly make reference to another Asian group. Given that Asian Americans may pridefully or oppressively distinguish themselves from other Asian Americans, this can be perceived as an insult. It also may significantly decrease the therapist's credibility. For example, a sansei Japanese American client seeking therapy does not feel comforted when the therapist mentions that they recently had the opportunity to travel to Vietnam. This client may not follow the connection the therapist makes. More likely than not this client may interpret this as a possible indication that the therapist lacks specific cultural knowledge and the ability to appreciate the cultural differences among Asian Americans.

Ethnic Match

Although data exist to support better therapy outcomes when therapist and client match by ethnicity (Flaskerud, 1986; S. Sue et al., 1991), this is not a guarantee for successful therapy. The diversity among people of Cambodian, Chinese, Filipino, Indian, Japanese, Korean, Laotian, Taiwanese, Thai, and Vietnamese has been distilled to a homogenous label, Asian American, therefore client and therapist may be matched only on this homogenous label, which corresponds to more of how this country thinks about race rather than the reality of ethnicity. For example:

Ms. Chhetri, a first generation Indian woman who has been in the United States since the beginning of her adolescence, sought help for increasing difficulties with sleeping, depression, and suicidal thoughts. She was in her senior year in college, and her parents were pressuring her to marry a young man she did not like and hardly knew. She had a boyfriend of her own choosing of whom her parents were uninformed. In an attempt to be culturally sensitive, the agency assigned this Asian woman an Asian therapist. This therapist, a fourth generation Japanese American knew little about the still common practice of arranged marriages in Indian families and had no specialized training for working with Asian or Asian American clients. She had grown up primarily in a white community, attended a primarily white college in the midwest, and knew little about Asian American cultures. The therapy did have value to this client, but not because of the therapist's Japanese background, but because they were a similar age, the therapist was particularly compassionate, and she obtained consultation to help her find resources and reading that were helpful to this client.

There are three conclusions from this example. First, not all Asians share the same history and cultural practices; in other words, not all Asians share the same ethnicity. Second, because someone is Asian does not mean they have the training to provide culturally sensitive service. Last, and not demonstrated by the therapist in the example, some Asian Americans may devalue Asian values and look down on other Asians who still want to be connected to Asian culture.

Nonverbal Behavior

Two nonverbal behaviors are subject to misunderstanding in the therapy setting: silence and head nodding. These behaviors in clients may be the result of culturally and familially transmitted interactions around the meaning of silence, restraint in communication, and demonstrations of respect. For example, the therapist may misinterpret silence or lack of talkativeness to mean a passive style in a negative sense and to assume it is a static interactional style across contexts. The therapist may not know how to distinguish between a passive, negative style and a restraint that communicates respect for their authority. Furthermore, the therapist may not know that this reluctance to talk may at other times reflect anger or disapproval of the therapist's behavior without direct confrontation. Likewise, the clients may not know how to interpret the silence or reluctance of a therapist to initiate questions and information. Not familiar with certain styles of therapy and having different expectations of therapist behavior in an authority role than that with which the therapist was trained to exhibit, a client might interpret the therapist's seeming passivity as disinterest or disapproval.

Head nodding in affirmation, smiling, or saying "yes," "oh, I see," or some variation does not necessarily mean agreement. It may be more a reflection of respect for authority, encouragement for the therapist to keep talking so that something valuable might come out, or even avoidance of conflict. Particularly with clients who have histories of trauma through social systems, seeming agreement may be a wise defense.

Ms. Min, a young Mien woman, had lost her baby in a car accident. She was severely depressed and had symptoms of an intermittent thought disorder. The circumstances that surrounded her leaving Laos and her subsequent experiences in an education camp in the Philippines for one year made her mistrustful of strangers, particularly persons in authority positions. Additionally, psychotherapy and its attendant conceptual systems of symptom explanation did not make sense to her. However, her attorney required her to seek psychological counseling as part of the legal process in the case she and her husband had filed against the driver of the other automobile. The community did not yet have a therapist of a similar ethnic match with the expertise needed for her symptom level and the anticipated legal process. Therapy was provided through a translator of a similar ethnic background. Even with the translator, also Mien, Ms. Min would seldom ask questions; seemingly be agreeable; and rarely, spontaneously tell her story.

Academic Performance or Work Performance

Many therapists use changes in academic or work performance to confirm the effects of stress. However, distress or pathology may not always be apparent from academic performance (S. Sue & Zane, 1985). This might be the case because of the emphasis placed on education for social and economic mobility in this country. A second explanation may be as viable. The importance of keeping family problems private may place increased importance on school performance to cover up the detection that anything is wrong or beyond the family's capacity to handle. On several occasions in Asian American studies classes I have taught, the importance of academic performance is apparent. Deaths in the immediate family or severe illness resulted in minor absence from school for these students. It was apparent they felt distressed by these events and may have benefited from dropping the quarter or taking incompletes, but there was a clear expectation from their parents that these events were not to impede their academic progress. Similarly, work performance may mask levels of distress in some individuals.

Not Returning to Therapy

Not returning to a scheduled appointment has solely been interpreted as premature termination in the literature and by therapists. Conceptual systems of suffering in many Asian cultures utilize suffering as normative and even redemptive. Thus, the expectation that life has hardships and will not always be easy may affect one's tolerance for discomfort. In turn, this may allow people to leave therapy once life is tolerable again, thinking therapy has been helpful, sooner than the therapist would wish. Additionally, the distinction between private and public lives and what is acceptable to share in those domains makes therapy a challenging situation for many Asian American clients. Although therapists and agencies guarantee confidentiality, going to a stranger for help, even if in the private sector, is still construed as going outside of the private sphere of one's life and going public with one's problems. Additionally, at the beginning of therapy, the contrived nature of therapy precludes an established relationship that would be accompanied by the rules of relationships. (The way in which people don't give notice for cancellation of an appointment may reflect on how they approach relationships in general.) Ending therapy as soon as possible allows one to retract problems into the private sector of their life. It is not necessarily a comment on therapy being terminated prematurely or being unsuccessful.

Conclusion

The basic foundation of relationships requires communication skills, trust, respect, and time. The healing nature of therapy is in part derived from the therapeutic relationship. Although a contrived and contractual relationship, its power derives from similar foundations upon which friendship is built, but with an agreed upon difference in expertise, confined space and time, and limits to the social contexts within which client and therapist agree to be in relationship. The process of developing the relationship is more complex. In working with Asian Americans, the therapeutic relationship is often cross-cultural; cross-racial; and increasingly, cross-national. As such, the reference point for what is normative in family functioning, individual development in relationship to significant others, conceptualization of illness and healing may be different and even conflictual between client and therapist. While generation, education, and language facility will guide the explicitness by which these differences might be observed, they are not absolutely coincidental or predictive. Differences in worldview between client and therapist challenges conventional training models of psychotherapy. This chapter was designed to supplement what is not offered in training programs for therapists who will work with Asian American clients.

References

Agbayani-Siewert, P., & Revilla, L. (1995). Filipino Americans. In P. G. Min (Ed.), *Asian Americans: Contemporary trends and issues* (pp. 134–168). Thousand Oaks, CA: Sage Publications.

Agtuca, J. (1993). *A community secret: The Filipina in an abusive relationship.* Seattle, WA: Seal Press.

Berg, I. K., & Miller, S. D. (1992). Working with Asian American clients: One person at a time. *Families in Society, 73*(6), 356–363.

Bradshaw, C. K. (1990). A Japanese view of dependency: What can amae psychology contribute to feminist theory and therapy? In L. S. Brown and M. P. P. Root (Eds.), *Diversity and complexity in feminist theory and therapy* (pp. 67–86). Thousand Oaks, CA: Sage Publications.

Chan, C. S. (1994). Asian American adolescents: Issues of sexuality. In J. Irvine (Ed.), *Sexual cultures: Adolescence, communities, and the constructions of identities* (pp. 89–99). Philadelphia, PA: Temple University Press.

Chung, R. C. Y. (1994). Help-seeking behavior among Southeast Asian refugees. *Journal of Community Psychology, 22*(2), 109–120.

Durvasula, R., & Sue, S. (1996). Severity of disturbance among Asian American outpatients. *Cultural Diversity and Mental Health, 2,* 43–51.

Flaskerud, J. H. (1986). The effects of culture-compatible interventions on the utilization of mental health services by minority clients. *Community Mental Health Journal, 22,* 127–141.

Furuto, S. M., Biswas, R., Chung, D. K., Murase, K., & Ross-Sheriff, F. (1992) (Eds.), *Social work practice with Asian Americans.* Thousand Oaks, CA: Sage Publications.

Heras, P. (1992). Cultural considerations in the assessment and treatment of child sexual abuse. *Journal of Child Sexual Abuse, 1*(3), 119–124.

Hirayama, H., & Hirayama, K. (1996). The sexuality of Japanese Americans. *Journal of Social Work and Human Sexuality, 4,* 81–98.

Ho, C. K. (1990). An analysis of domestic violence in Asian American communities: A multicultural approach to counseling. In L. S. Brown and M. P. P. Root (Eds.), *Diversity and complexity in feminist therapy* (pp. 129–150). New York: The Haworth Press.

Ima, K., & Hohm, C. F. (1991). Child maltreatment among Asian and Pacific Islander refugees and immigrants: The San Diego case. *Journal of Interpersonal Violence, 6,* 267–285.

Kinzie, J., Boehnlein, J. K., Leung, P. K., Moore, L. J., Riley, C., & Smith D. (1990). The prevalence of posttraumatic stress disorder and its clinical significance among Southeast Asian refugees. *American Journal of Psychiatry, 147,* 913–917.

Kitano, H. H. L. (1989). A model for counseling Asian Americans. In P. B. Pedersen, J. G. Draguns, W. J. Lonner, and J. E. Trimble (Eds.), *Counseling across cultures* (3rd ed., pp. 139–152). Honolulu: University of Hawaii Press.

Kleinman, A. M., Eisenberg, I., & Good, B. (1978). Culture, illness and care: Clinical lessons from anthropologic and cross-cultural research. *Annals of Internal Medicine, 88,* 251–258.

Lee, C. C., Oh, M. Y., & Mountcastle, A. R. (1992). Indigenous models of helping in nonwestern countries: Implications for multicultural counseling. *Journal of Multicultural Counseling and Development, 20,* 1–10.

Leong, F. T. L. (1986). Counseling and psychotherapy with Asian-Americans: Review of the Literature. *Journal of Counseling Psychology, 33,* 196–206.

Loo, C., Tong, B., & True, R. (1989). A bitter bean: Mental health status and attitudes in Chinatown. *Journal of Community Psychology, 17,* 284–296.

Marcelino, E. P. (1990). Towards understanding the psychology of the Filipino. In L. S. Brown and M. P. P. Root (Eds.), *Diversity and complexity in feminist therapy* (pp. 105–128). Thousand Oaks, CA: Sage Publications.

Min, P. G. (1995). *Asian Americans: Contemporary trends and issues.* Thousand Oaks, CA: Sage Publications.

Mollica, R. F., Wyshak, G., & Lavelle, J. (1987). The psychosocial impact of war trauma and torture on Southeast Asian refugees. *American Journal of Psychiatry, 144,* 1567–1572.

Morishima, J. K. (1975). *Report of the Asian American Assessment Colloquy.* Washington, DC: Child Development Associate Consortium.

Pine, J. P., Cervantes, J., Cheung, F., Hall, C. C. I., Holroyd, J., LaDue, R., Robinson, L. V., & Root, M. P. P. (1990). *Guidelines for providers of psychological services to ethnic, linguistic, and culturally diverse populations.* Washington, DC: American Psychological Association, Office of Ethnic Minority Affairs.

Prizzia, R., & Villaneuva-King, O. (1977). *Central Oahu Community Mental Health Needs Assessment Survey, Part III, A survey of the general population.* Honolulu: Management Planning and Administration Consultants.

Rimonte, N. (1989). Domestic violence among Pacific Asians. In Asian Women United (Eds.), *Making waves: An anthology of writings by and about Asian American women* (pp. 327–337). Boston: Beacon Press.

Rimonte, N. (1994). A question of culture: Cultural approval of violence against women in the Pacific-Asian community and the cultural defense. *Harvard Law Review, 43,* 1311–1326.

Root, M. P. P. (1985). Guidelines for facilitating therapy with Asian American clients. *Psychotherapy: Theory, Research, and Practice, 22,* 349–356.

Rumbaut, R. G. (1995). Vietnamese, Laotian, and Cambodian Americans. In P. G. Min (Ed.), *Asian Americans: Contemporary trends and issues* (pp. 232–270). Thousand Oaks, CA: Sage Publications.

Sue, D., & Sue, S. (1987). Cultural factors in the clinical assessment of Asian Americans. *Journal of Consulting and Clinical Psychology, 55*(4), 479–487.

Sue, D. W. (1981). *Counseling the culturally different theory and practice.* New York: John Wiley & Sons.

Sue, D. W., Ivey, A. E., & Pederson, P. B. (1996). *A theory of multicultural counseling and therapy.* Pacific Grove: Brooks/Cole.

Sue, D. W., & Sue, D. (1990). *Counseling the culturally different: Theory & practice* (2nd ed.). New York: John Wiley & Sons.

Sue, S. (1976). Conceptions of mental illness among Asian and Caucasian-American students. *Psychological Report, 38,* 703–708.

Sue, S. (1977). Community mental health services to minority groups: Some optimism, some pessimism. *American Psychologist, 32,* 616–624.

Sue, S., Fujino, D. C., Hu, L., Takeuchi, D. T., & Zane, N. (1991). Community mental health services for ethnic minority groups: A test of the cultural responsiveness hypothesis. *Journal of Consulting and Clinical Psychology, 59,* 533–540.

Sue, S., & McKinney, H. (1975). Asian-Americans in the community mental health care system. *American Journal of Orthopsychiatry, 45,* 111–118.

Sue, S., & Morishima, J. K. (1982). *The mental health of Asian Americans.* San Francisco: Josey-Bass.

Sue, S., Sue, D. W., & Takeuchi, D. T. (1995). Psychopathology among Asian Americans: A model minority? *Cultural Diversity and Mental Health, 1,* 39–51.

Sue, S., & Zane, N. W. S. (1985). Academic achievement and socioeconomic adjustment among Chinese university students. *Journal of Counseling Psychology, 32,* 570–579.

Sue, S., & Zane, N. W. S. (1987). The role of culture and cultural techniques in psychotherapy: A reformulation. *American Psychologist, 42,* 37–45.

True, R. H. (1990). Psychotherapeutic issues with Asian American women. *Sex Roles, 22*(7–8), 477–486.

Tsai, M., Teng, L. N., & Sue, S. (1980). Mental status of Chinese in the United States. In A. Kleinman and T. Y. Lin (Eds.), *Normal and deviant behavior in Chinese culture.* Hingham, MA: Reidel.

Uehara, E. S., Takeuchi, D. T., & Smukler, M. (1994). Effects of combining disparate groups in the analysis of ethnic differences: Variations among Asian American mental health service consumers in level of community functioning. *American Journal of Community Psychology, 22*(1), 83–89.

Yu, M. (1993). Divorce and culturally different older women: Issues of strategies and interventions. *Journal of Divorce & Remarriage, 21*(1–2), 41–54.

Yung, J. (1995). *Unbound feet: A social history of Chinese women in San Francisco.* Berkeley, CA: University of California Press.

Zane, N. W., Enomoto, K., & Chun, C. A. (1994). Treatment outcomes of Asian- and White-American clients in outpatient therapy. *Journal of Community Psychology, 22,* 177–191.

12
Psychotherapy with Southeast Asian American Clients

Kazumi Nishio and Murray Bilmes

Since the fall of Saigon in 1975, the influx of Southeast Asian refugees to the United States has been enormous, especially in the western and southern states. Approximately 250,000 Southeast Asian refugees were admitted to the United States from the spring of 1975 through the fall of 1979 (U.S. Department of Health, and Welfare, 1979). Between 1980 and 1984 more than 450,000 additional refugees arrived in the United States from the same area (Bureau of Census, 1985, 1986). Immigration of these refugees has slowed considerably since then, but they are still trickling into the country as part of the family reunification (U.S. Committee for Refugees, 1987). At present, few mental health agencies exclusively and effectively serve Asian American clients. Those that do are mainly located in big cities.

Not all of these visible new Americans, however, live in cities where Asian American mental health services are available and in which Southeast Asians are on the staff. In such places where special services do not exist, traditional mental health service workers are called on to work with these new clients.

In the Santa Rosa area (Sonoma County, California), for example, about 2,500 Asian refugees are currently struggling to adjust to life in a new, culturally unfamiliar country (Indochinese American Council, 1986). Mental health problems, such as depression, violence (within and outside the family), alcoholism, drug abuse, gambling, schizophrenia, suicidal attempts, and psychosomatic symptoms are prevalent (Nishio, 1982). However, there are no mental health services designed specifically to meet the special needs of these people. The clients are generally unfamiliar with Western mental health approaches, and the counselors who treat them have little training to help them understand such culturally different clients. Thus the Asian refugee, in spite of urgent and critical needs, is largely neglected.

Nishio, K., & Bilmes, M. (1987). Psychotherapy with Southeast Asian American clients. *Professional Psychology: Research and Practice, 18,* 342–346. Copyright 1987 by the American Psychological Association. Reprinted by permission.

This article attempts to provide pertinent background information on Southeast Asian culture and practical suggestions for counselors who work with these clients.

The term *Southeast Asian American* includes people of various ancestry— Vietnamese, Lao, Cambodian, Hmong, Mien, and other ethnic groups. Each of these peoples has a distinct language, group identity, history, and tradition. However, Southeast Asian Americans share common cultural values such as family orientation, interdependency, and religious and philosophical teachings.

The following brief explanation of demographic features and discussion of attitudes and cultural values should not be regarded either as definitive or as applicable to all cases. The life experiences of individual Southeast Asian Americans may, of course, differ greatly.

Demographic Features of Southeast Asian Refugees

The first wave of refugees came to the United States during the evacuation of Saigon in 1975. Many of these newcomers were fairly well-educated Vietnamese, employees of the U.S. government or of American-sponsored industry, Vietnamese government officials, and professionals (Chan, 1981). Among the Vietnamese were ethnic Chinese. Initially, the smaller numbers of refugees from Cambodia and Lao were also mainly U.S. government employees or Royal Lao government figures. Many spoke some English.

Subsequent waves of refugees, who came from rural farming areas, were less sophisticated, often belonging to lower socioeconomic groups, unable to speak English and without knowledge of the Western way of life. Many had passed through extreme ordeals, escaping under life-threatening conditions and subsequently enduring long stays in refugee camps in Thailand and Malaysia with uncertainty about their future (Nicassio, 1985). These were involuntary immigrants who had virtually no choice but to come to the United States, and even now, many are still separated from their families, who remain in refugee camps.

The number of Cambodian refugees increased dramatically when the second wave arrived. During the period 1971 to 1980, 7,739 Cambodian immigrants were counted by the Census Bureau, whereas in the shorter period of 1981 to 1984, 66,542 new Cambodian immigrants reached the United States (Bureau of Census, 1985, 1986). This population had suffered the massacres of the Pol Pot regime, many experiencing extreme atrocities with hellish physical and emotional traumas.

In the treatment of Southeast Asian refugees, knowledge of certain characteristics of these ethnic members is important. Necessary knowledge includes recognition of the differences among refugee groups, of the social and economic status of the patients, awareness of the degree of knowledge they may have of Western culture, their English-speaking ability, individualized experiences of trauma, and their membership in the family support system and in the ethnic community.

Attitude Toward Therapy

Psychotherapy is foreign to most Indochinese refugees. Life difficulties such as marital problems, children's behavioral problems, and problems of interpersonal relationships are often met stoically. This attitude toward life problems tests many Western therapists, who tend to try to "fix" the problem of "change" the client. However, if these ethnic Asians cannot simply endure misfortune, they are likely to find solace or seek help from family members, friends, or relatives. Sometimes they will go to the shaman, priest, or leader of their ethnic community for advice, or they may engage in rituals to eliminate evil spirits thought to be causing their problems (Egawa & Tashima, 1982; Moon & Tashima, 1982). Psychotherapists providing intangible services for a fee are unknown in most of the Asian nations from which these refugees come. Because many do not perceive mental health treatment as relevant to their problems or discomfort, such services in the United States remain outside their repertory of choice.

When Moon and Tashima (1982) asked 396 Asian refugees (Cambodians, Vietnamese, Hmong, Lao, Mien, and ethnic Chinese from Vietnam) from whom they would seek help for depression and other problems related to family, marriage, finance, isolation, work, and so forth, the refugees did not select providers from the outside (psychiatrists, counselors, teachers, and social workers). Lao and Mien refugees, for example, would in case of need turn to members of their communities for aid. Ethnic Chinese and Vietnamese respondents would rely on themselves, family, or friends. When marital problems were the issue, many Hmong would look to other family members to help them resolve their difficulties, but they would not seek such help in the case of depression, isolation, and financial problems. Among Cambodians, friends were the primary source of help for depression and isolation, and the ethnic community was the main source for assistance in marital problems. For problems diagnosed here as psychological problems, very little consideration was given to professional help by all examined ethnic groups.

In most cases, when Asian refugees come to a traditional mental health agency—typically a hospital or a county mental health service—they perceive the referral as a choice initiated by physicians, social service workers, the court, or other public health personnel, not as their own choice. They will seek mental health help only as a last resort, and they tend to have little faith in the process.

Case Example 1: A Vietnamese family was referred to therapy with a Western-trained American psychotherapist after an adolescent daughter's hospitalization following "bizarre behavior." In one session, because the therapy was supposed to focus only on the daughter, the fact that the patient's grandfather had died just four hours previously was not brought out. Also, following a later session when the therapist focused on the dynamic of wife and husband as a possible affecting factor on the daughter's behavior, the couple failed to keep the subsequent appointment. The couple told the therapist over the telephone that they would come to see him only as long as the marital issue was not addressed.

In this case the family treated the therapy session as if it were a transaction between themselves and a governmental agency, going through the required motions with suspicion. Disclosed feelings of sadness over the father's death or discussing private marital problems with a stranger was unthinkable. As far as the family was concerned, these issues, as well as other private emotions, were irrelevant in the context of curing the child's mental illness.

Somatization of Symptoms

Among Asians, many psychological problems are expressed as somatic complaints (Tung, 1978). Many Southeast Asian refugees believe that the health of the body and mind are inseparable. Illness of the mind, then, is treated by attending to the body (Moon & Tashima, 1982). Chien and Yamamoto (1982) stated, for example, that patients often attribute anxiety to kidney malfunction, hormonal imbalance, or malnutrition. Some refugees attribute mental illness to a metaphysical cause—within *yin-yan,* an imbalance of male and female light and darkness, or hot and cold in bodily functions (Tung, 1978). The spirit world and supernatural forces such as "bad wind" are also believed to affect physical and mental health (Indochinese Cultural & Service Center, 1982). Each cultural subgroup has its own malevolent spirits that, as with Cambodians' ancestral spirits, cause mental illnesses.

In addition to the concept of the inseparability of body and mind, shame and the stigma of mental illness also affect the reporting and treatment of mental illnesses among Southeast Asian refugees. In this group a disproportionately large number of physical complaints in which emotional difficulties are suspected have been reported (Kinzie & Minson, 1983). Mental illness brings social disgrace to the family because each individual member is a reflection of the entire family (Indochinese Cultural & Services Center, 1982; Sato, 1975). Thus aside from supernatural forces. the only culturally acceptable expression of mental illness is through recognizable physical complaints such as headaches, stomach pains, seizures, and paralysis.

More than 60 percent of the Southeast Asian clients who brought physical complaints to a community health center in San Diego, California were diagnosed as having psychogenic problems (Egawa & Tashima, 1981). The most commonly presented problem (39 percent) at the Indochinese Psychiatric Clinic in Oregon was multiple somatic symptoms (Kinzie & Minson, 1983). Under extreme stress, it is true, any person may manifest conversion disorder (American Psychiatric Association, 1980). However, the prevalence of conversion disorder as well as the overpresence of psychosomatic illness among Southeast Asian refugee populations is significant (Nishio, 1982).

Case Example 2: A fifty-four-year~old Cambodian man became paralyzed.

Extensive medical examinations revealed no organic cause, and he was diagnosed as having a psychogenic conversion disorder. The man had been depressed since he came to the United States two years before the episode. He could not find a job and could not support his family. As he was ashamed of his inability to take care of his family and continue in his role of the household, the secondary gain of paralysis was great. He was able to receive welfare assistance, and his wife stayed by his bedside for twenty-four hours a day as a required helper. He did not seem to possess the desire to get well. Because he and his family members did not recognize and acknowledge the psychological side of his physical condition, they insisted that Western medicine should be able to cure what they perceived as a purely physical illness. By the time the patient was referred to a psychotherapist, his condition was severely aggravated. When the therapist suggested an indigenous healer to perform a ritual to get rid of the demon, the patient insisted his condition was too advanced for such a remedy. The patient's refusal to help and his failure to follow the prescribed muscle exercises eventually led to serious physical atrophy.

Independence Versus Interdependence

Western culture almost invariably values independence. Dependence, on the other hand, is a key concept applicable to human relations in many Asian countries. A person asks another person's benevolence and receives indulgent support from other people (Doi, 1962). In return, the recipient is obligated to be dutiful and to repay the favor. This interdependency is the basis of a strong sense of family and community.

Many Asians live in an extended family situation. In the case of refugees, not only the grandparents, uncles, and aunts but also acquaintances often live together in this country. Limited housing, of course, sometimes forces this closeness upon them, but a wish to maintain interdependent relationships is a strong factor in maintaining such close living arrangements. The welfare of the family or community often has priority over individual needs (Sue & Sue, 1972). If independence is encouraged too sharply by a Western therapist, it may weaken or even destroy important sources of support and belongingness.

Case Example 3: A Laotian couple was referred to psychotherapy by a minister of their church. The husband was alcoholic and beat his wife. When the couple first went to a Western psychotherapist, the therapist encouraged the wife to leave her husband and lead an independent life. The couple immediately quit therapy and went to an Asian therapist. That therapist first acknowledged the dependency of the wife and the supremacy of the man over the wife. Gradually, after the trust relationship was built, the merit of a more independent wife was pointed out: for example, if the wife took more responsibility, she would be less of a burden on her husband, and he would have more time for himself.

Practical Suggestions

As seen in Case Example 1, the Asian American patient often regards therapy as a businesslike transaction that should be devoid of emotion and revelation of private matters. If the therapist pushes for more open feelings and seeks inner thought too early in the session, the patient quickly threatens to drop out. It is necessary to accept the patient's polite front as part of the self and not regard it as resistance. The patients may regard therapists as teachers, and Asian refugees are more likely, especially in the beginning, to expect wise and concrete guidance and advice rather than to seek insight into their own behavior.

One has to be aware, however, that acceptance of advice in the session does not necessarily mean the patient will follow the advice, especially if it requires open communication of feelings. Education concerning how to benefit from psychotherapy becomes essential. Let them experience a small success and some relief. Encourage them, if they are ready, to talk about the tragic and horrifying experience of escaping from the enemies in their own country. Many refugees report lighter feelings after venting these living memories, and they appreciate the interest and concern that Western therapists show to them. Many of these new Americans are learning English and want to communicate their histories and their needs to the best of their ability. The extensive use of an interpreter during the intake interview and the history-taking and information-gathering sessions, although often necessary, especially in the case of older clients who have no English-speaking ability, may hinder the establishment of an alliance between client and therapist. The patient usually does not come to the institution per se; the patient comes to see the counselor or therapist as somebody he or she knows and has come to trust. To help build that trust and to establish a personal relationship, with or without an interpreter, the therapist may show his or her interest and concern for the patient by making visits to the ethnic community, which plays a vital role in the patient's life, as well as to the patient's home.

The patient in Case Example 2 did not seek help until his condition became extreme. He also presented his mental problems in the form of physical illness—a culturally sanctioned expression of mental illness. As showing one's weakness is shameful, the therapist must not too eagerly suggest that the client is being treated for emotional illness and minimize the physical complaints. Medication and injection are important to Southeast Asian peoples. Educating medical doctors about the prevalence of psychosomatic disorders among Asian refugees may prompt earlier referral to psychotherapy. The use of indigenous healers in early stages should also be considered, as it is a common belief that bad spirits cause mental disturbances. Ethnic community leaders are often able to help the therapist find those who can perform rituals in conjunction with psychotherapy. Sometimes therapists can create their own rituals, which may have a salutary effect if they are performed with sincerity. Hollow rituals, on the other hand, will soon be recognized as false by the patients. Relaxation techniques, breathing exercises, hypnosis, meditation, and biofeedback can be used. Phrases like "too much stress" and "too much worry" are readily accepted to describe the connection between physical and psychological conditions.

The Western value of independence often is not useful to the Asian refugee, as indicated in Case Example 3. Traditional interdependency among family and community has to be respected in the right circumstances.

As Asian refugee women observe American women's freedom and independence, a desire to emulate the American woman may lead to conflicts with their own cultural values. Sometimes such women, in imitating the behavior of Western women, become demanding or promiscuous. Thus it is important to point out the responsibilities that come with independence and freedom. In Case Example 3 the strength of the wife "behind the scenes" was discussed so as to enable her to bring out this strength appropriately while developing an understanding of how inadequate her husband was feeling in this new country. In time the couple achieved a new balance, and the husband stopped beating his wife. His drinking problem also stopped when his wife and the therapist took a strong stance indicating that drinking was not acceptable.

It is not easy for Western therapists to side with chauvinistic husbands who regard their wives as part of the property. It may require considerable patience and understanding on the part of the therapist to tolerate Confucius's teaching and centuries-old traditions.

Sometimes it may be advisable to match male therapists with male patients and female therapists with female patients because in Asian cultures the gap between male and female roles is great. Male patients may not feel that female therapists are important enough or powerful enough to be of use to them. Female patients may be shy and become easily intimidated by male therapists, especially the bearded ones. However, it would be a disservice to perpetuate this female-inferior attitude among Southeast Asian refugees. It is well to learn in time that one great virtue of living in this country is to be able to acknowledge the equality and the importance of men and women.

Conclusions

In this article, only a few of the many cultural values and culturally based attitudes toward therapy are discussed. Yet even these present a complex picture for the Western therapist. It is not easy to work with patients who do not believe in Western modes of therapy. It may be wise to incorporate indigenous modes of healing, when appropriate, into the treatment process. Education as well as letting them experience a little success may gradually build patients' confidence in the therapeutic process. Making a personal connection and initially occupying the role of teacher may be the best means through which the therapist can help the Asian refugee accept and use mental health services. Therapists need to be aware of culturally accepted ways of expressing mental problems, such as through psychosomatic disorders, because mental illness carries a strong stigma and produces a deep sense of shame. It is well to remember that many of these clients believe that the body and mind are inseparable. The importance of the ethnic community to the Asian refugees must not be neglected because it plays a significant part in their mental health.

It may sometimes be trying for the Western therapist to have to understand and accept cultural values that he or she personally opposes. But once the Western therapist realizes that the Asian refugee values the concept of dependency or interdependency more than that of independence, the more easily he or she can understand the social principles inherent in that concept. However, when the concept manifests itself in the subjugation of wife to husband, the therapist may experience difficulty in accepting it. A constructive attitude may be achieved if the therapist does not totally accept the refugee's concept or demand absolute adherence to Western values. Sensitivity and awareness of differences can possibly bring about a new state of balance.

It may take more than the usual therapeutic skill and facility with language to reach the Asian refugee's heart. If the therapist shows concern, learns the different characteristics of each group along with the patient's unique cultural values, and understands his or her history and plight, the therapist will be able to touch and aid many refugees who are in desperate need of help.

References

American Psychiatric Association (1980). *Diagnostic and statistical manual of mental disorders* (3rd. ed.). Washington DC: Author.

Bureau of Census (1985). *Statistical abstract of the United States.* Washington, DC: U.S. Department of Commerce.

Bureau of Census (1986). *Statistical abstract of the United States.* Washington, DC: U.S. Department of Commerce.

Chan, K. (1981). Education for Chinese and Indochinese. *Theory Into Practice, 20*(1), 35–44.

Chien, C., & Yamamoto, J. (1982). Asian-American and Pacific-Islander patients. In F. Acosta, J. Yamamoto, & L. Evans (Eds.), *Effective psychotherapy for low-income and minority patients.* New York: Plenum.

Doi, L. T. (1962). *Amae*—A key concept for understanding Japanese personality structure. *Psychologia, 5,* 1–7.

Egawa, J. E., & Tashima, N. (1981). *Alternative service delivery models in Pacific/Asian American communities.* San Francisco: Pacific Asian Mental Health Research Project.

Egawa, J. E., & Tashima, N. (1982). *Indigenous healers in Southeast Asian refugee communities.* San Francisco: Pacific Asian Mental Health Research Project.

Indochinese American Council (1986). *Refugee statistics in Sonoma County.* Santa Rosa, CA: Indochinese American Council.

Indochinese Cultural & Service Center (1982). *Southeast Asian health care.* Portland, OR: Indochinese Culture & Service Center.

Kinzie, D. J., & Minson, S. (1983). Five-year's experience with Indochinese refugee psychiatric patients. *Journal of Operational Psychiatry 14* (2), 105–111.

Moon, A., & Tashima, N. (1982). *Help seeking behavior and attitudes of Southwest Asian refugees.* San Francisco: Pacific Asian Mental Health Research Project.

Nicassio, P. M. (1985). The psychological adjustment of the Southeast Asian refugee. *Journal of Cross-Cultural Psychology, 16* (2), 153–173.

Nishio, K. (1982). *Southeast Asian refugee mental health project.* Unpublished manuscript.

Sato, M. (1975). The shame factor: Counseling Asian Americans. *Journal of the Asian American Psychological Association, 5* (1), 20–24.

Sue, D., & Sue, S. (1972). Counseling Chinese-Americans. *Personnel and Guidance Journal, 50,* 637–644.

Tung, T. M. (1978). *Health and disease: The Indochinese perspective.* Paper presented at the annual Health, Education, and Welfare Mental Health Projects Grantee Conference. San Francisco.

U.S. Committee for Refugees (1987). *World refugee survey; 1986 in reviews.* Washington, DC: American Council for Nationalities Service.

U.S. Department of Health, and Welfare (1979). *The Congress Indochinese refugee assistance program.* Washington, DC: Social Security Administration, Office of Refugee Affairs.

The Asian American Client
Cases and Questions

1. You are a college counselor working at a prestigious university. A quiet and reserved traditional Chinese American male student seeks your help with study problems. He appears depressed, states that he suffers from headaches, has difficulty sleeping, and has lost several pounds over the last few weeks. You are aware that he has had a thorough medical exam with insignificant physical problems. Your sessions also reveal conflicts between the parents' wish that their son continue in premed and his own desire and interest in the social sciences. His vocational tests suggest he is in the wrong major and would be much happier in the field of anthropology.

   a) If we assume that the young man is somaticizing his psychological conflicts, what particular Asian American factors might be operating to affect the manner of symptom formation and why?

   b) What kind of potential familial problem might arise if you were to counsel the student to change majors and go against the wishes of his parents? (Hint: It is important to understand the primacy of the traditional Asian family, the value of interdependence, and the emphasis on respect for parents.)

   c) From your understanding of Asian American culture, what type of culturally relevant approach might you take in working with the student? Please provide a rationale for your approach.

2. You are a middle school counselor who has just had a thirteen-year-old female Vietnamese student referred to you because of suspected child abuse. In your first meeting with the student, you notice large bruises throughout her right arm and extending to the neck. As a counselor, you are aware that you are legally required to report any case of "suspected" child abuse within forty-eight hours. The youngster admits that her parents are responsible for the bruises, but she denies they abused her saying they were only using traditional Vietnamese healing methods.

   a) If you discovered that the bruises resulted from culturally accepted practices, would it make any difference to you? In other words, does culture justify the practice if it results in the harm of a child?

   b) If you wanted to talk with the family regarding their daughter, what cultural factors might work against their ability to share with you their thoughts and feelings? How might you approach them in a way that would minimize such potential barriers?

c) What other type of information would you want to obtain before proceeding in this case? Where would you seek the information?

3. You are a community psychologist employed by an agency that provides psychological services to a population of middle-class Japanese American families, among others. A Young Buddhist Association (YBA) has asked you to speak on "resolving intergenerational conflict" at its next meeting. (Your agency is aware that generational conflict has become a major problem in this community.)

   a) What do you think are some of the causes of the intergenerational conflict being experienced by these young people and their parents?
   b) Other than your talk, what services do you feel qualified to render these young Japanese Americans and their families?
   c) How do you think these services will be received by the YBA members and their families?

4. You are a high school counselor in a large suburban high school. A Japanese American student whom you have seen for academic advising on several occasions has just shared with you his involvement as a marijuana dealer. Although attempting to hide his emotions, the student is clearly distraught. He is particularly concerned that a recent arrest of a marijuana supplier will eventually lead authorities to him.

   a) How *might* the student's cultural background affect his feelings as he shares this problem?
   b) What kind of input from you as a counselor do you think this student wants/needs most?
   c) Can you anticipate any prejudicial reaction on the part of the school administration (if the student's behavior is uncovered) as a result of the student's racial/ethnic background?

5. You are a high school counselor asked by the Dean of Guidance to organize and moderate a number of value clarification groups. You plan to set up six groups of eight students each from a list of volunteers, although seven students were referred by teachers because they are nonparticipators in class. Six of the seven students referred by teachers are Asian Americans.

   a) Will the composition of your six groups be determined by the fact that six of seven teacher referrals are Asian American?
   b) What goals do you have for your six groups and for the individual members of these groups?
   c) How will your own cultural/educational background affect the way you relate to the six Asian American students?

The Asian American Client
Role Playing Exercise

Divide into groups of four or five. Assign each group member to a role and the responsibilities associated with the role as follows:

Role	Responsibility
1. Counselor	1. Assume role as a counselor or mental health worker who is assigned an Asian American client. Attempt to build rapport with the client.
2. Client	2. Assume role of an Asian American client (Chinese, Japanese, or Indo-Chinese refugee). To play this role effectively, it will be necessary for the student to (a) identify cultural values of Asian Americans, (b) identify sociopolitical factors that may interfere with counseling, and (c) portray these aspects in the counseling session. It is best to select a few powerful variables in the role play. You may or may not be initially antagonistic to the counselor, but it is important for you to be sincere in your role and your reactions to the counselor.
3. Observers	3. Observe interaction and offer comments during feedback session.

This exercise is most effective in a racially and ethnically mixed group. For example, an Asian American student can be asked to play the Asian American client role. However, this is probably not possible in most cases. Thus, students who play the client role will need to thoroughly read the articles for the group they are portraying.

Identifying the barriers that could interfere with counseling is an important aspect of this exercise. We recommend that a list be made of the group's cultural values and sociopolitical influences prior to the role playing. For example, how might restraint of strong feelings, preference for structure and activity, and trust/mistrust be manifested in the client?

Role playing may go on for a period of five to fifteen minutes, but the time limit should be determined prior to the activity. Allow ten to fifteen minutes for a feedback session in which all participants discuss (within the group) how they felt in their respective roles, how appropriate were the counselor responses, what else they might have done in that situation, and so forth.

Rotate and role-play the same situation with another counselor trainee *or* another Asian American client with different issues, concerns, and problems. In the former case, the group may feel that a particular issue is of sufficient importance to warrant reenactment. This allows students to see the effects of other counseling responses and approaches. In the latter case, the new exposure will allow students to get a broader view of barriers to counseling.

If videotaping equipment is available, we recommend that the session be taped and processed in a replay at the end. We have found this to be a powerful means of providing feedback to participants.

PART 5

The Hispanic American Client

Introduction

There is no single label that adequately describes the ethnically diverse groups that make up the Hispanic American population. This population includes Mexican Americans, Puerto Ricans, Cuban Americans, and Central and South Americans, each representing a distinct land of origin linked by common language and cultural heritage. When viewed as a combined population, they are the fastest growing ethnic minority in America. During the 1980s, the group increased five times as fast as the rest of the nation, reaching 22.3 million by 1988 (U.S. Bureau of the Census, 1990 C.P.H.-1-6). At its present growth rate, some are predicting that the group will surpass African Americans as America's largest ethnic minority.

Hispanic Americans are not only unique in their size and growth rate, but as a rule, they have also tended to cluster in fewer parts of the country than other ethnic groups. For instance, nearly 90 percent of the population is found in nine states: California, Texas, New York, Florida, Illinois, New Jersey, Arizona, New Mexico, and Colorado. Moreover, the vast majority of the population is congregated in major urban centers. It is precisely these phenomena—close clustering and rapid growth—that have produced a combination of strengths and challenges for the Hispanic American community.

From a cultural viewpoint, the densely populated Hispanic American community has proven to be a mecca for preserving and enhancing the culture. As is true in the case of all human groupings, culture plays an essential role in the life of the Hispanic American; it allows the distinct traits—knowledge, beliefs, values, religion, customs—of the group to be passed on from one generation to the next. It is in part because of this unique population pattern that the Hispanic American culture has persisted and evolved in America, providing its members with a sense of strength and security.

Their size and demography have also proven to be a source of strength in the political arena. According to the Hispanic American Almanac (1984) 40 percent of all congressional seats and 71 percent of the 270 electoral votes needed to elect our president are found in the nine states that are heavily populated by Hispanic Americans. "The growth in numbers and the increased political sophistication of Hispanics has meant an increase in the number of Hispanic elected officials on almost all levels of government" (p. 151). These trends were also reported by the U.S. Bureau of the Census for 1990 and are projected to continue into the year 2010 (U.S. Bureau of the Census, 1996).

High growth rate has also produced its share of problems. Hispanic Americans suffer many of the same problems that confront other ethnic minorities in inner cities. Poor schools, overcrowded classrooms, and campus violence have become a fact of life in many Latino communities (Castex, 1994; For Latinos, 1987; Rosado & Elias, 1993). Low-paying jobs and high unemployment help to lower the overall standard of living for many Hispanic

Americans. The U.S. Bureau of the Census has reported that 26 percent of Latino families live in poverty compared to 10 percent of non-Latino families (Current Population Report, Series P-60, No. 175). Further, it places the median income for all Hispanic American families at $23,400, while that of non-Hispanic families stands at $33,000 (Schick & Schick, 1991). As Schick and Schick (1991) indicate, members of this group are far more likely to be victims of crime than their White counterparts.

To a large degree, this situation can be explained by a cycle of poverty set in motion with the early immigration of Latinos to this country. Ancestral immigrants of many present-day Hispanic Americans came to the United States from nonindustrial, agrarian-based countries that for the most part were unskilled and Spanish speaking. (A major exception was the first wave of the Cuban population, many of whom were middle-class and skilled when they migrated.) Their life-style, customs, and language set them apart from the dominant society, making them the object of stereotyping, prejudice, and discrimination. Thus, many Latinos were forced to join the millions of other American ethnic minorities in competition for scarce jobs and low pay. The pattern was set, and each new generation has been condemned to the perpetual cycle of poverty and group discrimination.

The task of addressing the problems of this group has often been complicated by a lack of clarity over how to conceptualize them. Castex (1994), in the first article in this section, "Providing Services to Hispanic/Latino Populations: Profiles in Diversity," views this as a primary issue facing helping professionals. Many are unsure of the unique service needs that are particular to a given Hispanic/Latino subgroup (Mexican American, Cuban, Puerto Rican). They are also uncertain of similarities that might exist across the diverse subgroups that may affect the services delivered to the broader Hispanic/Latino population. Castex provides an excellent profile on the Hispanic/Latino that addresses these concerns. She explores such topics as "ethnic group concept," "national origin," "language," "family name," and "religion." Information and suggestions for working with the Hispanic/Latino client are discussed within each of the topical areas.

Rogler, Malgady, and Blumenthal, in the second article in this section, "What Do Culturally Sensitive Mental Health Services Mean? The Case of Hispanics," focus on the treatment that Hispanics have historically received from the mental health profession. They raise serious concerns over the mental health profession's lack of sensitivity to the Hispanic client. They identify three broad approaches for improving cultural sensitivity—increased accessibility to treatment, selecting culturally suited treatments, and modifying treatment to fit the culture. In each approach, the authors offer helpful information on how to increase the clinician's sensitivity and overall effectiveness with the Hispanic client.

In the final article in this section, "Counseling Cuban Americans," Altarriba and Bauer provide insight into Cuban American history and culture that is essential for working with Cuban Americans. Special emphasis is given to understanding the Cuban American's attitude toward professional treatment. Key factors for designing a culturally sensitive treatment model are discussed. They also propose a framework for assessing the quality of treatment in relations to the clients: worldview, relationship to family, and cultural values and beliefs.

References

Castex, G. M. (1994). Providing Services to Hispanic/Latino Populations: Profiles in Diversity. *Social Work, 39,* 288–296.

For Latinos, a growing divide. (1987, August 10). *U.S. News & World Report,* 47–49.

Rosado, J. W., & Elias, M. J. (1993). Ecological and Psychocultural Mediator in the Delivery of Services for Urban, Culturally Diverse Hispanic Clients. *Professional Psychology: Research and Practice, 24,* 450–459.

Schick, F. L., & Schick, R. (1991). *Statistical handbook on U.S. Hispanics.* Phoenix, AZ: The Oryz Press.

U.S. Bureau of the Census. (1990). *1990 Census of population and housing, summary population and housing characteristics, United States* (CPH-1-6). Washington, DC: U.S. Government Printing Office.

U.S. Bureau of the Census. (1993). *The Hispanic Population in the United States: March, 1993* (Current Population Reports, Series P20-475). Washington, DC: U.S. Government Printing Office.

U.S. Bureau of the Census. (1996). *Statistical Abstract of the United States, 1996.* Washington, DC: U.S. Government Printing Office.

13
Providing Services to Hispanic/Latino Populations: Profiles in Diversity

Graciela M. Castex

Many social workers are uncertain about what to expect when providing services to the culturally diverse group of clients known as Hispanics or, alternatively, as Latinos. The Hispanics/Latinos are a newly formed composite group, and people trained to approach ethnicity solely from a perspective that stresses cultural transmission as the primary element in ethnic group formation may lack the analytical tools necessary to understand this group's behaviors and strategies. This article briefly profiles the Hispanic/Latino population and places the group in the context of theories of ethnic group processes that emphasize their ontology as agents of social interaction with other groups and social institutions. At more length, key social characteristics of Hispanics/Latinos— such as differences in race, language, national origin, religion, self-ascription, and immigration and citizenship status—are discussed, along with their direct impact on practice.

Social workers in many settings find themselves providing services to clients characterized as Hispanics or Latinos, a group with which they may have had little experience. Although the literature makes frequent reference to Hispanics as a very diverse group, there has been little discussion of the socially important differences and similarities among Hispanics and how these differences and similarities may affect the provision of services. Instead, discussions about the provision of social services to Hispanic people often quickly focus on cultural attributes taken as common among subgroups, primarily Mexican Americans (or Chicanos), Puerto Ricans, and Cubans. Questions that may arise in the mind of the practitioner are, What is the Hispanic population?

If subgroups are diverse, in what ways are they diverse, and in what ways are they similar? What does it mean for culturally and racially diverse peoples to be perceived as members of a single ethnic group, and what are the implications of a client's ascription to this diverse group for practice?

Hispanic clients pose increasing challenges for social workers. This already large group is growing rapidly, and indicators such as age distribution and low median income levels indicate a rapidly increasing need for social services. The high numbers of recent immigrants, who often have limited English (Moore & Pachon, 1985) and experience a host of cultural factors that differentiate them from others in the population, add to the complexity of the challenge.

This article profiles the Hispanic/Latino population in the United States. It very briefly places the interactions of this group in the context of contemporary theories of ethnicity and discusses the diversity and similarities among members of the Hispanic/Latino group by examining key social features. The common experience of ascription to an ethnic minority in the United States has served as a primary unifying force that gave impetus—in a bidirectional process with state institutions—to the creation and maintenance of the Hispanic/Latino group.

Hispanics: A Statistical Profile

In April 1990, according to the U.S. Bureau of the Census, there were approximately 22 million people of Hispanic origin (referred to as Hispanics in the census literature) living in the United States out of a total population of 248.7 million. Hispanics, with 9.0 percent of the population, constituted the second largest minority group in the country after black Americans, with 12.1 percent. Because some census respondents identified themselves as both black and Hispanic, however, non-Hispanic blacks are only 11.8 percent of the nation's population. Furthermore, although census estimates are not available, the general assumption is that Hispanics are more likely to be undercounted than non-Hispanics (U.S. Bureau of the Census, 1991b, 1991c, 1991d).

The social needs of Hispanics are underlined by their standing in four social indexes:

1. poverty: In 1992, 26.2 percent of Hispanic families had incomes below the poverty level, compared with 10.3 percent of non-Hispanic families. Twelve percent of the children in the United States were Hispanic in 1992, but 21 percent of the children living in poverty were Hispanic; of all Hispanic children, 39.9 percent lived in poverty in 1992 (U.S. Bureau of the Census, 1993a).
2. income: The 1992 median income of non-Hispanic white households ($33,388) was 46.1 percent higher than that of Hispanic households ($22,848) (U.S. Bureau of the Census, 1993b).
3. family composition: Hispanics had a higher ratio of single-parent families (30 percent) than non-Hispanics (20 percent), and the ratio rose to 43 percent for the Puerto Rican–origin Hispanic subgroup (U.S. Bureau of the Census, 1991a).

4. demographics: The Hispanic population is young compared with non-Hispanics, with median ages in 1990 of 26.0 and 33.5 years, respectively; 30 percent of Hispanics and 21 percent of non-Hispanics are less than 15 years of age. Although accurate long-range demographic forecasts are difficult (one census projection predicts a Hispanic population of 128.3 million by 2050), short-range phenomena such as a high proportion of group members at or near childbearing age, a relatively high fertility rate, and high documented and undocumented net immigration rates guarantee a continued rapid growth of the Hispanic population during the next generation (U.S. Bureau of the Census, 1993c, 1993d).

Ethnic Group Concept

The Hispanic/Latino group, created by a federal order in the late 1970s, constitutes a valid social category that can be called an ethnic group and is increasingly regarded as such by those so ascribed. However, this usage may be counterintuitive for those trained to equate a list of cultural traits—a "culture"—with the ascription of ethnic status. But the U.S. government defined and formally created the Hispanic ethnic group on May 4, 1978. According to the Office of Management and Budget (1978), a Hispanic is "a person of Mexican, Puerto Rican, Cuban, Central or South American or other Spanish culture or origin, regardless of race" (p. 19269).

This definition largely focuses on the countries of origin and assumes that people in those countries have a common "Spanish culture," which is also shared by some people living in the United States. Although "Hispanic" was chosen by the federal government as the name of the group, many people so ascribed preferred to call themselves by another name, such as Latino or Latina. The formation of the Hispanic group should not be seen as unique; Native Americans and African Americans are two other examples, and similar phenomena are common in other countries.

The creation of an ethnic group in a dialectic with the state is a common social process. For the Hispanics in the United States, the process was bidirectional, involving state institutions and those so ascribed, to identify, control, and provide needed services to members of the new group (Castex, 1990; Enloe, 1981; Hayes-Bautista & Chapa, 1987; Nelson & Tienda, 1985).

If ethnic groups are regarded primarily as bearers of cultural traits, the bulk of which are passed from generation to generation, practitioners might assume that the federal government characterized Hispanics as belonging to a single group because they shared many significant cultural traits. Because this population is culturally diverse, from this culture-based perspective (which current anthropological and sociological ethnicity theory largely rejects) the designation "Hispanic" might be regarded as confusing at best.

The standard perspective among social theorists regarding the nature and functioning of ethnic groups—which began to be rigorously established in the late 1960s and early 1970s by Barth (1969), Cohen (1974), and Vincent (1974), among others—considers ethnicity to arise from groups interacting with other groups and social structures. In this perspective no ethnic group can exist without other groups to interact with: An ethnic group cannot exist in isolation. Ethnic identity is always expressed in dynamic processes of interaction with others. Barth (1969) pointed out that although particular cultural traits (for example, language or religion) may be important in the formation of a group and in the maintenance of group boundaries, no one can predict which traits will prove important in advance or which will continue to be ethnically significant in the future. Others have expanded Barth's arguments, elucidating the ways in which the state and other social structures affect ethnic group mobilization, maintenance, demobilization, and the joining together or splitting apart of groups to form new groups (Enloe, 1981; Horowitz, 1985; Wolf, 1982).

This perspective has directly or indirectly begun influencing discussions of ethnicity and cultural awareness in social work (Green, 1982; Pinderhughes, 1988, 1989). An understanding of Hispanic, or any other, ethnicity is impossible in the older paradigm; members of ethnic groups were presumed to "carry" a whole list of cultural traits, which sound suspiciously like stereotypes. The alternative viewpoint, however, emphasizes the need not only to value but also to expect diversity in a group. This view conditions exceptions and encourages development of strategies that avoid stereotypes when addressing the needs of the client.

Hispanic Ethnicity in Practice

Social workers need to keep in mind many features and issues deriving from the Hispanic client's ethnic status, in addition to the client's individual needs. Practitioners should prepare intellectually, emotionally, and clinically in anticipation of serving the Hispanic client. Prime features often regarded as ethnically significant and certainly important when interacting with clients include (but are not limited to) national origin, language, family names, religion, racial ascription, and immigration or citizenship status.

National Origin

Hispanics come from 26 nations according to the federal definition. There are significant differences among these nationalities; the languages, economic resources, educational systems, status structures, and customs vary dramatically from country to country. In addition, individual countries are often very ethnically diverse. The countries included by the Census Bureau are in North America (United States, Mexico), Central America (Guatemala, Honduras, El

Salvador, Belize, Nicaragua, Costa Rica, Panama), the Caribbean (Cuba, Puerto Rico, Dominican Republic), South America (Venezuela, Colombia, Ecuador, Peru, Bolivia, Chile, Paraguay, Argentina, Uruguay, Brazil, French Guiana, Suriname, and Guyana; the last three, lacking Spanish origin, are sometimes referred to as non-Hispanic South America, and the state language of Brazil is Portuguese), and Europe (Spain).

A social worker probably encounters clients coming from fewer countries, however. Persons describing themselves as of Mexican origin on the 1990 census constituted 60.4 percent of the Hispanic total, Puerto Ricans were 12.2 percent, and Cubans were 4.7 percent of the total. The catchall "other Hispanic" category covered 22.8 percent of Hispanics and included persons from all the other defined countries as well as some very old Hispanic communities in the United States (U.S. Bureau of the Census, 1991b).

The historical experiences of each country with the United States and the European colonialists are very different and can affect the ethnic self-identification of clients. Immigrants' attitudes toward the United States especially may be conditioned by these histories; long-time Dominican residents in New York, for example, sometimes express reluctance to become U.S. citizens; they still associate the United States with the suppression of the popular revolt in the Dominican Republic in 1965 and the subsequent military occupation by U.S. forces (personal communication with A. Goris, Hunter College instructor, Department of Puerto Rican Studies, March 17, 1992). Similarly complex feelings may be described by Mexicans, Nicaraguans, Salvadorans, Chileans, and Cubans. The feelings may not always be negative, but the actions of the state may evoke reactions dating from before the client's emigration or may even have contributed to the emigration. National background also affects the ease of obtaining legal residence status or, at times, refugee status. Practitioners working with Hispanic clients need to do the following:

- Ask where the client is from. What is the client's nationality?
- Ask if the client is a member of an ethnic group within that nationality.
- Become familiar with the group history and the history of the group's migration.
- Identify formal or informal providers of services directed toward members of this national group, such as religious and civic organizations, sports clubs, political organizations, and political officeholders.

Language

Many non-Hispanics assume that most Hispanics speak the same language—Spanish—or that their near forebears spoke it. This assumption follows the 19th century tendency to equate language, nationality, and ethnic status, even though the relationship of language and ethnicity has always been complex in the United States (Smith, 1989; Worsley, 1984). In fact, the home language of 3.05

million of the 14.61 million Hispanics counted in the 1980 census was not Spanish (Moore & Pachon, 1985).

Hispanics in the United States and residents of the 25 other countries of origin speak five major European languages (Spanish, Portuguese, French, Dutch, and English). They also speak such major Native American languages (each with millions of speakers) as Quechua, Mayan (a family of languages), Aymara, and Guarani, as well as many other Native American languages and creole dialects. Such language diversity is not a trivial point: Spanish may be a second language for many Spanish-speaking Hispanic immigrants. Immigrants from highland Guatemala (Mayan), highland Peru and Bolivia (Quechua and Aymara), and coastal Honduras (Garifuna, a creole language; Castex, in press) are common in the United States.

The assumption that Hispanics are normally fluent and literate in Spanish sometimes has damaging practical consequences for individual Hispanics, particularly in work-related situations. For example, a monolingual Spanish caseload should not be assigned to students or workers whose facility with the language is limited to discussions of the weather.

Similarly, not all Hispanic clients are fluent in Spanish. The situation may be even more complex, however. An agency sensitive to the needs of its clients, for example, may have materials and forms printed in Spanish, and the social worker may presume that all clients can read them. But some clients may not be literate in Spanish. Or some may speak both English and Spanish but may only be able to read English, making discussions of forms and legal documents very complex.

In addition, Hispanic clients speak a number of regional Spanish dialects. Speech in any language can serve as a social marker, however. The social worker should be sensitive, therefore, to situations in which the speech of the interviewer may indicate a status that differs from the client's. The interviewer's social status as indicated by Spanish usage may be higher or lower than that indicated by his or her English usage (Green, 1982; Kadushin, 1983).

The social worker attempting to communicate with Hispanic clients will find it helpful to

- find out what language the client communicates best in.
- be sensitive to the possibility that people who are in crisis or who are experiencing powerful emotions may have additional difficulties communicating in a second or third language.
- use trained people as interpreters or translators if such action seems appropriate and review literature on interviewing techniques when using interpreters.

Family Names

Many Hispanics have surnames that differ from those traditionally regarded as Spanish. While "Juan Garcia" is used colloquially as the Spanish equivalent of "John Smith," some Hispanics really are named Smith. And some Garcias in the United States are not Hispanic. The founding father of Chile was named O'Higgins, and the names of the current presidents of Peru, Argentina, and Chile—Fujimori, Menem, and Aylwin—are Japanese, Syrian, and Welsh in origin, respectively. Especially since 1800 there have been waves of migration to Latin America and the Caribbean from all over the world, particularly from Italy, France, Germany, and the Middle East but also from East Asia, Eastern Europe, and sub-Saharan Africa.

Regarding a surname as an indicator of ethnic status reached the height of absurdity when the Census Bureau tried to develop statistics on Hispanics on the basis of Spanish surnames. In preparing for the 1970 census, Spanish surnames were defined as any surname listed more than 25 times in the 1962 Havana, Cuba, telephone directory, thus excluding Cubans named Johnson or Lipshitz. The Havana list supplemented a 1950 list derived from the Mexico City and San Juan, Puerto Rico, directories. Had Eamon de Valera's mother not returned to Ireland from Brooklyn when he was a child, the first president of the Irish Republic would have been counted as Hispanic because his name began with "de." The "Martin" problem signaled the surname system's collapse, as thousands of people of British ancestry became "hispanized" because their last name appeared more than 25 times in a telephone directory (U.S. Bureau of the Census, 1975).

An additional source of confusion for practitioners may result from the Spanish language naming system, which differs from traditional English practice. Patrilineal descent is traced in naming through the second to the last name. The mother's maiden name (her father's) becomes a child's last name. In other words, Juan Garcia Jones's father's name is Garcia and his mother's name is Jones. Juan will pass on the Garcia name to his children as their second to last name, and so on.

Under Spanish common law, women do not acquire their husband's name on marriage. Garcia's mother, Señora Jones, is legally a Jones, not a Garcia. Forms including a husband's name—Señora Jones de Garcia—rarely have other than honorific status. Passports, airline tickets, and such are often issued in maiden names, which some countries require women to use when signing official documents. Therefore, social workers can make no assumptions about marital status or feminist attitudes because a couple uses different surnames.

Social workers will find it useful to

- make no firm assumptions about language use, ethnic status, or recent heritage based on a name.
- ask a client how to pronounce or spell a name.
- remember that persons in the same household may have different surnames. (Married names may have no legal standing, and the extended family may include aunts, uncles, cousins, grandparents, grandchildren, even godchildren and godparents, living together.)

- keep in mind that some people may not use their legal names because they fear attention from immigration authorities.

Racial Ascription

Racial ascription is generally regarded as cultural rather than biological among social theorists. The particular biological traits that significantly determine racial ascription vary from society to society. Skin color, hair texture, class status, and other traits may all interact differentially to determine racial ascription; therefore, ascription is primarily a cultural phenomenon. A white Dominican, for example, may be *trigueño* (mixed, literally "wheat-colored") in Puerto Rico and black in Georgia (Harris, 1964; Mintz, 1971; Stephens, 1989).

Hispanics are racially diverse by any system of definition. Individual Hispanics might be characterized in the United States as white or European American, Native American, African American, East Asian, South Asian, and perhaps other racial types. In many countries, discrimination based on ascription as an *indio* (Native American) may be the most socially significant racial designation. But even then, to live like a *blanco* (white or European) is often to become one (Comitas, 1967; Harris, 1964).

The U.S. census of 1990 identifies Hispanics as a category separate from race. When asked to identify race in a separate question, Hispanic respondents identified themselves as follows: white, 11.5 million; black, 770,000; American Indian, 165,000; Asian, 305,000; other race, 9.5 million. These figures communicate a significant message: Whereas 51.7 percent of the Hispanic population identified itself as white, 42.7 percent of the Hispanics self-identified as another race. Hispanics constitute 97.5 percent of the other race category for the nation as a whole. Most of these self-identified racially as Hispanic, Latino, Chicano, La Raza, mestizo, or some other term that referred to Hispanic origin (U.S. Bureau of the Census, 1991d).

Clients who may have become classified as African American only after their arrival in the United States may be experiencing serious racial discrimination for the first time. As a result, the practitioner must keep in mind the need to consult with the client regarding his or her racial status and to be sensitive to the possibility that he or she may have experienced a dramatic change in social status because of the U.S. system of racial ascription. Such a change can affect self-esteem, relations with others, and real opportunities.

Religion

Perhaps the majority of Hispanics are Roman Catholics, but there are very large (and growing) Protestant Hispanic populations both in the United States and in the countries of origin, as well as significant populations of other faiths. In addition, the beliefs and practices of many Hispanics have been influenced by or derive directly from African and Native American belief systems that may be syncretized with Christian or Catholic beliefs in forms such as *santeria*. For example, the *botanicas* (stores that sell herbal medicines and religious images) are communal centers in the expression of the spiritist beliefs that inform *santeria* (Borello & Mathias, 1977).

The cultural component and practices of Hispanic believers may differ quite extensively from the practices of non-Hispanic coreligionists in the United States (McCready, 1985). Hispanics and the once largely Irish hierarchy of the Catholic Church in the United States, for example, have had a long and complex struggle to achieve mutual understanding (to put the matter politely). Although differences between Hispanic Methodists and non-Hispanic Methodists may exist, most Protestant denominations are relatively less hierarchical and therefore in practice more open to different styles of observance (Weyr, 1988).

The Catholic Church and other denominations have developed many programs to address the social needs of Hispanics. These vary locally and run the gamut from soup kitchens to legal assistance for immigrants. Umbrella organizations encompassing other faiths have also been active, especially in working with immigrants and refugees. When making referrals, religious institutions may be important resources. It is important to keep in mind that

- religious institutions involving a variety of faiths may provide organizational support for and leadership to Hispanic communities.
- if it appears relevant, social workers should determine clients' religious affiliations, if any.
- social workers should make no assumptions about clients' experiences in their native country. For example, some Hispanics have experienced severe religious discrimination in their country of origin.

Ascription by Self or Others

Most Hispanics, when asked to describe their cultural heritage or ethnic identity, will first respond with a reference to their nationality (such as Mexican, Puerto Rican, Peruvian), even in the second or third immigrant generation. If one were to ask them about any broader self-identification, the term Hispanic would until recently rarely be heard; Latino or Latina is more common (Hayes-Bautista & Chapa, 1987).

When determining ethnic status, however, it is useful to look at the social context in which it is expressed. A single person can have many ethnicities, including a national ethnicity and a supraethnicity, when dealing with large-scale social institutions such as national or international systems or encompassing state structures. (Changes in state structures almost invariably radically affect ethnic expression. Contemporary Yugoslavia and the former

Soviet Union, British India in 1947, and Austria–Hungary in 1918 are striking examples.)

Hispanics are a composite group with enough feelings of similarity to aid coalition forming when confronting large-scale structures, which in turn may find it convenient to regard Hispanics as a single group (Greeley, 1977; Royce, 1982). In other situations this large-scale sense of selfhood need not be called into play—in a neighborhood of Hispanics, nationality might be the identifying factor; in a neighborhood of Mexican Americans, other local or ancestral criteria might come into play.

The state and the larger society, the "others," have named the Hispanic. In many respects, naming is the result of and a response to oppression and exploitation: One might speak of "greaser" or "wetback" ethnicity. By a purification of terms, such terms have come to refer to the more acceptable Hispanic or Latino ethnicity.

There are problems with the term "Hispanic." It reminds many persons so ascribed of the colonial exploitation of the Spanish state; many Hispanics have no ancestors from the Iberian Peninsula. The term "Latino," however, also excludes the Native American, African, Asian, or non-Latin European backgrounds of many Hispanics. But ethnicity may transcend terminology in the search for symbolic effectiveness. In situations in which ethnic identification may be important, the social worker might find it helpful to let people identify themselves, to remember that ascriptions may vary by social context, and to remember that individuals may not see themselves as members of the group they have been placed in.

Immigration or Citizenship Status

One great division in the Hispanic community is between those who have the legal right to both live and remain in the United States ("documented") and those who do not ("undocumented"). In addition, there are numerous classifications of documented status (such as refugee status) that affect access to public services. Legal status affects mobility, employment availability, the ability to assert rights, and even the ability to plan for the future on more than a day-to-day basis.

The date of entry into the United States is a key piece of information for those providing services to almost any immigrant. A verifiable entry date may render the undocumented client eligible for a regularization of status under various laws that offer protection and amnesties. For all immigrants, date of entrance communicates information about the opportunities in the United States at the time of migration and conditions in the country of origin at that time.

All noncitizens, even undocumented noncitizens, have rights, however. These include a child's right to schooling, the right to basic medical care, and the right to due process. Immigrants' rights group are sources of materials setting forth the rights of noncitizens and the policies of local governments and agencies in defense of those rights (National Center for Immigrant Students, 1991; New York Department of City Planning, 1990).

No matter how the client looks, sounds (even if there is no trace of a Spanish accent), or behaves, a social worker should consider whether or not documentation status is affecting the issues a client brings to the relationship. Social workers will find it useful to

- become acquainted with the services available to aid documented and undocumented people with various statuses.
- be sensitive to the possibility that clients who appear evasive or resistant to suggestions may be frightened about revealing undocumented status. Social workers can emphasize the degree of confidentiality that they can offer clients and include some legal advice about agency, local, and federal policies.
- keep abreast of current immigration regulations.

Conclusion

During the 19th century and early in the 20th century, Hispanics were legally discriminated against in the United States; they have always suffered from oppression, violence, and disrespect (Moore & Pachon, 1985). This suppression of group members, sanctioned by the state at various levels as well as by other social institutions and combined with the mounting rate of post–World War II immigration, led to the creation of the population we now call Hispanic or Latino. The population began to form a group as part of multidirectional interactions among component groups as well as interactions among the new group, federal and state authorities, and other institutions that were attempting to address perceived needs and pressures in an administratively convenient manner (Enloe, 1981; Moore & Pachon, 1985; Weyr, 1988). This process has led to an increasing group consciousness both organizationally and symbolically, as indicated by the ethnic self-identification in the 1990 census.

Yankauer (1987), reviewing a series of articles on terminology, commented that "whatever cohesion exists within the diverse groups covered by the term 'Hispanic,' it is the product of prejudice and discrimination directed against them" (p. 15). When confronted with the special needs and challenges of a large and growing population, the government began labeling, and the component groups tended to band together to more effectively confront the state and other discriminatory groups or institutions. Individuals tend to identify themselves as Hispanic or not depending on the level of interactions with other systems. Large systems tend to elicit responses of the amalgamated group; interactions at the neighborhood and more personal levels are likely to elicit more restricted identification. Peeling the onion of Hispanic ethnicity may well lead to additional ethnicities, depending on the group or institution with which it is interacting.

References

Barth, F. (1969). Introduction. In F. Barth (Ed.), *Ethnic groups and boundaries* (pp. 3–38). Boston: Little, Brown.

Borello, M. A., & Mathias, E. (1977, August–September). Botanicas: Puerto Rican folk pharmacies. *Natural History,* pp. 65–73.

Castex, G. M. (1990). An analysis and synthesis of current theories of ethnicity and ethnic group processes using the creation of the Hispanic group as a case example. *Dissertation Abstracts International, 51,* 07A (University Microfilms No. 90-33820).

Castex, G. M. (in press). Hondurans. In K. T. Jackson (Ed.), *Encyclopedia of New York City.* New Haven, CT: New York Historical Society and Yale University.

Cohen, A. (1974). Introduction: The lesson of ethnicity. In A. Cohen (Ed.), *Urban ethnicity* (pp. ix–xxiv). London: Tavistock.

Comitas, L. (1967). Education and social stratification in Bolivia. *Transactions of the New York Academy of Sciences, 9*(7, Series 2), 935–948.

Enloe, C. H. (1981). The growth of the state and ethnic mobilization: The American experience. *Ethnic and Racial Studies, 4,* 123–136.

Greeley, A. (1977). Minorities: White ethnics. In J. B. Turner (Ed.-in-Chief), *Encyclopedia of social work* (17th ed., Vol. 2, pp. 979–984). Washington, DC: National Association of Social Workers.

Green, J. W. (1982). *Cultural awareness in the human services.* Englewood Cliffs, NJ: Prentice Hall.

Harris, M. (1964). *Patterns of race in the Americas.* New York: W. W. Norton.

Hayes-Bautista, D. E., & Chapa, J. (1987). Latino terminology: Conceptual bases for standardized terminology. *American Journal of Public Health, 77,* 61–68.

Horowitz, D. L. (1985). *Ethnic groups in conflict.* Los Angeles: University of California Press.

Kadushin, A. (1983). *The social work interview.* New York: Columbia University Press.

McCready, W. C. (1985). Culture and religion. In P.S.J. Cafferty & W. C. McCready (Eds.), *Hispanics in the United States: A new social agenda* (pp. 49–61). New Brunswick, NJ: Transaction Books.

Mintz, S. (1971). Groups, group boundaries, and the perception of race. *Comparative Studies in Society and History, 13,* 437–450.

Moore, J., & Pachon, H. (1985). *Hispanics in the United States.* Englewood Cliffs, NJ: Prentice Hall.

National Center for Immigrant Students. (1991). Immigrant students' right of access. *New Voices, 1*(1), 4.

Nelson, C., & Tienda, M. (1985). The structuring of Hispanic ethnicity: Historical and contemporary perspectives. *Ethnic and Racial Studies, 8,* 49–74.

New York Department of City Planning, Office of Immigrant Affairs. (1990). *Immigrant entitlements made (relatively) simple* (DCP No.90-14). New York: Author.

Office of Management and Budget. (1978, May 4). Directive 15: Race and ethnic standards for federal statistics and administrative reporting. *Federal Register, 43,* 19269.

Pinderhughes, E. (1988). Significance of culture and power in the human behavior curriculum. In C. Jacobs & D. D. Bowles (Eds.), *Ethnicity & race: Critical concepts in social work* (pp. 152–166). Silver Spring, MD: National Association of Social Workers.

Pinderhughes, E. (1989). *Understanding race, ethnicity, and power.* New York: Free Press.

Royce, A. P. (1982). *Ethnic identity.* Bloomington: Indiana University Press.

Smith, A. (1989). The origins of nations. *Ethnic and Racial Studies, 12,* 340–367.

Stephens, T. M. (1989). The language of ethnicity and self-identity in American Spanish and Brazilian Portuguese. *Ethnic and Racial Studies, 12,* 138–145.

U.S. Bureau of the Census. (1975). *Comparison of persons of Spanish surname and persons of Spanish origin in the United States* (Technical Paper 38). Washington, DC: U.S. Government Printing Office.

U.S. Bureau of the Census. (1991a). *The Hispanic population in the United States: March 1990* (Current Population Reports, Series P-20, No. 449). Washington, DC: U.S. Government Printing Office.

U.S. Bureau of the Census. (1991b). *Resident population distribution for the United States, regions, and states, by race and Hispanic origin: 1990* (Press Release CB91-100). Washington, DC: Author.

U.S. Bureau of the Census. (1991c). *Census Bureau releases counts on specific racial groups* (Press Release CB91-215). Washington, DC: Author.

U.S. Bureau of the Census. (1991d). *Census Bureau releases 1990 Census counts on Hispanic population groups* (Press Release CB91-216). Washington, DC: Author.

U.S. Bureau of the Census. (1993a). *Poverty in the United States: 1992* (Current Population Reports, Series P-60, No. 185). Washington, DC: U.S. Government Printing Office.

U.S. Bureau of the Census. (1993b). *Money income of households, families, and persons in the United States: 1992* (Current Population Reports, Series P-60, No. 184). Washington, DC: U.S. Government Printing Office.

U.S. Bureau of the Census. (1993c). *Population projections of the United States, by age, sex, race, and Hispanic origin* (Current Population Reports, Series PS-25, No. 1104). Washington, DC: U.S. Government Printing Office.

U.S. Bureau of the Census. (1993d). *Hispanic Americans today* (Current Population Reports, Population Characteristics, Series P-23, No.183). Washington, DC: U.S. Government Printing Office.

Vincent, J. (1974). The structuring of ethnicity. *Human Organization, 33,* 375–378.

Weyr, T. (1988). *Hispanic U.S.A.: Breaking the melting pot.* New York: Harper & Row.

Wolf, E. (19S2). *Europe and the people without history.* Berkeley: University of California Press.

Worsley, P. (1984). *The three worlds: Culture and world development.* Chicago: University of Chicago Press.

Yankauer, A. (1987). Hispanic/Latino—What's in a name? *American Journal of Public Health, 77,* 15–17.

14

What Do Culturally Sensitive Mental Health Services Mean? The Case of Hispanics

*Lloyd H. Rogler, Robert G. Malgady,
Guiseppe Costantino, and Rena Blumenthal*

Two events converged in the decade of the 1960s to focus attention on the need for culturally sensitive mental health services for economically disadvantaged minority populations. First was the rise of the civil rights movement, when Blacks and other minority groups insisted that the institutional structure of American society be more responsive to their needs and less exclusionary of their participation as citizens in a pluralistic democracy. Second was the nationwide development of community mental health programs. As these programs expanded to cover new, economically disadvantaged catchment areas with populations that had never before received professional mental health care, many of the deficiencies of traditional service systems and therapies became evident. Traditional therapies, based largely on the therapeutic needs of middle-class clients, often proved to be of questionable effectiveness with minority persons living in inner-city neighborhoods, thus prompting pleas for culturally sensitive modalities.

Culturally sensitive mental health services are especially important for Hispanics, because they are the most rapidly growing minority population in the United States. According to census figures, the Hispanic population was 14.6 million in 1980, and it has had a 6.1 percent annual growth rate since 1970. Moreover, demographic studies of the Hispanic population indicate that Hispanics are younger, less educated, poorer, and more likely to live in inner-city neighborhoods than the general population and that they confront language problems. This constellation of characteristics makes Hispanics vulnerable to mental health problems requiring psychotherapeutic services.

Rogler, L. H., Malgady, R. G., Costantino, G., & Blumenthal, R. (1987). What do culturally sensitive mental health services mean? *American Psychologist, 24,* 565–570. Copyright © 1987 by the American Psychological Association. Reprinted by permission.

The past two decades have witnessed an explosive growth in the literature focusing on Hispanic mental health. This literature is pervasively critical, documenting the multiple barriers that, in the face of massive need, keep Hispanics from receiving adequate mental health care (Rogler et al., 1983). At the core of the literature's criticism is the charge, once again, that mental health services targeted for Hispanics are not culturally sensitive. Thus, the question arises: What do culturally sensitive mental health services mean? To answer this question, we examined the use of the concept by mental health practitioners and researchers in their work with Hispanics. In doing so, we uncovered three broad approaches to cultural sensitivity: first, rendering traditional treatments more accessible to Hispanics; second, selecting an available therapeutic modality according to the perceived features of Hispanic culture; and third, extracting elements from Hispanic culture and using them to modify traditional treatments or as an innovative treatment tool. The first purpose of this article is to describe the components of cultural sensitivity within each of the three approaches mentioned above. The second purpose is to examine the relationship between culture and therapy in the literature on Hispanics by posing a fundamental question: Must the content of all culturally sensitive therapies stand in an isomorphic, mirror-like relationship to the client's culture? Inferences drawn from the literature and our own research justify raising this question.

Increased Accessibility of Treatment

The first and most basic approach to culturally sensitive mental health care involves increasing the accessibility of traditional treatments of Hispanic clients. This issue can be understood in the context of Freidson's (1970) argument that two characteristics of a cultural subpopulation are likely to influence the utilization of the professional medical system. The first involves the level of congruence between the client's and the professional's understanding of illness and treatment—the greater the level of accord, the more likely it is that the client will seek out and retain professional services. The second characteristic involves the ethnic group's lay referral system, which ranges from a loose/truncated system, allowing the individual great leeway in personal health decisions, to a cohesive/extended system, pressing the individual to act according to the values of the cultural milieu. The least utilization of health services occurs in communities that have a marked incongruence between cultural and professional values combined with a cohesive/extended lay referral structure. Such a lay referral system is likely to inhibit the use of professional services and to provide alternative routes to coping with health needs in a culturally congruent way.

Research suggests that many Hispanics fit into this categorization (Rogler et al., 1983). Thus, an accessible treatment program for Hispanics should increase the congruence between professional mental health values and indigenous Hispanic values and also incorporate elements of the lay referral system to forward its own purpose.

A variety of attempts have been made in recent years to develop more accessible treatment programs for Hispanics in diverse mental health settings. Karno and Morales (1971), for example, described the creation of a mental health clinic specially modified to the perceived needs of Hispanics. Preventive services, consultation with other community agencies, and crisis intervention were incorporated into the program along with traditional services. Although they did not provide evidence, Karno and Morales (1971) stated that "in a context of cultural and linguistic familiarity and acceptance" Mexican Americans respond just as well to traditional treatment as Anglos. Scott and Delgado (1979) discussed the issues arising during the development of a mental health program for Hispanics within a community clinic. They believed that the program became effective after the recruitment of a bilingual/bicultural staff, integration of the program into the structure of the host facility, and coordination of the program's effort with the needs of the Hispanic community. Abad, Ramos, and Boyce (1974), describing their experience in establishing a mental health clinic in a community mental health center in New Haven, emphasized the need to gain the support of local religious and political leaders prior to commencing the effort. To succeed, the clinic had to maintain a credible presence in the institutional structures affecting the Puerto Ricans' lives. Similar programs were described by Cuellar, Harris, and Naron (1981) within an inpatient institutional setting and by Normand, Iglesias, and Payn (1974) and Rodriguez (1971) on a small-group basis within large hospital settings.

The lowest common denominator of cultural sensitivity with Hispanics is generally that of linguistic accessibility. Indeed, for many treatment innovators, the primary efforts have been focused on the hiring of bilingual/bicultural staff, thus overcoming the most blatant communication barriers that exist between clients and staff. The importance of even such minimal outreach efforts is dramatized by the innovative use of paraprofessionals by Acosta and Cristo (1981). Assuming that Hispanics' needs for mental health services would likely continue to exceed the availability of Hispanic therapists, they developed a bilingual interpreter program in a psychiatric clinic. The interpreters were recruited from the same neighborhoods as the clients and were trained in key concepts of psychotherapy and the nomenclature used in clinical settings. They also acted as cultural consultants, explaining to English-speaking therapists the

This research was supported by Grant 2R01 MH30569-06A from the Center for Minority Group Mental Health Programs (National Institute of Mental Health) to L. H. Rogler, Director of the Hispanic Research Center, Fordham University, and also by Grant 1R01 MH33711 from the Center for Minority Group Mental Health Programs to G. Costantino, Research Associate of the Hispanic Research Center. We wish to thank Janet Cohen and Stasia Madrigal for their editorial assistance.

Correspondence concerning this article should be addressed to Lloyd H. Rogler, Hispanic Research Center, Thebaud Hall, Fordham University, Bronx, NY 10458.

meanings conveyed by patients during therapy. In spite of the awkwardness inherent in introducing a third party into a therapeutic relationship, the success of this program in increasing accessibility of services seems to justify the approach: The percentage of Spanish-speaking patients admitted to the clinic doubled with such efforts. Indeed, there is additional evidence, both longitudinal and cross-sectional, that such innovations do increase utilization rates in Hispanic communities (Bloom, 1975; Trevino, Bruhn, & Bunce, 1979).

By reaching out to the ethnic network in the community, the professional system has found that it can attract Hispanics to use and retain its services, advance professional conceptions of mental health, and partially bypass alternative coping patterns indigenous to Hispanic culture. At the same time, by incorporating members of the ethnic network into the professional system, key elements of the lay culture are assimilated. All such forms of increasing accessibility therefore represent the first approach to providing culturally sensitive mental health services.

Selection of Treatments to Fit Hispanic Culture

In addition to treatment accessibility, another area of concern calling for cultural sensitivity has been the treatment Hispanics receive once they enter the mental health system. Without such a concern, the incongruous, but nevertheless conceivable, situation could occur of Hispanics having greater access to culturally inappropriate therapeutic modalities. The possibility of this occurring was noted in the development of a mental health clinic for Puerto Ricans in New Haven (Abad et al., 1974, p. 590). Thus the second approach to cultural sensitivity is the selection of a therapy modality to coincide with perceived Hispanic cultural characteristics.

Some researchers and therapists have argued that treatment decisions ought not to preclude the use of psychoanalytic concepts and techniques with ethnic minority clients. Maduro and Martinez (1974) claimed that "more self-aware individuals are needed to confront insidious social realities in the outer world, as well as unconscious themes in the inner world" (p. 461). They believed that Jungian dream work is congruent with Mexican culture, in that folk healers often specialize in the interpretation of dreams, and that such traditional analytic treatments are accessible and appropriate to their Hispanic clientele. Nonetheless, the attitudes of Maduro and Martinez represent a minority opinion. Frontline mental health practitioners working in inner-city, economically depressed, Hispanic neighborhoods were among the first to level criticism at insight-oriented psychoanalytic therapy as both uneconomical and irrelevant to the context of Hispanic life (Ruiz, 1981; Sue & Sue, 1977). Their widely shared image of the psychologically distressed Hispanic was of a person pressured and harassed by problems of poverty, slum life, and lack of acculturation into American society. The image of such a client taking his or her place on the proverbial psychoanalytic couch for a long-term therapy designed to nurture insight into repressed impulses caricatured psychoanalysis as an absurdly inconsequential modality. For this reason, few psychoanalytic therapists sought to address Hispanic's emotional problems, and a pervasive view developed that insight-oriented techniques were too esoteric to respond to the massive stresses impinging on the majority of Hispanic clients.

Bluestone and Vela's (1982) work stands as an exception to this pattern of neglect, for they proposed that a series of culturally informed adjustments can be made in the use of insight-oriented therapy with Puerto Ricans living at the bottom of the socioeconomic heap. Notwithstanding such adjustments, they recognized that suitable candidates for insight-oriented intervention must be relatively free from external chaos, display a persistent motivation to remain in therapy, have a long-term outlook on life, and possess a capacity for insight. The issue remains, however, that even with a liberal interpretation of these qualifications, traditional insight therapy would be an inappropriate modality for most members of economically disadvantaged, inner-city Hispanic communities. Ruiz (1981) made this point rather bluntly, speaking in reference to treatment of inner-city Hispanic clients: "Do they need brilliant insights into the etiology of . . . paranoia? Do they need to become more introspective or psychodynamically oriented? The answers to these questions are negative" (p. 202).

As an alternative to insight-oriented therapies, others have suggested individualized treatment selection: Culturally sensitive therapy must accord with the needs of the individual client. However, in broadly discussing cultural traits, one can easily fall into the trap of disregarding the substantial differences between Hispanic subcultures (Gurak & Rogler, 1980) and individual differences within specific groups. In this context the work of Ruiz (1981) is a valuable contribution to clarification of the concept of cultural sensitivity. Ruiz acknowledged the diversity of subcultures that fall under the catch-all phrase "Hispanic" and the difficulty of identifying as a Hispanic a person who is bicultural or sufficiently assimilated to be considered Anglo. Clearly, treatment decisions cannot be based on a simplistic criterion such as a Spanish surname. Ruiz believed that culturally sensitive treatment plans should be based on the objective assessment of the degree of biculturalism that the individual client manifests, and he provided rich examples of integrated treatment plans that may span the continuum from the "most Hispanic" to the "most Anglo" client. Prior to selection of a therapy modality for a given client, the therapist conducts an assessment of the client's linguistic skills in English and Spanish (both dominance and preference) and of the client's general level of acculturation.

Ruiz illustrated his point by describing the disposition of a case classified at the "most Hispanic" extreme—a non-English-speaking, unacculturated Mexican living in an impoverished, inner-city, Hispanic community. The initial assessment included a detailed medical history in Spanish (involving family members) and a physical examination to rule out organic etiology. Next, Ruiz focused on the hierarchy of the client's need, first stressing the immediacy of counseling aimed at the basic problems—such as health, housing, immigration status, and economic survival—that confronted the client on a daily basis. Based on the client's social immersion within a complex extended-family network (as is common within Mexican American communities), a family-oriented therapy with the goal of stress reduction was administered by a Spanish-speaking and bicultural therapist. Ruiz insightfully argued that disposition to treatment by psychodynamic or even behavior modification techniques was premature.

Acculturation refers to the complex process whereby the behaviors and attitudes of the migrant change toward the dominant group as a result of exposure to a cultural system that is significantly different. A variety of acculturation measures have been published recently for diverse Hispanic subcultures, including Mexican Americans (Cuellar, Harris, & Jasso, 1980), Cubans (Szapocznik, Scopetta, & King, 1978), and Puerto Ricans (Inclan, 1979). Following such assessments, the therapist is able to make a more judicious decision about the particular treatment to be given.

However, acculturation signifies a process of change with multiple components. Some components change more rapidly than others, as shown by the Rogler and Cooney (1984, pp. 71–98) study of intergenerationally linked Puerto Rican families. This means that treatment decisions based on the client's level of acculturation still confront some ambiguity. From one moment to the next, the therapist with a transcultural orientation may need to address issues pertaining to the client's traditional culture, the culture of the host society, or some emergent product of both cultures. Nevertheless, the point to be stressed is that individualizing the treatment process is the primary and preferred mode of dealing with the problem.

Thus, the second approach to the delivery of culturally sensitive mental health services involves distinguishing between those acculturated Hispanics who can be treated as if they were Anglos and those who require some sort of special treatment modality reflecting their adherence to Hispanic culture. It is the treatment of this latter population that leads to the third approach to culturally sensitive treatment.

Modifying Treatments to Fit Hispanic Culture

If the therapy is selected to fit the client, aspects of the therapy can also he adapted to fit the client's culture. A clear example of using an element from the client's ethnic culture to complement and modify the provision of conventional therapy is given in Kreisman's (1975) account of treating two Mexican American female schizophrenics who thought of themselves as *embrujadas* (bewitched). The essence of Kreisman's treatment modification was merely to concur that they were indeed bewitched. The therapist's acknowledgment of bewitchment and of the need for folk remedies broke through the plateau that had been reached in conventional therapy, thus enabling further therapeutic progress. In this context, elements of the client's culture were incorporated into the treatment without abandoning or compromising the therapist's chosen modality.

A somewhat different example of using an element of the client's culture is provided by the language-switching techniques employed by Pitta, Marcos, and Alpert (1978), who postulated that emotional expression is freer and more spontaneous in one's native tongue, whereas the use of a second language fosters intellectual defenses and control. The language in which therapy is conducted is chosen according to both patient characteristics and phase of treatment, and language-switching is used as a therapeutic technique. The medium into which this technique is incorporated is a traditional, insight-oriented psychotherapy that is in no other way modified for the needs of the ethnic client. Again, neither the conception of therapy nor the therapeutic role is altered, but an ethnic characteristic of the client is introduced to buttress the treatment modality.

One of the most ambitious programmatic efforts made to adapt treatment modalities to the perceived traits of a Hispanic population is that of Szapocznik and his collaborators (Szapocznik et al., 1979). They developed objective measures of Cuban value orientations and acculturation that are used to guide therapeutic intervention. According to their theory of intrafamily tension and stress, the greater the disparity in acculturation between family members, the greater the family tensions and stresses. Szapocznik et al. (1978) maintained that the treatment of the acculturation problems of Cuban families should stand in an isomorphic, mirror-like relationship to the clients' cultural background: "Cubans' value structure must be matched by a similar set of therapeutic assumptions" (p. 116). The selection of family therapy as the treatment was predicated on the notion that Cubans are family oriented. Having determined through their research that the Cuban value system prizes lineality, Szapocznik et al. had the family therapist assume a position of authority to restore or reinforce parental authority over the children. Szapocznik and his colleagues outlined a detailed sequence of therapeutic interventions deduced from their findings on the cultural characteristics of Cuban clients and implemented in compliance with the assumption that therapeutic content should mirror the culture.

More recently, Szapocznik, Kurtines, and Fernandez (1980) recognized that other treatment modifications with Hispanic clients need not follow a rigid isomorphic pattern with respect to the culture. Sometimes the objective of treatment is to change culturally prescribed behavior. For example, Boulette (1976) observed the ubiquity of the "subassertiveness" pattern common among Mexican American women. This pattern, judged to be psychologically dysfunctional, became the target for a therapeutic program to train Mexican American women to be more assertive. The ultimate purpose was for the women to overcome the somatic complaints and symptoms of depression and anxiety thought to result from culturally prescribed submissiveness. Other Hispanic groups have similar cultural patterns (Rogler & Hollingshead, 1985). Boulette's therapeutic approach raises important issues when placed in the context of the lives of persons who are rooted in first-generation, traditional ethnic culture and who are at the bottom rung of the socioeconomic ladder. In such a context, Hispanics pervasively experience gender-based role segregation (Rogler & Cooney, 1984, pp. 99–124). Among spouses, there is a sharp distinction between *trabajo de hombre* (men's work) and *trabajo de mujer* (women's work) as well as sex-based differences in leisure patterns and inequities in power tending to favor the husbands. How does the development of assertiveness interact with such role segregation? Will the women's assertiveness clash with the culturally prescribed submissiveness imbedded in role segregation? The questions can be raised, but the research required to answer them is not available.

Nonetheless, contrasted with earlier accounts prescribing that therapeutic activities and structure should mirror Hispanic culture, Boulette's antithetical view raises intriguing questions. Once the cultural characteristics of a minority ethnic group have been adequately documented, how should the characteristics be taken into account during treatment? Is effective therapy necessarily that which attempts the preservation of traditional cultural elements, or should acculturation, assimilation, or adaptation to the host society sometimes take priority? Perhaps advocacy on behalf of preserving traditional cultural elements, no matter how well intentioned, ought not always or exclusively shape the nature of therapeutic interventions. On the other hand, the values of the host society similarly should not be idealized as reflecting universal standards of mental health.

It is our contention that when therapy modalities are modified to address the needs of Hispanic clients, the adapted therapy need not isomorphically reflect the client's cultural characteristics. We suggest that therapeutic gains can be made when traditional cultural patterns are bent or redirected according to predetermined therapeutic goals. Thus, the first step in the process of treatment modification is to determine the ethnic group's traits of likely therapeutic relevance and then employ them directly or transform them as needed. Isomorphic reinforcement of cultural traits implies that they are necessarily adaptive, whereas, on the other hand, departures from this assumption imply that some cultural traits serve as an obstacle to therapy and that acculturation to the values of the host society is an additional and valid standard of adjustment. It also assumes that cultural elements can be modified within the treatment according to the implicit goals of the therapy without impugning their value and purpose as functional cultural traits in the immigrant's society of origin. The modifications imply the development of hypotheses reflecting the intricacies of the many possible connections between various cultural traits and the therapies administered. The ultimate aim should be relief from psychological distress and the adaptation of the Hispanic client to the new host society in such a way that ethnic identity and pride are not negated or belied.

Developing a Culturally Sensitive Modality With Children

A third approach to cultural sensitivity, modification of treatment, also is in evidence when specific elements from the client's culture are used as the vehicle for therapeutic intervention. *Cuento* or folktale therapy, a recent innovation (Costantino, Malgady, & Rogler, 1986), provides an illustration. Cuento therapy is a modeling technique based on the principles of social learning theory, but it takes as its medium the folktales of Puerto Rican culture and focuses them on psychologically distressed Puerto Rican children.

Although much of the aforementioned literature has dealt with the mental health of Hispanic adults, little attention has been directed to second-generation Hispanic children who, trapped between two cultures, are at high risk of mental disorder. For this reason, we attempted the development of cuento therapy. The therapy was administered by bilingual/bicultural therapists in a mental health clinic with a catchment area that is predominantly Puerto Rican. The objective in telling folktales to the children was to transmit cultural values, foster pride in the Puerto Rican cultural heritage, and reinforce adaptive behavior.

To conduct the therapy, the therapist read the folktales in both English and Spanish to the children and led a group discussion on the meaning or moral of the story, highlighting the "good" and "bad" behaviors of the characters. The stories quickly captured the attention of the children, who identified readily with the characters portrayed. In the next step of the intervention, the group participants role-played the various characters in the story. This activity was videotaped, and afterward the children viewed themselves on tape and discussed the role-playing activities with the therapist in relation to their own personal problems. The therapist then proposed new scenarios for role playing, and the children acted out solutions to problems presented in the scenarios. The therapist verbally reinforced adaptive behavior and corrected behavior that was maladaptive.

To examine the question of whether therapy should isomorphically reflect the culture, some of the children were told folktales as they appeared in original folklore, thus replicating cultural elements without changing them. Departing from the isomorphic assumption, other children were told folktales that had been changed in order to convey the knowledge, values, and skills useful in coping with the demands of the sociocultural environment of the host society's inner-city neighborhoods. In the adaptation of stories, moral issues were retained from the original story, but other changes were made: Cultural objects comprising the setting changed from a rural tropical scene to an urban, Hispanic neighborhood; culturally based interpersonal patterns also were changed—for example, authoritarian control of a younger sibling by an older one was transformed into the problem of maladaptive influences from peers in an urban setting and the overcoming of fear in resisting such influences.

The interested reader is invited to turn elsewhere for a full statement of the experimental design and procedures used to evaluate cuento therapy and the study's findings (Costantino, Malgady, & Rogler, 1985). Here, it is important to note that cuento therapy, compared to traditional group therapy and nonintervention, significantly reduced trait anxiety. Moreover, the therapy group with cuentos adapted to American society evidenced a greater reduction in trait anxiety, and this effect remained stable one year after the intervention. Thus, there is empirical justification for the development of both therapies that take elements unchanged from the clients' culture and those that adapt such elements to the host society.

Conclusions

The three approaches to cultural sensitivity presented here can be viewed metaphorically as a pyramidal structure. At the base lie the numerous programs that have made efforts to improve the accessibility of mental health services to Hispanic populations. Moving up the pyramid, we find programs that have gone several steps further in this process and that choose treatments according to the cultural characteristics of Hispanics. At the top are those programs modifying traditional therapy modalities according to an understanding and evaluation of ethnic characteristics or creatively deriving the therapeutic vehicle from the cultural milieu. Although our analysis of culturally sensitive treatment was prompted by Hispanic concerns, in principle we believe that this pyramidal structure can be extended to other migrant and culturally different groups.

The development of new therapeutic modalities out of specifically relevant cultural traits is always an ambitious and difficult task. Efforts to render therapeutic modalities culturally sensitive, no matter how persuasive or attractive they are, must ultimately attend to the final objective of relieving the client of psychological distress and of improving his or her level of effective functioning in the society. It should no longer be sufficient for a clinician merely to assert cultural sensitivity on the basis of good intentions alone: As an alternative, we invite our colleagues to situate their clinical innovations in the pyramidal framework developed here. From our attempt to order conceptually the many uses and meanings of cultural sensitivity, it is the concept of therapeutic isomorphism that emerges as a major contribution to the field. Thus, we invite our colleagues also to attend to the distinction we have drawn between isomorphic reinforcement and departures from isomorphism in the interest of the clients' well-being, not only in working with Hispanic clients but with any culturally different clientele.

To attend to such issues, research must be conducted. As Padilla, Ruiz, and Alvarez (1975) stated, "An innovative treatment program is self-defeating unless validating research is conducted . . . to guide the development of programs with the greatest probability of success" (p. 900). It is particularly important that innovative modalities, such as cuento therapy, not become part of the vast pool of untested therapies, but the task of validation should not deter us from creating new, culturally sensitive therapeutic programs.

References

Abad, V., Ramos, J., & Boyce, E. (1974). A model for delivery of mental health services to Spanish-speaking minorities. *American Journal of Orthopsychiatry, 44* (4), 584–595.

Acosta, F., & Cristo, M. (1981). Development of a bilingual interpreter program. An alternative model for Spanish-speaking services. *Professional Psychology, 12* (4), 474–482.

Bloom, B. (1975). *Changing patterns of psychiatric care.* New York: Human Sciences Press.

Bluestone, H., & Vela, R. (1982). Transcultural aspects in the psychotherapy of the Puerto Rican poor in New York City. *Journal of the American Academy of Psychoanalysis, 10* (2), 269–283.

Boulette, T. (1976). Assertive training with low income Mexican American women. In M. R. Miranda (Ed.), *Psychotherapy with the Spanish-speaking: Issues in research and service delivery* (pp. 67–72). Los Angeles: University of California, Spanish Speaking Mental Health Research Center.

Costantino, G., Malgady, R., & Rogler. L. (1985). *Cuento therapy: Folktales as a culturally sensitive psychotherapy for Puerto Rican children* (Hispanic Research Center Monograph No. 12). Maplewood, NJ: Waterfront Press.

Costantino, G., Malgady, R., & Rogler, L. (1986). Cuento therapy: A culturally sensitive modality for Puerto Rican children. J*ournal of Consulting and Clinical Psychology, 54,* 639–645.

Cuellar, I., Harris, L, & Jasso, R. (1980). An acculturation scale for Mexican American normal and clinical populations. *Hispanic Journal of Behavioral Sciences, 2,* 199–217.

Cuellar, I., Harris, L., & Naron, N. (1981). Evaluation of a bilingual bicultural treatment program for Mexican American psychiatric inpatients. In A. Baron (Ed.), *Explorations in Chicano psychology* (pp. 165–186). New York: Praeger.

Freidson, E. (1970). *Profession of medicine.* New York: Dodd, Mead.

Gurak, D., & Rogler, L. (1980). New York's new immigrants: Who and where they are. The Hispanics. *New York University Education Quarterly, 11* (4), 20–24.

Inclan, J. (1979). *Family organization. acculturation and psychological symptomatology in second generation Puerto Rican women of three socioeconomic classes.* Unpublished doctoral dissertation, New York University.

Karno, M., & Morales, A. (1971). A community mental health service for Mexican Americans in a metropolis. *Comprehensive Psychiatry, 12* (2), 116–121.

Kreisman, J. (1975). The curandero's apprentice: A therapeutic integration of folk and medicinal healing. *American Journal of Psychiatry, 132* (1), 81–83.

Maduro, R., & Martinez, C. (1974). Latino dream analysis: Opportunity for confrontation, *Social Casework, 55,* 461–469.

Normand, W., Iglesias, J., & Payn, S. (1974). Brief group therapy to facilitate utilization of mental health services by Spanish-speaking patients. *American Journal of Orthopsychiatry, 44* (1), 37–42.

Padilla, A., Ruiz, R., & Alvarez, R. (1975). Community mental health services for the Spanish-speaking/surnamed populations. *American Psychologist, 30,* 892–905.

Pitta, P., Marcos, L., & Alpert, M. (1978). Language switching as a treatment strategy with bilingual patients. *American Journal of Psychoanalysis, 38,* 255–258.

Rodriguez, I. (1971). Group work with hospitalized Puerto Rican patients. *Hospital and Community Psychiatry, 22* (7), 219–220.

Rogler, L., & Cooney, R. (1984). *Puerto Rican families in New York City: Intergenerational processes* (Hispanic Research Center Monograph No. 11). Maplewood, NJ: Waterfront Press.

Rogler, L., & Hollingshead, A. (1985). *Trapped: Puerto Rican families and schizophrenia.* Maplewood, NJ: Waterfront Press.

Rogler, L., Santana-Cooney, R., Costantino, G., Fancy, B., Grossman, B., Gurak, D., Malgady, R., & Rodriguez, O. (1983). *A conceptual framework for mental health research on Hispanic populations* (Hispanic Research Center Monograph No.10). New York: Fordham University.

Ruiz, R. (1981). Cultural and historical perspectives in counseling Hispanics. In D. Sue (Ed.), *Counseling the culturally different* (pp. 186–215). New York: Wiley.

Scott, J., & Delgado, M. (1979). Planning mental health programs for Hispanic communities. *Social Casework, 60,* 451–455.

Sue, D. W., & Sue, D. (1977). Barriers to effective cross-cultural counseling. *Journal of Counseling Psychology, 24,* 420–429.

Szapocznik, J., Kurtines, W., & Fernandez, T. (1980). Bicultural involvement and adjustment in Hispanic American youths. *International Journal of Intercultural Relations, 4,* 353–365.

Szapocznik, J., Scopetta, M., Hervis, O., Ladner, R., Alegre, C., Truss, C., Santisteban, D., & Rodriguez, A. (1979). The Spanish Family Guidance Center of Miami. *Research Bulletin, 4,* (Available from Fordham University, Hispanic Research Center, Thebaud Hall, Bronx, NY 10458).

Szapocznik, J., Scopetta, M., & King, O. (1978). Theory and practice in matching treatment to the special characteristics and problems of Cuban immigrants. *Journal of Community Psychology, 6,* 112–122.

Trevino, F., Bruhn, J., & Bunce, H. (1979). Utilization of community mental health services in a Texas-Mexican border city. *Social Science and Medicine, 13* (3a), 331–334.

15

Counseling Cuban Americans

Jeanette Altarriba & Lisa M. Bauer

Cuban Americans are fast becoming one of America's largest ethnic minorities. The term "Cuban American" refers to those individuals who are Cuban born or of Cuban parentage and who live in the United States (Jaffe, Cullen, & Boswell, 1980). Since 1959, the time of the Castro Revolution, there has been a large increase in the number of Cuban-born people living in the United States. Self-selection in previous waves of migration and the nature of migration policies and immigration laws have played a major role in determining who has emigrated from Cuba and in what numbers (Boswell & Curtis, 1983). For many, the decision to leave Cuba was influenced by political and economic factors (Rogg, 1974). By 1990, Cubans comprised roughly 6.8 percent of all those of Hispanic origin living in the United States. Largely as a result of the Mariel boatlift in 1980 and the recent exodus in 1994, this population has increased to the point of making them the third largest Hispanic minority group in the country. The largest minority group is Mexican-Americans followed by Puerto Ricans (Garwood, 1992).

Not surprisingly, those who have immigrated to this country in the past thirty years have brought a large portion of their culture and tradition with them. Often, it is these very traditions that can be used as an effective means of psychological counseling. However, counselors and practitioners may not be aware of the cultural traits of this group or the methods by which these traditions may be applied in a counseling setting. As this minority group struggles to acculturate in an Anglo society, it is increasingly important for mental health workers to consider cultural values and beliefs when assessing and treating these clients.

The aim of this chapter is to describe several factors that are important in designing a culturally-sensitive treatment model for Cuban American clients. Cultural sensitivity refers to a treatment model built on a set of ideas that complement the client's value structure. A description of the background, cultural values, and belief systems of Cuban Americans is provided along with a review of various treatment methods that have been used successfully with culturally diverse clients.

Characteristics of Cuban Americans and Implications for Counseling

Migration

Most Cubans migrated to the United States under different circumstances than did Mexicans and Puerto Ricans. For Cuban Americans, migration to the United States is a more recent event than the migration of either Puerto Ricans or Mexicans. Also, many Cubans immigrated to the United States as political exiles. The Cubans experienced economic hardships and political or philosophical differences with the revolution in Cuba (Marín & Marín, 1991). However, the population of Cubans that entered the United States as a result of the boatlift from Mariel in 1980 was significantly different in social and psychological aspects from the population that arrived in the early 1960s. In 1980 Fidel Castro decided to allow anyone who wanted to leave Cuba to exit through the port of Mariel. It became apparent that a much larger proportion of the population wished to leave than the government had anticipated. Fidel Castro decided to force all those that had gone to Cuba to pick up relatives to also transport "undesirables" to the United States. This group included mentally ill persons, persons with criminal records, and those with ailments such as leprosy. Approximately 4 percent of these immigrants were hard-core criminals (Boswell & Curtis, 1983). These people are often referred to as *Marielitos,* a term usually used as a negative descriptor. As a result of the different waves of migration, Cuban Americans are somewhat socially and psychologically diverse. Members of this population will be referred to here simply as Cuban Americans.

Place of Residence

In 1990, about 90 percent of all Cuban Americans lived in the following six states: Florida, New Jersey, New York, California, Illinois, and Texas (U.S. Bureau of the Census, 1990). Large cities attracted Cuban immigrants presumably due to the increased economic opportunities available. Florida was a choice by many because of its proximity to Cuba and its similarity of climate. Also, there were Cubans who had arrived earlier in Miami who could help the immigrants settle in the existing Cuban communities (Boswell & Curtis, 1983).

Cuban American communities have been in existence since the 1960s. In New York and in Miami, Cuban Americans formed ethnic communities of extended families and friends who assisted each other economically and socially. As political exiles, it is not uncommon for Cuban Americans living in Miami and other parts of the United States to still dream of returning to their homeland and reuniting with their family members who remain in Cuba.

Socioeconomic Characteristics

As mentioned, Cuban Americans have centered themselves in large cities in part because of the economic opportunities available. Boswell and Curtis (1983) note that Cuban Americans have attained a high socioeconomic level compared to other Hispanic groups and considering the relatively short time they have been in the United States. This high level of attainment can still be seen today as demonstrated by the following demographic information.

In 1993, it was reported that Cuban American males comprised 20.3 percent of Hispanic professional and managerial workers. The figure for Cuban Americans is larger than that reported for Mexican American males (8.7 percent) and Puerto Rican males (15.5 percent) living in the United States. Cuban American females comprised 18.4 percent of Hispanic professional and managerial workers. The mean family income for Cuban Americans in 1992 was $39,632 while the average family income for Mexican Americans and Puerto Ricans was $29,251 and $26,618, respectively (Montgomery, 1994).

The economic status of Cuban Americans has approached that of people of non-spanish descent. In 1993, Cuban American males comprised 20.3 percent of Hispanic professional and managerial workers. The total percent for males of Spanish origin (i.e., Puerto Rican, Mexican American, Cuban American, and all others) was 11.6. A total of 27.9 percent of non-Hispanics and 29.2 percent of non-Hispanic Whites were professional and managerial workers. The total percent for females of Hispanic origin was 15.4 percent while it was 29.8 percent and 30.9 percent for non-Hispanic and non-Hispanic Whites, respectively (Montgomery, 1994). For mean family income, Cuban Americans again fall between non-Hispanic Americans ($45,681 for non-Hispanics and $48,201 for non-Hispanic Whites) and the total population of Hispanic descent ($30,332) (Montgomery, 1994).

In summary, Cuban Americans are doing quite well in regards to socioeconomic conditions. Their average income and occupational status approach that of people of non-Hispanic origin.

Educational Characteristics

Education is one of the main factors influencing the rate of assimilation of immigrant children into a new society. American values are inculcated into the youth, and cultural values and traditions are transmitted through education. Cuban Americans occupy an intermediate position between those of non-Hispanic origin and the total of Hispanic origin with respect to educational achievement. In 1993, 16.5 percent of the Cuban American population ages 25 to 34 had completed four years of college or more as compared to 9.0 percent for the total of Hispanic origin and 22.9 percent for those not of Hispanic origin. In 1993, 5.9 percent of the Puerto Rican population and 8.0 percent of the Mexican American population between the ages of 25 and 34 had four years of college or more. In addition, in 1988, the median number of school years completed by Cuban Americans was 13.4 while that for total Hispanic population and those of non-Hispanic descent was 12.4 and 12.9, respectively (U.S. Bureau of the Census, 1988).

Education is highly valued by individuals of Cuban descent. Cuban Americans encourage their children to attend school and further their education by obtaining college and graduate degrees. In fact, the Cuban community in Miami has established its own private elementary and secondary schools in which classes are taught in Spanish and emphasis is placed on the Cuban culture and traditional values.

Value Orientations

The family and family cohesiveness play a significant role in traditional Cuban American society (Boswell & Curtis, 1983; Comas-Díaz, 1993). A sense of self-confidence and security arises from the close family bond. Bean and Tienda (1987) explained that cohesiveness within the ethnic community is also an important factor in the integration of Cuban Americans in this country. Group cohesiveness facilitates adjustment and a successful transition into new surroundings. A Cuban American client from a traditional setting is likely to consult with the family in times of trouble and will find it difficult to rely on impersonal, secondary relationships for help.

Respect for family members and for the reputation of the family as a whole is important for the traditional Cuban family. There is a double standard applied for men and women at work and at home. There are tasks that are undertaken solely by women such as child rearing and housekeeping. The role of the man is to provide income for the household, and he is also to make the major family decisions. The cultural pattern of *machismo* is demonstrated by a male's show of virility, courage, and manliness. The women of the family are to be kept at home and daughters are often prohibited from dating unless accompanied by a family member or close friend.

In the past ten to fifteen years, there have been changes in the traditional patterns, mostly due to women entering the workforce in increasing numbers. Women contribute more to the financial structure of the family and are making more decisions in the household. In the workplace, most Cuban Americans value economic independence and achievement. "Cubans have not remained segregated in a secondary labor market, have been the most successful of all groups (Latin American and Hispanic immigrants) and are demonstrating strong tendencies toward integration into the larger society . . ." (Bean & Tienda, 1987, p. 33). Cuban Americans still continue making great strides in the labor market as the number of Cuban Americans who have obtained college degrees has steadily increased.

Hispanics tend to prefer interpersonal relationships in in-groups that are nurturing, loving, intimate, and respectful. Their cultural value of *allocentrism* emphasizes these needs. Allocentrism is associated with high levels of conformity, mutual empathy, willingness to sacrifice for the welfare of the group, trust among members of the group, and high levels of personal interdependence (Marín & Marín, 1991).

Another Hispanic cultural value is termed *simpatía* and emphasizes the need for behaviors that promote pleasant and nonconflicting social relationships. This value encourages the Cuban American to show a certain level of conformity and to avoid conflictive circumstances (Triandis, Mann, Lisansky, & Betancourt, 1984). The influences on the individual of allocentrism and *simpatía* should be recognized by the therapist as part of the patient's culture.

Religion is also an important part of life for traditional Cuban Americans in the United States and is a way of maintaining cultural identity. The majority of Cuban Americans are Catholic, but there are also a number of Protestant groups and an even smaller number of Cuban Jews. Religion is seen more as personal rather than institutional. *Santería,* a combination of Catholic and African traditions, became more popular as refugees sought to maintain their cultural identity (Curtis, 1980). This is a folk religion that combines ritual, magical, and medical beliefs. It is principally characterized by the worship of saints or *santos* taken from the Catholic religion. The saints also represent African tribal deities stemming from the Yoruba tribe of Nigeria. The Yoruba religious traditions were introduced into Cuba through the presence of African slaves. Those that practice *Santería* are called *Santeros.* The followers of this religion often erect yard shrines in honor of the saints. The shrines often contain a statue of a particular saint along with other articles such as fruits and leaves. Worshipers attempt to satisfy the saints by making offers of food or money or through animal sacrifice. Sandoval (1979) notes that *Santería* also serves as a system of mental health for many Cubans. The religion has an adaptive nature in that it can meet a variety of needs of its followers. For traditional Cuban Americans, many religious practices take place outside of the structure of the church, and often, church attendance is low.

Family Characteristics

The traditional Cuban American family provides a sense of security and identity for its members. Respect or *respeto* is an important value in these families. Generally, elders are treated courteously and respectfully. Respect must be maintained for the family as a whole, and no act should be performed that could damage the family's reputation. Family relationships are very close and an individual is likely to seek help with a problem from a family member rather than a secondary source. Close relationships are also maintained with relatives and godparents known as *compadres.* These individuals are chosen by the parents for the child and are expected to look after the child should anything happen to the natural parents. The *compadre* may also give economic aid to the child as well as guidance on personal matters. The *compadres* may or may not be relatives of the child but they should live close to the family.

The household usually includes relatives outside of the nuclear family. The extended members of the household often partake in the rearing and socialization of the children and sometimes live within the same structure as the nuclear family. Thus, counselors should note that an extensive family support system normally exists, making the Cuban American individual less likely to go out of the home to seek solutions to their problems. When they do seek psychological aid, they are often reluctant to divulge all of their thoughts and feelings. This may arise out of guilt for seeking help outside of the family on personal matters.

A therapist, therefore, may see clients and their close family relations together in a treatment session. The client may feel more secure in the treatment surroundings if accompanied by a close family member who is aware of the problem. It would serve a client better to build a counseling system consisting of the entire family and to note the family's sensitivity to external pressures (Szapocznik, Scopetta, & King, 1978).

Communication in counseling can also be enhanced through the use of group or family therapy. Individuals in a group with others culturally similar to themselves tend to feel accepted and more relaxed. Clients may feel less reluctant to communicate their thoughts and feelings in this type of setting. Bernal and Flores-Ortiz (1982) present several guidelines for family therapy with Hispanics that may be helpful in engaging Cuban Americans in family therapy. Patients should be welcomed in their own language, and a handshake is also recommended. This initial contact helps the patient feel at ease and one hopes it begins to set up trust between the patient and the therapist. The father is usually the focal point in the presentation of the problem, but the wife and children should also be asked to express the problem as they view it. After problem identification, it is important for the therapist to understand the family system. The therapist should ask about the role of family members and the development of the family through marriage, births, and so forth. In summary, the importance of language, family, and cultural values cannot be overemphasized in the therapeutic setting. Language issues are discussed further in the following section.

Language

Initially, language was a handicap that early Cuban Americans encountered when they entered the United States. Spanish is the official language in Cuba and few immigrants had training in English. The vast majority of first-generation Cuban Americans speak Spanish as their main language; Boswell and Curtis (1983) noted that Spanish remains the dominant language spoken in Cuban American homes. However, second- and third-generation Cuban Americans are likely to speak Spanish and English and may often switch between languages. Altarriba and Santiago-Rivera (1994) provided a review regarding the use of language in therapy. They suggested that the strategic use of language switching and language mixing in the counseling environment may be extremely useful when treating bilingual clients. For example, clients may choose to describe certain painful issues in their nondominant language distancing themselves from the emotionally-laden content of those issues. A form of bilingual therapy may prove to be highly successful for Cuban American clients.

Attitudes Toward Counselors

Szapocznik et al., (1978) emphasized the importance of matching treatment to the special characteristics of Cuban immigrants. Matching patient-therapist expectations is crucial for the effective delivery of mental health care (Heitler, 1976). Studies conducted by Pomales and Williams (1989) and Ponce and Atkinson (1989) have found that less acculturated Hispanic Americans perceive counselors with a greater degree of ethnic similarity as more favorable sources of help than Anglo-American counselors. Scott (1975) reported several factors that influence a client's decision to choose among or between different modes of therapy. Reasons for preferential mental health care use include language, transportation difficulties, and a perceived lack of cultural fit between personal beliefs and practices and those of the host society. Often, Cuban Americans may attribute health problems to supernatural causes or interpersonal conflicts and seek the advice of faith healers who identify with the Cuban culture.

Traditional practices and beliefs about mental illness held by Cuban Americans stem directly from those held in Cuba. Sandoval (1979) explained that in Cuba, prior to the revolution, psychiatrists treated institutionalized individuals while psychologists and counselors were unknown or inaccessible. The majority of those with emotional problems sought help within the family or from general medical practitioners. However, attitudes toward counseling are slightly different among Cuban Americans.

As previously stated, Cuban Americans and Hispanics in general place a great deal of importance on the family as a main source of emotional support and guidance. Rogg (1974) asked Cuban American respondents who they would turn to for psychological help if someone in the family had a serious nervous or mental problem. Approximately 75 percent of her sample responded that they would turn to the family doctor, family and friends as the first, second, or third choice of help. The family was important because of close bonds built on understanding and love, while the family doctor was cited as a qualified authority able to provide advice on physical and mental problems. A full 56 percent of Cuban American respondents reported that they would not turn to a therapist in private practice.

Assessment and Treatment of the Cuban American Client

A careful review of the literature on multicultural counseling revealed the absence of any models that specifically dealt with treating the Cuban American client. This section describes how existing perspectives may be extended for treating this population. We have chosen the following three perspectives for our discussion: the Worldview, the Social/Environmental Change Agent Model, and the Ecological Structural Family Therapy Model. These can be easily adapted for use with Cuban American clients, and the suggested modifications stem from the discussion of the major psychological and social characteristics described in the first part of this chapter. Additionally, we propose a framework for the assessment and the treatment of Cuban American clients that emphasizes many of the major factors expressed in these three perspectives.

Worldview

A worldview, according to Ibrahim (1991) and Sue (1978, 1981) includes an individual's entire philosophy of life and the ways of interacting with the world and with other people. Individual worldviews may vary within groups and ethnic cultures. Therefore, when engaging in therapy sessions with a client, one needs to consider the characteristics of each client. An objective assessment of a client's worldview may be obtained by using the Scale to Assess World Views (SAWV) (Ibrahim & Kahn, 1987). The SAWV was designed to aid the counselor in comprehending the client's worldview, understanding what experiences and problems led to the client seeking professional assistance, and to aid in clarifying the client's individual worldview instead of that of his or her family, minority group, or society as a whole (Ibrahim, 1991).

The SAWV assesses where the individual falls within a range in each of the following categories: human nature, social relationships, nature, time orientation, and activity orientation (Ibrahim, 1991). An understanding of an individual's worldview will greatly enhance the therapist's knowledge of a client's self-identity, beliefs, and value system. This knowledge of a particular individual's orientation and culture will no doubt facilitate any therapeutic encounter (Lonner & Ibrahim, 1989; Tyler, Sussewell, & Williams-McCoy, 1985). When treating Cuban Americans, counselors should take into consideration the differences between the values of their own culture and those of Cuban Americans, which may be in direct contrast to each other. Many Cuban Americans have the following beliefs:

(1) *Nature*—With respect to a Person-Nature orientation, many Cuban Americans believe that people are one with nature. Nature is one's partner in life and if anything, a person must subjugate himself or herself for nature's benefit. In this sense, people are seen as having little control over the forces of nature.

(2) *Time*—Most Cuban Americans prefer a present-centered orientation with reference to time. The past and the future play only minor roles in deciding behavior and actions.

(3) *Activity*—Cuban immigrants will often prefer a stance characterized by activity that is spontaneous and expressive in terms of emotions and desires.

(4) *Social Relations*—Finally, in terms of social relations, traditional Cuban Americans endorse lineality or the idea that relationships are hierarchical. An individual may be subordinate to another and may defer to authority on many occasions.

Keep these values in mind when counseling a Cuban American. However, the client's individual worldview should be emphasized over that of the client's racial, cultural, or religious group. A counselor should ask the Cuban American client to elaborate on his or her worldview in reference to the listed dimensions and others such as language preference and views of the family and mental illness, as those listed can only be used as a guideline.

Social/Environmental Change Agent Role Model

Smith (1985) noted that conventional psychotherapy places a great deal of emphasis on the idea that a patient's problems arise from within rather than stemming from the external environment (e.g., the outside factors to which a racial or ethnic minority member must adjust). Katz (1985) also criticized the use of psychotherapy and suggested that clients should be urged to change those environmental conditions that are creating specific problems rather than maintaining a focus exclusively on the client. An alternative to the traditional view of psychotherapy is that of the Social or Environmental Change Agent Role Model (see Atkinson, Thompson, & Grant, 1993; chapter 16 of the current text). Atkinson et al. noted that a counselor can function as an agent or role model for change or as a consultant or advisor to a client acting to strengthen a patient's support systems. At least three factors should be considered when a counselor is deciding what roles and strategies to adopt when working with a minority client (Atkinson, Morten, & Sue, 1993):

(1) the client's level of acculturation,
(2) the perceived cause and development of the problem on the part of the client and therapist (internally caused v. externally caused), and
(3) the specific goals to be attained in the helping process.

There are at least eight specific roles that a counselor may adopt including advisor, advocate, facilitator of indigenous support systems, facilitator of indigenous healing systems, consultant, change agent, counselor, and psychotherapist (for further discussion, see Atkinson, Thompson, & Grant, 1993).

The client's gender, age, language, religion, expectations of the counselor, and so forth, also will determine an appropriate role for the therapist. However, unlike the worldview perspective, this model places the counselor in a position to actively attempt to change the client's social environment, which seems to be contributing to the client's problems. The counselor can help change an environment by including the Cuban American client's family in therapy sessions, thereby strengthening the family support system. Many Cuban Americans place an emphasis on family, therefore it might serve the client better if the counselor builds a counseling system consisting of the entire family. There will also be less external pressure from the family if the therapist can effectively communicate to the family that it is acceptable to receive counseling, because most Cuban Americans perceive seeking outside professional counseling as a stigma. In cases in which the Cuban American has newly arrived, perhaps the best role for a therapist to adopt would be the advocate role. It is extremely important for the counselor to determine the level of acculturation because this factor will generally lead to the specification of the most beneficial role a counselor should adopt.

Ecological Structural (Ecostructural) Family Therapy

The Ecological Structural (Ecostructural) Family Therapy model, developed by Aponte (1974); emphasizes the role of the family in the treatment of Hispanic clients. Treatment modalities may include effective reorganization and even restructuring of the family and the extended family. The goal of this type of therapy is to change those negative aspects of the family environment that may be causing the client difficulty. The locus of a client's dysfunction is not only internal but also external in the environment in which the client interacts with other people (Szapocznik et al., 1978).

In this model, the family is viewed as the most influential part of the individual's life. The term "structural" refers to the idea that the problem the Cuban American is experiencing is due to the manner of family organization when dealing with intrafamilial and extrafamilial matters. The ecological approach assumes that the dysfunction lies within the interactions that occur between the individual and the ecological systems that impinge on the individual. Therefore, this model states that the dysfunctional behavior is supported in the ecology and the responsibility for the dysfunction is shared by the whole ecology (Szapocznik et al., 1978). Consequently, the model suggests that the system should be reorganized and restructured such that the dysfunction is not supported.

An assessment of the interaction between the individual and the ecology should be conducted at the onset of therapy. The assessment includes looking at the boundaries between systems, the relations between systems, the strength of the relationships between the systems, the family hierarchical structure and how the authority is portrayed within that structure, potential contradictions in requests, and the overall system and its inherent relationships that appear to be the most desirable to restructure.

The main goal for the therapist should be to help facilitate functional interactions between the individual members of the family. In addition, the therapist should promote positive interactions among family members so that the interactions become positive reinforcers and the individuals experience effective ways of handling their environment. Family members should learn to recognize and feel comfortable within their roles in the family.

Ecological Family Therapy effectively matches the value orientations and belief structure of Hispanics and specifically Cuban Americans given the hierarchical nature of their family structure and the importance placed on family relationships. For this model to be effective for the client, the client must be present and doing-oriented, be a member of the hierarchical family structure, and lack the confidence to interact with the extrafamilial environment. These are important requirements as the therapist tries to organize and structure the family and extrafamilial systems. The Cuban American may feel unable to control or modify his or her environment, therefore it is up to the therapist to assume a position of authority and assist in structuring situations such that the client develops functional patterns of interactions.

This model also takes into consideration the high regard for interpersonal relationships that most Cuban Americans hold. It focuses on group cohesiveness, close family bonds, and level of acculturation. Some of the dysfunctional patterns of interaction among Cuban American family members may be due to intergenerational acculturation differences that cause feelings of alienation. In this case, the parents may be much less acculturated than the children, and they may be concerned that their authority is being challenged. The Ecological Structural Family Therapy matches the cultural values of Cuban Americans, therefore this model should prove useful when treating clients whose problems stem from familial and extrafamilial interactions.

General Framework for the Assessment and Treatment of the Cuban American Client

In this final section, we propose a framework for the assessment and the treatment of Cuban American clients that emphasizes many of the major factors expressed in the previous three perspectives. The emphasis of this general framework is on the identification of a client's worldview, the client's relationship with his or her family, and the need to identify the client's cultural values and beliefs. A summary of this general approach can be found in table 15.1.

In assessing and treating Cuban American clients the literature indicates that certain cultural factors must be taken into consideration. Among these are close family bonds, highly interpersonal relationships, *simpatía,* language, and acculturation. These are important aspects to cover when working with a Cuban American client. The therapist should get to know and understand the client's problems by looking at the client's values and the environment in which he or she interacts. This can be accomplished by assessing the client's worldviews and asking just a few questions about his or her background and current social environment. This procedure will allow the therapist to get a feel for how the client views the world.

The assessment of worldviews can be accomplished by using the Scale to Assess World Views (Ibrahim, 1991; Ibrahim & Kahn, 1987). As previously discussed, this scale measures the client's worldviews by looking at the range

Table 15.1

Assessment Topics to be Explored Prior to Treatment of the Cuban American Client

I. Gain general information about the client's current social environment and reasons for seeking counseling.
II. Evaluate the client's worldview using the Scale to Assess World Views (SAWV).
III. Engage the client in a discussion of the following topics:
   A. Describe the quality of your relationship with your family members.
   B. Characterize the nature of the majority of your social relationships.
   C. What is your language preference?
   D. What is your generation of descent?
   E. Which race do you most closely identify with?
IV. Design a treatment program taking these factors into consideration.
V. Discuss the treatment plan with client. Make revisions where appropriate.

they fall in under the categories of human nature, social relationships, nature, time orientation, and activity orientation. The assessment of the client's worldviews is important because the worldviews are a byproduct of the individual's process of socialization.

In addition to assessing the client's worldview, the therapist should inquire about issues related to the counseling process. The therapist may choose to engage the client in relevant discussions by asking the client to: (1) describe the quality of their relationship with family members; (2) characterize the nature of the majority of their social relationships; (3) discuss language preferences; (4) state generation of descent; and (5) discuss which race they most closely identify with.

Inquiries regarding family relationships, social relationships, language preferences, and generation of descent can provide the therapist with a lot of information about the client in a relatively short time. The first question (see table 15.1), regarding the quality of familial relationships can suggest many things. The Cuban American culture supports strong family relationships, and the client may be experiencing problems coping with the lack of a strong family support system. The client may also be more acculturated than other family members and therefore feel alienated.

The second topic of discussion regarding social relationships is focusing on the Cuban American value of *simpatía,* which emphasizes the need for behaviors that promote pleasant and nonconflicting relationships. This question also addresses whether the client holds Cuban American values. However, most individuals, Cuban or not, like to have positive social relationships and perhaps the problem lies more within the individual or the individual's interactions with the environment.

The client's language preference is extremely important because language could be a barrier that could directly or indirectly affect proper treatment of the client. Language preference may also aid in identifying the client's level of acculturation.

The interest in the client's generation of descent is for purposes of determining the degree of acculturation. As an individual becomes more adjusted to the new society, he or she learns to incorporate the society's customs, rituals, and beliefs into his or her belief system. Therapists must be aware of the family tensions that may arise as a result of the differing rates of assimilation and adjustment among individuals in a family or group, to accurately assess problem situations.

There are people of various races who are of Hispanic descent. Nearly 9 percent of the United States population is of Hispanic origin (U.S. Bureau of the Census, 1992). Ninety-six percent of Hispanics were White by race, approximately 2 percent were Blacks, and another 2 percent were of other races (U.S. Bureau of the Census). It is possible for an individual to be a Black Hispanic, an Asian Hispanic, or of any combination of race and ethnicity. The possibility of an individual being of one ethnicity and another race poses many questions for the U.S. Census Bureau and for counselors. A recent U.S. Bureau of the Census (1992) publication addressed the difficulties in deciding how overlapping groups should be classified in population surveys and whether Black Hispanics are more closely related to other Blacks or to other Hispanics in terms of various socioeconomic factors.

It was found that Black Hispanics are more closely related to other Blacks than to Hispanics in terms of labor force participation. However, Black Hispanics were more similar to White Hispanics rather than to other Blacks in terms of unemployment. In terms of high school graduation, Hispanic Blacks are more similar to other Blacks than to White Hispanics. There is no difference, however, among Black Hispanics, non-Hispanic Blacks, or White Hispanics in terms of college graduation.

From these data we can see that there may or may not be differences between the various races of people of Hispanic origin depending upon the factors being investigated. Therefore, it is important for the counselor to take into consideration not only the client's Hispanic ethnicity, but also the race that the client most closely associates with.

By assessing the client's individual worldviews, language preference, level of acculturation, and patterns of family interaction, the therapist is in a better position to implement a specific treatment plan to counsel the individual. This approach takes into consideration the differences between individuals in the family unit and their differing rates of assimilation and acculturation. An individual may have a Cuban American "one-with-nature" worldview and at the same time have an Anglo-Saxon "future-oriented" view of time. In summary, it would be ill-advised to assume that all Cuban American clients have the same worldviews, regardless of other factors in their lives.

Finally, the therapist should discuss the designed treatment program with the client and attempt to make sure that the client is comfortable with what the therapist feels are the appropriate processes to follow and final goals. At this point, if the client feels uncomfortable with the plan, goal adjustments can be made in an attempt to minimize any miscommunication.

Conclusions

To engage Cuban Americans in beneficial therapy, it is helpful for the counselor to have well-developed skills in family therapy and to demonstrate a high level of cultural sensitivity. The therapist should make all attempts to evaluate the client's specific history, including language spoken; family background; and more specifically, the client's cultural identity. It is helpful if counselors have a good understanding of the Spanish language to address culturally-related problems and communicate effectively with non-English speaking family members. It is imperative that a clear understanding exists of the social and psychological characteristics of the Cuban American society. Cultural values should form the basis of any treatment program. A proper awareness of the most effective and culturally acceptable solutions to the problems of a specific minority population should lead to the greatest benefits for the client.

Exercises

The following exercises will give students some insight into the problems experienced by Cuban Americans in counseling. Students will be able to practice their problem-solving techniques as they demonstrate their knowledge of the psychological and sociocultural context of Cuban Americans.

A. Divide the class into groups of four or five. Have each group read the following description and answer the questions that follow. After fifteen minutes, have each group present their answers out loud to the rest of the class. Class discussions should be encouraged.

   Mari is a twenty-year-old White Cuban who entered a mental health center with her mother for counseling. Mari had emigrated from Cuba with her mother and two younger brothers, four months earlier. She was shy and reluctant to speak to the counselor but eventually was able to discuss her feelings of depression. Mari's mother had encouraged her to seek help as she noticed Mari's loss of appetite and irregular sleeping patterns. Mari explained that she felt alienated from her peers at school because of the language barrier that existed. Her English was not very good and the counselor had a difficult time understanding the situation. Mari also complained that she felt out of place because of her physical appearance. Their father had left them when they arrived in the United States, therefore the family had financial difficulties and Mari could not afford to buy clothing that was in style. She could not obtain a job because of her poor English skills.

1. What is the main problem with the counselor's communication skills?
2. What are possible options available to Mari to improve her English?
3. What types of employment can Mari secure that require minimal English?
4. Discuss some ways in which Mari can work on improving her self-esteem and self-image.

B. Choose two students to play the roles of mother and daughter. Have them each read the following passages and act out their characters in front of the class. Afterwards, have the class answer the questions that follow.

Mrs. Celia Hernandez is forty-eight years old and was born in Cuba. She immigrated to Miami, Florida, in 1960 with her husband Juan. They have four children, Juan Jose, twenty; Margó, seventeen; Angel, twelve; and Ricardo, eight. Celia is a traditional mother and wife. She does not work outside of the home and her main concern is the children's welfare. She does not allow Margó to date and always listens in on her telephone conversations. Celia insists that Juan Jose accompany Margó to and from school every day. Consequently, Juan Jose must miss hours from work and has lost several jobs because of the inconvenience.

Margó insists that she is old enough to date and insists on her privacy with the telephone. She has tried to explain to her mother that she can take a bus to school or go with a friend so not to burden Juan Jose. She explains that she is an excellent student and always helps at home. She feels she should be allowed to go out with friends and relax every now and then.

1. What are the main issues involved in this situation?
2. Should Celia try to develop interests outside of the home? Explain the benefits of following this suggestion. Are there any possible consequences?
3. What other alternatives could Margó propose in this situation?
4. Would you recommend family therapy? Why or why not?

C. Have each student generate a list of questions that would be helpful in eliciting useful information from Cuban American clients in counseling. Some possible questions include:
1. What was the year of migration to this country?
2. Did any family members remain in Cuba?
3. What religious practices are followed by the family?

References

Altarriba, J., & Santiago-Rivera, A. L. (1994). Current perspectives on using linguistic and cultural factors in counseling the Hispanic client. *Professional Psychology: Research and Practice, 25,* 388–397.

Aponte, H. J. (1974, March). Psychotherapy for the poor: An ecostructural approach to treatment. *Delaware Medical Journal,* 1–7.

Atkinson, D. R., Morten, G., & Sue, D. W. (1993). *Counseling American minorities: A cross-cultural perspective* (4th ed.). Madison, WI: Brown & Benchmark.

Atkinson, D. R., Thompson, C. E., & Grant, S. K. (1993). A dimensional model for counseling racial/ethnic minorities. *The Counseling Psychologist, 21,* 257–277.

Bean, F. D., & Tienda, M. (1987). *The Hispanic population of the United States.* New York: Russell Sage Foundation.

Bernal, G., & Flores-Ortiz, Y. (1982). Latino families in therapy: Engagement and evaluation. *Journal of Marital and Family Therapy, 8,* 357–365.

Boswell, T. D., & Curtis, J. R. (1983). *The Cuban American experience.* New Jersey: Rowman and Allanheld.

Comas-Díaz, L. (1993). Hispanic/Latino communities: Psychological implications. In D. R. Atkinson, G. Morten, & D. W. Sue (Eds.), *Counseling American minorities: A cross-cultural perspective* (4th ed., pp. 241–296). Madison, WI: Brown & Benchmark.

Curtis, J. R. (1980). Miami's Little Havana: Yard shrines, cult religion and landscape. In R. B. Browne (Ed.), *Rituals and ceremonies in popular culture* (pp. 105–119). Bowling Green, OH: Bowling Green University Popular Press.

Garwood, A. N. (Ed.). (1992). *Hispanic Americans: A statistical sourcebook.* Boulder, CO: Numbers & Concepts.

Heitler, J. B. (1976). Preparatory techniques in initiating expressive psychotherapy with lower-class, unsophisticated patients. *Psychological Bulletin, 83,* 339–352.

Ibrahim, F. A. (1991). Contribution of cultural worldview to generic counseling and development. *Journal of Counseling and Development, 70,* 13–19.

Ibrahim, F. A., & Kahn, H. (1987). Assessment of worldviews. *Psychological Reports, 60,* 163–176.

Jaffe, A. J., Cullen, R. M., & Boswell, T. D. (1980). *The changing demography of Spanish Americans.* New York: Academic Press.

Katz, J. H. (1985). The sociopolitical nature of counseling. *The Counseling Psychologist, 13,* 615–625.

Lonner, W. J., & Ibrahim, F. A. (1989). Assessment in cultural counseling. In P. B. Pedersen, J. G. Draguns, W. J. Lonner, & J. E. Trimble (Eds.), *Counseling across cultures* (pp. 229–234). Honolulu: University of Hawaii Press.

Marín, G., & Marín, B. V. (1991). *Research with Hispanic populations.* Newbury Park, CA: Sage Publications.

Montgomery, P. A. (1994). *The Hispanic population in the United States: March 1993.* U.S. Bureau of the Census, Current Population Reports, Series P20-475. Washington, DC: U.S. Government Printing Office.

Pomales, J., & Williams, V. (1989). Effects of level of acculturation and counseling style on Hispanic students' perceptions of counselor. *Journal of Counseling Psychology, 36,* 79–83.

Ponce, F. Q., & Atkinson, D. R. (1989). Mexican-American acculturation, counselor ethnicity, counseling style, and perceived counselor credibility. *Journal of Counseling Psychology, 36,* 203–208.

Rogg, E. M. (1974). *The assimilation of Cuban exiles: The role of community and class.* New York: Aberdeen Press.

Sandoval, M. C. (1979). Santería as a mental health care system: An historical overview. *Social Science and Medicine, 13,* 139–151.

Scott, C. (1975). Competing health care Systems in an inner city area. *Human Organization, 34,* 108–109.

Smith, E. M. J. (1985). Ethnic minorities: Life stress, social support, and mental health issues. *The Counseling Psychologist, 13,* 537–579.

Sue, D. W. (1978). Worldviews and counseling. *The Personnel and Guidance Journal, 56,* 458-462.

Sue, D. W. (1981). *Counseling the culturally different.* New York: Wiley & Sons.

Szapocznik, J., Scopetta, N. A., & King, O. E. (1978). Theory and practice in matching treatment to the special characteristics and problems of Cuban immigrants. *Journal of Community Psychology, 6,* 112–122.

Triandis, H. C., Mann, G., Lisansky, J., & Betancourt, H. (1984). Simpatía as a cultural script of Hispanics. *Journal of Personality and Social Psychology, 47,* 1363–1375.

Tyler, F. B., Sussewell, D. R., & Williams-McCoy, J. (1985). Ethnic validity in psychotherapy. *Psychotherapy, 1,* 133–151.

U.S. Bureau of the Census. (1988). *The Hispanic population in the United States: March 1988.* Washington, DC: U.S. Government Printing Office.

U.S. Bureau of the Census. (1990). *Persons of Spanish Origin in the United States: March 1990.* Washington, DC: U.S. Government Printing Office.

U.S. Bureau of the Census, Current Population Reports, P23-182. (1992). *Exploring Alternative Race-Ethnic Comparison Groups in Current Population Surveys.* Washington, DC: U.S. Government Printing Office.

The Hispanic American Client
Cases and Questions

1. You are a counselor at a large predominantly European American university that has a Hispanic student enrollment of 10 percent. You are meeting with a Hispanic American student who has just explained that he is homesick for his family and that he is having difficulties fitting in with the diverse cultures on the campus.

   a) How will you develop a rapport with this student?
   b) What common experiences might your client have with other Hispanic Americans?
   c) Would you relate differently to your client if he was Mexican American, Puerto Rican, or Cuban American? If so, how? If not, why not?

2. You are a counselor at a large state university that has publicly stated support for all its federally mandated affirmative action programs. Recently, however, the Sociology Department's graduate admission procedure has been under fire by the campus newspaper for its practice of reserving 20 percent of its new admissions for Hispanic American students (the state in which the school is located is composed of 20 percent Hispanic Americans).

   a) How do you feel about the selection procedure described?
   b) What action would you take in view of your feelings?
   c) What impact would you expect this to have on your ability to relate to Hispanic American students?

3. You are a counselor in a state-run rehabilitation agency. A Puerto Rican paraplegic enters your office looking very sullen and begins to question your ability to help her. She points out that you cannot possibly understand her problems since you are not encumbered, as she is, by the forces of multiple oppression.

   a) How will you respond to her charges?
   b) What doubts do you have about your ability to work with this client?
   c) What are some of the cultural factors in which you need to be sensitive in working with this client?

4. You are a counselor in an urban elementary school with a student enrollment that is 60 percent European America and 40 percent Mexican American. Several physical confrontations have occurred in the school cafeteria recently, apparently the result of insult trading between European Americans and Mexican Americans over "Mex" and "Gringo" food. The school principal has asked you to work with some of the students involved.

a) How do you plan to work (what is your role) with these students?

b) Do you anticipate any difficulty in establishing a relationship with either the European American or Mexican American students? How will you deal with the difficulty?

c) What community resources might you want to tap in dealing with this problem?

The Hispanic American Client
Role Playing Exercise

Divide into groups of four or five. Assign each group member to a role and the responsibilities associated with the role as follows:

Role	Responsibility
1. Counselor	1. Assume role as a counselor or mental health worker who is assigned a Hispanic American client. Attempt to build rapport with the client.
2. Client	2. Assume role of a Hispanic American client. To play this role effectively, it will be necessary for the student to (a) identify cultural values of Hispanic American, (b) identify sociopolitical factors that may interfere with counseling, and (c) portray these aspects in the counseling session. It is best to select a few powerful variables in the role play. You may or may not be initially antagonistic to the counselor, but it is important for you to be sincere in your role and your reactions to the counselor.
3. Observers	3. Observe interaction and offer comments during feedback session.

This exercise is most effective in a racially and ethnically mixed group. For example, a Hispanic American can be asked to play the Hispanic American client role. However, this is probably not possible in most cases. Thus, students who play the client role will need to thoroughly read the articles for the group they are portraying.

Identifying the barriers that could interfere with counseling is an important aspect of this exercise. We recommend that a list be made of the group's cultural values and sociopolitical influences prior to the role playing.

Role playing may go on for a period of five to fifteen minutes, but the time limit should be determined prior to the activity. Allow ten to fifteen minutes for a feedback session in which all participants discuss (within the group) how they felt in their respective roles, how appropriate were the counselor responses, what else they might have done in that situation, and so forth.

Rotate and role-play the same situation with another counselor trainee *or* another Hispanic American client with different issues, concerns, and problems. In the former case, the group may feel that a particular issue is of sufficient importance to warrant reenactment. This allows students to see the effects of other counseling responses and approaches. In the latter case, the new exposure will allow students to get a broader view of barriers to counseling.

If videotaping equipment is available, we recommend that the session be taped and processed in a replay at the end. We have found this to be a powerful means of providing feedback to participants.

PART 6
Implications for Minority Group/Cross-Cultural Counseling

16

Current Issues and Future Directions in Minority Group/Cross-Cultural Counseling

In the first three chapters we defined some of the terms used in cross-cultural counseling, discussed the need to recognize within-group differences among racial/ethnic minority groups, and examined how the counseling profession has responded to the needs of racial/ethnic minority people. Chapters 4 through 15 provided information about the counseling needs and experiences of the four major racial/ethnic minority groups in the United States. In this chapter we will examine ethical standards, models for practice, training models, and research ideas that have implications for cross-cultural counseling in the future.

Ethical Considerations in Cross-Cultural Counseling

In the late 1960s ethnic minority psychologists and counselors began expressing concern that counseling an ethnically different client without proper training and experience was unethical. This view received a major boost in 1973 when the American Psychological Association (APA) Vail Conference Follow-Up Commission declared:

> that the provision of professional services to persons of culturally diverse backgrounds by persons not competent in understanding and providing professional services to such groups shall be considered unethical; that it shall be equally unethical to deny such persons professional services because the present staff is inadequately prepared, that it shall be the obligation of all service agencies to employ competent persons or to provide continuing education for the present staff to meet the service needs of the culturally diverse population it serves. (Korman, 1973, cited in Midgette & Meggert, 1991, p. 139)

Nondiscrimination and the need for multicultural competence are codified in the ethical standards of the APA and the American Counseling Association (ACA). Although the entire APA *Ethical Principles of Psychologists and Code of Conduct* has implications for multicultural counseling, the following points relate directly to multicultural counseling practice, training, and research, and merit reprinting in a book of this nature:

- Psychologists respect and protect human and civil rights, and do not knowingly participate in or condone unfair discriminatory practices. (Preamble).
- Psychologists are cognizant of the fact that the competencies required in serving, teaching, and/or studying groups of people vary with the distinctive characteristics of those groups. (Principle A: Competence).
- Psychologists strive to be aware of their own belief systems, values, needs and limitations and the effect of these on their work. (Principle B: Integrity).
- Psychologists are aware of cultural, individual, and role differences, including those due to age, gender, race, ethnicity, national origin, religion, sexual orientation, disability, language, and socioeconomic status. Psychologists try to eliminate the effect on their work of biases based on those factors, and they do not knowingly participate in or condone unfair discriminatory practices. (Principle D: Respect for People's Rights and Dignity).
- Where differences of age, gender, race, ethnicity, national origin, religion, sexual orientation, disability, language, or socioeconomic status significantly affect psychologists' work concerning particular individuals or groups, psychologists obtain the training, experience, consultation, or supervision necessary to ensure the competence of their services, or they make appropriate referrals. (Standard 1.08).
- In their work-related activities, psychologists do not engage in unfair discrimination based on age, gender, race, ethnicity, national origin, religion, sexual orientation, disability, socioeconomic status, or any basis proscribed by law. (Standard 1.10).
- Psychologists do not knowingly engage in behavior that is harassing or demeaning to persons with whom they interact in their work based on factors such as those persons' age, gender, race, ethnicity, national origin, religion, sexual orientation, disability, language, or socioeconomic status. (Standard 1.12).
- Psychologists attempt to identify situations in which particular interventions or assessment techniques or norms may not be applicable or may require adjustment in administration or interpretation because of factors such as individuals' gender, age, race, ethnicity, national origin, religion, sexual orientation, disability, language, or socioeconomic status. (Standard 2.04[c]). (American Psychological Association, 1992)

Similarly, the entire *Code of Ethics and Standards of Practice* of the ACA are relevant to providing services in a multicultural setting; however, the following sections are particularly pertinent:

- Association members recognize diversity in our society and embrace a cross-cultural approach in support of the worth, dignity, potential, and uniqueness of each individual. (Preamble)

- Counselors do not condone or engage in discrimination based on age, color, culture, disability, ethnic group, gender, race, religion, sexual orientation, marital status, or socioeconomic status. (Section A.2.a.).
- Counselors will actively attempt to understand the diverse cultural backgrounds of the clients with whom they work. This includes, but is not limited to, learning how the counselor's own cultural/ethnic/racial identity impacts her/his values and beliefs about the counseling process. (Section A.2.b).
- Counselors are aware of their own values, attitudes, beliefs, and behaviors and how these apply in a diverse society, and avoid imposing their values on clients. (A.5.b).
- Counselors will demonstrate a commitment to gain knowledge, personal awareness, sensitivity, and skills pertinent to working with a diverse client population. (C.2.a).
- [Counselors] take steps to maintain competence in the skills they use, are open to new procedures, and keep current with the diverse and/or special populations with whom they work. (C.2.f).
- Counselors do not discriminate against clients, students, or supervisees in a manner that has a negative impact based on their age, color, culture, disability, ethnic group, gender, race, religion, sexual orientation, or socioeconomic status, or for any other reason. (C.5.a).
- Counselors, as either employers or employees, do not engage in or condone practices that are inhumane, illegal, or unjustifiable (such as considerations based on age, color, culture, disability, ethnic group, gender, race, religion, sexual orientation, or socioeconomic status) in hiring, promotion, or training. (D.1.i).
- Counselors recognize that culture affects the manner in which clients' problems are defined. Clients' socioeconomic and cultural experience is considered when diagnosing mental disorders. (E.5.b).
- Counselors are cautious when selecting tests for culturally diverse populations to avoid inappropriateness of testing that may be outside of socialized behavioral or cognitive patterns. (E.6.b).
- Counselors are cautious in using assessment techniques, making evaluations, and interpreting the performance of populations not represented in the norm group on which an instrument was standardized. They recognize the effects of age, color, culture, disability, ethnic group, gender, race, religion, sexual orientation, and socioeconomic status on test administration and interpretation and place test results in proper perspective with other relevant factors. (E.8).
- Counselors design and conduct research that reflects cultural sensitivity appropriateness. (G.1.a).
- Counselors are sensitive to diversity and research issues with special populations. They seek consultation when appropriate. (G.1.f).
- Counselors respect diversity and must not discriminate against clients because of age, color, culture, disability, ethnic group, gender, race, religion,

sexual orientation, marital status, or socioeconomic status. (Standard of Practice - 1). (American Counseling Association, 1995)

Although these ethical codes make it clear that psychologists and counselors are not to discriminate against clients, students, and research subjects based on their race, ethnicity, or culture, and that psychologists and counselors are to use culturally appropriate tests and obtain training to adequately serve diverse clients, the codes have been criticized for being insensitive to ethnic minority issues. Addressing the APA ethical standards, Payton (1994) acknowledges that while successive versions of the APA ethics code have shown increasing sensitivity to issues raised by psychologists from diverse populations:

> diverse groups and all who share their concerns should be alerted to a profound philosophical shift represented by the new code. If, as it seems, psychologists have abandoned their moral tradition of endorsing the primacy of fundamental human rights, progress of diverse groups within the APA may be hampered. The current code may be the beginning steps of moving back to the future. (p. 320)

In supporting her argument, Payton points out that all earlier versions of the Code stated at the outset of the Preamble that psychologists respect the dignity and worth of individuals, a proclamation that has aided disfranchised groups within the APA in their struggle for equal treatment. She compares this to the current Preamble, which begins with a statement declaring the profession's commitment to developing scientific knowledge based on research. Payton also points out that the Code limits its aspirations and principles to psychologists' work-related activities, implying that a psychologist could eschew racism at work while embracing it outside the office.

Other concerns have also been raised with specific aspects of the APA and ACA ethical codes. Ethical codes define principles (i.e., obligations) that guide professionals that are arrived at by consensus of an ethics committee and the membership of the organization. It can be argued that the APA and ACA ethical codes (as well as the codes of other mental health professional organizations) reflect the values of middle-class European Americans and not those of ethnic minorities (DuBose, Hamel, & O'Connell, 1994; Ibrahim, 1996; Pedersen, 1995). As such, they typically reflect the values of the society and culture in which they are established. In particular, these codes have been criticized for placing a heavy emphasis on autonomy and individualism and that many ethnic minority cultures place greater emphasis on community and collectivism.

Meara, Schmidt, and Day (1996) argue that concerns about the shortcomings of principle ethics (defining obligatory behavior) can best be addressed through virtue ethics. Rather than defining obligations, virtue ethics "sets forth a set of ideals to which professionals aspire." Although Meara et al. acknowledge that virtue ethics, like principle ethics, can vary from culture to culture, they cite the following reasons why virtue ethics may enhance the practice of counseling in a multicultural society:

First, the stating of virtues fosters self- and other-awareness by making explicit what is often implicit. Such awareness could reduce ethnocentrism and increase cross-cultural understanding. Second, explicit statement of virtues provides a frame of reference for asking whether and how other cultures are similar or different. Cultures may differ in the virtues they espouse, in the relative importance placed on different virtues, or in the ways particular virtues such as prudence, integrity, respectfulness, and benevolence are defined and expressed in the common-sense practices of everyday life. Third, once questions about other virtues or ways of being virtuous are considered, we can evaluate what virtues (if any) are appropriate for the profession in this time and place and decide if and how we might want to develop them. (p. 54)

While accepting the premise that virtue ethics may provide a more culturally sensitive approach than principle ethics, Ibrahim (1996) takes Meara et al. (1996) to task for framing their discussion of principle and virtue ethics within the mainstream cultural values of the United States. Drawing on Pedersen's (1995) discussion of relativism, absolutism, and universalism in ethics, Ibrahim argues that what is needed is a universalist approach to ethics in professional psychology. Briefly, the relativist position examines the ethics of each culture separately, the absolutist position applies the ethics of the dominant culture to all cultures, and the universalist position looks for ethical guidelines common across cultures while acknowledging those that are unique to each culture (Pedersen, 1995, pp. 35–36). According to Ibrahim, psychology needs to develop an ethical code that reflects both the shared worldview and unique cultural values of the public it serves.

We are pleased to see that current ethical standards are being scrutinized for their applicability across diverse groups. We agree with Meara et al. (1996) that the increasingly multicultural nature of our society calls for psychologists and counselors to continually reexamine the virtues to which they and the members of the communities they serve aspire. Ibrahim (1996) also makes an important point that the profession should strive to identify universal values. Being a counselor or psychologist in a multicultural society demands sensitivity to ethical issues beyond those directly addressed by a rigid set of professional ethical standards. In particular, the heavy stress on individual autonomy found in the ethical codes of professional mental health organizations may need to be moderated when working with ethnic minority clients.

Theories/Models That Guide Cross-Cultural Counseling Practice

Three-Dimensional Model for Counseling Racial/Ethnic Minority Clients

In chapter 3 it was noted that a great deal of criticism has been directed at the conventional counseling role of psychotherapy. Time-bound, space-bound, cathartic psychotherapy may be irrelevant to the life experiences and needs of many ethnic minorities. Rather than demanding that the client adapt to the counselor's culture, critics argue that the counselor should adjust to and work within the client's culture. The counselor needs to get out of the office and meet the client in the client's environment and become actively involved in social programs and activities in racial/ethnic minority communities (Wilson & Calhoun, 1974).

While some racial/ethnic minority clients may come to the attention of counselors in schools and social service agencies, others will go unserved unless counselors reach out to them. By reaching out to the client in his/her environment, the counselor is in a better position to: a) build credibility and rapport, b) understand the cultural experience of the client, c) directly observe the environmental factors that contribute to the client's problem, and d) respond to the client's needs at the time they are experienced.

In addition to getting out into the client's environment, we believe the counselor needs to engage in viable alternatives to the conventional psychotherapy role. In general, these alternative roles should involve the counselor more actively in the client's life experiences than does the conventional role. An alternative role might take on a provocative, preventative, or remedial focus. The alternative roles to be discussed are: (1) advocate, (2) change agent, (3) consultant, (4) adviser, (5) facilitator of indigenous support systems, and (6) facilitator of indigenous healing methods. There is considerable overlapping of these six role functions, but each includes some aspects that makes it different from the others and the conventional psychotherapy and counseling roles. We also offer a brief discussion of how conventional psychotherapy and conventional counseling can be applied more effectively with ethnically diverse clients than they have in the past.

Advocate

All ethnic minority individuals by definition are oppressed to some degree by the dominant society. Some ethnic minority individuals and groups have developed skills that help them deal with discrimination. Others, particularly recent immigrants, may lack the English-speaking skills and economic power to confront and/or deflect oppressive environments. In these situations the client or clients may need an advocate rather than a psychotherapist.

In this role the counselor represents a client or group of clients who have brought a particular form of discrimination to the counselor's attention. Being an empathic counselor who suggests alternative ways of coping with discrimination may not be enough; the counselor may need to also actively pursue alternative courses of action with or for the client, including making a personal contact for the client who is overwhelmed by the bureaucracy. As an advocate, the counselor speaks on behalf of the client, often confronting the institutional sources of oppression that are contributing to the client's problems. Not infrequently the injustice involves the institution employing the counselor. If the client's goals are in conflict with those of the institution, the counselor must decide to represent the client and not the institution or the system, presumably within ethical restrictions imposed by the profession. The counselor need not represent a particular client or group of clients; rather, the entire minority culture experiencing an injustice may function as the client. The advocate, because an ethnic minority client is involved, has the added responsibility for making certain that the minority person can benefit fully from the social and economic resources of the majority culture without losing what is unique and valued in his/her own culture.

The advocate role is extremely important for counselors in ethnically diverse schools (Esquivel & Keitel, 1990), particularly those with recent immigrants. The National Coalition of Advocates for Students (1988) has developed a number of recommendations for advocacy on behalf of immigrant students. School counselors (and other school personnel) are urged to advocate that their school: (1) ensure that all school personnel understand that immigrant children have a legal right to free, appropriate public education; (2) restructure those policies and practices that sort immigrant students into programs that prepare them for inferior futures; (3) ensure that immigrant students (and all students) experience a school environment free of victimization, harassment, and intergroup conflict; and (4) ensure a more equitable allocation of resources to those (typically inner city) schools that serve immigrant students.

Change Agent

According to Egan (1985), "change agent refers to anyone who plays an important part in designing, redesigning, running, renewing, or improving any system, subsystem, or program" (p. 12). As a change agent, the counselor attempts to change the social environment that oppresses racial/ethnic minorities and helps the client identify the external sources of his or her problem and methods of resolving the problem. Rather than encouraging the client to "own the problem," the counselor helps the client become aware of the oppressive forces creating the problem. Together the counselor and client develop a strategy for eliminating or reducing the effect of the oppression on the client's life. This is often done by facilitating the formation of racial/ethnic minority political groups. Through political power, racial/ethnic minorities and other disenfranchised groups are able to bring about change in their social and physical environment. The counselor serving as a change agent frequently assumes a low-visibility profile, often finding it useful to mobilize other influential persons in the offending institution to bring about change (Waltz & Benjamin, 1977).

In the mid-1970s, the Division 17 Professional Affairs Committee of the APA suggested that college counselors need to accept responsibility for changing university environments to benefit all ethnic minority students.

> Problems of institutional racism are paramount on a university campus. Counseling alone on discrimination issues will be ineffective. Counseling

psychologists must involve themselves in affirmative action programs, sponsor symposia and workshops on racism in society, and actively involve themselves in programs of cultural awareness. (Ivey, 1976, p. 10–11)

Lewis and Lewis (1977) identified four ways the counselor can serve as a change agent. The counselor can assess community needs, coordinate activities and resources, provide training in skill building, and advocate change. Ponterotto (1987) has described a multimodal approach to counseling Mexican Americans that includes a change agent component and that appears equally applicable to other ethnic groups. The change agent component of the approach involves identifying the social, environmental, and institutional factors that are oppressing the client but that are external to his/her control. The counselor helps the client organize a plan for confronting the situation and identify agencies that could facilitate elimination of the problem.

As a change agent, the counselor also can work directly with majority clients in an attempt to move them toward the goal of reducing racist attitudes. Katz and Ivey (1977) described a racism-awareness training program that involves a reeducation process designed, ". . . to raise [the] consciousness of White people, help them identify racism in their life experience from which their racist attitudes and behaviors have developed, and move them to take action against institutional and individual racism" (p. 487). The six phases of the program are designed to help participants to:

1. Increase their understanding of racism in society and themselves.
2. Confront discrepancies existing between the myths and reality of American ideology and behavior.
3. Sort through some of their feelings and reactions that were triggered by phases 1 and 2.
4. Confront the racism in the White culture that their own actions support.
5. Understand and accept their Whiteness.
6. Develop specific action strategies to combat personal and institutional racism (p. 487).

Katz and Ivey's suggestion that racism is a White problem and that White counselors should assume a major role in dealing with it makes sense. European American counselors are, in some respects, in the best position to confront the majority population with their own stereotypic attitudes and behaviors.

Consultant

According to Hansen, Hines, and Meier (1990), consultation involves a collegial relationship between the consultant and the consultee (or client), who work together to affect the behavior of a third party. A distinction between the change agent role and the consultant role is that a primary goal of the former is to alleviate existing problems while a primary goal of the latter is to prevent the problems from developing.

In the consultant role, counselors can help ethnic minority clients learn skills needed to interact successfully with the dominant society. For example, some minority clients lack assertiveness skills. According to Wood and Mallinckrodt (1990):

> members of many ethnic minority groups have values about assertive responding that differ markedly from those of the dominant culture. The resulting inability to perform skills valued by the dominant culture may place ethnic minority persons at a significant disadvantage for coping in the majority society (p. 5).

LaFromboise and Rowe (1983) proposed social skills training as a strategy for helping American Indians learn to relate to non-Indians. They suggest that a skills training approach is particularly applicable to American Indian clients because: (1) "it is less culturally biased than alternative approaches stemming from the academic tradition" (p. 590); (2) it can be used to prevent as well as remediate problems; (3) it involves the use of modeling in small group settings, a procedure compatible with American Indian methods of transmitting knowledge; (4) it has been found to be more effective than alternative treatments; and (5) it is applicable to the kinds of problems American Indians are currently experiencing.

Adviser

Some ethnic minority individuals, particularly recent immigrants, simply are not aware of the kind of discrimination they may face or the kinds of problems they may encounter as a result of overt or covert racism. In this case the counselor may be of most assistance by advising these individuals about the problems they or their families may encounter; the goal is to prevent problems. The consultant role differs from the adviser role in that in the former role, the client (often high in acculturation) initiates contact with the counselor to seek help in preventing a problem; as an adviser, the counselor initiates contact with the client (often low in acculturation) to advise the client of unanticipated problems.

The role of adviser has been eschewed historically by the counseling profession. For the past four decades the counseling literature has criticized advise-giving while promoting such alternative counselor behaviors as listening, facilitating, and supporting. In reality, however, advise may be exactly what recent immigrants need in order to prevent problems before they develop. An example of advise-giving would be to advise recent immigrants of the discrimination they will face on the job market and that their children may face in school. Further, the counselor should advise recent immigrants what they and their children might do to reduce the impact of such discrimination.

Facilitator of Indigenous Support Systems

It is probably accurate to state that every culture in the world has developed some form of social support to help prevent and remediate psychological and relationship problems. Counseling can be thought of as a social support system that evolved as our economic base shifted from agriculture to industry to technology and as people became more mobile and removed from their family support systems (Tyler, 1961). Like counseling, social support systems often provide a medium for advice-giving, consultation, modeling, catharsis, reinforcement, and advocacy. Thus, social support systems serve many of the same functions as counselors, but support systems are more socially acceptable within many cultures than is professional counseling.

When people begin immigrating to the United States in large numbers from any country, as they did from Vietnam in 1975, their indigenous social support systems are often in disarray and nonfunctional. However, these preexisting social support systems frequently can be adapted to fit the new situation, or new support systems can emerge in the context of the new cultural milieu. Examples of indigenous social support systems that play an important role in many ethnic minority communities include extended ethnic community centers, family networks, neighborhood social networks, ethnic churches, and ethnic advocacy groups.

Counselors can facilitate the development of indigenous support systems by publicly acknowledging the important role they play, by supporting government and private funds to build ethnic community centers, and by encouraging ethnic organizations (e.g., ethnic churches, ethnic service organizations) to provide such services. Counselors can also facilitate the use of indigenous support systems by referring clients to them.

Facilitator of Indigenous Healing Methods

In their review of intervention and treatment research with ethnic minorities, S. Sue, Chun, and Gee (1995) concluded that "culture-specific treatment should be available to ethnic clients especially those who are unacculturated or who hold very traditional ethnic values that are discrepant from Western values" (p. 278). Just as all cultures have developed support systems to help prevent psychological and relationship problems, all cultures have developed methods of intervening with these problems once they develop. While the psychological healing methods of various cultures may have common elements (Torrey, 1972; Tseng & McDermott, 1975), each has evolved within a cultural context and is effective because members of that culture believe in its efficacy. According to Wohl (1995), "If the explanatory models [beliefs about problem etiology and treatment] of the clinician and the patient are far apart and the distance between them is not negotiated, treatment will flounder . . ." (p. 81). Individuals who believe in a healing regimen are likely to follow it and invest themselves in making it successful.

Conventional counseling may be ineffective for someone who believes that their psychological problems are the result of an "evil eye" or an inappropriate diet. For this reason, Cayleff (1986) suggests that:

> When counseling ethnic and racial minorities, certain belief systems of the client must be considered if quality care is to be given. This entails understanding and

honoring folk belief systems such as (a) the humoral hot-cold theory of physical and mental disease . . . , (b) *curanderismo* . . . and belief in folk disease . . . , and (c) religious healing rituals and practices. (p. 345)

Understanding and honoring folk belief systems does not mean that the counselor must begin incorporating these healing methods in his/her own practice. It does mean that the counselor must accept that healing methods from the client's culture are more likely to be effective with the client than are conventional psychotherapeutic strategies from the dominant culture (Berthold, 1989).

Frequently, counselors are unaware of or are disdainful of these procedures, preferring to engage the client in the very counseling process so heavily criticized by minority representatives. Counselors may be able to best serve their minority clientele by attempting to facilitate rather than discourage use of indigenous support systems. According to Cayleff (1986), counselors violate the ethical principle of beneficence (doing good by preventing harm) if they fail to honor the client's belief system (p. 345).

The counselor can facilitate indigenous healing methods by (1) referring the client to an indigenous healer and (2) incorporating the healing methods of the indigenous culture in his/her counseling practice. Referring the client to an indigenous healer requires that the counselor be familiar with healers from various cultures and their credibility within the racial/ethnic community. Incorporating the healing methods of various cultures into a counseling practice is more problematic. First, it is doubtful if individual counselors can become skilled in the healing method of multiple cultures. We caution against such activity without proper training and indoctrination by indigenous healers. Second, and most important, healing methods from various cultures can involve contradictory beliefs, creating concern about the integrity of the counselor's own belief system.

Conventional Counseling

The Education and Training Committee of Division 17 (1984) of the APA has defined counseling psychology as:

a psychological specialty in which practitioners help others improve their well-being, alleviate their distress, resolve their crises, and increase their ability to solve problems and make decisions. Counseling psychologists enable and facilitate psychological growth and development by helping others better use existing resources and skills, or by guiding them in developing new ways to help themselves. (p. 1)

This definition of counseling psychology suggests that counselors help clients remediate existing problems, prevent problems, and make decisions. The remediation of existing problems is a healing function that we will discuss under the next heading, conventional psychotherapy. In this section, Conventional Counseling, we focus on the role of helping clients make decisions and prevent problems.

Helping clients make decisions is a universal process that applies across the various cultures within the United States. This process involves listing alternatives, considering the possible consequences of each alternative, weighing the probability of each alternative, and choosing an alternative. In helping racial/ethnic minority clients to make decisions, however, it is extremely important that the counselor is sensitive to cultural values and to oppressive forces that may impinge on decision making. It is also extremely important that the counselor be aware of his/her own cultural biases that may be influencing the client's decision-making and to acknowledge these biases to the client.

Many Hispanic Americans and Asian Americans live in intact families and many African Americans in extended families, therefore preventative counseling with families may be particularly relevant for ethnic minority clients (Lefley, 1994). Lefley suggests that family psychoeducation may be particularly useful for ethnic minority clients. However, she also cautions that although "communication skills, behavior management techniques, and problem-solving strategies are needed by all families, . . . they must be geared to the conceptual framework of a particular culture" (p. 232). For example, she suggests that egalitarian problem-solving techniques, assessment of enmeshment in dominant cultural terms, and inadequate attention to spiritual factors may be problematic and in need of adjustment when working with ethnic minority clients.

Conventional Psychotherapy

While the exclusive use of psychotherapy as the intervention of choice with racially/ethnically diverse clients is inappropriate, the elimination of psychotherapy as a counseling tool with special populations would be equally ill-advised (Wohl, 1995). Ethnically diverse clients can experience the same mental disorders that afflict nonminority clients. Further, many ethnically diverse clients are bicultural and feel comfortable with conventional forms of psychotherapy. Thus, when the goal of counseling is to remediate an existing psychological problem, the counselor may want to provide psychotherapy if the client is bicultural and if the problem is no longer being maintained by external sources of oppression.

When providing psychotherapy for racial/ethnic minority clients, counselor credibility may be more important than knowledge of the client's indigenous culture per se, particularly for highly acculturated clients. S. Sue and Zane (1987) have suggested that although knowledge of a client's culture and techniques generated by this knowledge are important when working with ethnically diverse clients, their primary importance in psychotherapy may be to establish therapist credibility. These authors argue that knowledge of a client's culture and culturally specific forms of intervention may be distal to therapeutic outcome. More directly related to therapeutic outcome, they argue, are therapist credibility and giving, two processes particularly relevant when working with ethnically diverse clients. Credibility is a function of ascribed status and achieved status. Ascribed status is assigned by others; achieved status is primarily a function of the therapist's skills. S. Sue and Zane suggest that three factors are significantly linked to achieved status:

1. *Conceptualization of the problem.* If the client's problems are conceptualized in a manner that is incongruent with the client's belief systems, the credibility of the therapist is diminished.
2. *Means for problem resolution.* If the therapist requires from the client responses that are culturally incompatible or unacceptable, the achieved credibility of the therapist is diminished.
3. *Goals for treatment.* If the definitions of goals are discrepant between therapist and client, credibility of the therapist will be diminished. (p. 41)

Wohl (1995) points out the importance of addressing resistance in conventional psychotherapy with a culturally different client, but cautions against misinterpreting wariness on the part of ethnic minority clients due to past discrimination as clinical resistance. Equally important, Wohl suggests that therapists must be aware of their own countertransference tendencies. These tendencies include avoiding racial/ethnic issues out of fear of offending the client and offending the client by communicating conscious and unconscious racist attitudes. He points out that in "interethnic, intercultural situations, one must pay much more attention to the work of establishing the basis for a communicative relationship than in those where this factor is not evident" (p. 79). On acknowledging race/ethnicity as a factor in interracial psychotherapy, Wohl suggests that there are several alternatives:

> One would have therapists introduce the topic of race and its possible impact on the therapeutic relationship openly at the outset of psychotherapy. Presumably this would lead to an exploration of the patient's attitudes about and difficulties with ethnic conflict and ethnic identity. . . . The other position holds that therapists should be willing to discuss racial issues but provides no specific technical guidance about how they are to be introduced and by which participant. . . . The fine line in this instance, then, is to balance out readiness to deal with a problem that is believed to be a part of the therapeutic interaction against the sense that generally it is better to wait until one has evidence that the issue exerts sufficient pressure within the patient that would make dealing with it fruitful. Above all, it is important to avoid the comfort of an intellectualized discussion of race and the evils of racism. (p. 86)

S. Sue et al. (1995) concluded, after reviewing ethnic minority treatment and intervention research, that having a bilingual therapist is vital to an ethnic minority client not proficient in English, that having an ethnically similar therapist may be advantageous to an ethnic minority client, that therapists who are not familiar with the cultures of their ethnic minority clients should consult with mental health professionals who are, and for ethnic minority clients who are not familiar with the psychotherapy process, pretherapy intervention may be important.

Selecting an Appropriate Role

Selecting from among these various roles the most appropriate one for a particular client and a particular problem can be a difficult and confusing task. Atkinson, Thompson, and Grant (1993) have addressed this problem by suggesting that at least three factors need to be taken into account when selecting an appropriate role. These three factors are: (1) locus of problem etiology, (2) client's level of acculturation, and (3) goal of counseling. Locus of problem etiology refers to a continuum of problem causes that range from external to internal. Externally caused problems are those imposed on the client by the environment; in the case of racial/ethnic minority clients these externally imposed problems are often a function of oppression. Job discrimination based on racial/ethnic bias is an example of an externally imposed problem. Mood swings, irrational fear, and weak impulse control are examples of problems assumed to have an internal source. Although some psychologists (e.g., behaviorists) might argue that all client problems have an external source, most client problems are treated by psychologists as if they had an internal etiology.

Level of acculturation refers to the extent to which the client has adopted the culture of mainstream, dominant society. Recent immigrants are often low in acculturation, although even third and fourth generations after immigration may have avoided adopting dominant cultural values. Persons high in acculturation have adopted the attitudes, values, and behaviors of dominant society; they may have retained cultural values from their indigenous culture (and are therefore bicultural) or they may have lost most of their ancestral cultural values.

The goals of counseling also can be portrayed as a continuum ranging from preventative on one end to remedial on the other. Atkinson et al. (1993) suggest that counselors can determine the best role to use with an ethnic minority client by conceptualizing the etiology, acculturation, and goals continua as a cube or three-dimensional model (see figure 16.1). The intersections of these three continua form the corners of the cube and each corner is associated with one of eight roles a counselor might assume when working with a racial/ethnic minority client.

Atkinson et al. (1993) caution against using the three-dimensional model as a cookbook for making this determination; in reality, clients and their problems are seldom identified with the extremes of these continua and therefore no single role is clearly most appropriate. They also express concern that counselors not interpret the model as justification for ignoring minority cultural background when the client is highly acculturated. Highly acculturated individuals may still retain strong ties to their indigenous culture. Also, as racial/ethnic minorities they cannot escape the oppression and discrimination of a racist society. Given these caveats, however, the three-dimensional model can be a useful way to conceptualize racial/ethnic minority clients and their

Figure 16.1

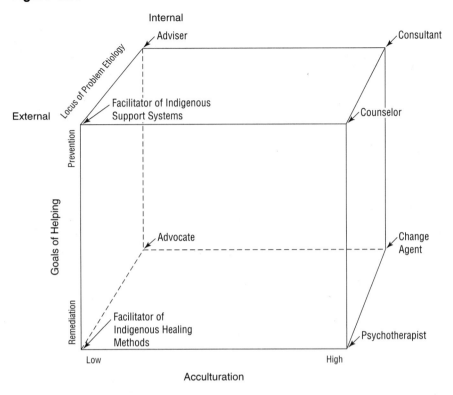

problems and can help counselors determine the best role or combination of roles to use when working with them.

Helms' Interactional Model

Another model of cross-cultural counseling that emerged during the 1980s that has important implications for counseling practice in the future is Helms' Black/White Interaction Model (Helms, 1990, 1995). This model grew out of Helms' work with Black racial identity development (see chapter 2) and White racial identity development (Helms, 1984, 1990). Helms (1990) postulates that White racial identity formation is a two-phase developmental process in which, "Phase 1, the abandonment of racism, begins with the Contact stage and ends with the Reintegration stage. Phase 2, defining a positive White identity, begins with the Pseudo-Independent stage and ends with the Autonomy stage" (p. 55). Briefly, in the Contact stage the individual is oblivious to his/her own racial identity. This is followed by the Disintegration stage, in which the individual first acknowledges his/her White identity. The individual then moves to the

Reintegration stage, in which he/she idealizes Whites and denigrates Blacks. In the subsequent Pseudo-Independent stage, the individual begins to question the attitude that Blacks are innately inferior to Whites. As the individual searches for a more positive attitude toward Whites, he/she enters the Immersion/Emersion stage and begins an honest appraisal of racism and what it means to be White. In the final stage, Autonomy, the individual assumes a multicultural identity and nonracist attitudes (Helms, 1990, p. 51–52).

Although a full discussion of Helm's Black/White Interaction Model is beyond the scope of this text, a key concept is that the relationship between the counselor and client stages of racial identity development (rather than racial similarities or differences per se) are predictive of counseling outcome. According to Helms (1995), the basic premises of the racial identity interaction model are:

> (a) racial identity statuses structure people's reactions to one another as well as to external events, (b) people form harmonious or disharmonious alliances with one another based on the tenor of their expressed racial identity, (c) racial reactions occur within the context of direct or vicarious interpersonal activities, and (d) patterns of reactions within an interpersonal context can be classified according to quality. (p. 191)

Four types of relationships are possible for same race and cross-race dyads: parallel, crossed, progressive, and regressive. In a *parallel* relationship, the counselor and client share similar racial attitudes about Blacks and Whites. In a *crossed* relationship, the counselor and client hold opposing racial attitudes about Blacks and Whites. "A *progressive* relationship is one in which the counselor's stage of racial consciousness is at least one stage more advanced than the client's; a *regressive* relationship is one in which the client's stage of development is at least one stage more advanced than the counselor's" (Helms, 1990, p. 141). Examples of each type of relationship are presented in table 16.1 (numerous other combinations within each type are possible, however).

Although a few studies have been conducted on Helms' Black/White Interaction Model, more research is needed to determine its validity. Research is also needed to determine if the model can be generalized to racial/ethnic groups other than Blacks and Whites. Assuming that the Model is supported by future research, it will have important implications for the practice of counseling and the training of counselors (to be discussed in the next section). With respect to counseling practice, it is clear that for both ethnically similar and ethnically dissimilar counseling dyads, progressive relationships are likely to be most productive and regressive relationships likely to be least productive (and perhaps even harmful). This suggests that counselors should assess their own and their clients' racial identity development and refer the client to a more appropriate counselor in the case of a regressive counseling relationship. It also suggests that counselors, Black or White, at higher levels of racial identity development will be able to establish productive relationships with more clients

Table 16.1

Examples of the Four Types of Counseling Relationships Based on Racial Identity Stages

	Stages of Identity			Common Affective Issues	Counseling Process	
	Counselor's	Client's	Type of Relationship		Counselor/Strategies	Counseling Outcome
				Black Dyads		
1.	Preencounter	Preencounter	Parallel	Anger about being assigned to a Black person. Guilt about negative feelings.	Both will use strategies designed to deny and avoid issues to reinterpret whatever happens in a manner consistent with perceived negative stereotypes.	Client terminates with little symptom remission. Counselor "pushes" client out of counseling.
2.	Immersion	Preencounter	Crossed (Progressive)	Counselor may feel angry and rejecting; client feels fearful and and intimidated.	General non-acceptance of one another; counselor may be low in empathy, use much advice giving; client is passive and tries not to become involved in the process.	If counselor can act as positive role model, client may develop positive feelings about Blackness; self-esteem is enhanced.
3.	Preencounter	Immersion	Regressive (Crossed)	Counselor shares White society's fear, weariness and anxiety; client displaces anger.	Client attempts to reform counselor; counselor attempts to avoid issues.	Short relationships; client's anger may be enhanced, counselor's anxiety may be increased.
4.	Encounter	Preencounter	Progressive	Counselor feels excited and apprehensive about working with Black client; client feels angry and apprehensive and distrusting.	Social discussion in which counselor tries to prove he/she is Black; client tries to prove he/she isn't.	Long relationships if counselor uses enthusiasm to engage client; limited symptom remission if counselor avoids doing therapy.

Table 16.1—*Continued*

Examples of the Four Types of Counseling Relationships Based on Racial Identity Stages

Stages of Identity			Counseling Process		
Counselor's	*Client's*	*Type of Relationship*	*Common Affective Issues*	*Counselor/Strategies*	*Counseling Outcome*
			White Dyads		
1. Contact	Contact	Parallel	Counselor and client exhibit curiosity and naivete about racial issues.	Information sharing, avoidance of negative affect related to racial matters.	Discussion of racial issues is aborted because neither knows how to resolve them.
2. Contact	Reintegration	Crossed (Regression)	Mutual dislike because they don't empathize with one another's racial attitudes.	Argumentative attempts to reeducate each other.	Premature termination; client's symptoms may be aggravated because he/she doesn't respect counselor.
3. Autonomous	Disintegration	Progressive	Counselor may be empathic and accepting; client needs to deal with self-concept issues and confused feelings.	Counselor attempts to encourage self-awareness and understanding of racial dynamics.	Potential for client insight and knowledge acquisition is good.
4. Disintegration	Autonomous	Regressive	Friction; low levels of empathy and understanding.	Counselor attempts to protect and nurture client inappropriately.	Premature termination; client perceives counselor as inexpert.

Table 16.1—*Continued*

Examples of the Four Types of Counseling Relationships Based on Racial Identity Stages

Stages of Identity			Counseling Process		
Counselor's	Client's	Type of Relationship	Common Affective Issues	Counselor/Strategies	Counseling Outcome
			Mixed Dyads		
1. Preencounter	Reintegration	Parallel	Mutual anxiety: counselor wants to prove competence; client displaces anger previously denied.	Abusive relationship; client tests and manipulates; counselor is unassertive and task oriented.	Relationship may be long-lasting because it reinforces stereotypes; little symptom remission.
2. Immersion	Reintegration	Crossed	Direct overt expression of hostility and anger by both.	Debates; refusal to become involved with one another.	Short-lived; leaves both feeling frustrated about original beliefs.
3. Internalization	Disintegration	Progressive	Client's self-concept issues, feelings of confusion, and helplessness are the focus.	Counselor attempts to model positive adjustment and to elicit denied feelings.	Potential for client cross-racial skill development and improved self-confidence is good.
4. Disintegration	Internalization	Regressive	Counselor experiences pain and/or anxiety about cross-racial issues.	Counselor interacts with undue reserve, uneasiness, and incongruence; client senses counselor's discomfort.	Premature termination client will seek counselor more in tune with her/his needs.

Note: From *Black and White Racial Identity: Theory, Research, and Practice* (pp. 142–143) by J. E. Helms, 1990, New York: Greenwood Press. Copyright 1990 by J. E. Helms. Reprinted with permission.

than those at the Preencounter (Black counselor) or Contact (White counselor) stages of development.

Theory of Multicultural Counseling and Therapy

As multicultural counseling and therapy (MCT) became increasingly influential in the mental health professions, a number of scholars expressed the need for theory development to organize the burgeoning literature in the field (Ivey, Ivey, & Simek-Morgan, 1993; Pedersen, 1994; Ponterotto & Casas, 1991; D.W. Sue & D. Sue, 1990). They noted that work in multicultural counseling was often based upon inconsistent formulations and lacked a conceptual framework to guide practice considerations. Furthermore, they pointed out that current theories of counseling/therapy originate from a European American context, are culture-bound, and are inadequate to describe and explain the richness and complexity of culturally different populations in the United States. Theory often guides conceptualizations of normality and abnormality and helping techniques and strategies are derived from these formulations, therefore European American orientations (psychodynamic, existential/humanistic, and cognitive/behavioral) potentially neglect or trivialize Asian, African, and other non-Western contributions (D.W. Sue, 1995).

Attempting to critically integrate research and work in multicultural psychology, D. W. Sue, Ivey, and Pedersen (1996) recently proposed a theory of MCT that operates from six major propositions and forty-seven corollaries. A few of the assumptions underlying MCT theory are summarized here. Any attempt to briefly describe the theory does not do it justice. The interested reader is encouraged to seek out the original sources for a more critical analysis.

1. One of the primary assumptions guiding the theory is that culture is central to all theories of normal and abnormal development, and failure to acknowledge this leads to inaccurate diagnosis and treatment. As mentioned earlier, the APA and ACA ethical codes and standards of practice place high value upon autonomy and individualism. It is clear, however, that many culturally different groups value "collectivism" and "interdependence." An unenlightened therapist who equates autonomy with maturity may unknowingly and inaccurately label traditional Asian American clients as "overly dependent" if they seek parental or family input before making decisions.

2. European American conceptions of mental health must be balanced by non-Western perspectives. Theories of counseling and therapy arise from European American culture and reflect the values, mores, customs, philosophies, and language of that group. As such they represent worldviews embedded in a particular cultural context; non-Western worldviews of helping, indigenous to another culture, must be seen as equally legitimate. Failure to acknowledge and adjust counselor practice

accordingly may deprive racial/ethnic minority clients culturally relevant services and/or result in cultural oppression (D.W. Sue, 1978).

3. MCT theory offers a "both/and" rather than an "either/or" view of theory and practice. In other words, diverse theories and counseling practices provide different perspectives of the same phenomenon. For example, humanistic/existential approaches emphasize the "feeling self"; cognitive approaches the "thinking self"; and behavioral approaches the "behaving self." MCT theory views the totality of human existence to be comprised of not only biological, thinking, feeling, and behaving selves, but social, cultural, and political ones as well. Thus, a wholistic view of counseling means that all can exist under the same umbrella. MCT theory is a metatheory of counseling and psychotherapy and offers an organizational framework for understanding the numerous helping approaches developed by humankind.

4. Human development is embedded in *multiple levels* of experiences— individual, group, and universal—and in *multiple contexts,* including individual, family, and cultural milieu. In other words, people (a) are unique, (b) share commonalities with their reference groups (race, culture, ethnicity, gender, sexual orientation, etc.), and (c) share many universal qualities by virtue of being *Homo sapiens.* Traditional counseling and therapy have historically tended to relate to clients at only the individual or universal levels, thereby negating group identities. Likewise, the totality of contexts (individual, family, and society) must be the focus of any effective treatments. Remedial work aimed only at the client addresses merely the "individual context" and may fail to acknowledge that the source of problems potentially resides in systemic forces.

5. The effective MCT practitioner is one who uses modalities and defines goals consistent with the life experiences and cultural values of the client. No single approach is equally effective across all populations and life situations. The ultimate goal of the helping professions must be to expand the repertoire of helping responses available to the counselor or therapist regardless of theoretical orientation. As a result, MCT theory also stresses the importance of multiple helping roles developed by many culturally different groups and societies. The conventional counselor/therapist role is seen as only one of many others available to the helping professional.

MCT theory as proposed by D. W. Sue, Ivey, and Pedersen (1996) is an attempt to lay the groundwork for a systematic theory of multicultural helping. From their theory, they attempt to derive research, training, and practice implications for the mental health profession. Some of these derivations challenge traditional mental health practices and appear quite revolutionary. However, because of its newness, there has been no direct formal testing of the propositions and corollaries. While the theory was formulated from the existing research literature on multicultural psychology, it appears that the future impact of MCT theory will ultimately reside in the validity of its underlying assumptions.

Counselor Education

In chapter 2 we pointed out that one of the reasons ethnic minorities have underutilized mental health services is due to the lack of ethnically similar counselors. In this section, we will document the history of ethnic minority underrepresentation in psychology and counseling and examine methods that programs might use to increase the number of ethnic minority students they enroll and graduate. We will also look at the mandate for training all counselors, regardless of ethnicity, in multicultural counseling, and how programs go about providing that training.

Underrepresentation of Ethnic Minorities in Psychology

It is probably safe to say that very few professional psychology and counselor education programs have intentionally discriminated against minority applicants in their admission's policies and procedures in recent years. However, racial/ethnic minority representation in professional psychology and counselor education has not improved significantly since the 1970s. Surveys of psychology departments and APA members in the 1970s consistently revealed that racial/ethnic minorities were underrepresented in the profession (Kennedy & Wagner, 1979; Padilla, Boxley, & Wagner, 1973; Parham & Moreland, 1981; Russo, Olmedo, Stapp, & Fulcher, 1981; Stang & Peele, 1977). By 1980, ethnic minorities still made up only 3.1 percent of all APA members, 5 percent of all graduate faculty in psychology, approximately 8 percent of those awarded Ph.D.'s in psychology, and approximately 10 percent of those enrolled in graduate psychology programs (Russo et al., 1981). Enrollment in doctoral programs did not improve during the 1980s. Kohout and Pion (1990) reported that African American enrollment in doctoral psychology programs actually dropped slightly between 1977 (3.5 percent) and 1987 (3.4 percent) while enrollment for ethnic groups edged up slightly (Asian American, 1.2 percent to 1.7 percent; American Indians, 0.3 percent to 0.6 percent; and Hispanics 1.5 percent to 3.5 percent). The most recent figures (rounded to the nearest whole percent) indicate that African Americans make up 5 percent, Hispanics 5 percent, Asian Americans 4 percent, and American Indians 1 percent of the enrollment in doctoral psychology programs (Kohout & Wicherski, 1993), even though collectively they made up 25 percent of the U.S. population that same year. Kohout and Wicherski (1993) found that ethnic minorities were even more underrepresented among the full-time faculty in health service provider subfields of graduate departments of psychology. African Americans made up 5 percent, Hispanics 2 percent, Asian Americans 1 percent, and American Indians less than 1 percent, of the faculty in clinical, counseling, and school psychology training programs in the early 1990s. Based on data like these, Aponte and Clifford (1995) concluded that "at best, . . . any increase of ethnic persons in the field of psychology has been at a rate that continues to fall further [*sic*] behind the rate of increase of ethnic groups in the U. S. population, and, at worst, appears to be flat or decreasing in the face of increasing ethnic group populations" (p. 285).

Racial/ethnic minorities also have been underrepresented among students and faculty in counselor-education programs. Atkinson (1983a) surveyed counselor education programs and found that Asian Americans were underrepresented as faculty and that Blacks and Hispanics were underrepresented as students and faculty. A more recent survey of racial/ethnic minority representation among counselor education faculty revealed that the situation has become worse, not better. Young, Chamley, and Withers (1990) found that Asian American representation in the general population was 1.9 times higher than their representation on counselor education faculty, Black representation in the general population was 2.7 times higher than on counselor education faculty, and Hispanics representation in the population at large was 4.3 times higher than on counselor education faculty.

These data and data from other mental health fields prompted organizations like the National Institute of Mental Health, the APA Council of Representatives, and the Presidential Commission on Mental Health to call for an increase in the number of minority mental health professionals (Ridley, 1985; Young et al., 1990). Korchin (1981) identified five reasons, paraphrased below, why the racial/ethnic minorities representation in the mental health professions must be increased:

1. It is morally right to do so.
2. Minority mental health workers are better able than are their nonminority colleagues to understand minority clients.
3. Minority mental health workers are more motivated than are their nonminority colleagues to work with minority clients.
4. Minority mental health workers are needed as identification figures for minority clients.
5. Minority mental health workers can enrich the knowledge of their nonminority colleagues by sharing their knowledge of human diversity.

After three decades of nondiscrimination and affirmative action, ethnic parity in professional psychology remains an elusive goal. Drastic steps are needed if ethnic parity is to be achieved among psychology students and faculty in the foreseeable future. Unfortunately, by the mid-1990s strong opposition to affirmative action was being exercised in the legislative and judicial branches of state and federal government (Dellios, 1994). We believe affirmative action efforts are needed more than ever if mental health training programs are to meet the needs of the rapidly growing ethnic minority population. Furthermore, as will become evident in the next section, we believe that admissions procedures need not give "preferential" treatment to ethnic minority applicants, but they do need to reflect the strengths that minorities bring to the profession.

Recruiting, Admitting, and Supporting Ethnic Minority Counselor Trainees

According to the APA, "there are only about 15 or 20 programs that really have been proactive in developing training and in recruitment and retaining of minority students in psychology" (Moses, 1990). One reason that psychology departments and counselor education programs have not enrolled and graduated significant numbers of racial/ethnic minority students in the past is that they fail to recognize counselor-trainee selection as a three-phase process involving recruitment, admission, and support (Atkinson, 1981). Even an admission policy designed to increase minority enrollment will be unsuccessful if the applicant pool includes only a few ethnically diverse applicants. Further, as victims of oppression, racial/ethnic minorities often need supplemental economic, social, and emotional support that nonminorities may not need in order to complete a degree in counseling.

Affirmative action recruitment efforts should be designed to identify and solicit applications, not only from those minority individuals who already have definite plans to enroll in a counselor training program, but also from those individuals who have ruled out graduate education in counseling for reasons unrelated to their qualifications (e.g., lack of knowledge about financial support available to them). Such a recruitment effort is affirmative in the true sense of the word. It reaches out to those who might settle for a less appealing vocation because their oppressive experience has conditioned them to settle for less than what they actually desire. It includes recruitment literature that identifies: (1) the counselor-education faculty's commitment to enroll a diversified student population, (2) racial/ethnic minority representation on the faculty, (3) the numbers or proportions of racial/ethnic minority students, (4) aspects of the training program (e.g., course content, field-work settings, research focus) that provide a multicultural experience, and (5) support services (e.g., tutorial, financial, social) that are available to minorities (for specific recommendations regarding information that should be sent to applicants, see Ponterotto, Burkard, et al., 1995). It includes active recruitment by students and faculty at college career days, professional conventions, and day-to-day encounters. It also includes personal contacts with interested minority persons by department heads and individual faculty to communicate a real interest in enrolling racial/ethnic minorities.

Counselor training programs need to develop admission policies and procedures that will admit as many minority applicants as is legally, morally, and ethically possible to eliminate the current underrepresentation of minorities in the field of counseling. Traditional admission criteria of undergraduate GPA and graduate aptitude test scores have been found to discriminate against racial/ethnic minorities (Bernal, 1980) and to be unreliable predictors of counseling performance (Rowe, Murphy, & DeCsipkes, 1975). New and/or additional criteria need to be identified by counselor education programs that will ensure minorities are adequately represented in their student populations.

As most psychologists and counselor educators are aware, the U.S. Supreme Court decision in *Bakke v. Regents of the University of California* ruled out the use of quotas as a means of ensuring minority admissions. What tends to be overlooked, however, was the court's approval of some admission's procedures designed to ensure minority representation. Citing the Harvard undergraduate admission policy as an example, the Court held that a "representational" admission policy designed to ensure representation from diverse groups was acceptable as long as it did not involve quotas.

Atkinson, Brown, and Casas (1996) described a number of procedures that can be used to recruit, select, and support ethnic minority students and faculty in counselor training programs. These authors argue that admission policies and procedures need to reflect criteria related to the changing national demographics and to the strengths that ethnic minority psychologists can bring to the profession. For example, experience with two or more U.S. ethnic populations is a criterion that can be met by any student or faculty applicant, but one that almost all ethnic minority applicants meet. Similarly, expressed and/or demonstrated interest in research with ethnic minority populations and concerns is another criterion that might reflect the strengths of ethnic minority applicants without the application of separate criteria.

Although the admission criteria discussed by Atkinson et al. (1996) are by design applicable to all applicants, special efforts may be needed to recruit ethnic minority applicants. When European American students and faculty are selected from large pools of applicants while ethnic minorities are selected from small pools, the majority of applicants who meet admissions standards are likely to be European Americans. Training programs need to make every effort possible to increase their pool of ethnic minority applicants to increase the number of ethnic minority students they enroll. Atkinson et al. suggest that programs offer courses of interest to ethnic minority applicants, provide recruitment materials that express an interest in ethnic minority issues, make personal contact with ethnic minority students, target predominantly ethnic minority colleges for recruitment, and mentor ethnic minority undergraduates in research in order to recruit ethnic minority applicants. They propose similar procedures to recruit ethnic minority faculty.

A variety of support services are needed to ensure that racial/ethnic minorities, once admitted, are able to complete their graduate education in counseling. Special fellowship funds need to be developed and administered for underrepresented groups that could not otherwise attend graduate school (Bernal, 1980). Whenever feasible, racial/ethnic minorities should be employed as research and teaching assistants, because these positions involve not only a financial remuneration but serve as apprenticeships for skills needed as a professional counselor and/or researcher. In addition to financial support, counselor training programs should provide tutorial support to those individuals who may have experienced an inferior education due to their minority status.

Ethnic minority role models are often not available on counselor education faculties, therefore nonminority faculty need to expand their advising role for minority students to include the functions of mentor (Walton, 1979). The results of a study by Atkinson, Neville, and Casas (1991), suggest that European American psychology faculty can serve successfully as mentors for racial/ethnic minority graduate students. As a minority-student mentor, the faculty member attempts to minimize the trauma of graduate education and maximize the supportive services for each minority advisee. For emotional/psychological support, many counseling programs have arranged to have support groups offered for their minority students. Atkinson et al. (1996) suggest that it is particularly important for faculty to involve ethnic minority students in their research projects because "research collaboration/supervision provides an opportunity to (a) learn research skills needed for the dissertation, (b) establish a mentoring relationship between the faculty member and the student, and (c) socialize the student to the academic role" (pp. 244–245).

In summary, counselor-trainee selection involves recruitment, admission, and support. If counseling programs are to reduce the underrepresentation of racial/ethnic minorities in the counseling profession, expanded effort in all three areas will be needed in the future.

Mandate for Training in Cross-Cultural Counseling

In addition to training more ethnically diverse counselors and psychologists, all mental-health practitioners, regardless of their ethnicity, need to be trained to work with culturally diverse clients. In view of the increasingly multicultural makeup of American society described in chapter 1, it seems highly unlikely that counselors being trained today (especially those being trained for educational settings) will escape contact with culturally different clients. It is imperative, therefore, that counselors of all cultural backgrounds be at least minimally prepared to work with clients who differ culturally from themselves.

Although APA, ACA, and other professional counseling organizations were slow to respond to the demands to train counselors and psychologists to work with culturally diverse clients, both the APA and ACA now mandate training in multicultural counseling through their accreditation policies. According to Hills and Strozier (1992), pressure for training psychologists in multicultural counseling was evident at numerous APA conferences dating back to the mid-1960s, beginning with the Chicago conference in 1965 and running through the Vail Conference in 1973, Austin Conference in 1975, Dulles Conference in 1978, Atlanta Conference in 1986, and Utah Conference in 1987. By 1979, APA had codified its commitment to muticultural training by adding Criterion II to the criteria for accreditation of doctoral programs in professional psychology.

Criterion II specified, among other things, that "Programs must develop knowledge and skills in their students relevant to human diversity, such as people with handicapping conditions; of differing ages, genders, ethnic and racial backgrounds; religions, and life-styles; and from differing social and individual backgrounds" (Committee on Accreditation, 1980).

The current *Guidelines and principles for accreditation of programs in professional psychology* (APA, 1996) include statements that direct programs to demonstrate respect for racial/ethnic diversity, to train psychologists to be multiculturally competent, and to train psychologists from racially/ethnically diverse backgrounds. These directives appear under Domain A (Eligibility) and D (Cultural and Individual Differences and Diversity) of the *Guidelines:*

- The program engages in actions that indicate respect for and understanding of cultural and individual diversity. . . . The phrase "cultural and individual diversity" refers to diversity with regard to personal and demographic characteristics. These include, but are not limited to, age, color, disabilities, ethnicity, gender, language, national origin, race, religion, sexual orientation, and social economic status.
- Respect for and understanding of cultural and individual diversity is reflected in the program's policies for the recruitment, retention, and development of faculty and students, and in its curriculum and field placements. The program has nondiscriminatory policies and operating conditions, and it avoids any actions that would restrict program access or completion on grounds that are irrelevant to success in graduate training or the profession. (APA, 1996, p. 5).
- The program has made systematic, coherent, and long-term efforts to attract and retain students and faculty from differing ethnic, racial, and personal backgrounds into the program. Consistent with such efforts, it acts to ensure a supportive and encouraging learning environment appropriate for the training of diverse individuals and the provision of training opportunities for a broad spectrum of individuals. Further, the program avoids any actions that would restrict program access on grounds that are irrelevant to success in graduate training.
- The program has and implements a thoughtful and coherent plan to provide students with relevant knowledge and experiences about the role of cultural and individual diversity in psychological phenomena as they related to the science and practice of professional psychology. The avenues by which these goals are achieved are to be developed by the program. (APA, 1996, pp. 9–10).

The APA has also created a mandate for training in multicultural counseling skills in other policy documents. The current APA Ethical Principles state that:

> Where differences of age, gender, race, ethnicity, national origin, religion, sexual orientation, disability, language, or socioeconomic status significantly affect

psychologists' work concerning particular individuals or groups, psychologists obtain the training, experience, consultation, or supervision necessary to ensure the competence of their services, or they make appropriate referrals. (APA, 1992, p. 1601)

Furthermore, the *Guidelines for the providers of psychological services to ethnic, linguistic, and culturally diverse populations* in 1993 by the APA in effect mandates that APA members receive training in multicultural skills (American Psychological Association, 1993). These APA professional mandates are clear: psychology training programs must provide training in multicultural counseling (Atkinson et al. 1996; Ridley, Mendoza, & Kanitz, 1994).

Similarly, to be accredited by the Council for Accreditation of Counseling and Related Educational Programs (CACREP, the accrediting arm of ACA), a counseling program's goals must reflect (a) "current knowledge . . . concerning the counseling and human development needs of a multicultural society" and (2) "the present and projected needs of a multicultural society for which specialized counseling and human development activities have been developed" (Accreditation procedures, 1988, p. 25). Further, in order to be accredited by CACREP, the curriculum of a counselor training program must provide knowledge and skill in human growth and development "within cultural contexts" and in social and cultural foundations of "societal subgroups" (Accreditation procedures, 1988, p. 25).

Training Program Response to Mandate

Although professional organizations have clearly mandated that programs need to provide multicultural training, the mandate has been criticized for being vague and lacking in substance. Some authors (Atkinson, 1994; D. W. Sue, Arredondo, & McDavis, 1992) have argued that specific standards are needed that can guide program development and ensure that counselor trainees receive training for selected multicultural counseling skills. In spring, 1990, the APA Committee on Accreditation created a subcommittee on Cultural and Individual Differences to review Criterion II of the APA "Criteria for Accreditation." The subcommittee came up with a number of recommendations but stopped short of defining content that programs need to teach. "The Committee [on Accreditation] respects differences among programs in terms of their goals and methods to achieve those goals" (The nature, 1991, p. 5). However, the vagueness of the accreditation guidelines and other professional mandates have been blamed for the lack of uniformity of multicultural training provided by the various training programs (J. M. Jones, 1985; Rickard & Clements, 1993). Some programs require coursework in multicultural counseling, others offer a multicultural counseling course as an elective, and still others claim that they have integrated multiculturalism into all their courses. Further complicating the situation is the lack of research on multicultural training that might contribute to the establishment of training guidelines (Ridley, et al., 1994).

Is the training in multicultural counseling that psychologists and counselors are receiving adequate? Surveys conducted in the late 1970s indicated that few clinical psychology training programs were offering courses in multicultural counseling at that time (APA, 1982; Bernal & Padilla, 1982). More recent studies indicate a positive trend. A survey of clinical psychology training programs in 1990 revealed that 62 percent offered courses related to multicultural counseling and 26 percent required these courses for the doctoral degree; comparable figures for 1980 were 41 percent and 9 percent, respectively (Bernal & Castro, 1994). An even more recent survey of directors of training of APA-approved counseling psychology programs by Hills and Strozier (1992) found that 87 percent of the programs surveyed offer at least one course on multicultural counseling; 59 percent required students to take at least one multicultural course; and 45 percent offered a specialization in multicultural counseling. Respondents indicated that the greatest pressure to offer multicultural coursework came from members of their own faculty, followed by APA. These data suggest that APA programs are responding to the accreditation requirements for training in multicultural counseling, although a large proportion apparently still do not require that students take these courses.

Furthermore, students have a different view of how adequately they are being trained to work with culturally diverse clients. A survey (Mintz, Bartels, & Rideout, 1995) of predoctoral counseling and clinical psychology interns found that 58 percent indicated no course in Cross-Cultural/Ethnic Issues/Counseling was offered by their academic program (clinical interns were more likely than counseling interns to report that no such course was offered). Similarly, Allison, Crawford, Echemendia, Robinson, and Knepp (1994) reported that 66 percent of counseling and clinical psychologists who had completed their Ph.D.'s between 1985 and 1987 had received their training in programs in which a course focusing the provision of services on diverse (defined to include sexual orientation, economic disadvantage, physical-sensory challenge, and ethnicity) populations was not offered. Forty-six percent of the respondents to the Allison et al. survey indicated that issues relevant to diverse populations were either infrequently or never covered. Also, 46 percent indicated that their supervision during their doctoral program infrequently or never addressed cultural issues.

Although the apparent discrepancy between the first two studies (Bernal & Castro, 1994; Hills & Strozier, 1992) and the latter two studies (Allison et al., 1994; Mintz et al., 1995) could be due to sampling bias in one or more of the studies, it does raise concerns that the percent of programs offering a course in multicultural counseling reported by directors of training may be inflated. At the least it suggests that directors of training and psychology interns have different views about curriculum content with respect to multicultural issues (Bluestone, Stokes, & Kuba, 1996). Directors of training may feel that students are receiving adequate training for multicultural counseling, while students confronted with an ethnically and culturally diverse internship clientele may feel their training has not adequately prepared them for the challenge.

Issues in Defining and Teaching Cross-Cultural Counseling

Defining, Identifying, and Operationalizing Cross-Cultural Counseling Competence

One of the reasons professional organizations such as the APA and ACA have not developed specific standards for multicultural training is that multicultural counseling competencies have yet to be clearly defined and agreed upon by the profession.

Pope-Davis, Reynolds, Dings, and Ottavi (1994) offered the following definition of multicultural competence:

> an appreciation of and sensitivity to the history, current needs, strengths, and resources of communities and individuals who historically have been underserved and underrepresented by psychologists. . . . Specifically, these competencies entail the following: an awareness of one's own biases and cultural assumptions, content knowledge about cultures different from one's own culture, an accurate self-assessment of one's multicultural skills and comfort level, an appropriate application of cultural knowledge to the counseling process, and an awareness of the cultural assumptions underlying the counseling process. (p. 466)

Important aspects of cross-cultural counseling competence were identified earlier by the Educational and Training Committee of APA Division 17. In their position paper, the committee identified consciousness raising (attitudes and beliefs), knowledge, and skills as three important curriculum areas for a cross-cultural counseling program. Under attitudes and beliefs they list four competencies that a cross-cultural counselor should have. The culturally skilled counseling psychologist:

1. has moved from being culturally unaware to being aware and sensitive to his/her own cultural heritage and to valuing and respecting differences.
2. is aware of his/her own values and biases and how they may affect minority clients.
3. is comfortable with differences that exist between the counselor and client in terms of race and beliefs.
4. is sensitive to circumstances that may dictate referral of the minority client to a member of his/her own race/culture.

The Committee also identified four types of knowledge a cross-cultural counselor should have. The culturally skilled counseling psychologist:

1. will have a good understanding of the sociopolitical systems operation in the United States with respect to its treatment of minorities.
2. must possess specific knowledge and information about the particular group he/she is working with.

3. must have a clear and explicit knowledge and understanding of the generic characteristics of counseling and therapy.
4. is aware of institutional barriers that prevent minorities from using mental health services.

Finally, the Committee identified three skills that a cross-cultural counselor should have:

1. is able to generate a wide variety of verbal and nonverbal responses.
2. is able to send and receive both verbal and nonverbal messages accurately and "appropriately."
3. is able to exercise institutional skills on behalf of his/her client when appropriate. (D. W. Sue et al., 1982)

The Professional Standards Committee of the American Association for Counseling and Development (a division of the American Association for Counseling and Development) published a position paper that proposes thirty-one multicultural counseling strategies (D. W. Sue et al., 1992). The Professional Standards Committee recently revised the earlier statement and provided examples of how these multicultural counseling strategies can be operationalized (Arredondo et al., 1996). This document is an extremely important step in the effort to define and operationalize multicultural counseling, and we have reprinted the section from it on Multicultural Counseling Competencies in the Appendix.

There is often confusion about the relationship between cross-cultural competence and cultural sensitivity. Ridley, Mendoza, Kanitz, Angermeier, and Zenk (1994) pointed out that cross-cultural competency is a general phrase, denoting a cluster of related, but different, constructs. They define cultural sensitivity as a perceptual schema, or more specifically:

> the ability of counselors to acquire, develop, and actively use an accurate cultural perceptual schema in the course of multicultural counseling. . . . The schema serves to alert the counselor to cultural variables in the context of counseling, organizes cultural stimuli in meaningful ways, and appropriately channels this information to initiate some type of culturally responsive action. (pp. 130–131)

Zayas, Torres, Malcolm, and DesRosiers (1996) surveyed nonminority members of APA and the National Association of Social Workers and asked them how they defined ethnically sensitive therapy. Respondents' definitions were examined for similarities and four overlapping dimensions emerged: (a) being aware of the existence of differences, (b) having knowledge of the client's culture, (c) distinguishing between culture and pathology in assessment; and (d) taking culture into account in therapy.

Need for Assessing Multicultural Competence

Although multicultural competence has yet to be fully operationalized, four instruments assessing the multicultural counseling competencies identified by

D. W. Sue et al. (1982) have appeared in the professional literature since 1990: the Cross-Cultural Counseling Inventory-Revised (CCCI) (LaFromboise, Coleman, & Hernandez, 1991), the Multicultural Counseling Awareness Scale-Form B (MCAS) (Ponterotto, Sanchez, & Magids, 1991), the Multicultural Counseling Inventory (MCI) (Sodowsky, Taffe, Gutkin, & Wise, 1994), and the Multicultural Awareness-Knowledge-and-Skills Survey (MAKSS) (D'Andrea, Daniels, & Heck, 1991). However, the validity of all four of these instruments has been questioned. Based on their review of all four instruments, Ponterotto, Rieger, Barrett, and Sparks (1994) recommended that:

> none of them be incorporated in counseling training for any purpose other than research and continuing validation. . . . It is premature to use these instruments to assess students' readiness for entering doctoral study; readiness for graduation; or readiness for practicum, internship, or professional employment. (p. 321)

We find ourselves in agreement with this judgment particularly with regard to the MCAS, MCI, and MAKSS, which ask respondents to rate their own cross-cultural competence.

Coleman (1996) proposed the use of a counselor's portfolio as an alternative means of assessing multicultural counseling competence. A counselor's portfolio is roughly analogous to the artist's portfolio, in which the artist places examples of his/her work. According to Coleman:

> the first step in developing a portfolio is to determine its purpose or goal and how it will be used. Once that goal is determined, the developer can go on to the second step, which is to identify what evidence will be most effective at demonstrating the acquisition of the goal. . . . The purpose and use of a portfolio will be determined by the learner in relationship to his or her audience, whether that be an instructor, a supervisor, a prospective employer, clients, or colleagues. (p. 220)

Referring to the D. W. Sue et al. (1982) position paper, Coleman suggests that counselors should include self-selected evidence of their multicultural awareness, knowledge, and skills in their personal portfolio. Portfolio submissions might include written work, audiotapes, and videotapes. The portfolio itself might be an expandable file folder, a CD-ROM, or some other means of storing data.

The portfolio concept is appealing given the lack of agreement about what constitutes multicultural competence and the psychometric inadequacies of existing assessment instruments. However, there are problems associated with the use of a portfolio for evaluation purposes. For one thing, Coleman (1996) points out that development and review of the portfolio can take a great deal of time on the part of the student and the supervisor. Also, because each student's portfolio submissions are unique, the reliability of scoring or evaluating materials is a concern. Despite these limitations, the counselor portfolio has promise for assessing multicultural competence, at least until more clearly defined multicultural awareness, knowledge, and skills are empirically established.

Curriculum Controversy

In addition to lack of consensus about the cross-cultural counseling competencies that need to be taught, there is some controversy about how training in cross-cultural counseling should be incorporated into the curriculum. Copeland (1982) identified four curriculum models that have been employed by cross-cultural counseling programs: (a) separate course, (b) interdisciplinary, (c) integrated, and (d) area of concentration. Briefly, in the separate-course model, multicultural issues are addressed in a specialty course but ignored in other courses. In the interdisciplinary model, students are encouraged to take courses in ethnic studies and other human-service-oriented fields to sensitize them to the needs of ethnic and other minority groups. Under the integrated model, the goals of cross-cultural training are integrated into all the counseling courses. Under the area of concentration model, the training program offers several courses that focus on one or several minority groups. In addition to the separate course, interdisciplinary, integrated, and area of concentration (subspecialty) models described by Copeland (1982), Ridley, Mendoza, and Kanitz (1992) identify the traditional program design and the workshop design. The traditional program assumes that existing counseling theories and practices are generalizable across ethnic groups, and few (if any) accommodations are needed for training counselors who will work with ethnically diverse clients. The workshop design is essentially an add-on to the traditional program design in that training for multicultural counseling takes place in periodic workshops that are offered in addition to a traditional training program.

Each of these models has certain strengths and weaknesses. The traditional model, for all practical purposes, ignores training for multicultural counseling. The workshop model can address specific populations and multicultural concerns, but does not integrate this knowledge into other aspects of the trainee's education and experiences. The area of concentration and interdisciplinary models provide for in-depth study of one or several ethnic groups but may not result in the kind of generalized understanding of ethnic and other minority groups that is the goal of cross-cultural training. The separate course model is easy to employ but may be viewed as ancillary to the core training program. Also, a single separate course usually can only introduce trainees to multicultural issues and does not provide the in-depth training needed to actually work with culturally different clients (D'Andrea, Daniels, & Heck, 1991). The integration model meets all the goals of cross-cultural training but may be the most difficult to achieve because it requires that all the counseling faculty be sensitive to cross-cultural issues that relate to the courses they teach and be willing to incorporate these issues into their course content.

The mandate by professional organizations that multicultural training be provided all psychologists and counselors has, for all practical purposes, focused attention on the separate course and integrated infusion models of training (Bernal & Castro, 1994; Carey, Reinat, & Fontes, 1990). For APA accredited programs, the integrated model is the only viable model for addressing Domain D of the most recent APA accreditation guidelines (Bluestone et al., 1996).

Although the APA and ACA have not adopted specific standards for multicultural counseling training, a number of authors have attempted to identify the elements of a multicultural training program. S. Sue, Akutsu, and Higashi (1985) have identified three important elements of any cross-cultural counseling training program. According to these authors, training in cross-cultural counseling should include knowledge of various cultural groups and history of their treatment in this country, experience counseling clients of various racial/ethnic groups, and training in devising innovative treatment strategies. Copeland (1983) listed four components of a cross-cultural training program: a consciousness-raising component, a cognitive understanding component, an affective component, and a skills component (p. 13). Similarly, Bernal (quoted in Bales, 1985) stated that a multicultural training program for psychologists should have the following goals:

> Understanding the social, historical, and cultural background and characteristics of minority groups; conveying a positive attitude toward these groups and a desire to learn from them, gaining theoretical knowledge and expertise in the scientific study of sociocultural variables, as well as in culturally appropriate intervention strategies; and communicating fluently in the appropriate language. (p. 7)

According to Bernal and Padilla (1982), a multicultural approach to training psychologists includes certain important components and a particular training philosophy.

The components include a concern for cultural sensitivity, a better understanding of racism and its consequences for mental health, knowledge about the merits and dangers of customs of different cultures as they affect their members in terms of universal standards of mental health, an increase in opportunities for students to work with clients of ethnically similar and dissimilar backgrounds, and enlargements of the numbers of minority students and faculty. The multicultural training philosophy acknowledges that it is vital for trainees to have a broad-based historical and cultural understanding of minority groups; to develop positive attitudes toward them; to gain theoretical knowledge and expertise in the scientific study of sociocultural variables; to become experienced in the application of primary, secondary, and tertiary preventative strategies that are culturally appropriate; and to be able to communicate fluently in their client's language (Bernal & Padilla, 1982, p. 786).

Multicultural Counseling Training Models

A number of models for training counselors in cross-cultural counseling have appeared in the professional literature since 1970. The early models described simulation exercises, fieldwork experiences, training workshops, or courses that could be used to prepare counselors to work with ethnic minorities. These early models often involved one-shot experiences and were not theory based and will not be discussed in this text (for an overview of these training activities, see Leong and Kim, 1991). More recently, developmental training models have been described that are comprehensive and theory based; several of these will be briefly discussed.

Developmental Models

In addition to being intuitively appealing, developmental models provide for the selection and sequencing of learning materials and experiences, rather than just a potpourri of exercises and workshops (Bennett, 1986). Carney and Kahn (1984) were among the first authors to propose a developmental model of training in cross-cultural counseling. Their model consists of five stages; counselor trainee characteristics and appropriate learning environments are identified and described for each stage. In Stage One, the trainee has limited knowledge about other cultural groups and feels conflicted by the disparity between his/her own ethnocentrism and the egalitarian values of the counseling profession. At this stage, the trainer provides information on the history of America's cultural groups. In Stage Two, the trainee begins to become aware of his/her own ethnocentric attitudes and behavior but the trainee still employs ethnocentric counseling approaches. The trainer at this stage provides information about barriers to cross-cultural counseling, ethnocentrism in counseling, and alternative world views. In Stage Three the trainee feels guilty and responsible for injustices and espouses an attitude of "colorblindness." The trainer at this stage encourages self-review and exploration of the colorblindness. In Stage Four, the trainee begins to identify as a cross-cultural change agent and attempts to blend new cross-cultural knowledge, attitudes, and skills with his/her indigenous attitudes and behavior. In this stage, the trainer places the trainee in direct counseling experiences in multicultural settings and acts as a supervisor. In Stage Five, the trainee "assumes a self-directed activist posture in expanding own cross-cultural knowledge, attitudes, and skills, and in promoting cultural pluralism in society at large" (p. 113). The trainer in Stage Five acts as a peer consultant to help the trainee reach his/her goals.

About the same time that Carney and Kahn (1984) were formulating their developmental model of counselor training, Bennett (1986) was germinating his developmental model for training in *intercultural* sensitivity. Designed for individuals experiencing international cultural differences, but not intended specifically for counselors, his model has obvious application to the multicultural context here in the United States. The model defines six stages of development (denial, defense, minimization, acceptance, adaptation, integration) as an individual moves from ethnocentrism to "ethnorelativism" (defined by Bennett to be the antonym of ethnocentrism). Bennett describes developmental training activities that can be used at each stage to encourage intercultural sensitivity.

Lopez et al. (1989) also proposed that learning cultural sensitivity is a developmental process, but concluded that it consisted of only four stages. In the first stage, "unawareness of cultural issues," the counselor does not entertain cultural hypotheses (i.e., does not recognize the potential for cultural interpretations of the client's problem). Participation in a cross-cultural counseling course, coursework, supervision, or personal experience "may serve as an impetus for therapists to begin valuing the cultural context of their clients' lives" (p. 372). At this point the counselor moves into the second stage of development, the "heightened awareness of culture" stage. In this stage the counselor is aware of how important cultural factors are in fully understanding clients but feels unprepared to work with culturally different clients. The authors suggest that "with proper supervision, student-therapists can learn that they have the capability of understanding and helping someone from a distinct cultural group" (p. 373). However, after working with several ethnic minority clients, counselors then move into the third, or "burden of considering culture," stage. In this stage the counselor becomes hypervigilant about cultural factors and their clinical effectiveness may be diminished because they feel they must be constantly on the alert for cultural issues. To move supervisees on to the fourth stage, supervisors must "provide a supportive atmosphere and allow student-therapists to voice their sense of feeling burdened" (p. 374). In the fourth stage, "toward cultural sensitivity," counselors are able to entertain cultural hypotheses and to test these hypotheses before accepting cultural explanations.

Perhaps the most parsimonious training model based on White racial identity development (WRID) is that described by Sabnani, Ponterotto, and Borodovsky (1991). Sabnani et al. examined the Hardiman (1982), Helms (1984), and Ponterotto (1988) models and integrated the common themes into a six-stage model.

Stage 1: Lack of awareness of self as a racial being
Stage 2: Interaction with members of other cultures
Stage 3: Breakdown of former knowledge regarding racial matters; conflict
Stage 4: Prominority stance
Stage 5: Pro-White, antiminority stance
Stage 6: Internalization (Sabnani et al., 1991, p. 82)

Sabnani et al. propose that the training of White counselors for cross-cultural counseling should involve a matching of goals and tasks to the first five stages of WRID. They define the goals and tasks for each stage under three headings used by D. W. Sue et al. (1982): Beliefs/attitudes, knowledge, and skills. Table 16.2 summarizes the key points of their model.

Support for the Sabnani et al. (1991) training model was provided by Ottavi, Pope-Davis, and Dings (1994). Ottari et al. found that variation in scores of White counseling graduate students on the Multicultural Counseling Inventory (Sodowsky et al., 1994), above and beyond that accounted for by

Table 16.2
Cross-Cultural Counseling Training Goals and Tasks

	Beliefs/Attitudes		Knowledge		Skills	
	Goals	Tasks	Goals	Tasks	Goals	Tasks
Stage 1 Preexposure/ Precontact	Awareness of one's own cultural heritage Awareness of the cultural heritage of minority groups	Awareness group experience[ab] "Ethnic dinners"[b] Tours/exhibits of other cultures' crafts/areas Intercultural sharing[c] Multicultural action planning (low level of active involvement)[c] Free drawing test[h] Public and private self-awareness exercise[g] Value statements exercise[h] Decision awareness exercise[g]	Knowledge of the cultural heritage of other minority groups	Research into the history of other cultures Intercultural sharing[c] Multicultural action planning (low level of active involvement)[c] Ethic literature reviews Field trips Case studies[c] Culture assimilator[ijk]	Beginning development of counseling skills	Regular counselor training tasks (microskills training)[def]

Table 16.2—*Continued.*
Cross-Cultural Counseling Training Goals and Tasks

	Beliefs/Attitudes		Knowledge		Skills	
	Goals	*Tasks*	*Goals*	*Tasks*	*Goals*	*Tasks*
Stage 2 Conflict	Awareness of one's stereotypes and prejudicial attitudes and the impact of these on minorities Awareness of the conflict between wanting to conform to White norms while upholding humanitarian values Dealing with feelings of guilt and depression or anger	Critical incidents exercise[h] Implicit assumptions checklist We and you exercise[h] Exercise for experiencing stereotypes[c] Stereotypes awareness exercise[g] Less structured cross-cultural encounter groups	More extensive knowledge of other cultures Knowledge of the concepts and prejudice and racism Knowledge of the impact of racism on minorities and the privileges of being White	MAP-investigative[e] Tours to other communities Research on racism in the past and present Classes in multicultural issues presenting survey data on minorities Films	Develop more client-specific methods of intervention	Critical incidents method[l] Role-playing exercise[h] Role-playing a problem in a group[h]

Table 16.2—*Continued.*

Cross-Cultural Counseling Training Goals and Tasks

	Beliefs/Attitudes		Knowledge		Skills	
	Goals	*Tasks*	*Goals*	*Tasks*	*Goals*	*Tasks*
Stage 3 Prominority Antiracism	Awareness of overidentification and of paternalistic attitudes, and the impact of these on minorities	Interracial encounters[m] Cross-cultural encounter groups Responsible feedback exercise[h] Anonymous feedback from the group exercise[h]	Further immersion into other cultures	Guided self-study Exposure to audiovisual presentations[g] Interviews with consultants and experts[g] Lectures Minority student panels[b] Research into the impact of race on counseling	Continue developing culturally emic and etic approaches to counseling	Role-playing exercises Communication skills training Facilitating interracial groups (FIG)[b] Counseling ethnic minorities (CEM)[b]
Stage 4 Retreat into White Culture	Awareness of and dealing with one's own fear and anger	Cross-cultural encounter groups Lump sum[h]	Knowledge of the development of minority identity and White identity	Research into minority identity development models Research into White identity development models	Building culturally etic (transcendent) approaches	Microskills Ponterotto and Benesch (1988)

Table 16.2—Continued.
Cross-Cultural Counseling Training Goals and Tasks

	Beliefs/Attitudes		Knowledge		Skills	
	Goals	Tasks	Goals	Tasks	Goals	Tasks
Stage 5 Redefinition and Integration	Develop an identity which claims Whiteness as a part of it	Feedback-related exercises (see Stage 3)	Expand knowledge on racism in the real world; Expand knowledge on counseling methods more appropriate to minorities	Visits to communities with large minority populations; Research on ways to transform White-based counseling methods to one more credible to minorities	Deepen more culturally emic approaches; Face more challenging cross-cultural counseling interactions	Facilitating interracial groups (FIG)[b]; Counseling ethnic minorities individually (CEMI)[b]; Triad model[g]; Cross-cultural practica

Note: References for exercises suggested in Table 16.2 are indicated by letters, as follows: a. Parker & McDavis, 1979; b. McDavis & Parker, 1977; c. Parker, 1988; d. Ivey & Authier, 1978; e. Egan, 1982; f. Clarkhuff & Anthony, 1979; g. Pedersen, 1988; h. Weeks et al., 1977; i. Brislin et al., 1986; j. Albert, 1983; k. Merta, Stringham, & Ponterotto, 1988; l. Sue, 1981; m. Katz & Ivey, 1977. From White racial identity development and cross-cultural counselor training. *The Counseling Psychologist,* 1991, *19,* 76–102 by Sabnani, H. B., Ponterotto, J. G., & Borodovsky, L. G. (1991). Copyright 1991 by Sage Publications, Inc. Reprinted by permission of Sage Publications, Inc.

demographic, educational, and clinical variables, were explained by scores on the White Racial Identity Attitude Scale (Helms & Carter, 1990). Although more research is needed to validate the Sabnani et al. training model, it is more appealing than earlier training models that prescribe a common experience for all counselor trainees.

Successful Programs

Several counselor training programs have gained recognition for their efforts to provide training in cross-cultural counseling. Arredondo (1985) describes three types of cross-cultural training programs that have been implemented in American universities: (a) specifically funded projects, (b) specializations integral to existing counseling-psychology programs, and (c) continuing-education conferences. She lists the DISC (Developing Interculturally Skilled Counselors) program at the University of Hawaii as an example of the first type. For existing counseling-psychology programs that have integrated a cross-cultural focus, she lists: Boston University; Teachers College; Columbia University; the University of California, Santa Barbara; California State University, Northridge; Syracuse University; The University of Massachusetts at Amherst; and Western Washington University at Bellingham. For universities sponsoring continuing-education conferences on cross-cultural counseling, she lists Teachers College, Columbia University, and Boston University.

As part of their Delphi survey of fifty-three experts in cross-cultural counseling, Heath, Neimeyer, and Pedersen (1988) asked respondents to identify the top cross-cultural counseling programs in the United States. The top five programs in this survey were Syracuse University; University of Hawaii; Teachers College; Columbia University; University of California, Santa Barbara; and Western Washington University. Ponterotto and Casas (1987) surveyed eighteen "leading multicultural counseling specialists" to determine their rankings of leading cross-cultural training programs. In order of nominations received, the five leading programs were housed at Syracuse University; Boston University; Western Washington University; University of Hawaii; and University of California, Santa Barbara. The common core-elements shared by these five programs were: (1) at least one faculty member seriously committed to cross-cultural counseling research and/or training, (2) at least one course on multicultural issues is offered, and (3) more racial-ethnic diversity on the faculty and student body than is typical at most training programs. We would hope that the first two elements soon become part of *every* counselor training program.

Ponterotto, Alexander, and Grieger (1995) published a multicultural competency checklist for counselor training programs. The checklist contains twenty-two items that can be used to assess how well a training program is addressing multicultural issues in six areas: minority representation, curriculum, counseling practice and supervision, research, student and faculty competency evaluation, and physical environment. Although not endorsed by any

Table 16.3

Mean Rank Orders for Academic Programs

Mean Rank	Item
3.95	Philosophy of the program
5.77	Multicultural curriculum
6.40	Faculty with multicultural expertise
8.36	Openness of students and faculty
9.02	Diversity of faculty
9.05	Specific course content
9.20	Diverse student population
9.85	Exploration of culturally sensitive approaches
10.94	Professional development for faculty around multicultural issues
12.26	Larger university environment supportive
12.38	Financial assistance for minority students
13.64	Multicultural field placements for students
13.73	Faculty involved in multicultural research
13.74	Various definitions of multicultural
13.81	Departmental structures for addressing multicultural concerns
14.10	Program facilitates self-awareness
14.57	Students involved in multicultural research
14.69	Supervision
14.91	Support services for students
14.95	Evaluation of students around multicultural issues
15.18	Availability of multicultural resource material
17.32	Department has community involvement
18.17	Degrees or minors granted in multicultural subject areas

From Speight, S. L., Thomas, A. J., Kennel, R. G., & Anderson, M. E. (1995). Operationalizing multicultural training in doctoral programs and internships. *Professional Psychology: Research and Practice, 26,* 401–406. Reprinted with permission.

professional psychological organization at this point, the checklist may be of value to programs that wish to conduct a self-evaluation in the area of multicultural training.

Speight, Thomas, Kennel, and Anderson (1995) conducted a Delphi survey of ninety-one experts in multicultural counseling in order to identify the attributes of multicultural counseling programs and internships. In the initial Delphi questionnaire, the expert panelists identified attributes in response to an open-ended questionnaire. In the second Delphi questionnaire these same panelists were asked to rank order the importance of each attribute. The mean rank orders for academic programs and internships are presented in tables 16.3 and 16.4, respectively. The authors of this study suggest that "these specific elements may function as objectives for academic programs or internships as

Table 16.4

Mean Rank Orders for Internships

Mean Rank	Item
4.78	Staff has multicultural training
4.85	Philosophy/commitment of internship site
6.76	Supervision of interns addresses multicultural issues
7.30	Diversity of clients that interns serve
7.84	Diversity of clinical staff
7.97	Assessment/diagnosis issues with diverse clients is addressed
8.23	Counseling process issues
8.81	Evaluation of interns around multicultural issues
9.43	Diversity of interns
9.56	Specific training topics
9.81	Prerequisite training of interns
10.36	Elements of multicultural training program
11.14	Internship facilitates self-awareness of interns
12.27	Internship site utilizes community contact people
13.06	Supervisor and counselor relationship reflects diversity
13.80	Site interacts with community
14.07	Structured support mechanisms for interns
14.75	Internship site is flexible regarding services provided
15.23	Multicultural research conducted

From Speight, S. L., Thomas, A. J., Kennel, R. G., & Anderson, M. E. (1995). Operationalizing multicultural training in doctoral programs and internships. *Professional Psychology: Research and Practice, 26,* 401–406. Reprinted with permission.

they endeavor to enrich, expand, or initiate their multicultural training efforts" (p. 406).

Effects of Training on Trainee Competence

Are students who receive training in multicultural counseling more multiculturally competent than those who don't receive it? In one of the first attempts to link multicultural training to self-perceived competence, Parker, Valley, and Geary (1986) cited student course evaluations as evidence that multicultural training enhanced knowledge of, and cultural sensitivity to, ethnic minorities. Several more studies found self-reports of multicultural competence to be related to previous coursework, experience, and supervision in multicultural counseling. D'Andrea et al. (1991) administered the MAKSS to counselor education students before and after participation in a comprehensive multicultural counselor training course and found substantially improved levels of multicultural counseling awareness, knowledge, and skills after completion of the course. Pope-Davis, Reynolds, Dings, and Ottavi (1994) found a direct relationship between predoctoral interns' self-reported multicultural knowledge and skills on the Multicultural Counseling Awareness Scale-Revised and the amount of supervision for multicultural counseling they had received, their attendance at multicultural workshops, and the number of multicultural courses they had taken. Similarly, Pope-Davis, Reynolds, Dings, and Nielson (1995) reported a direct relationship between multicultural workshop, practicum, and client contact hours and self-ratings of multicultural competence on the MCI for counseling and clinical graduate students. They also found that counseling psychology students (who completed an average of 1.6 multicultural counseling courses) rated themselves as more multiculturally competent than clinical students (who completed an average of 0.9 multicultural counseling courses). In a national survey of counseling and clinical psychologists who had received their Ph.D.'s between 1985 and 1987, Allison et al. (1994) found that the number of therapy cases with an ethnic minority client during training was predictive of self-reported competence to work with ethnic minority populations. However, enrollment in a diversity course was not predictive of either self-reported competence to work with ethnic minorities or number of ethnic minorities in the respondent's current caseload. Neville et al. (1996) found that counseling students increased their self-perceived multicultural competence (as measured by the MAKSS) and moved to higher levels of White racial identity attitudes (as measured by the WRIAS) after having completed a diversity-related graduate course. In considering the results of these studies, remember that given the questionable validity of these self-report instruments (i.e., MAKSS, MCAS-R, and MCI), self-ratings of competence may not be related to client or observer ratings of cross-cultural competence.

Two studies using more objective measures of cross-cultural competence also have been reported in the professional literature. Mio (1989) exposed counselor education students to either a cultural exchange experience with immigrant and refugee students or library research on a particular cultural group. Judges rated papers the counseling students wrote about their experiences and concluded that the one-to-one exchange of ideas produced more sensitivity to the target cultural group than only studying factual information about the group.

In the most sophisticated study of multicultural training to date, Wade and Bernstein (1991) randomly assigned Black female clients to counselors who had or had not received four hours of culture sensitivity training. At the conclusion of counseling, clients rated counselors who received the culture sensitivity training higher on expertness, trustworthiness, attractiveness, unconditional regard, and empathy than counselors who did not receive the training. Also, clients assigned to counselors who received the culture sensitive training returned for more follow-up sessions and reported greater satisfaction with counseling than did the comparison group.

In summary, although the APA, ACA, and other professional mental health associations have yet to define specific standards, these organizations through their accreditation policies have established a strong mandate for training professionals to provide multicultural counseling. Position papers by the Educational Training Committee of APA Division 17 and the Professional Standards Committee of the AMCD have identified general cross-cultural counseling competencies that are being taught in counselor training programs but are not operationalized. Also, an increasing number of training programs are providing individual courses related to multicultural counseling and attempting to integrate multicultural content into the program curriculum. Furthermore, although they are in need of empirical validation, training models based on developmental stages of racial awareness appear to offer promise for the future. Finally, there is some evidence that counselors and their culturally diverse clients perceive the counselor who received multicultural training to be more multiculturally competent than those who received no training.

Counseling Research

Paucity of Research on Racial/Ethnic Minorities

Sattler (1970) reviewed the research examining the effect of experimenter race on experimentation, testing, interviewing, and psychology in 1970, and found only three studies related to counselor-client interaction. While a fairly large number of studies examining race/ethnicity or culture as an independent variable have been published since Sattler completed his review (see subsequent reviews by Abramowitz & Murray, 1983; Atkinson, 1983b, 1985: Atkinson & Lowe, 1995; Casas, 1984, 1985; Harrison, 1975; Leong, 1986; Ponterotto, 1988; Sattler, 1977), they still represent only a small proportion of the studies being published in the counseling journals. For example, in his review of articles published in the *Journal of Counseling Psychology* from 1976 to 1986 (inclusive), Ponterotto (1988) found that only 5.7 percent focused on racial/ethnic minority variables. Similarly, Graham (1992) examined articles published between 1970 through 1989 (inclusive) in six APA journals and found a declining number of studies involving African American participants.

There are several reasons for the relatively low percentage of counseling studies that examine race/ethnicity or culture as an independent variable. One explanation is that a majority-controlled counseling research establishment may not view race/ethnicity or culture as important factors in counseling. Another reason may be that majority researchers believe that the topic is a highly controversial one and prefer to conduct research on less controversial subjects. As Gardner (1971) points out, ". . . many blacks have called for a moratorium on all further efforts by white investigators to study and explain the psychological and social characteristics of blacks" (p. 78). Similar requests have been made by other minority professionals who believe that forays by majority researchers into minority cultures have resulted in reinforced stereotypes rather than enlightened understanding (Mio & Iwamasa, 1993).

In addition, S. Sue et al. (1995) point out that "lack of available funding for ethnic research, the belief among some that psychotherapy was unimportant because massive social and political interventions were needed in order to address race and ethnic relations, and difficulties in conducting ethnic research" contributed to the paucity of research on ethnic minorities in the past. They suggest that even today, researchers who wish to examine the ethnic variable in counseling and psychotherapy research face a number of obstacles. According to S. Sue et al.:

> researchers still face difficulties in finding adequate and representative samples to study. These difficulties include the relatively small size of the populations and the unwillingness of some ethnic minorities (e.g., illegal immigrants in the United States) to become research subjects. . . . These difficulties in finding adequate samples may have two unfortunate consequences. First, researchers may simply be unable to find a representative sample of ethnic minority populations. . . . Second, investigators may lump diverse groups together in order to achieve adequate sample sizes. (p. 269)

S. Sue et al. point out that researchers often have to use ethnic minority students in analog research designs because ethnic minority clients are not available or unwilling to participate in a study.

African American males are understandably reluctant to participate in any activity that smacks of experimentation. Perhaps the most tragic violation of human rights to occur under the auspices of a research project in this country involved Black men in Macon County, Alabama (J. H. Jones, 1981). The study, which came to be known as The Tuskegee Study, was initiated in 1932 by the United States Public Health Service. A total of 399 syphilitic Black men in the late stage of the disease were examined but their condition not treated over a forty-year period (despite the availability of penicillin in the 1940s) so that the progress of the disease could be tracked (European studies in the late 1890s had already documented the course of the disease). As an incentive to participate in the study, the men received free physical examinations, free transportation to the clinics, free treatment for other minor ailments, hot meals the days they were examined, and a guarantee that their survivors would receive a burial stipend when they died. At least forty-eight of these men died (some estimates range as high as 100) and numerous others were permanently maimed as a direct result of the disease. A number of other studies with potentially harmful effects have been conducted on inmates (a majority of whom are members of racial/ethnic minorities) in federal and state prisons either without the subject's knowledge or with direct or indirect coercion.

Whatever the reasons for the relatively low percentage of studies that examine race/ethnicity or culture as an independent variable, it is clear that more research is needed. In challenging APA members to advance psychology's role in minority issues, J. M. Jones (1990) listed as a top priority the need to "aggressively and effectively expand the publication of ethnic minority relevant material in APA journals" (p. 23).

Proposed Research Model for Minority Group/Cross-Cultural Research

The suggestion has been made that the impacts of the preconceptions or prejudices of the experimenter on cross-cultural counseling research can be minimized when the researcher feels "comfortably polycultural" (Vontress, 1976, p. 2). However, the danger of cultural bias on the part of a single researcher, no matter what his/her race/ethnicity, socioeconomic background, sex, sexual orientation, and so forth, is always present. It seems unlikely that any researcher has totally escaped the impact of cultural stereotyping that may be present as unrecognized bias in the design, implementation, and/or data analysis of a research project.

The possibility of unrecognized bias can be reduced, however, when research teams are composed of at least one representative from each cultural group included in the study. We are proposing, in effect, that whenever two or more cultural groups are represented in a research design, each group have an advocate from their group on the research team. Objectivity might also be enhanced if the research team included a person whose cultural background was not directly related to the variables under study. Thus, a research team examining the effectiveness of Black or White counselors with Black or White clients might include a Hispanic American researcher as well as African American and European American investigators.

The APA hosted a conference on professional training at Vail, Colorado, in 1973; one recommendation developed at the conference was that ". . . counseling of persons of culturally diverse backgrounds by persons who are not trained or competent to work with such groups should be regarded as unethical" (Pedersen, 1976, p. 35). We would like to recommend that a similar ethical restriction be placed on minority group/cross-cultural researchers.

Other steps that can be taken to reduce cultural bias in cross-cultural counseling research include having a member(s) of the ethnic group(s) to be studied on the human subjects committee that reviews the research, the funding review committee (if it is a funded study), and the journal editorial board if the study description is submitted for publication. When members of the group(s) being studied do not already sit on these reviewing agencies, the reviewing agency should be required to appoint ad hoc members for the review of cross-cultural studies.

The Need for Theory-Based Research

There are a number of methodological shortcomings of the cross-cultural counseling research to date. Some of the criticisms include: (a) designs in which client and therapist race or ethnicity are not fully crossed (S. Sue, 1988), (b) using measures that are not applicable to counseling (Atkinson, 1985), (c) failing to take intra-group differences into account (Atkinson, 1983b, 1985; Casas, 1985), and (d) selecting subjects on the basis of accessibility rather than representation (Abramowitz & Murray, 1983; Casas, 1985). A majority of cross-cultural studies to date have also failed to link their hypotheses to an adequate theoretical base. Ponterotto (1988) analyzed the cross-cultural counseling studies published in the *Journal of Counseling Psychology* between 1976 and 1986 and found that less than one-third of them tied their research hypotheses to theory.

After examining the cross-cultural counseling research published in the 1980s, Atkinson and Thompson (1992) concluded that racial identity development, acculturation, and social influence theories were being used as the bases of some studies. They also point out, however, that theory was lacking from many studies of racial/ethnic/cultural variables in counseling, despite the fact that a number of current psychological theories appear to have relevance to cross-cultural issues. Atkinson and Thompson suggested that with regard to within-group variability, some of the personality constructs that may be a function of oppression experienced by racial/ethnic minorities and those hypothesized to be a function of culture should be examined. As examples of the former, they cited cultural mistrust (Terrell & Terrell, 1981, 1984) and self-efficacy (Bandura, 1982). As examples of the latter they identified field dependence/independence (Witkin, 1962) and locus of control (Rotter, 1966). Other theoretical constructs that they judged to have relevance for cross-cultural counseling research included social cognitive theory (Bandura, 1986), balance theory (Heider, 1958), cognitive dissonance theory (Festinger, 1957), the Elaboration Likelihood Model (ELM) (Petty & Cacioppo, 1986a, 1986b), and attribution theory (Kelley, 1973).

Ridley, Mendoza, Kanitz, Angermeier, and Zenk (1994) challenged researchers to test their model of cultural sensitivity (described briefly earlier in this chapter). As a first step, Ridley et al. urged researchers to construct instruments to measure cultural sensitivity and the subprocess that contribute to the counselor's ability to use cultural schemata. They also encouraged researchers to develop instruments to measure the prerequisites of culturally responsive behavior, culturally responsive behavior itself, and the effects of culturally responsive behavior. Another line of research related to their model would examine how cultural schemata are developed, changed, and made more plastic. Finally, they encourage research examining how the cultural schemata and behaviors of experienced, culturally sensitive counselors differ from those of novice counselors.

Attribution theory deserves special attention. Parham and McDavis (1987) suggested that although many problems experienced by Black men can be attributed to external sources, it is important that counselors promote an attribution of internal responsibility for solving the problem. A similar theme has been sounded by Neighbors, Braithwaite, and Thompson (1995), who suggest that "asking African-Americans to take a major role in solving their own health problems through an examination of life-style and behavior is consistent with the black self-help tradition and the black power movement"

(p. 285). Brickman et al. (1982) labeled external attribution of causing, and internal attribution for solving, problems the "compensatory" model of helping. Brickman et al. hypothesized that "many of the problems characterizing relationships between help givers and help recipients arise from the fact that the two parties are applying [attribution] models that are out of phase with one another" (p. 375). These authors identified four models of helping (moral, medical, compensatory, enlightenment) based on attributions people make regarding responsibility for a problem and responsibility for solving the problem. How important is it that counselors offer their ethnically similar and dissimilar clients models of helping that are consistent with the client's model? What role does culture play in shaping attributions about the responsibility of a problem and the responsibility for solving it? These are questions that cross-cultural counseling researchers might address.

A closely related topic has to do with the attributions clients and counselors make about the causes of psychological problems. Medical anthropologists have concluded that shared beliefs between a healer and patient about the etiology of the patient's health problem play a major role in the healing relationship (Kleinman, 1980; Torrey, 1972). Torrey provides a graphic example of this point:

> A psychoanalyst trying to cure a patient who does not believe in oedipal conflicts and a witchdoctor trying to cure a patient who does not believe in spirit possession will be equally ineffective unless they can persuade the patient to accept their theory of causation. (p. 21)

Future research might examine the role that culture plays in determining etiology attributions and how these attributions affect counseling process and outcome.

Research also is needed to assess the effectiveness of activist counseling roles when dealing with minority clientele. Are counselors who serve as advocates, change agents, and so forth, actually perceived by minority clients as more helpful than counselors who function in a more conventional role? More important, what is the actual impact of counselors functioning in these roles?

When research is done with ethnic minority populations, appropriate generalization of the findings can be maximized by following several of the suggestions that Phinney (1996) has offered:

> First . . . authors should describe ethnic samples thoroughly in terms of all variables that may be relevant, such as social class, geographic region, and level of acculturation, so that readers can determine the particular subgroups involved. It is important also to indicate how participants were assigned to an ethic category, for example, on the basis of school records, appearance, last name, self-report, or some other means. . . . In cases of group comparisons, all possible efforts should be made to match the groups being compared, to minimize confounding with the many demographic variables that co-vary with ethnicity. . . . The best way to control for ethnicity is to hold it constant, that is to study processes within groups rather than make comparisons across groups. (p. 924)

If this book helps to stimulate research activity with ethnic minorities that is theory-based and that addresses some of the problems of past research, it will have served an important purpose. We hope it also contributes to practitioners becoming more multiculturally competent and training programs becoming more multiculturally focused. Despite the current trend toward ethnocentrism in U.S. society, we remain optimistic that the barriers to cross-cultural counseling can be bridged.

References

Abramowitz, S. I., & Murray, J. (1983). Race effects in psychotherapy. In J. Murray & P. R. Abramson (Eds.), *Bias in psychotherapy* (pp. 215–255). New York: Praeger.

Accreditation procedures manual and application. (1988). Alexandria, Va.: Council for Accreditation of Counseling and Related Educational Programs.

Allison, K. W., Crawford, I., Echemendia, R., Robinson, L., & Knepp, D. (1994). Human diversity and professional competence: Training clinical and counseling psychology revisited. *American Psychologist, 49,* 792–826.

American Counseling Association. (1995). *Code of ethics and standards of practice.* Alexandria, VA: Author.

American Psychological Association. (1982). *Survey of graduate departments of psychology.* Washington, DC: Author.

American Psychological Association. (1992). Ethical principles of psychologists and code of conduct. *American Psychologist, 47,* 1597–1611.

American Psychological Association. (1993). Guidelines for the providers of psychological services to ethnic, linguistic, and culturally diverse populations. *American Psychologist, 48,* 45–48.

American Psychological Association. (1996). *Guidelines and principles for accreditation of programs in professional psychology.* Washington, DC: Author.

Aponte, J. F., & Clifford, J. (1995). Education and training issues for intervention with ethnic groups. In J. F. Aponte, R. Young Rivers, & J. Wohl (Eds.), *Psychological interventions and cultural diversity* (pp. 283–300). Boston: Allyn and Bacon.

Arredondo, P. (1985). Cross-cultural counselor education and training. In P. Pedersen (Ed.), *Handbook of cross-cultural counseling and therapy.* Westport, Conn.: Greenwood Press.

Arredondo, P., Toporek, R., Brown, S. P., Jones, J., Locke, D. C., Sanchez, J., & Stadler, H. (1996). Operationalization of the Multicultural Counseling Competencies. *Journal of Multicultural Counseling and Development, 24,* 42–78.

Atkinson, D. R. (1981). Selection and training for human rights counseling. *Counselor Education and Supervision, 21,* 101–108.

Atkinson, D. R. (1983a). Ethnic minority representation in counselor education. *Counselor Education and Supervision, 23,* 7–19.

Atkinson, D. R. (1983b). Ethnic similarity in counseling psychology: A review of research. *The Counseling Psychologist, 11*(3), 79–92.

Atkinson, D. R., (1985). A meta-review of research on cross-cultural counseling and psychotherapy. *Journal of Multicultural Counseling and Development, 13,* 138–153.

Atkinson, D. R. (1994). Multicultural training: A call for standards. *The Counseling Psychologist, 22,* 300–307.

Atkinson, D. R., Brown, M. T., & Casas, J. M. (1996). Achieving ethnic parity in counseling psychology. *The Counseling Psychologist, 24,* 230–258.

Atkinson, D. R., & Lowe, S. M. (1995). The role of ethnicity, cultural knowledge, and conventional techniques in counseling and psychotherapy. In J. G. Ponterotto, J. M. Casas, L. A. Suzuki, & C. M. Alexander (Eds.), *Handbook of multicultural counseling* (pp. 387–414). Thousand Oaks, CA: Sage Publications.

Atkinson, D. R., Neville, H., & Casas, A. (1991). The mentorship of ethnic minorities in professional psychology. *Professional Psychology: Research and Practice, 22,* 336–338.

Atkinson, D. R., & Thompson, C. E. (1992). Racial, ethnic, and cultural variables in counseling. In S. D. Brown & R. W. Lent (Eds.), *Handbook of Counseling Psychology* (2nd ed), New York: John Wiley & Sons.

Atkinson, D. R., Thompson, C. E., & Grant, S. K. (1993). A three-dimensional model for counseling racial/ethnic minorities. *The Counseling Psychologist, 21,* 257–277.

Bales, J. (1985). Minority training falls short. *APA Monitor, 16*(11), 7.

Bandura, A. (1982). Self-efficacy mechanism in human agency. *American Psychologist, 37,* 122–147.

Bandura, A. (1986). *Social foundations of thought and action: A social cognitive theory.* Englewoods Cliff, N. J.: Prentice-Hall, Inc.

Bennett, M. J. (1986). A developmental approach to training for intercultural sensitivity. *International Journal of Intercultural Relations, 10,* 179–186.

Bernal, M. E. (1980). Hispanic issues in psychology: Curricula and training. *Hispanic Journal of Behavioral Sciences, 2,* 129–146.

Bernal, M. E., & Castro, F. G. (1994). Are clinical psychologists prepared for service and research with ethnic minorities? Report of a decade of progress. *American Psychologist, 49,* 797–805.

Bernal, M. E., & Padilla, A. M. (1982). Status of minority curricula and training in clinical psychology. *American Psychologist, 37,* 780–787.

Berthold, S. M. (1989). Spiritualism as a form of psychotherapy: Implications for social work practice. *Social Casework, 70,* 502–509.

Bluestone, H. H., Stokes, A., & Kuba, S. A. (1996). Toward an integrated program design: Evaluating the status of diversity training in a graduate school curriculum. *Professional Psychology: Research and Practice, 27,* 394–400.

Brickman, P., Rabinowitz, V. C., Karuza, J. Jr., Coates, D., Cohn, E., & Kidder, L. (1982). Models of helping and coping. *American Psychologist, 37,* 368–384.

Carey, J. C., Reinat, M., & Fontes, L. (1990). School counselors' perceptions of training needs in multicultural counseling. *Counselor Education and Supervision, 29,* 155–169.

Carney, C. G., & Kahn, K. B. (1984). Building competencies for effective cross-cultural counseling: A developmental view. *The Counseling Psychologist, 12,* 111–119.

Casas, J. M. (1984). Policy, training and research in counseling psychology: The racial/ethnic minority perspective. In S. Brown & R. Lent (Eds.), *Handbook of counseling psychology* (pp. 785–831). New York: John Wiley.

Casas, J. M. (1985). A reflection of the status of racial/ethnic minority research. *Counseling Psychologist, 13*(4), 581–598.

Cayleff, S. E. (1986). Ethical issues in counseling gender, race, and culturally distinct groups. *Journal of Counseling and Development, 64,* 345–347.

Coleman, H. L. K. (1996). Portfolio assessment of multicultural counseling competency. *The Counseling Psychologist, 24,* 216–229.

Committee on Accreditation. (1980). *Criteria for accreditation of doctoral programs and internships in professional psychology.* Washington, DC: American Psychological Association.

Copeland, E. J. (1982). Minority populations and traditional counseling programs: Some alternatives. *Counselor Education and Supervision, 21,* 187–193.

Copeland, E. J. (1983). Cross-cultural counseling and psychotherapy: A historical perspective, implications for research and training. *Personnel and Guidance Journal, 62,* 10–15.

D'Andrea, M., Daniels, J., & Heck, R. (1991). Evaluating the impact of multicultural counseling training. *Journal of Counseling and Development, 70,* 143–150.

Dellios, H. (December 4, 1994). Scholars plot affirmative action's end. *San Francisco Examiner,* A-1, A-14.

DuBose, E. R., Hamel, R. P., & O'Connell, L. J. (Eds.). (1994). *A matter of principles?: Ferment in U. S. Bioethics.* Valley Forge, PA: Trinity Press International.

Education and Training Committee of Division 17 (1984). "What is a counseling psychologist?" (Available from the American Psychological Association, 1200 Seventeenth Street, N. W., Washington, DC 20036.)

Egan, G. (1985). *Change agent skills in helping and human service settings.* Monterey, CA: Brooks/Cole Publishing Co.

Esquivel, G. B., & Keitel, M. A. (1990). Counseling immigrant children in the schools. *Elementary School Guidance and Counseling, 24,* 213–221.

Festinger, L. (1957). *A theory of cognitive dissonance.* Stanford, CA: Stanford University Press.

Gardner, L. H. (1971). The therapeutic relationship under varying conditions of race. *Psychotherapy: Theory, Research and Practice, 8*(1), 78–87.

Graham, S. (1992). "Most of the subjects were White and middle class": Trends in published research on African Americans in selected APA journals, 1970–1989. *American Psychologist, 47,* 629–639.

Hansen, J. C., Hines, B. S., & Meier, S. (1990). *Consultation: Concepts and practices.* Englewood Cliffs, NJ: Prentice Hall.

Hardiman, R. (1982). White identity development: A process-oriented model for describing the racial consciousness of White Americans. *Dissertation Abstracts International, 43,* 104A. (University Microfilms No. 82-10330).

Harrison, D. K. (1975). Race as a counselor-client variable in counseling and psychotherapy: A review of the research. *Counseling Psychology, 5*(1), 124–133.

Heath, A. E., Neimeyer, G. J., & Pedersen, P. B. (1988). The future of cross-cultural counseling: A delphi poll. *Journal of Counseling and Development, 67,* 27–30.

Heider, F. (1958). *The psychology of interpersonal relations.* New York, John Wiley & Sons.

Helms, J. E. (1984). Toward a theoretical explanation of the effects of race on counseling: A Black and White model. *The Counseling Psychologist, 12,* 153–165.

Helms, J. E. (1990). *Black and White racial identity: Theory, research, and practice.* Westport, CT: Greenwood.

Helms, J. E. (1995). An update of Helms's White and people of color racial identity models. In J. G. Ponterotto, J. M. Casas, L. A. Suzuki, and C. M. Alexander (Eds.), *Handbook of Multicultural Counseling* (pp. 181–198). Thousand Oaks, CA: Sage Publications.

Helms, J. E., & Carter, R. T. (1990). Development of the White racial identity inventory. In J. E. Helms (Ed.), *Black and White racial identity: Theory, research, and practice* (pp. 67–80). Westport, CT: Greenwood Press.

Hills, H. I., & Strozier, A. L. (1992). Multicultural training in APA-approved counseling psychology programs: A survey. *Professional Psychology: Research and Practice, 23,* 43–51.

Ibrahim, F. A. (1996). A multicultural perspective on principle and virtue ethics. *The Counseling Psychologist, 24,* 78–85.

Ivey, A. E. (1976). *Counseling psychology, the psychoeducator model and the future.* Paper prepared for APA Division 17 Professional Affairs Committee.

Ivey, A. E., Ivey, M. B., & Simek-Morgan, L. (1993). *Counseling and psychotherapy: A multicultural perspective.* Boston: Allyn Bacon.

Jones, J. H. (1981). *Bad blood: The Tuskegee syphilis experiment.* New York: The Free Press.

Jones, J. M. (1985). The sociopolitical context of clinical training in psychology: The ethnic minority case. *Psychotherapy, 22,* 453–456.

Jones, J. M. (1990, September). A call to advance psychology's role in minority issues. *APA Monitor,* p. 23.

Katz, J. H., & Ivey, A. (1977). White awareness: The frontier of racism awareness training. *Personnel and Guidance Journal, 55,* 485–489.

Kelley, H. H. (1973). The processes of causal attribution. *American Psychologist, 28,* 107–128.

Kennedy, C. D., & Wagner, N. N. (1979). Psychology and affirmative action: 1977. *Professional Psychology, 10,* 234–243.

Kleinman, A. (1980). *Patients and healers in the context of culture.* Berkeley, CA: University of California Press.

Kohout, J., & Pion, G. (1990). In G. Stricker, E. Davis-Russell, E. Bourg, E. Duran, W. R. Hammond, J. McHolland, K. Polite, & B. E. Vaughn (Eds), *Toward ethnic diversification in psychology education and training* (pp. 105–111). Washington, DC: American Psychological Association.

Kohout, J., & Wicherski, M. (1993). *Characteristics of graduate departments of psychology: 1991–92.* Washington, DC: Education Directorate, American Psychological Association.

Korchin, S. J. (1981). Clinical psychology and minority problems. *American Psychologist, 35,* 262–269.

LaFromboise, T. D., Coleman, H. L. K., & Hernandez, A. (1991). Development and factor structure of the Cross-Cultural Counseling Inventory-Revised. *Professional Psychology: Research and Practice, 22,* 380–388.

LaFromboise, T. D., & Rowe, W. (1983). Skills training for bicultural competence: Rationale and application. *Journal of Counseling Psychology, 30,* 589–595.

Lefley, H. P. (1994). Service needs of culturally diverse patients and families. In H. P. Lefley & M. Wasow (Eds.), *Helping families cope with mental illness* (pp. 223–242). USA: Harvard Academic Publishers.

Leong, F. T. L. (1986). Counseling and psychotherapy with Asian-Americans: Review of the literature. *Journal of Counseling Psychology, 33,* 196–206.

Leong, F. T. L., & Kim, H. H. W. (1991). Going beyond cultural sensitivity on the road to multiculturalism: Using the intercultural sensitizer as a counselor training tool. *Journal of Counseling & Development, 70,* 112–118.

Lewis, M. D., & Lewis, J. A. (1977). The counselor's impact on community environments. *Personnel and Guidance Journal, 55,* 356–358.

Lopez, S. R., Grover, K. P., Holland, D., Johnson, M. J., Kain, C. D., Kanel, K., Mellins, C. A., & Rhyne, M. C. (1989). Development of culturally sensitive psychotherapists. *Professional Psychology: Research and Practice, 20,* 369–376.

Meara, N. M., Schmidt, L. D., & Day, J. D. (1996). Principles and virtues: A foundation for ethical decisions, policies, and character. *The Counseling Psychologist, 24,* 4–77.

Midgette, T. E., & Meggert, S. S. (1991). Multicultural counseling instruction: A challenge for faculties in the 21st century. *Journal of Counseling & Development, 70,* 136–141.

Mintz, L. B., Bartels, K. M., & Rideout, C. A. (1995). Training in counseling ethnic minorities and race-based availability of graduate school resources. *Professional Psychology: Research & Practice, 26,* 316–321.

Mio, J. S. (1989). Experiential involvement as an adjunct to teaching cultural sensitivity. *Journal of Multicultural Counseling & Development, 17,* 38–46.

Mio, J. S., & Iwamasa, G. (1993). To do, or not to do: That is the question for White cross-cultural researchers. *The Counseling Psychologist, 21,* 197–212.

Moses, S. (1990, December). Sensitivity to culture may be hard to teach. *APA Monitor,* p. 39.

National Coalition of Advocates for Students. (1988). *New voices: Immigrant students in U.S. public schools.* Boston, MA: Author. (ERIC Document Reproduction Service No. ED 297 063).

Neighbors, H. W., Braithwaite, R. L., & Thompson, E. (1995). Health promotion and African-Americans: From personal empowerment to community action. *American Journal of Health Promotion, 9,* 281–287.

Neville, H. A., Heppner, M. J., Louie, C. E., Thomson, C. E., Brooks, L., & Baker, C. E. (1996). The impact of multicultural training on White racial identity attitudes and therapy competencies. *Professional Psychology: Research & Practice, 27,* 83–89.

Ottari, T. M., Pope-Davis, D. B., & Dings, G. (1994). Relationship between White racial identity attitudes and self-reported multicultural counseling competencies. *Journal of Counseling Psychology, 41,* 149–154.

Padilla, E. R., Boxley, R., & Wagner, N. (1973). The desegregation of clinical psychology training. *Professional Psychology, 4,* 259–265.

Parham, T. A., & McDavis, R. J. (1987). Black men, an endangered species: Who's really pulling the trigger? *Journal of Counseling & Development, 66,* 24–27.

Parham, W., & Moreland, J. R. (1981). Non-White students in counseling psychology: A closer look. *Professional Psychology, 12,* 499–507.

Parker, W. M., Valley, M. M., & Geary, C. A. (1986). Acquiring cultural knowledge for counselors in training: A multifaceted approach. *Counselor Education & Supervision, 26,* 61–71.

Payton, C. R. (1994). Implications of the 1992 ethics code for diverse groups. *Professional Psychology: Research & Practice, 25,* 317–320.

Pedersen, P. B. (1976). The field of intercultural counseling. In P. Pedersen, W. J. Lonner, & J. G. Draguns (Eds.), *Counseling across cultures.* Honolulu: The University of Hawaii Press.

Pedersen, P. B. (1994). *Culture-centered counseling: A search for accuracy.* Newbury Park, CA: Sage.

Pedersen, P. B. (1995). Culture-centered ethical guidelines for counselors. In J. G. Ponterotto, J. M. Casas, L. A. Suzuki, & C. M. Alexander (Eds.), *Handbook of multicultural counseling* (pp. 34–49). Thousand Oaks, CA: Sage Publications.

Petty, R. E., & Cacioppo, J. T. (1986a). *Communication and persuasion: Central and peripheral routes to attitude change.* New York: Springer-Verlag.

Petty, R. E., & Cacioppo, J. T. (1986b). The elaboration likelihood model of persuasion. In L. Berkowitz (Ed.), *Advances in experimental social psychology* (Vol. 19, pp. 123–205). New York: Academic Press.

Phinney, J. S. (1996). When we talk about American ethnic groups, what do we mean? *American Psychologist, 51,* 918–927.

Ponterotto, J. G. (1987). Counseling Mexican Americans: A multimodel approach. *Journal of Counseling and Development, 65,* 308–312.

Ponterotto, J. G. (1988). Racial consciousness development among white counselor trainees: A stage model. *Journal of Counseling and Development, 16,* 146–156.

Ponterotto, J. G., Alexander, C. M., & Grieger, I. (1995). A multicultural competency checklist for counseling training programs. *Journal of Multicultural Counseling and Development, 23,* 11–20.

Ponterotto, J. G., Burkard, A., Yoshida, R. K., Cancelli, A. A., Mendez, G., Wasilewski, L., & Susman, L. (1995). Prospective minoirty students' perceptions of application packets for professional psychology programs: A qualitative study. *Professional Psychology: Research and Practice, 26,* 196–204.

Ponterotto, J. G., & Casas, J. M. (1987). In search of multicultural competence within counselor education programs. *Journal of Counseling and Development, 65,* 430–434.

Ponterotto, J. G., & Casas, J. M. (1991). *Handbook of racial/ethnic minority counseling research.* Springfield, IL: Charles C Thomas.

Ponterotto, J. G., Rieger, B. P., Barrett, A., & Sparks, R. (1994). Assessing multicultural counseling competence: A review of instrumentation. *Journal of Counseling and Development, 72,* 316–322.

Ponterotto, J. G., Sanchez, C. M., & Magids, D. M. (1991, August). *Initial development and validation of the Multicultural Counseling Awareness Scale (MCAS).* Paper presented at the annual meeting of the American Psychological Association, San Francisco, CA.

Pope-Davis, D. B., Reynolds, A. L., Dings, J. G., & Nielson, D. (1995). Examining multicultural counseling competencies of graduate students in psychology. *Professional Psychology: Research and Practice, 26,* 322–329.

Pope-Davis, D. B., Reynolds, A. L., Dings, J. G., & Ottavi, T. M. (1994). Multicultural competencies of doctoral interns at University counseling centers: An exploratory investigation. *Professional Psychology: Research and Practice, 25,* 466–470.

Rickard, H. C., & Clements, C. B. (1993). Critique of APA Accreditation Criterion II: Cultural and individual differences. *Professional Psychology: Research and Practice, 24,* 123–126.

Ridley, C. R. (1985). Imperatives for ethnic and cultural relevance in psychology training programs. *Professional Psychology: Research and Practice, 16,* 611–622.

Ridley, C. R., Mendoza, D. W., & Kanitz, B. E. (1992). Program designs for multicultural training. *Journal of Psychology and Christianity, 11,* 326–333.

Ridley, C. R., Mendoza, D. W., & Kanitz, B. E. (1994). Multicultural training: Reexamination, operationalization, and integration. *The Counseling Psychologist, 22,* 227–289.

Ridley, C. R., Mendoza, D. W., Kanitz, B. E., Angermeier, L., & Zenk, R. (1994). Cultural sensitivity in multicultural counseling: A perceptual schema model. *Journal of Counseling Psychology, 41,* 125–136.

Rotter, J. B. (1966). Generalized expectancies for internal versus external locus of reinforcement. *Psychological Monographs, 80,* 1–28.

Rowe, W., Murphy, H. B., & DeCsipkes, R. A. (1975). The relationship of counselor characteristics and counseling effectiveness. *Review of Educational Research, 45,* 231–246.

Russo, N. F., Olmedo, E. L., Stapp, J., & Fulcher, R. (1981). Women and minorities in psychology. *American Psychologist, 36,* 1315–1363.

Sabnani, H. B., Ponterotto, J. G., & Borodovsky, L. G. (1991). White racial identity development and cross-cultural counselor training. *The Counseling Psychologist, 19,* 76–102.

Sattler, J. M. (1970). Racial experimenter effects in experimentation, testing, interviewing and psychotherapy. *Psychological Bulletin, 73,* 137–160.

Sattler, J. M. (1977). The effects of therapist-client racial similarity. In A. S. Burman & A.M. Razin (Eds.), *Effective psychotherapy* (pp. 252–290). New York: Pergamon Press.

Sodowsky, G. R., Taffe, R. C., Gutkin, T. B., & Wise, S. L. (1994). Development of the Multicultural Counseling Inventory: A self-report measure of multicultural competencies. *Journal of Counseling Psychology, 41,* 137–148.

Speight, S. L., Thomas, A. J., Kennel, R. G., & Anderson, M. E. (1995). Operationalizing multicultural training in doctoral programs and internships. *Professional Psychology: Research and Practice, 26,* 401–406.

Stang, D. J., & Peele, D. (1977). The status of minorities in psychology. In E. L. Olmedo & S. Lopez (Eds.), *Hispanic mental health professionals* (pp. 31–42). Los Angeles: Spanish Speaking Mental Health Research Center.

Sue, D. W. (1978). Eliminating cultural oppression in counseling: Toward a general theory. *Journal of Counseling Psychology, 25,* 419–428.

Sue, D. W. (1995). Toward a theory of multicultural counseling and therapy. In J.A. Banks & C.A. McGee Banks (Eds.), *Handbook of research on multicultural education* (pp. 647–659). New York: Macmillan.

Sue, D. W., Arredondo, P., & McDavis, R. J. (1992). Multicultural counseling competencies/standards: A call to the profession. *Journal of Multicultural Counseling and Development, 20,* 64–88.

Sue, D. W., Bernier, J. E., Durran, A., Feinberg, L., Pedersen, P., Smith, E. J., & Vasquez-Nuttal, E. (1982). Position paper: Cross-cultural counseling competencies. *The Counseling Psychologist, 10*(2), 45–52.

Sue, D. W., Ivey, A. E., & Pedersen, P. B. (1996). *A theory of multicultural counseling and therapy.* Pacific Grove, CA: Brooks/Cole.

Sue, D. W., & Sue, D. (1990). *Counseling the culturally different* (2nd ed.). New York: John Wiley & Sons.

Sue, S. (1988). Psychotherapeutic services for ethnic minorities: Two decades of research findings. *American Psychologist, 43,* 301–308.

Sue, S., Akutsu, P. D., & Higashi, C. (1985). Training issues in conducting therapy with ethnic-minority-group clients. In P. Pedersen (Ed.), *Handbook of cross-cultural counseling and therapy.* Westport, Conn.: Greenwood Press.

Sue, S., Chun. C., & Gee, K. (1995). Ethnic minority intervention and treatment research. In J. F. Aponte, R. Young Rivers, & J. Wohl (Eds.), *Psychological interventions and cultural diversity* (pp. 266–282). Boston: Allyn and Bacon.

Sue, S., & Zane, N. (1987). The role of culture and cultural techniques in psychotherapy: A critique and reformulation. *American Psychologist, 42,* 37–45.

Terrell, F., & Terrell, S. L. (1981). An inventory to measure cultural mistrust among Blacks. *The Western Journal of Black Studies, 5,* 180–184.

Terrell, F., & Terrell, S. L. (1984). Race of counselor, client sex, cultural mistrust level, and premature termination from counseling among black clients. *Journal of Counseling Psychology, 31,* 371–375.

The nature, scope, and implementation of criterion II: Cultural and individual differences (1991, Summer). *APA CAPSULE, 1*–5.

Torrey, E. F. (1972). *The mind game: Witch doctors and psychiatrists.* New York: Emerson-Hall.

Tseng, W. S., & McDermott, J. F., Jr. (1975). Psychotherapy: Historical roots, universal elements, and cultural variations. *American Journal of Psychiatry, 132,* 378–384.

Tyler, L. E. (1961). *The work of the counselor* (2nd ed.). New York: Appleton-Century-Crofts.

Vontress, C. E. (1976). Racial and ethnic barriers in counseling. In P. B. Pedersen, W. J. Lonner, & J. G. Draguns (Eds.), *Counseling across cultures.* Honolulu: The University of Hawaii Press.

Wade, P., & Bernstein, B. L. (1991). Culture sensitive training and counselor's race: Effects on Black female clients' perceptions and attribution. *Journal of Counseling Psychology, 38,* 9–15.

Walton, J. M. (1979). Retention, role modeling, and academic readiness: A perspective on the ethnic minority student in higher education. *Personnel and Guidance Journal, 58,* 125–127.

Waltz, G. R., & Benjamin, L. (1977). *On becoming a change agent.* Ann Arbor: Eric Counseling and Personnel Services Information Center.

Wilson, W., & Calhoun, J. F. (1974). Behavior therapy and the minority client. *Psychotherapy: Theory, Research and Practice, 11*(4), 317–325.

Witkin, H. A. (1962). A cognitive-style approach to cross-cultural research. *International Journal of Psychology, 2,* 233–250.

Wohl, J. (1995). Traditional individual psychotherapy and ethnic minorities. In J. F. Aponte, R. Y. Rivers, & J. Wohl (Eds.), *Psychological interventions and cultural diversity* (pp. 74–91). Boston: Allyn and Bacon.

Wood, P. S., & Mallinckrodt, B. (1990). Culturally sensitive assertiveness training for ethnic minority clients. *Professional Psychology: Research and Practice, 21,* 5–11.

Young, R. L., Chamley, J. D., & Withers, C. (1990). Minority faculty representation and hiring practices in counselor education programs. *Counselor Education and Supervision, 29,* 148–154.

Zayas, L. H., Torres, L. R., Malcolm, J., & DesRosiers, F. S. (1996). Clinician's definitions of ethnically sensitive therapy. *Professional Psychology: Research & Practice, 27,* 78–82.

APPENDIX

Multicultural Counseling Competencies

I. Counselor Awareness of Own Cultural Values and Biases
A. Attitudes and Beliefs
1. Culturally skilled counselors believe that cultural self-awareness and sensitivity to one's own cultural heritage is essential.

Explanatory Statements

- Can identify the culture(s) to which they belong and the significance of that membership including the relationship of individuals in that group with individuals from other groups institutionally, historically, educationally, and so forth (include A, B, and C Dimensions as do the other suggestions in this section).
- Can identify the specific cultural group(s) from which counselor derives fundamental cultural heritage and the significant beliefs and attitudes held by those cultures that are assimilated into their own attitudes and beliefs.
- Can recognize the impact of those beliefs on their ability to respect others different from themselves.
- Can identify specific attitudes, beliefs, and values from their own heritage and cultural learning that support behaviors that demonstrate respect and valuing of differences and those that impede or hinder respect and valuing of differences.
- Actively engage in an ongoing process of challenging their own attitudes and beliefs that do not support respecting and valuing of differences.
- Appreciate and articulate positive aspects of their own heritage that provide them with strengths in understanding differences.
- In addition to their cultural groups, can recognize the influence of other personal dimensions of identity (PDI) and their role in cultural self-awareness.

Pages 57–74 of Arriedondo, P., Toporek, R., Brown, S. P., Jones, J., Locke, D. C., Sanchez, J., & Stadler, H. (1996). Operationalization of the multicultural competencies. *Journal of Multicultural Counseling and Development, 24,* 42–78.

2. Culturally skilled counselors are aware of how their own cultural background and experiences have influenced attitudes, values, and biases about psychological processes.

   Explanatory Statements
   - Can identify the history of their culture in relation to educational opportunities and its impact on their current worldview (includes A and some B Dimensions).
   - Can identify at least five personal, relevant cultural traits and can explain how each has influenced the cultural values of the counselor.
   - Can identify social and cultural influences on their cognitive development and current information processing styles and can contrast that with those of others (includes A, B, and C Dimensions).
   - Can identify specific social and cultural factors and events in their history that influence their view and use of social belonging, interpretations of behavior, motivation, problem-solving and decision methods, thoughts and behaviors (including subconscious) in relation to authority and other institutions and can contrast these with the perspectives of others (A and B Dimensions).
   - Can articulate the beliefs of their own cultural and religious groups as these relate to sexual orientation, able-bodiedness, and so forth, and the impact of these beliefs in a counseling relationship.

3. Culturally skilled counselors are able to recognize the limits of their multicultural competency and expertise.

   Explanatory Statements
   - Can recognize in a counseling or teaching relationship, when and how their attitudes, beliefs, and values are interfering with providing the best service to clients (primarily A and B Dimensions).
   - Can identify preservice and in-service experiences which contribute to expertise and can identify current specific needs for professional development.
   - Can recognize and use referral sources that demonstrate values, attitudes, and beliefs that will respect and support the client's developmental needs.
   - Can give real examples of cultural situations in which they recognized their limitations and referred the client to more appropriate resources.

4. Culturally skilled counselors recognize their sources of discomfort with differences that exist between themselves and clients in terms of race, ethnicity, and culture.

Explanatory Statements

- Able to recognize their sources of comfort/discomfort with respect to differences in terms of race, ethnicity, and culture.
- Able to identify differences (along A and B Dimensions) and are nonjudgmental about those differences.
- Communicate acceptance of and respect for differences both verbally and nonverbally.
- Can identify at least five specific cultural differences, the needs of culturally different clients, and how these differences are handled in the counseling relationship.

B. Knowledge

1. Culturally skilled counselors have specific knowledge about their own racial and cultural heritage and how it personally and professionally affects their definitions of and biases about normality/abnormality and the process of counseling.

Explanatory Statements

- Have knowledge regarding their heritage. For example, A Dimensions in terms of ethnicity, language, and so forth, and C Dimensions in terms of knowledge regarding the context of the time period in which their ancestors entered the established United States or North American continent.
- Can recognize and discuss their family's and culture's perspectives of acceptable (normal) codes of conduct and what are unacceptable (abnormal) and how this may or may not vary from those of other cultures and families.
- Can identify at least five specific features of culture of origin and explain how those features affect the relationship with culturally different clients.

2. Culturally skilled counselors possess knowledge and understanding about how oppression, racism, discrimination, and stereotyping affect them personally and in their work. This allows individuals to acknowledge their own racist attitudes, beliefs, and feelings. Although this standard applies to all groups, for White counselors it may mean that they understand how they may have directly or indirectly benefited from individual, institutional, and cultural racism as outlined in White identity development models.

Explanatory Statements

- Can specifically identify, name, and discuss privileges that they personally receive in society due to their race, socioeconomic background, gender, physical abilities, sexual orientation, and so on.
- Specifically referring to White counselors, can discuss White identity development models and how they relate to one's personal experiences.
- Can provide a reasonably specific definition of racism, prejudice, discrimination, and stereotype. Can describe a situation in which they have been judged on something other than merit. Can describe a situation in which they have judged someone on something other than merit.
- Can discuss recent research addressing issues of racism, White identity development, antiracism, and so forth, and its relation to their personal development and professional development as counselors.

3. Culturally skilled counselors possess knowledge about their social impact on others. They are knowledgeable about communication style differences, how their style may clash with or foster the counseling process with persons of color or others different from themselves based on the A, B, and C Dimensions, and how to anticipate the impact it may have on others.

Explanatory Statements

- Can describe the A and B Dimensions of Identity with which they most strongly identify.
- Can behaviorally define their communication style and describe both their verbal and nonverbal behaviors, interpretations of others' behaviors, and expectations.
- Recognize the cultural bases (A Dimension) of their communication style, and the differences between their style and the styles of those different from themselves.
- Can describe the behavioral impact and reaction of their communication style on clients different from themselves. For example, the reaction of an older (1960s) Vietnamese male recent immigrant to continuous eye contact from the young, female counselor.
- Can give examples of an incident in which communication broke down with a client of color and can hypothesize about the causes.
- Can give three to five concrete examples of situations in which they modified their communication style to compliment that of a culturally different client, how they decided on the modification, and the result of that modification.

C. Skills

1. Culturally skilled counselors seek out educational, consultative, and training experiences to improve their understanding and effectiveness in working with culturally different populations. Being able to recognize the limits of their competencies, they (a) seek consultation, (b) seek further training or education, (c) refer to more qualified individuals or resources, or (d) engage in a combination of these.

Explanatory Statements

- Can recognize and identify characteristics or situations in which the counselor's limitations in cultural, personal, or religious beliefs, or issues of identity development require referral.
- Can describe objectives of at least two multicultural-related professional development activities attended over the past 5 years and can identify at least two adaptations to their counseling practices as a result of these professional development activities.
- Have developed professional relationships with counselors from backgrounds different from their own and have maintained a dialogue regarding multicultural differences and preferences.
- Maintain an active referral list and continuously seek new referrals relevant to different needs of clients along A and B Dimensions.
- Understand and communicate to the client that the referral is being made because of the counselor's limitations rather than communicating that it is caused by the client.
- On recognizing these limitations, the counselor actively pursues and engages in professional and personal growth activities to address these limitations.
- Actively consult regularly with other professionals regarding issues of culture to receive feedback about issues and situations and whether or where referral may be necessary.

2. Culturally skilled counselors are constantly seeking to understand themselves as racial and cultural beings and are actively seeking a nonracist identity.

Explanatory Statements

- Actively seek out and participate in reading and in activities designed to develop cultural self-awareness, and work toward eliminating racism and prejudice.
- Maintain relationships (personal and professional) with individuals different from themselves and actively engage in discussions allowing for feedback regarding the counselor's

behavior (personal and professional) concerning racial issues. (For example, a White counselor maintains a personal/professional relationship with a Latina counselor that is intimate enough to request and receive honest feedback regarding behaviors and attitudes and their impact on others, "I seem to have difficulty retaining Latina students in my class, given how I run my class, can you help me find ways that I may make it a more appropriate environment for Latina students?" or "When I said ___, how do you think others perceived that comment?") This requires the commitment to develop and contribute to a relationship that allows for adequate trust and honesty in very difficult situations.

- When receiving feedback, the counselor demonstrates a receptivity and willingness to learn.

(See Appendix A for strategies to achieve the competencies and objectives for Area I.)

II. Counselor Awareness of Client's Worldview
A. Attitudes and Beliefs

1. Culturally skilled counselors are aware of their negative and positive emotional reactions toward other racial and ethnic groups that may prove detrimental to the counseling relationship. They are willing to contrast their own beliefs and attitudes with those of their culturally different clients in a nonjudgmental fashion.

Explanatory Statements

- Identify their common emotional reactions about individuals and groups different from themselves and observe their own reactions in encounters. For example, do they feel fear when approaching a group of three young African-American men? Do they assume that the Asian-American clients for whom they provide career counseling will be interested in a technical career?
- Can articulate how their personal reactions and assumptions are different from those who identify with that group. (e.g., if the reaction on approaching three young African-American men is fear, what is the reaction of a young African-American man or woman in the same situation? What might be the reaction of an African-American woman approaching a group of White young men?)
- Identify how general emotional reactions observed in oneself could influence effectiveness in a counseling relationship. (Reactions may be regarding cultural differences as well as along A and B Dimensions).

- Can describe at least two distinct examples of cultural conflict between self and culturally different clients, including how these conflicts were used as "content" for counseling. For example, if a Chicana agrees to live at home rather than board at a 4-year college to support her mother, can a counselor be nonjudgmental?

2. Culturally skilled counselors are aware of their stereotypes and preconceived notions that they may hold toward other racial and ethnic minority groups.

Explanatory Statements

- Recognize their stereotyped reactions to people different from themselves. (e.g., silently articulating their awareness of a negative stereotypical reaction, "I noticed that I locked my car doors when that African-American teenager walked by.")
- Consciously attend to examples that contradict stereotypes.
- Can give specific examples of how their stereotypes (including "positive" ones) referring to the A and B Dimensions can affect the counselor-client relationship.
- Recognize assumptions of those in a similar cultural group but who may differ based on A or B Dimension.

B. Knowledge

1. Culturally skilled counselors possess specific knowledge and information about the particular group with which they are working. They are aware of the life experiences, cultural heritage, and historical background of their culturally different clients. This particular competency is strongly linked to the minority identity development models available in the literature.

Explanatory Statements

- Can articulate (objectively) differences in nonverbal and verbal behavior of the five major cultural groups most frequently seen in their experience of counseling.
- Can describe at least two different models of minority identity development and their implications for counseling with persons of color or others who experience oppression or marginalization.
- Understand and can explain the historical point of contact with dominant society for various ethnic groups and the impact of the type of contact (enslaved, refugee, seeking economic opportunities, conquest, and so forth) on current issues in society.
- Can identify within-group differences and assess various aspects of individual clients to determine individual differences as well as

cultural differences. For example, the counselor is aware of differences within Asian Americans: Japanese Americans, Vietnamese Americans, and so forth; differences between first generation refugees versus second or third generation; differences between Vietnamese refugees coming in the "first wave" in 1975 versus Vietnamese refugees coming to the United States in 1990.

- Can discuss viewpoints of other cultural groups regarding issues such as sexual orientation, physical ability or disability, gender, and aging.

2. Culturally skilled counselors understand how race, culture, ethnicity, and so forth may affect personality formation, vocational choices, manifestation of psychological disorders, help-seeking behavior, and the appropriateness or inappropriateness of counseling approaches.

Explanatory Statements

- Can distinguish cultural differences and expectations regarding role and responsibility in family, participation of family in career decision making, appropriate family members to be involved when seeking help, culturally acceptable means of expressing emotion and anxiety and so forth (primarily along A Dimension and portions of B Dimension).
- Based on literature about A Dimensions, can describe and give examples of how a counseling approach may or may not be appropriate for a specific group of people based primarily on an A Dimension.
- Understand and can explain the historical point of contact with dominant society for various ethnic groups and the impact of the type of contact (e.g., enslaved, refugee, seeking economic opportunities, conquest) on potential relationships and trust when seeking help from dominant culture institutions.
- Can describe one system of personality development, the population(s) on which the theory was developed, and how this system relates or does not relate to at least two culturally different populations.
- Can identify the role of gender, socioeconomic status, and physical disability as they interact with personality formation across cultural groups.

3. Culturally skilled counselors understand and have knowledge about sociopolitical influences that impinge on the life of racial and ethnic minorities. Immigration issues, poverty, racism, stereotyping, and powerlessness may affect self-esteem and self-concept in the counseling process.

Explanatory Statements

- Can identify implications of concepts such as internalized oppression, institutional racism, privilege, and the historical and current political climate regarding immigration, poverty, and welfare (public assistance).
- Can explain the relationship between culture and power. Can explain dynamics of at least two cultures and how factors such as poverty and powerlessness have influenced the current conditions of individuals of those cultures.
- Understand the economic benefits and contributions gained by the work of various groups, including migrant farm workers, to the daily life of the counselor and the country at large.
- Can communicate an understanding of the unique position, constraints, and needs of those clients who experience oppression based on an A or B Dimension alone (and families of clients) who share this history.
- Can identify current issues that affect groups of people (A and B Dimensions) in legislation, social climate, and so forth, and how that affects individuals and families to whom the counselor may be providing services.
- Are aware of legal legislation issues that affect various communities and populations (e.g., in California it is essential for a counselor to understand the ramifications of the recent passage of Proposition 187 and how that will affect not only undocumented individuals, but also families and anyone that has Chicano features, a Mexican-American accent, and speaks Spanish. In addition, the counselor must be aware of how this will affect health issues, help-seeking behaviors, participation in education, and so forth.)
- Counselors are aware of how documents such as the book *The Bell Curve* and affirmative action legislation affect society's perception of different cultural groups.

C. Skills

1. Culturally skilled counselors should familiarize themselves with relevant research and the latest findings regarding mental health and mental disorders that affect various ethnic and racial groups. They should actively seek out educational experiences that enrich their knowledge, understanding, and cross-cultural skills for more effective counseling behavior.

Explanatory Statements

- Can discuss recent research regarding such topics as mental health, career decision making, education and learning, that focuses on issues related to different cultural populations and as represented in A and B Dimensions.

- Complete (at least 15 hours per year) workshops, conferences, classes, in-service training regarding multicultural counseling skills and knowledge. These should span a variety of topics and cultures and should include discussions of wellness rather than focusing only on negative issues (medical model) related to these cultures.
- Can identify at least five multicultural experiences in which counselor has participated within the past 3 years.
- Can identify professional growth activities and information that are presented by professionals respected and seen as credible by members of the communities being studied (e.g., the book *The Bell Curve* may not represent accurate and helpful information regarding individuals from non-White cultures).
- Can describe in concrete terms how they have applied varied information gained through current research in mental health, education, career choices, and so forth, based on differences noted in A Dimension.

2. Culturally skilled counselors become actively involved with minority individuals outside the counseling setting (e.g., community events, social and political functions, celebrations, friendships, neighborhood groups) so that their perspective of minorities is more than an academic or helping exercise.

Explanatory Statements

- Can identify at least five multicultural experiences in which the counselor has participated within the past 3 years. These include various celebrations, political events, or community activities involving individuals and groups from racial and cultural backgrounds different from their own, such as political fundraisers, Tet celebrations, and neighborhood marches against violence.
- Actively plan experiences and activities that will contradict negative stereotypes and preconceived notions they may hold.

(See Appendix B for strategies to achieve the competencies and objectives for Area II.)

III. Culturally Appropriate Intervention Strategies
A. Beliefs and Attitudes

1. Culturally skilled counselors respect clients' religious and spiritual beliefs and values, including attributions and taboos, because these affect worldview, psychosocial functioning, and expressions of distress.

Explanatory Statements

- Can identify the positive aspects of spirituality (in general) in terms of wellness and healing aspects.
- Can identify in a variety of religious and spiritual communities the recognized form of leadership and guidance and their client's relationship (if existent) with that organization and entity.

2. Culturally skilled counselors respect indigenous helping practices and respect help-giving networks among communities of color.

Explanatory Statements

- Can describe concrete examples of how they may integrate and cooperate with indigenous helpers when appropriate.
- Can describe concrete examples of how they may use intrinsic help-giving networks from a variety of client communities.

3. Culturally skilled counselors value bilingualism and do not view another language as an impediment to counseling ("monolingualism" may be the culprit).

Explanatory Statements

- Communicate to clients and colleagues values and assets of bilingualism (if client is bilingual).

B. Knowledge

1. Culturally skilled counselors have a clear and explicit knowledge and understanding of the generic characteristics of counseling and therapy (culture bound, class bound, and monolingual) and how they may clash with the cultural values of various cultural groups.

Explanatory Statements

- Can articulate the historical, cultural, and racial context in which traditional theories and interventions have been developed.
- Can identify, within various theories, the cultural values, beliefs, and assumptions made about individuals and contrast these with values, beliefs, and assumptions of different racial and cultural groups.
- Recognize the predominant theories being used within counselor's organization and educate colleagues regarding the aspects of those theories and interventions that may clash with the cultural values of various cultural and racial minority groups.
- Can identify and describe primary indigenous helping practices in terms of positive and effective role in at least five A or B Dimensions, relevant to counselor's client population.

2. Culturally skilled counselors are aware of institutional barriers that prevent minorities from using mental health services.

Explanatory Statements

- Can describe concrete examples of institutional barriers within their organizations that prevent minorities from using mental health services and share those examples with colleagues and decision-making bodies within the institution.
- Recognize and draw attention to patterns of usage (or non-usage) of mental health services in relation to specific populations.
- Can identify and communicate possible alternatives that would reduce or eliminate existing barriers within their institutions and within local, state, and national decision-making bodies.

3. Culturally skilled counselors have knowledge of the potential bias in assessment instruments and use procedures and interpret findings in a way that recognizes the cultural and linguistic characteristics of the clients.

Explanatory Statements

- Demonstrate ability to interpret assessment results including implications of dominant cultural values affecting assessment/ interpretation, interaction of cultures for those who are bicultural, and the impact of historical institutional oppression.
- Can discuss information regarding cultural, racial, gender profile of normative group used for validity and reliability on any assessment used by counselor.
- Understand the limitations of translating assessment instruments as well as the importance of using language that includes culturally relevant connotations and idioms.
- Use assessment instruments appropriately with clients having limited English skills.
- Can give examples, for each assessment instrument used, of the limitations of the instrument regarding various groups represented in A and B Dimensions.
- Recognize possible historical and current sociopolitical biases in *DSM (Diagnostic & Statistical Manual of Mental Disorders)* system of diagnosis based on racial, cultural, sexual orientation, and gender issues.

4. Culturally skilled counselors have knowledge of family structures, hierarchies, values, and beliefs from various cultural perspectives. They are knowledgeable about the community where a particular cultural group may reside and the resources in the community.

Explanatory Statements

- Are familiar with and use organizations that provide support and services in different cultural communities.
- Can discuss the traditional ways of helping in different cultures and continue to learn the resources in communities relevant to those cultures.
- Adequately understand the client's religious and spiritual beliefs to know when and what topics are or are not appropriate to discuss regarding those beliefs.
- Understand and respect cultural and family influences and participation in decision making.

5. Culturally skilled counselors should be aware of relevant discriminatory practices at the social and the community level that may be affecting the psychological welfare of the population being served.

Explanatory Statements

- Are aware of legal issues that affect various communities and populations (e.g., in Proposition 187 California described earlier).

C. Skills

1. Culturally skilled counselors are able to engage in a variety of verbal and nonverbal helping responses. They are able to send and receive both verbal and nonverbal messages accurately and appropriately. They are not tied down to only one method or approach to helping, but recognize that helping styles and approaches may be culture bound. When they sense that their helping style is limited and potentially inappropriate, they can anticipate and modify it.

Explanatory Statements

- Can articulate what, when, why, and how they apply different verbal and nonverbal helping responses based on A and B Dimensions.
- Can give examples of how they may modify a technique or intervention or what alternative intervention they may use to more effectively meet the needs of a client.
- Can identify and describe techniques in which they have expertise for providing service that may require minimal English language skills (e.g., expressive therapy).
- Can communicate verbally and nonverbally to the client the validity of the client's religious and spiritual beliefs.
- Can discuss with the client (when appropriate) aspects of their religious or spiritual beliefs that have been helpful to the client in the past.

2. Culturally skilled counselors are able to exercise institutional intervention skills on behalf of their clients. They can help clients determine whether a " problem" stems from racism or bias in others (the concept of healthy paranoia) so that clients do not inappropriately personalize problems.

Explanatory Statements

- Can recognize and discuss examples in which racism or bias may actually be imbedded in an institutional system or in society.
- Can discuss a variety of coping and survival behaviors used by a variety of individuals from their A and B Dimensions to cope effectively with bias or racism.
- Communicate to clients an understanding of the necessary coping skills and behaviors viewed by dominant society as dysfunctional that they may need to keep intact.
- Can describe concrete examples of situations in which it is appropriate and possibly necessary for a counselor to exercise institutional intervention skills on behalf of a client.

3. Culturally skilled counselors are not averse to seeking consultation with traditional healers or religious and spiritual leaders and practitioners in the treatment of culturally different clients when appropriate.

Explanatory Statements

- Participate or gather adequate information regarding indigenous or community helping resources to make appropriate referrals (e.g., be familiar with the American Indian community enough to recognize when, how, and to whom it may be appropriate to refer a client for indigenous healers).

4. Culturally skilled counselors take responsibility for interacting in the language requested by the client and, if not feasible, make appropriate referrals. A serious problem arises when the linguistic skills of the counselor do not match the language of the client. This being the case, counselors should (a) seek a translator with cultural knowledge and appropriate professional background or (b) refer to a knowledgeable and competent bilingual counselor.

Explanatory Statements

- Are familiar with resources that provide services in languages appropriate to clients.
- Will seek out, whenever necessary, services or translators to ensure that language needs are met.

- If working within an organization, actively advocate for the hiring of bilingual counselors relevant to client population.

5. Culturally skilled counselors have training and expertise in the use of traditional assessment and testing instruments. They not only understand the technical aspects of the instruments but are also aware of the cultural limitations. This allows them to use test instruments for the welfare of culturally different clients.

Explanatory Statements

- Demonstrate ability to interpret assessment results including implications of dominant cultural values affecting assessment and interpretation, interaction of cultures for those who are bicultural, and the impact of historical institutional oppression.
- Can discuss information regarding cultural, racial, and gender profile of norm group used for validity and reliability on any assessment used by counselor.
- Understand that although an assessment instrument may be translated into another language, the translation may be literal without an accurate contextual translation including culturally relevant connotations and idioms.

6. Culturally skilled counselors should attend to, as well as work to eliminate, biases, prejudices, and discriminatory contexts in conducting evaluations and providing interventions, and should develop sensitivity to issues of oppression, sexism, heterosexism, elitism, and racism.

Explanatory Statements

- Recognize incidents in which clients, students, and others are being treated unfairly based on such characteristics as race, ethnicity, and physical ableness and take action by directly addressing incident or perpetrator, filing informal complaint, filing formal complaint, and so forth.
- Work at an organizational level to address, change, and eliminate policies that discriminate, create barriers, and so forth.
- If an organization's policy created barriers for advocacy, the counselor works toward changing institutional policies to promote advocacy against racism, sexism, and so forth.

7. Culturally skilled counselors take responsibility for educating their clients to the processes of psychological intervention, such as goals, expectations, legal rights, and the counselor's orientation.

- Assess the client's understanding of and familiarity with counseling and mental health services and provide accurate information regarding the process, limitations, and function of the services into which the client is entering.
- Ensure that the client understands client rights, issues, and definitions of confidentiality, and the expectations placed on that client. In this educational process, counselors adapt information to ensure that all concepts are clearly understood by the client. This may include defining and discussing these concepts.

(See Appendix C for strategies to achieve competencies and objectives in Area III. See Appendix D for strategies to achieve competencies and objectives in all three areas.)

Adapted from "Multicultural Counseling Competencies and Standards: A Call to the Profession" (Sue, Arredondo, & McDavis 1992).

References

Arredondo, P., & Glauner, T. (1992). *Personal Dimensions of Identity Model.* Boston, MA: Empowerment Workshops.

Helms, J. (1990). *White identity development.* New York: Greenwood Press.

Packer, A. H., & Johnston, W. B. (1987). *Workforce 2000: Work and Workers for the 21st Century.* Indiana: Hudson Institute.

Sue, D. W., Arredondo, P., & McDavis, R. J. (1992). Multicultural counseling competencies and standards: A call to the profession. *Journal of Counseling & Development, 70,* 477–483.

AUTHOR INDEX

Abad, V., 270, 271
Abbott, K. A., 205
Abramowitz, S. I., 73, 347, 350
Acosta, F., 270
Adams, E. M., 32
Adams, J. Q., 7
Adebimpe, V. R., 54, 56, 62, 73
Agbayani-Siewert, P., 220
Agtuca, J., 221
Akao, S. F., 168
Akutsu, P. D., 75, 336
Alegre, C., 274
Alexander, C. M., 33, 165, 343
Allen, B. P., 7
Allen, D. B., 169
Allen, P. G., 167
Allen, W., 121, 123
Allison, K. W., 331, 346
Allport, G., 13
Alonzo, W., 6
Alpert, M., 274
Altarriba, J., 68, 285
Alvarez, R., 275
American Counseling Association, 306
American Indian Health Care Association, 140
American Psychiatric Association, 238
American Psychological Association, 67, 139,
    174, 303, 304, 329, 330, 331
Anderson, C. H., 6
Anderson, M. E., 344, 345
Angermeier, L., 350
Antone, M., 148
Aponte, H. J., 289
Aponte, J. F., 59, 325
Archer, J., 53
Arkoff, A., 209
Arnold, B., 30
Arredondo, P., 330, 333, 343
Arredondo-Dowd, P. M., 95
Atkinson, D. R., 31, 42, 45, 68, 69, 73, 149,
    165, 174, 177, 286, 288, 316, 325, 326,
    327, 328, 330, 347, 349, 350
Attneave, C. L., 140, 144, 146, 160, 170, 171

Bach, P. J., 169
Bachman, R., 138
Bajaki, M., 26
Baker, C. E., 346
Bales, J., 336
Bandura, A., 350
Barnes, M., 53, 54, 59, 66
Barney, D. D., 55, 57, 60, 63
Barona, A., 29
Barresi, C. M., 8
Barrett, A., 334
Bartels, K. M., 331
Barter, E. R., 138, 141
Barter, J. T., 138, 141
Barth, F., 258
Basso, K., 169
Beals, J., 139
Bean, F. D., 283
Beatty, L., 117, 119
Beiser, M., 140, 160, 174
Belgarde, M., 169
Bell, C., 160
Bellah, R. N., 148
Benjamin, L., 309
Bennett, C. F., 3
Bennett, M. J., 337
Bennett, S. K., 150, 165
Berg, I. K., 225
Bergman, R. L., 144, 149
Berieda, M., 91, 93
Bernal, G., 285
Bernal, M. E., 7, 14, 69, 327, 331, 335, 336
Berne, E., 88
Bernier, J. E., 333, 334, 339
Bernier, Y., 74
Bernstein, B. L., 346
Berry, B., 34
Berry, G. L., 91, 96
Berry, J. W., 25, 26, 27, 28, 58
Berthold, S. M., 313
Betancourt, H., 284
BigFoot, D. S., 165, 169
BigFoot-Sipes, D. S., 150

Billson, J. M., 96, 97, 98
Bilmes, M., 235
Bishop, J. B., 163
Biswas, R., 216
Bjork, J., 140, 160
Black Caucus, 85
Black Perspectives, 83
Blackwell, J. E., 96
Blank, M. B., 69
Bloom, B., 271
Bloom, J., 139
Blos, P., 99, 102
Blue, A. W., 144, 164
Bluestone, H. H., 272, 331, 336
Blumenthal, R., 171, 268
Bobo, J. K., 169
Boehnlein, J. K., 215
Boll, T. J., 149
Bollin, G. G., 205
Borello, M. A., 263
Bornemann, T., 58
Bornstein, P. H., 169
Borodovsky, L. G., 68, 73, 338, 339
Boswell, T. D., 280, 281, 282, 283, 285
Botvin, G. J., 169
Boulette, T., 274
Bourne, P. G., 209
Bowen, M., 119
Bowman, P. J., 96
Boxley, R., 324
Boyce, E., 270, 271
Boyce, T., 138
Boyce, W., 138
Boyd-Franklin, N., 106, 118, 120, 122
Bradshaw, C. K., 220
Braithwaite, R. L., 89, 350
Brandon, P. R., 209
Brannon, R., 98
Brickman, P., 70, 351
Brigham, J. C., 13
Brinkley, D. F., 69
Brody, E., 58
Brooks, L., 346
Brown, B. B., 100, 101
Brown, M. T., 69, 327, 328, 330
Brown, R., 13
Brown, S. P., 333
Bruhn, J., 271
Bryde, J., 169
Buckard, A., 326
Bulhan, H. A., 164
Bunce, H., 271
Bureau of Indian Affairs, 137

Burgess, E. W., 25
Burman, W., 170
Burns, B. J., 53
Butler, Y., 140
Byerly, E. R., 3

Cacioppo, J. T., 350
Caldwell, C. H., 51, 54, 59, 60
Calhoun, J. F., 308
Campbell, P. R., 4
Campbell, S. M., 208
Cancelli, A. A., 326
Canino, I. A., 59
Cannon, M. S., 52
Carey, J. C., 335
Carney, C. G., 73, 337
Carpenter, A., 169
Carter, J. H., 59, 64, 68, 119, 120
Carter, R. T., 34, 42, 95, 343
Casas, A., 31, 328
Casas, J. M., 31, 67, 69, 72, 73, 74, 95, 322,
    327, 328, 330, 343, 347, 349, 350
Cass, V. C., 32
Castaneda, D. M., 56, 59
Castex, G. M., 251, 252, 257, 260
Castro, F. G., 69, 331, 335
Cayleff, S. E., 72, 312, 313
Cazenave, N. A., 91, 96, 97
Cervantes, J., 214, 227
Chamley, J. D., 325
Chan, C. S., 221
Chan, K., 236
Chapa, J., 16, 257, 263
Chapman, A. B., 89, 92
Chaudhuri, A., 139, 160
Cheatham, H. E., 95
Cheung, F., 214, 227
Cheung, F. H., 52, 73
Cheung, F. K., 53, 96
Cheung, L. R. L., 57
Cheung, M. K., 205
Chew, M., 23
Chi, C., 205
Chickering, A. W., 98
Chien, C., 238
Chin, J. L., 59, 208, 209
Chodorow, N., 102
Chou, E. L., 210
Chun, C., 22, 23, 52, 54, 65, 66, 68, 71, 218,
    312, 315, 347, 348
Chung, D. K., 216
Chung, R. C. Y., 58, 62, 63, 205, 217
Cimbolic, P., 117

Claiborn, C. D., 95, 118
Clark, C., 123
Clark, K., 96
Clarke, G., 205
Clements, C. B., 330
Clifford, F., 4
Clifford, J., 325
Coates, D., 70, 351
Cobbs, P., 123
Cohen, A., 258
Cohn, E., 70, 351
Colcord, C., 96
Coleman, H. L. K., 334
Comas-Díaz, L., 283
Comer, J., 120
Comitas, L., 262
Committee on Accreditation, 329
Conaway, L., 169
Condie, H., 208
Conner, J. W., 209
Conrad, R. D., 170
Constantino, G., 171
Cook, D. A., 14, 15
Cook, H., 205
Cooney, R., 273, 275
Cooper, C., 99
Cooper, M., 85
Copeland, E. J., 95, 335, 336
Corbine, J. L., 72
Cortes, D. E., 31, 58
Costantino, G., 268, 269, 270, 276, 277
Cox, C. I., 32
Cox, O. C., 7
Crawford, I., 331, 346
Cristo, M., 270
Cross, W. E., Jr., 32, 33, 37
Crouch, R. T., 59
Cuellar, I., 29, 30, 270, 273
Cullen, R. M., 280
Cummings, J. L., 142
Cummings, N. A., 142
Curtis, J. R., 280, 281, 282, 283, 284, 285
Curtis, L. A., 96
Cvetkovich, G., 169

D'Andrea, M., 334, 335, 345
Daniels, J., 334, 335, 345
Daniels, R., 207
Dauphinais, I., 165, 168
Dauphinais, L., 150
Dauphinais, P., 150, 162, 164, 165, 168, 176
Davenport, D. S., 90, 93
David, D. S., 98

David, K., 169
Davis, A., 88
Davis, J. E., 97
Davis, R., 96
Davis, U., 140
Day, J. D., 306, 307
de Anda, D., 29
Deardorff, K., 3
DeCsipkes, R. A., 327
DeLeon, P. H., 138, 140
Delgado, M., 270
Delk, J. I., 170
Dell, P. F., 145
Dellios, H., 325
Densmore, F., 173
DesRosiers, F. S., 333
DeVos, G., 205
Deyhle, D., 138
Dinges, N. G., 141, 144, 146, 160
Dings, G., 339
Dings, J. G., 332, 345, 346
Dixon, D. N., 150, 164, 189
Dobbins, J. E., 12
Doheny, V., 69
Doi, L. T., 239
Dole, A. A., 7
Domhoff, G. W., 103
Dona, G., 58
Donaldson, D. J., 148, 162
Donovan, D. M., 138
Dornbusch, S. M., 100, 101, 205
Downing, N. E., 32
Doyle, J. A., 98
Draguns, J. G., 174
DuBose, E. R., 306
DuBray, W. H., 184, 185
DuClos, C. W., 139
Due, D., 32
Dukepoo, P. C., 141
Dulles Conference Task Force, 149
Duran, B., 146
Duran, E., 146, 150
Durran, A., 74, 333, 334, 339
Durvasula, R., 215

Earley, B. F., 59
Eastman, K., 205
Echemendia, R., 331, 346
Echohawk, M., 140
Efrat, B., 151
Egan, G., 309
Egawa, J. E., 237, 238
Eisenberg, I., 218

Ekblad, S., 58
Elias, M. J., 251
Elmore, R. F., 152
Enloe, C. H., 257, 258, 265
Enomoto, K., 218
Epps, E. G., 11
Erikson, D. L., 98
Erikson, E., 102
Esquivel, G. B., 57, 60, 62, 309

Fabrega, H., Jr., 57
Fairchild, H. H., 7
Fairchild, H. P., 10
Fancy, B., 269
Farias, P., 58
Farley, R., 25
Farnsworth, D. L., 98
Farrell, M. P., 100
Fasteau, M. F., 98
Fchohawk, M., 160
Feagin, J. R., 7, 8
Feinberg, L., 74, 333, 334, 339
Fenz, W., 209
Fernandez, T., 30, 274
Festinger, L., 350
Fixico, M., 167
Flaskerud, J. H., 229
Fleming, C. M., 148, 162, 174
Flores-Ortiz, Y., 285
Fogg, N., 102
Fong, R., 206
Fong, S. L. M., 205
Fontana, A., 56, 64
Fontes, L., 335
Ford, R. C., 32
Fordham, S., 101, 102
Forman, B. D., 58, 59
Forman, D., 31
Foster, G. A., 103
Fox, J. R., 146
Fraleigh, D., 205
France, G., 164
Francisco, D., 148
Frank, J. D., 148
Franklin, C., 97, 103
Freedle, R., 32
Freidson, E., 269
Friedman, S., 56, 73
Fujino, D. C., 44, 53, 54, 215, 229
Fukuyama, M. A., 72, 209
Fulcher, R., 324
Furlong, M. J., 165
Furuto, S. M., 216

Gardner, J. W., 83
Gardner, L. H., 347
Garrett, J. T., 183, 185, 187, 189
Garrett, M. W., 183, 185, 187
Garwood, A. N., 280
Gary, L., 91, 96, 117, 119
Gay, G., 32
Geary, C. A., 345
Gee, K., 22, 23, 52, 54, 65, 66, 68, 71, 312, 315, 347, 348
Gest, T., 85
Ghee, K. L., 16
Gibbs, J. T., 96, 101, 102, 103, 149, 173
Gilchrist, L. D., 169
Gilligan, C., 102
Gim, R. H., 31
Gingerich, W., 191
Goff, B., 205
Goldenberg, I. I., 14
Goldstein, A. P., 92
Goldstein, M. S., 148, 162
Gonsalves, J., 95
Gonzalez, C. A., 52, 57, 58
Good, B., 218
Good Tracks, J. G., 190
Gordon, A. N., 105
Gordon, M. M., 11
Goris, A., 259
Gottesfeld, H., 64
Graham, S., 347
Grant, S. K., 149, 286, 288, 316
Gray, B. A., 52
Gray-Ray, P., 99
Greeley, A., 264
Green, J. W., 258, 260
Green, R., 167
Greenberg, G., 145
Greenberg, H., 145
Greene, R. L., 54, 62
Greenfield, T. K., 209
Grieger, I., 343
Grier, W., 123
Griffith, E. E. H., 52, 57, 58
Grossman, B., 269
Grotevant, H., 99
Grover, K. P., 338
Guillory, B., 150
Gurak, D., 269, 272
Gutierrez, J. M., 95
Gutkin, T. B., 334, 339

Hahn, A., 96
Halevy-Martini, J., 171

Haley, J., 119, 122
Hall, C. C. I., 214, 227
Hall, W. S., 32
Hallowell, A. I., 168
Hamel, R. P., 306
Hammerschlag, C. A., 161
Hampson, D., 160
Hanley, C. P., 32
Hanley, T. C., 32
Hannerz, U., 96
Hansen, J. C., 310
Hardiman, R., 338
Harris, L., 270, 273
Harris, L. C., 29
Harris, M., 262
Harris, S. M., 96, 97, 98, 100, 101
Harrison, A. A., 210
Harrison, D. K., 347
Harrison, R., 85
Hatch, M., 56, 73
Hatfield, D., 84
Hayes, S., 160, 163
Hayes, W., 116
Hayes-Bautista, D. E., 16, 257, 263
Heath, A. E., 23, 343
Heck, R., 334, 335, 345
Hee, S., 3
Heide, F., 350
Heinrich, R. K., 72
Heisberger, J., 164
Heitler, J. B., 286
Helmey-Van der Velden, E., 171
Helms, J. E., 14, 15, 22, 32, 33, 34, 43, 45,
   60, 95, 317, 318, 321, 338, 343
Hendricks, L. E., 96
Henkin, L. B., 58
Henwood, K. L., 8
Heppner, M. J., 346
Heras, P., 221
Hernandez, A., 334
Herring, R. D., 184, 190
Herskovits, M., 25
Hervis, O., 274
Hevesi, D., 84
Higashi, C., 75, 336
Highlen, P. S., 32
Hill, C. E., 177
Hills, H. I., 328, 331
Hines, B. S., 310
Hines, P. M., 106, 118
Hinkston, J. A., 33, 165
Hippler, A. E., 148
Hirayama, H., 221

Hirayama, K., 221
Ho, C. K., 219
Ho, D. Y. F., 22, 72, 206
Ho, M. K., 123
Hodgkinson, H. L., 184
Hohm, C. F., 222
Holden, G. W., 169
Holland, D., 338
Hollingshead, A., 275
Holroyd, J., 214, 227
Hornig, C. D., 56
Horowitz, A. V., 146
Horowitz, D. L., 258
Horwath, E., 56
Howard, M. O., 138
Howard-Pitney, B., 148
Hu, L. T., 44, 53, 54, 205, 215, 229
Huang, L. N., 173, 205
Huey, W. C., 105
Hughes, E. C., 7
Hunter, A. G., 97

Ibrahim, F. A., 287, 290, 306, 307
Iglesias, J., 270
Ima, K., 222
Inclan, J., 273
Indian Health Service, 139
Indian Nations at Risk Task Force, 137
Indochinese American Council, 235
Indochinese Cultural & Service Center, 238
Ino, S., 205
Iron Eye Dydley, J., 185, 186
Irvine, J. J., 103
Irvine, O., 139, 160
Ivey, A. E., 174, 217, 219, 224, 310, 322, 323
Ivey, M. B., 322
Iwamasa, G., 347

Ja, D. Y., 206
Jackson, B., 32
Jackson, J. S., 51, 54, 59, 60, 62
Jaco, E. G., 52
Jaffe, A. J., 280
Jasso, R., 29, 273
Jewell, D. P., 174
Jilek-Aall, L., 146, 162
Johnson, C., 85
Johnson, D., 146, 161
Johnson, J., 56
Johnson, M. E., 184
Johnson, M. J., 338
Johnson, R. A., 209
Johnson, S. D., Jr., 9

Jones, B. E., 52
Jones, C., 4
Jones, J., 118, 333
Jones, J. H., 330, 348
Jones, J. M., 12, 208
Jones-Webb, R. J., 56
Joseph-Fox, Y. K., 137, 141
Josselson, R., 99
June, L. N., 95
Jung, C., 147

Kadushin, A., 260
Kahn, H., 287, 290
Kahn, K. B., 73, 337
Kahn, M. W., 148
Kain, C. D., 338
Kallen, H. M., 11
Kanel, K., 338
Kanfer, F. H., 92
Kanitz, B. E., 335, 350
Kaplan, B., 146, 161
Karno, M., 270
Karuza, J., Jr., 70, 351
Katz, J. H., 70, 288, 310
Katz, R., 146, 147, 148, 151, 161, 164
Kaufman, J. A., 137, 141
Keefe, S. E., 24, 25
Keitel, M. A., 57, 60, 62, 309
Kelley, H. H., 350
Kelso, D. R., 146, 160
Kennedy, A., 26
Kennedy, C. D., 324
Kennel, R. G., 344, 345
Kenney, G. E., 205
Kidder, L., 70, 351
Kiesler, C. A., 151
Kim, H. H. W., 337
Kim, S. J., 31
Kim, U., 26, 27
King, M., 53
King, O. E., 273, 274, 285, 286, 289
Kinze, J. D., 205
Kinzie, D. J., 238
Kinzie, J. D., 139, 160, 215
Kirk, B. A., 209
Kitano, H. H. L., 205, 207, 208, 215, 218
Kivlahan, D. R., 138, 160
Kleinman, A. M., 218, 351
Kluckhohn, C., 5
Kluckhohn, F. R., 185
Knegge, R., 141
Knepp, D., 331, 346
Kochman, T., 97

Kohout, J., 69, 324
Korchin, S. J., 59, 325
Koss-Chioino, J. D., 62
Krate, R., 99, 103
Kreisman, J., 273
Kroeber, A. L., 5
Krug, M., 10
Kuba, S. A., 331, 336
Kunjufu, F., 99, 100
Kunkel, M. A., 31
Kurtines, W., 30, 274
Kutscher, R., 4
Kwon, J., 205

LaBarre, W., 161
Ladner, R., 274
LaDue, R., 214, 227
LaFromboise, P., 169
LaFromboise, R., 141, 167
LaFromboise, T. D., 75, 95, 118, 140, 143, 146, 147, 148, 150, 160, 162, 163, 164, 165, 167, 169, 174, 184, 188, 189, 190, 311, 334
Lambert, M. D., 138
Landay, J. S., 84
Lapchick, R., 100
Larrabee, M. J., 95
Lashley, K. H., 184
Lavelle, J., 215
LaVoie, J., 102
LEAP and UCLA Asian American Studies Center, 201
LeClere, F. B., 89, 92
Lee, C. C., 217, 218
Lefley, H. P., 56, 57, 61, 314
Leiderman, P. H., 205
Leigh, J. W., 166, 167
Lejero, L., 148
Lemann, N., 83
Leonard, P. Y., 96, 101
Leong, F. T. L., 52, 53, 54, 56, 58, 60, 62, 210, 215, 337, 347
Lettrell, M., 165
Leung, P. K., 215
Lew, L., 61
Lew, S., 29
Lewis, J. A., 310
Lewis, M. D., 310
Lewis, R. G., 191
Liberman, D., 141
Lichter, D. T., 89, 92
Lieberman, L., 6
Lieberman, M. A., 63

Liebow, E., 96
Lin, K., 58, 62, 63
Linton, R. W., 5, 25
Lippincott, J. A., 61
Lipscomb, W. D., 67
Lisansky, J., 284
Littlefield, A., 6
Little Soldier, L., 191
Littrell, J., 165
Liu, J. H., 208
Locke, B. Z., 52
Locke, D. C., 108, 333
Lockhart, B., 162
Locklear, V. S., 169
Locust, C., 160, 188
Lonner, W. J., 174, 287
Loo, C., 215, 217
Lopez, S. R., 338
Lothstein, L., 105
Louie, C. E., 346
Low, K. G., 174
Lowe, S. M., 68, 347
Lujan, P., 162
Lum, D., 167
Lyerly, R. J., 162
Lyles, M., 119, 120
Lyons, C., 169

MacAskill, R. L., 52
Madsen, R., 148
Maduro, R., 271
Magids, D. M., 334
Magoon, T. M., 53
Majors, R., 72, 96, 97, 98, 101
Maki, M., 208
Malcolm, J., 333
Maldonado, R., 30
Malgady, R. G., 31, 58, 171, 268, 269, 276, 277
Mallinckrodt, B., 311
Malson, M., 120
Manderscheid, R. W., 52
Mann, G., 284
Manson, S. M., 139, 141, 143, 144, 146, 160, 162
Manuel, J., 148
Marcelino, E. P., 220
Marcos, L., 274
Margullis, C., 61
Marin, B. V., 29, 281, 284
Marin, G., 29, 30, 31, 281, 284
Marsella, A. J., 58, 209
Marshal, M., 140

Marshall, M., 160
Martinez, C., 271
Maruse, K., 23
Marvin, R. L., 96
Mathias, E., 263
Maton, K. I., 107
Mayes, B., 120
McAdoo, H., 119, 123
McCarty, T. L., 168
McCauley, C., 13
McCready, W. C., 263
McDavis, R. J., 71, 72, 87, 88, 91, 102, 330, 333, 342, 350
McDermott, J. F., Jr., 312
McDiarmid, G., 144
McDonald, J. D., 140
McFadden, J., 67
McFee, M., 168
McKinney, H., 215
McLaughlin, D. K., 89, 92
McLemore, S. D., 11
McLeod, B., 210
McShane, D., 151
McWhirter, E. H., 103
Meara, N. M., 306, 307
Medicine, B., 141, 145, 146, 160
Meggert, S. S., 303
Meier, S., 310
Mellins, C. A., 338
Mencado, P., 165
Mendez, G., 326
Mendoza, D. W., 335, 350
Meredith, C. W., 209
Meredith, G. M., 205, 209
Messner, M. A., 100
Mickelson, R. A., 101
Midgette, T. E., 303
Miedzian, M., 106
Mierzwa, J. A., 61
Milazzo-Sayre, L. J., 52
Miller, B. D., 57
Miller, F. S., 45
Miller, J. A., 29
Miller, J. D. B., 15
Miller, S. D., 225
Miller, S. I., 162
Miller, W., 96, 169
Min, P. G., 214
Mindel, C., 116
Minerbrook, S., 85
Minson, S., 238
Mintz, L. B., 331
Mintz, S., 262

Minuchin, S., 117, 121
Mio, J. S., 67, 74, 75, 95, 346, 347
Mitchell, M., 151
Mizokawa, D. T., 208
Mohatt, G. V., 144, 148, 150, 161, 184, 188, 190
Mollica, R. F., 58, 215
Moncher, M. S., 169
Montgomery, P. A., 282
Montgomery, T. A., 96
Montoya, B., 144
Moon, A., 237, 238
Moore, B. M., 5
Moore, D., 99
Moore, J., 256, 260, 265
Moore, L. J., 215
Morales, A., 270
Moreland, J. R., 324
Morishima, J. K., 208, 216, 217, 226
Morris, D. R., 67, 74, 75
Morten, G., 42, 288
Morton, G., 165, 174, 177
Moses, L. G., 168
Moses, S., 69, 74, 326
Mountcastle, A. R., 217, 218
Moyerman, D. R., 31, 58, 59
Murase, K., 216
Murphy, H. B., 327
Murray, J., 73, 347, 350
Myers, L. J., 32

Nagel, J., 8
Naron, N., 270
National Center for Immigrant Students, 265
National Coalition of Advocates for Students, 309
National Indian Justice Center, 138
Neidert, L. J., 25
Neighbors, H. W., 51, 54, 59, 60, 62, 350
Neimeyer, G. J., 23
Neliegh, G., 160
Neligh, G., 142
Nelson, C., 257
Nelson, S., 140, 141, 159
Neville, H. A., 328, 346
New York Department of City Planning, 265
Nguyen, L. T., 58
Nicassio, P. M., 236
Nichols, M., 117
Nickerson, K. J., 45, 60
Nielson, D., 346
Niemeyer, G. J., 343
Nikelly, A., 72

Nisdorf, J. F., 205
Nishio, K., 235, 238
Normand, W., 270
Norment, L., 91, 92
Novak, M., 25

Oberg, K., 27
O'Connell, L. J., 306
Office of Management and Budget, 257
Ogbu, J. M., 101, 102
Ogbu, J. U., 59, 101
Oh, M. Y., 217, 218
Okazaki, S., 210
Oliver, W., 96, 97, 98
Olmeda, E., 26
Olmedo, E. L., 24, 324
Olstad, R. G., 208
O'Neil, J. M., 98
Ong, P., 3
Orlandi, M. A., 169
Orley, J., 58
Otero-Sabogal, R., 29
Ottari, T. M., 339
Ottavi, T. M., 332, 345

Pachon, H., 256, 260, 265
Padgett, D. K., 53
Padilla, A. M., 28, 29, 68, 160, 331, 336
Padilla, E. R., 324
Padilla, S., 275
Palinkas, L., 96
Pallak, M. S., 142
Palleja, J., 169, 170
Pang, V. O., 208
Paradis, C. M., 56, 73
Parham, T. A., 22, 33, 34, 71, 87, 88, 91, 95, 102, 342, 350
Parham, W., 324
Park, R. E., 25
Park, S. E., 210
Parker, W. M., 91, 93, 345
Pasquale, F., 141, 144, 160
Patrick, C., 53
Pattison, E. M., 139, 160
Payn, S., 270
Payton, C. R., 306
Pedersen, P. B., 23, 74, 95, 174, 177, 185, 217, 219, 224, 306, 307, 322, 323, 333, 334, 339, 343, 349
Pedigo, J., 184
Peele, D., 324
Penistone, E., 170
Perez-Stable, E. J., 29

Perkins, E., 96, 97
Perry, J. L., 108
Peskin, H., 205
Pettigrew, T., 96
Petty, R. E., 350
Phinney, J. S., 9, 24, 351
Pierce, H. P., 96
Pinderhughes, E. B., 103, 121, 258
Pine, J. P., 214, 227
Pion, G., 69, 324
Pitta, P., 274
Plake, B., 147
Pleck, J. H., 98
Plous, S., 84
Polgar, S., 168
Pomales, J., 31, 95, 118, 286
Ponce, F. Q., 286
Ponterotto, J. G., 32, 33, 72, 73, 74, 95,
    165, 310, 322, 326, 334, 338, 339, 343,
    347, 350
Pope-Davis, D. B., 332, 339, 345, 346
Poston, W. C., 165
Poston, W. S. C., 32
Poussaint, A. F., 90, 91
Power, S., 26
Powers, W. K., 145, 162
Price, M., 117, 119
Primeaux, M. H., 145, 160
Prizzia, R., 216
Putnam, J. S., 142

Rabinowitz, V. C., 70, 351
Ramos, J., 270, 271
Rando, T. A., 90
Rank, R. C., 105
Rappaport, H., 147, 150
Rappaport, J., 147, 148
Rappaport, M., 147, 150
Rapport, J., 166
Raspberry, W., 84
Ray, M. C., 99
Redfield, R., 25
Red Horse, Y., 144
Reibstein, L., 84, 85
Reich, C. A., 3
Reicher, S., 8
Reinat, M., 335
Reuveni, U., 170
Revilla, L., 220
Reyhner, J., 138
Reynolds, A. L., 32, 332, 345, 346
Reynolds, L. T., 6
Rhoades, E. R., 160

Rhodes, E. R., 140
Rhyne, M. C., 338
Richards, T. F., 163
Richardson, E. H., 190
Rickard, H. C., 330
Rickard-Figueroa, K., 29
Rideout, C. A., 331
Ridley, C. R., 74, 325, 335, 350
Rieger, B. P., 334
Riley, C., 215
Rimonte, N., 222
Ritter, P. L., 205
Rivera, G., 61, 62
Robbins, M., 148
Roberts, D. F., 205
Roberts, S. V., 85
Robinson, L. V., 214, 227, 331, 346
Robinson, S. P., 90
Rodriguez, A., 274
Rodriguez, I., 270
Rodriguez, O., 269
Rodriguez-Andrew, S., 64
Rogg, E. M., 280, 286
Rogler, L. H., 31, 58, 59, 171, 269, 270, 272,
    273, 275, 276, 277
Rolde, E., 146, 148, 161, 164
Romero, D., 68
Root, M. P. P., 7, 214, 215, 217, 225, 226, 227
Rosado, J. W., 251
Rose, P. I., 6, 14
Rosenheck, R., 56, 64
Rosenstein, M. J., 52
Ross-Sheriff, F., 216
Rotter, J. B., 350
Rouse, B. A., 64
Roush, K. L., 32
Rowe, W., 75, 150, 164, 165, 167, 168, 169,
    311, 327
Roy, C., 139, 160
Royce, A. P., 264
Ruhf, L., 171
Ruiz, A. S., 32
Ruiz, R. A., 72, 271, 272, 275
Rumbaut, R. G., 58, 215
Rumberger, R. W., 96
Rushton, J. P., 6
Russo, N. F., 324
Ryan, L., 167, 168, 172
Ryan, R., 167, 168, 172

Sabnani, H. B., 73, 338, 339
Sabo, D., 100
Sabogal, F., 29

Sack, W. H., 205
Sampath, B. M., 139, 160
Sampson, R. J., 102
Sanchez, A. R., 31, 53
Sanchez, C. M., 334
Sanchez, J., 333
Sanders, D., 184
Sandner, D. F., 162
Sandoval, M. C., 284, 286
Santana-Cooney, R., 269
Santiago-Rivera, A. L., 68, 285
Santisteban, D., 274
Sarason, S., 147, 175
Sato, M., 238
Sattler, J. M., 347
Schaefer, R. T., 6, 7, 8, 13
Schick, F. L., 252
Schick, R., 252
Schilling, R. F., 169, 170
Schinke, S. P., 105, 169, 170
Schlesinger, H. J., 53
Schlossberg, N. K., 90
Schmidt, L. D., 306, 307
Schoenfel, P., 171
Schoenfeld, L. S., 162
Schofield, W., 149
Scopetta, M., 273, 274
Scopetta, N. A., 285, 286, 289
Scott, C., 286
Scott, J., 270
Scott, N. E., 68
Segal, M., 13
Sessions, W. B., 96
Sheppard, H. L., 3
Shon, S. P., 206
Shore, J. H., 139, 160
Silverstein, B., 99, 103
Simek-Downing, L., 174
Simek-Morgan, L., 322
Simms, W. F., 143
Singer, M. K., 205
Skillings, J. H., 12
Sloan, D., 91, 93
Smart, D. W., 58
Smart, J. F., 58
Smith, A., 259
Smith, B., 143, 166
Smith, D., 215
Smith, E. J., 32, 74, 333, 334, 339
Smith, E. M., 93
Smith, E. M. J., 59, 70, 288
Smith, H. O., 69
Smukler, M., 216

Snipp, C. M., 137
Snowden, L. R., 52, 53, 56, 63, 73, 96
Sodowsky, G. R., 334, 339
Solomon, G., 164
Sparks, R., 334
Special Populations Subpanel on Mental
    Health, 138
Special Populations Task Force of the
    President's Commission on Mental
    Health, 52
Speck, R., 171
Speight, S. L., 32, 344, 345
Spence, J. T., 147
Spindler, G. E., 138, 167
Spindler, L. S., 138, 167
Stadler, H., 333
Stang, D. J., 324
Staples, L., 96, 97
Staples, R., 87, 88, 89, 90, 91, 92, 93, 116, 119
Stapp, J., 324
Steinberg, L., 100, 101
Stephens, T. M., 262
Stikes, C. S., 72
Stitt, C. L., 13
Stokes, A., 331, 336
Stoller, R. J., 102
Stone, G. L., 53
Stonequist, E. V., 25, 34
Strodtbeck, F. L., 185
Strozier, A. L., 328, 331
Stuart, R., 119
Sue, D., 58, 68, 122, 205, 206, 209, 215, 216,
    218, 219, 239, 271, 322
Sue, D. M., 205, 209
Sue, D. W., 32, 36, 38, 41, 52, 58, 60, 61, 67,
    68, 70, 71, 74, 122, 165, 174, 177, 206,
    209, 215, 216, 217, 218, 219, 224, 271,
    287, 288, 322, 323, 330, 333, 334, 339
Sue, S., 9, 22, 23, 36, 38, 41, 44, 52, 53, 54,
    61, 65, 66, 68, 71, 75, 169, 205, 210, 215,
    216, 217, 218, 225, 226, 229, 231, 239,
    312, 314, 315, 336, 347, 348, 349
Suicides of Young Indians, 139
Suinn, R. M., 29
Sullivan, W. M., 148
Sum, A., 102
Sumner, W. G., 12
Susman, L., 326
Sussewell, D. R., 287
Swidler, A., 148
Swinomish Tribal Mental Health Project,
    144, 150
Szapocznik, J., 30, 274, 285, 286, 289

Taffe, R. C., 334, 339
Takeuchi, D. T., 44, 53, 54, 65, 68, 215, 216, 229
Tashima, N., 23, 237, 238
Tata, S. P., 52, 54, 56, 60, 62
Tatum, B. D., 13
Taylor, M. C., 103
Teng, L. N., 217
Terrell, F., 44, 45, 60, 117, 350
Terrell, S. L., 44, 45, 117, 350
Tetrick, F. L., 69
Thomas, A. J., 344, 345
Thomas, C. W., 96
Thomas, K. R., 72
Thomas, R. K., 162
Thomason, T. C., 184, 190
Thompson, C. E., 45, 149, 286, 288, 316, 346, 350
Thompson, D., 139
Thompson, E. T., 7, 51, 54, 59, 60, 350
Thompson, R., 117
Thompson, S. D., 174
Thurman, P. J., 165
Tienda, M., 257, 283
Tippeconie, B., 142
Tipton, S. M., 148
Tong, B., 215, 217
Toporek, R., 333
Torres, L. R., 333
Torres-Matrullo, C., 59
Torrey, E. F., 72, 148, 312, 351
Trevino, F. M., 16, 271
Triandis, H. C., 17, 284
Trimble, J. E., 26, 141, 143, 144, 145, 146, 147, 148, 149, 150, 160, 162, 163, 169, 170, 173, 174, 184, 188, 190
Troiden, R. R., 32
True, R. H., 215, 217, 221
Truss, C., 274
Tsai, M., 217
Tseng, W. S., 312
Tung, T. M., 238
Tyler, F. B., 287
Tyler, I. M., 174
Tyler, L. E., 312

Uehara, E. S., 216
U.S. Bureau of the Census, 3, 4, 8, 43, 44, 89, 116, 137, 184, 201, 210, 235, 236, 251, 252, 256, 257, 259, 261, 262, 281, 283, 292
U.S. Committee for Refugees, 235
U.S. Congress, 139, 166

U.S. Department of Health and Welfare, 235
U.S. Department of Justice, 138
U.S. Senate Select Committee on Indian Affairs, 138

Valentine, C. A., 25
Valley, M. M., 345
Van Dijk, T. A., 12
Vasquez-Nuttal, E., 74, 333, 334, 339
Vela, R., 272
Vigil, P., 29
Villanueva, M., 150
Villaneuva-King, O., 216
Vincent, J., 258
Vontress, C. E., 32, 72, 349

Wade, P., 346
Wagner, D. J., 61
Wagner, N. N., 324
Wagner, N. S., 52, 54, 56, 60, 62
Wainrib, B. R., 102
Walker, J. R., 162
Walker, P. S., 138
Walker, R. D., 138, 160
Wallace, A., 146, 161
Walton, J. M., 328
Waltz, G. R., 309
Wampold, B., 73
Wang, L. L-C., 210
Ward, C. J., 26, 137
Warfield, J. L., 96
Washington, C. S., 96
Wasilewski, L., 326
Waters, M., 6
Watkins, C. E., 45
Watts, T. D., 96
Wax, R. H., 162
Weizmann, F., 7
Welch, W., 139
Westermeyer, J., 205
Weston, R. E., 105
Weyr, T., 263, 265
Whiteley, S., 31
Wicherski, M., 69, 324
Wilkinson, K., 99
Williams, C., 170
Williams, J., 84
Williams, T., 84
Williams, V., 31, 286
Williams-McCoy, J., 287
Wilson, A. N., 96, 97, 98
Wilson, F., 118
Wilson, N., 116

Wilson, R., 168
Wilson, W., 308
Winer, J. L., 164
Winkelman, M., 27
Wirth, L., 14, 15
Wise, S. L., 334, 339
Withers, C., 325
Witkin, H. A., 350
Wohl, J., 61, 71, 72, 312, 314, 315
Wolf, E., 258
Wood, P. S., 311
Worsley, P., 259
Worthington, R., 45
Wright, R., 96
Wyatt, G. E., 7
Wyshak, G., 215

Yamamoto, J., 238
Yankauer, A., 265
Yee, A. H., 7

Yeh, M., 65, 68, 205
Yoshida, R. K., 326
Yoshioka, R. B., 23
Young, C., 91, 92
Young, M., 26
Young, R. L., 325
Yu, M., 228
Yung, J., 220
Yurich, J. M., 90, 93

Zanbe, N. W. S., 44
Zane, N., 9, 65, 215, 229, 314, 315
Zane, N. W., 205, 218
Zane, N. W. S., 53, 54, 215, 216,
    225, 231
Zayas, L. H., 169, 170, 333
Zenk, R., 350
Zimmerman, M. A., 107
Zuckerman, M., 6, 7, 9
Zweigenhaft, R. L., 103

SUBJECT INDEX

Acculturation, 9, 11, 24–31, 58, 63, 206, 208, 218, 273, 274, 292, 316
Acculturative stress, 27–28
Adviser role, 311
Advocate role, 308–9, 351
Affirmative action, 326
African American, as term, 16
African American client, 83–135
  cases and questions, 127–28
  family therapy, 116–24
  Hispanic, 262, 292
  male adolescent, 95–111
  role playing exercise, 129–30
  women, 87–93
  See also Race/ethnicity; Racism
Allocentrism, 283–84
American Association for Counseling and Development, 333
American Counseling Association (ACA), 66–67, 74, 226, 328, 330, 336
  ethical code of, 303, 304–6, 322
American Indian client, 133–97
  cases and questions, 193–95
  cultural values of, 183–91
  healing perspective on, 159–77
  and mental health policy, 137–52
  role playing exercise, 196–97
  See also Race/ethnicity
American Personnel and Guidance Association (APGA), 66, 67
American Psychiatric Association, 68
American Psychological Association (APA), 66–67, 68, 74, 139, 174, 226, 313, 325
  ethical code of, 303–4, 306, 322
  and multicultural training, 328–30, 331, 332, 336, 347, 349
Asian American, as term, 15–16
Asian American client, 201–47
  cases and questions, 244–45
  obstacles to treatment, 215–32
  role playing exercise, 246–47
  sociocultural influences on, 205–10, 237–41
  See also Race/ethnicity

Assimilation, 11, 21, 25, 168, 188, 208, 218
Association for Multicultural Counseling and Development (AMCD), 67, 74–75, 347
Atlanta Conference, 328
Attribution theory, 350–51
Austin Conference, 67, 328
Autonomy stage, 317, 318, 320

Bakke v. Regents of the University of California, 327
Behavior therapy, 170, 173
Biculturalism, 11, 16, 29, 168, 188
Bilingual counselor, 68
Bilingual interpreter, 227, 270–71
Bilingualism, 11, 29, 285–86
Blacks. See African American client; Racism
Black Student Psychological Association, 67
Black/White Interaction Model, 317–22
Board of Social and Ethical Responsibility for Psychology (BSERP), 67
Bureau of Indian Affairs (BIA), 142

Caucasian, as term, 17
Census Bureau, racial/ethnic categories of, 8, 16, 262
Change agent role, 309–10, 351
Chicago Conference, 328
Communication
  barriers, 91, 122, 169, 270
  nonverbal, 122, 189–90, 230
Conformity stage, 33, 35, 36–37, 40–41
Consultant role, 310–11
Contact stage, 317, 320
Council for Accreditation of Counseling and Related Educational Programs (CACREP), 330
Counseling psychology, defined, 313–14
Counselors
  in activist roles, 309–13, 351
  bilingual, 68
  ethnically similar, 68–69, 164–65, 286
  racially/ethnically different, 17–18
  racist attitudes of, 72–74

Counselors (*cont.*)
    western-oriented, 71–72
    See also Cross-cultural counseling
Cross-cultural counseling
    defined, 17–18
    ethical codes in, 303–7, 322
    research, 347–52
    theories/models in, 307–24
    training in, 74–75, 149–51, 174–76,
        324–47
Cross-cultural psychology, defined, 17
Cultural awareness, 28
Cultural conflict, 58, 184–85, 208
Cultural differences, within-group, 23–24
Culturally deprived, 9–10
Culturally different, 10
Culturally disadvantaged, 9, 10
Culturally distinct, 10
Culturally sensitive therapy, 116–24, 337–38
Cultural mistrust, 44–45
Cultural pluralism, 11
Cultural racism, 12
Cultural values, 9, 60–62
    African American, 120–22
    American Indian, 183–91
    Asian American, 206–7, 209, 218–23
    Hispanic American, 283–86
Culture, defined, 5–6, 14
Culture shock, 27–28

Data collection, on racial and ethnic
    groups, 8
Discrimination, 59
Dissonance stage, 33, 35, 37, 41
Diversification trend, 3–4
Dulles Conference, 67, 149, 328

Ecological Structural (Ecostructural) Family
    Therapy model, 289–90
Emic, 17
Empowerment, 166–67
Enabling factors, 55, 63–66
Enculturation, 26
Ethnically similar counselors, 68–69,
    164–65, 286
Ethnic Heritage Studies Bill, 11
Ethnicity
    ascription of, 263–64
    defined, 7–8, 9, 257–58
    See also Race/ethnicity
Ethnic loyalty, 28
Ethnic minority group, defined, 14–15
Ethocentrism, 12

Etic, 17
Eurocentrism, 71, 73

Family therapy, 116–24, 173, 273, 285,
    289–90
Folk healers, 62–63, 144, 148, 188–89, 271,
    312–13

Hispanic American, as term, 16, 265
Hispanic American client, 251–300
    cases and questions, 297–98
    children, 276–77
    Cuban American, 274–93
    mental health services for, 268–78
    role playing exercise, 299–300
    sociocultural features of, 256–66

Identity formation, 102–3
    racial, 31–34, 208
Immersion stage, 32, 318, 319, 321
    See also Resistance/immersion stage
Immigration, 3, 11, 21, 57–58, 215, 235–36,
    260, 264–65, 280, 281
Indian Health Services (IHS), 140, 141–42, 173
Indian Self-Determination and Education
    Assistance Act, 143, 151
Indians. *See* American Indian client
Individuation stage, 99, 106–7
Institutional racism, 12
Integrative awareness status, 33
Internalization stage, 32, 33, 321
Introspection stage, 35, 38–39, 41

Language-switching technique, 274, 285–86
Latino
    as term, 16
    See also Hispanic American client
Loss and grieving, 90–91

Machismo, 283
Melting pot theory, 10, 11, 25
Mental health needs, 51–75
Minority, defined, 14, 15
Minority-group counseling
    defined, 18
    See also Cross-cultural counseling
Minority Identity Development (MID) model,
    34–42
Multicultural counseling, 18
    See also Cross-cultural counseling
Multicultural Counseling and Therapy (MCT)
    model, 217–18, 322–24
Multiracial/multiethnic/multicultural, 16

National Institute of Mental Health, 52, 140, 325
Native American client. *See* American Indian client
Need factors, 55
Network therapy, 170–71, 173
Nonverbal communication, 122, 189–90, 230

Office of Management and Budget (OMB), 8, 16
Oppression, defined, 14

Person-centered therapy, 168–69
Political refugees, 58, 215, 235–36, 280, 281
Population, diversification trend, 3–4
Predisposing factors, 55, 60–63
Preencounter stage, 32, 33, 319, 321
Prejudice and discrimination, 13, 162–63, 207–8, 265
    See also Racism
Prevalence rate, 56–57, 138–39
Pseudo-independent stage, 317, 318
Psychological acculturation, 26–27
Psychotherapy, conventional, 314–15

Race
    ascription, 262
    defined, 6–7, 9
    mixed race, 16
Race/ethnicity
    Census Bureau categories, 8, 16
    definition of terms, 3–15
    identity development, 31–34, 208
    and mental health needs, 51–75
    research on, 347–48
    terminology, 15–17
    withingroup differences, 21–45
Racism
    of counselors, 72–74
    defined, 12–13

historical perspective on, 118–19
prevalence of, 83–85
types of, 12, 73
    See also Prejudice and discrimination; Stereotypes
Reintegration stage, 317, 318, 320, 321
Resistance/immersion stage, 33, 35, 38, 41, 42
Rogerian therapy, 168–69

Santería, 284
Scale to Assess World Views (SAWV), 287, 290–91
Separation stage, 99, 106–7
Simpatía, 284, 291
Snyder Act, 142
Social/Environmental Change Agent Role Model, 288–89
Social skills therapy, 169–70, 311
Social support systems, 119–20, 170–71, 311–12
Somatic complaints, 238–39
Stereotypes, 13–14, 73, 84, 91–92, 202
Stress, 57–59, 217
Synergistic stage, 35, 39–40, 41–42

Third World, 15
Translators, 227, 270–71
Treatment rate, 51–56

Utah Conference, 328

Vail Conference, 67, 149, 303, 328
Value-free therapy, 147
Visible racial/ethnic group, 15

Women clients, 87–93, 221
Worldview, 287–88, 290–91